D1503823

MANAGING

CONSTRUCTION
THE
CONTRACTUAL VIEWPOINT

MANAGING CONSTRUCTION

THE
CONTRACTUAL VIEWPOINT

Keith Collier

Delmar
Publishers Inc.™

NOTICE TO THE READER

Publisher does not warrant or guarantee any of the products described herein or perform any independent analysis in connection with any of the product information contained herein. Publisher does not assume, and expressly disclaims, any obligation to obtain and include information other than that provided to it by the manufacturer.

The reader is expressly warned to consider and adopt all safety precautions that might be indicated by the activities described herein and to avoid all potential hazards. By following the instructions contained herein, the reader willingly assumes all risks in conection with such instructions.

The publisher makes no representations or warranties of any kind, including but not limited to, the warranties of fitness for particular purpose or merchantability, nor are any such representations implied with respect to the material set forth herein, and the publisher takes no responsibility with respect to such material. The publisher shall not be liable for any special, consequential or exemplary damages resulting, in whole or in part, from readers' use of, or reliance upon, this material.

Cover design by Barry Littman

Delmar Staff:

Senior Executive Editor: Mark W. Huth
Assistant Editor: Nancy Belser
Project Editor: Elena M. Mauceri

Production Coordinator: Karen Smith
Art/Design Coordinator: Cheri Plasse

For information address Delmar Publishers Inc.
3 Columbia Circle Drive, Box 15—015
Albany, New York 12203—5015

Printed in the United States of America
Published simultaneously in Canada
by Nelson Canada,
a division of The Thomson Corporation

10 9 8 7 6 5 4 3 2 1 XX 99 98 97 96 95 94

Library of Congress Cataloging-in-Publication Data

Collier, Keith, 1927-
    Managing construction : the contractual viewpoint / by Keith Collier.
        p.   cm.
        Rev. ed. of: Managing construction contracts. 1st ed. c1982.
        Includes index.
    ISBN 0-8273-5700-1
        1. Construction contracts--United States.   2. Construction industry--Law and legislation--United States.   I. Collier, Keith, 1927-   Managing construction contracts.   II. Title.
    KF902.C592   1994
    343.73'07869--dc20   93-3778
    [347.3037869]   CIP

NEW AND REVISED TITLES FOR 1994

Estimating for Commercial and Residential Construction / *Benedict*
ISBN: 0-8273-5498-3

Fundamental Structural Steel Design-ASD / *Burns*
ISBN: 0-8273-5705-2

Estimating with Timberline® Precision / *Reich*
ISBN: 0-8273-6002-9

Practical Surveying for Technicians / *Landon*
ISBN: 0-8273-3941-0

Reinforced Concrete Technology / *French*
ISBN: 0-8273-5495-9

To request more information on these publications, contact your local bookstore, or call or write to:

Delmar Publishers Inc.
3 Columbia Circle
P. O. Box 15015
Albany, NY 12212-5015

Phone: 1-800-347-7707 • 1-518-464-3500 • Fax: 1-518-464-0301

DEDICATION

To: F. Wools, L. Waterman, J. Hardy
and all other masters of building.

CONTENTS

PREFACE

ABOUT THIS BOOK

This book is called *Managing Construction: The Contractual Viewpoint* because it deals with management from the perspective of construction contracts. Also, to offer and generate ideas about the use of computers for particular applications in construction, several kinds of computer programs are indicated. Better contracts and improved understanding and a greater use of information (and of computer systems) are the means to more economical and effective contracting.

Prior to the 1960s there were few books on construction management. Among the first were the four volumes on "practical construction management" by George F. Deatherage. In the preface to the first volume, entitled *Construction Company Organization and Management*,[1] he said:

---

[1]George E. Deatherage, P.E., *Construction Company Organization and Management* (New York: McGraw-Hill, 1964).

According to a "Bibliography of Construction Management," by King Royer of the University of Florida, but 33 books were published in the decade following the year 1952. These were mainly in the category of general construction methods, estimating, and cost accounting. Periodicals have carried occasional articles on the subject, but the student of construction company organization and management found himself in an unenviable position because of the dearth of information on the subject.

In his first volume, Deatherage devoted about one-third of the pages to organization and management, and the remaining two-thirds to an examination of contracts. Since then, most books on construction management have had little to say about contracts. Yet, contracts precede management, and they deeply affect management. The administration of a fixed-price contract based on the AIA standard documents A101 and A201[2] is different from, say, the management of a cost-plus-fee contract drawn up by the owner's lawyer.

The Importance of Cost Estimating and Information

Most construction companies are small and their main focus is on work in the field. Many, however, do not have enough information about the contracts they enter, about the projects on which they work, about the costs they incur, and about management generally. One reason is the constantly pressing need to make estimates and bids, since a company often has to make several to get a job. Often, therefore, there is a reluctance to spend on other less immediate things. Cost estimates are essential; they are a primary information source for construction management.

By using a computer system, and every cost estimate as a source of information (even the unsuccessful ones), both estimating and construction management can be made more efficient.

The Importance of Computer Systems

The only practical way to deal with the large amounts of information and data needed for construction is to use computer systems. Since there is an abundance of computer system information elsewhere, this text will present suggestions about the many different kinds of application programs that can be used in construction.

Some Features of This Book

Key words are set in **boldface** to show they are found in the Glossary of Construction Terms.

A Summary of Main Points is provided in each chapter.

References and End Notes in each chapter provide sources of additional information.

Questions and Topics for Discussion are found at the end of each chapter.

There is an extensive Index, and an Instructor's Guide is available.

---

[2]AIA Document A101, *Owner-Contractor Agreement,* and AIA Document A201, *General Conditions of the Contract for Construction.* These documents are referred to extensively throughout this book.

ACKNOWLEDGMENTS

The quotations at the beginning of chapters were gleaned from many sources, including my own memory. In particular, I wish to acknowledge the following sources:

- *The Oxford Dictionary of Quotations,* 3d ed. (New York: Oxford University Press, 1979).
- *Instant Quotation Dictionary* (Mundelein, IL: Career Institute, 1972).

In addition, acknowledgment is due the following reviewers: Daniel E. Whiteman, University of Florida; John H. Erion, Jr., P. E., Bowling Green State University; Bruce D. Dallman, Ph.D., Indiana State University; Charles Matthewson, Southern Illinois University, Edwardsville; and Archibald Alexander, Perdue University.

Keith Collier
White Rock, British Columbia.

CHAPTER

1

CONSTRUCTION CONTRACTS AND MANAGEMENT

Ignorance of the law excuses no man.
John Selden (1584–1654)

This chapter reviews the essential ingredients of valid and enforceable contracts and how the nature and content of construction contracts determines how construction work is managed. Unless otherwise indicated, assume a fixed-price contract. Further, the nature of construction itself, and construction management through the estimating–planning–controlling cycle is examined.

1.1 CONSTRUCTION CONTRACTS

If books on construction management are few, those on contracts are fewer. Yet, all **construction work*** takes place within a contract; therefore, a brief survey of contracts will be useful.

Essential Ingredients of Contracts

If they are to be valid and enforceable by law, all contracts must contain certain elements.

1. *Mutual agreement* between the contracting parties as to the terms and conditions of the contract (i.e., a clear understanding between both parties what a contract is about; a meeting of minds)
2. *Genuine intention* of the parties to accept and fulfill their respective rights and duties under the contract (i.e., a

---

*Terms in the Glossary of Construction Terms are marked in boldface when they first appear and when particular attention to their meaning is required.

true intent to follow through with that to which they have agreed)

3. *Legal capacity* (ability) of the parties to make a valid contract (i.e., the parties are sensible adults, know what they are doing and have the legal right to do it)

4. *Consideration* of value exchanged between the parties (e.g., cash payment for construction work)

5. *Lawful object* (purpose) of the contract (e.g., to build a structure for a lawful purpose which conforms to laws and regulations).

Contract law is called residual,[1] since it mainly deals with things not dealt with by statute law, or legislated law. It is largely traditional common law modified by statute. Contracts are the means by which all commerce and business works. Considering how much the law impinges on individuals and construction, the courts interfere very little in the making of contracts. People make contracts every day, and yet the law remains unconcerned with most of them.

To be valid and enforceable all contracts must contain the aforementioned elements. In construction, lawful object is the least problematic, and mutual agreement is the most elusive. In the eyes of the law, valid means alive and with meaning; enforceable means it can be enforced at law. A contract may be valid but not enforceable. For example, if a contract is not in writing and not witnessed by a **third party,** there is no evidence to prove it exists, except affirmation by the contracting parties. If one of them decides to deny there is a contract, it will be one's word against the other's.

Mutual Agreement. Some problems in construction contracts arise from dishonesty, but probably most come from imperfect understanding. Mutual agreement is at the heart of a contract. An offer (**bid,** or **tender**) and its unconditional acceptance signifies mutual agreement. A counteroffer also requires unconditional acceptance. The law requires only certain agreements to be written and many are not. In construction all contract agreements should be written to avoid misunderstandings and disputes, because construction is complicated and closely related to land. The law considers land especially important and requires agreements about land to be in writing. Also, certain fraud statutes require all contracts of amounts above a certain figure to be in writing.

Standard forms of construction contract contain a printed agreement and the **general conditions of the contract.**[2] Usually drawings and specifications accompany them as other **contract documents.** Special, or supplementary conditions may be added to deal with particular matters, such as site conditions or special payment provisions. The contents of a written agreement, such as the standard **AIA** *Document A101,* set out and exemplify a contract's essential ingredients, which are

- The parties: the party of the first part, the owner (named in the agreement), and the party of the second part, the contractor (also named). Their capacity to contract is represented by their signatures.
- The agreement signed by the parties shows their genuine intention to be obligated by the contract.
- The consideration is the contract sum to be paid by the owner to the contractor for performance of the contract.[3]
- The legal object, represented by the name and location of the Project and the Work of the Contract as identified and shown on the drawings and described in the specifications (listed in the agreement

with the other contract documents) to be completed substantially by a stipulated date.

■ Contract time, shown by the dates of commencement and **substantial completion** stipulated in agreement.

Certain other important provisions and information are usual in a construction agreement, including the following:

■ Payment procedures
■ List of contract documents
■ Dates for starting and completing the work
■ Matters concerning termination and assignment of the contract and other required provisions

The contents of a standard form of agreement illustrates the essential elements of a contract. Other essential parts of a construction contract are found in the other documents governed by the agreement, including

■ Contract conditions
■ Drawings
■ Specifications.

Mutual agreement follows unconditional acceptance of an offer, although either may be imperfect. In construction, one person makes a bid and another accepts it. Or instead, there are some informal words, or perhaps a handshake to show offer and acceptance, and nothing on paper. A contract exists nevertheless, and may be evident from the oral agreement and the subsequent actions of the two parties. It probably is valid and enforceable providing neither party tries to deny it.

A bid as submitted is not a contract document unless the contract says it is. A bid should be declared a contract document if it contains information that may be required in the contract's administration or modification, such as

■ **Unit prices** provided by the **bidder**
■ **Cash allowances** required by the owner–designer
■ A list of proposed **subcontractors,** if required by the instructions to bidders

All such information in a bid should be specifically referred to in the agreement document along with a list of the other contract documents.

Consideration. Contract law does not say much about consideration, except that it must exist and be of some value. As to how much, the law is silent and leaves that up to the contracting parties. This exemplifies the attitude of the law to contracts generally: the utmost freedom to contract so that commerce and business may not be impeded. As with freedom everywhere, there exists the risk of abuse; therefore, the well-known exhortation regarding a contract to purchase: *Caveat emptor,* buyer beware.

Oral Contracts. Providing it has all the essentials mentioned, if a contract is oral (i.e., spoken) it is a valid contract. Exceptions include those contracts dealing with certain things (e.g., land, divorce) where statute law requires an agreement to be in writing. However, unless there is external evidence as to a contract's existence, it may not be enforceable should one party decide to repudiate the contract (i.e., deny that it ever existed).

Sometimes, external evidence of an oral contract may exist; such as a third party witnessing the agreement, or work begun and accepted. Nevertheless, it is better if a contract is in writing. A written contract can be informal, and for minor work an exchange of letters may suffice to set down the main points of an agreement: the parties' names, the work's description, the contract sum (consideration), and the date agreed to for completion, if any. For larger, more complex, and more expensive projects complete and detailed documents are necessary.

***Standard Contracts.* Standard forms of contract** help one to understand a contract's documents and to avoid misunderstandings; however, a standard contract is not always carefully read or fully understood because

- It is considered too long and too complicated
- The parties say they trust each other, so it is considered a mere formality
- A contractors' association endorsed the form of contract, so a contractor believes it must be reliable

To deal with specific conditions and requirements, a standard construction contract often needs modifying. If you know a standard contract well, you do not need to read every word every time; you do, however, need to make an initial investment in time and effort to study and learn the contents of standard contracts. This text will refer often to the most widely used standard contract documents: those of the American Institute of Architects (particularly AIA Document A101—Owner–Contractor Agreement and AIA Document A201—General conditions of the contract for construction). You should have copies of these documents on hand. Also, by way of contrast, where it is different, this text refers occasionally to the Canadian document, the Stipulated Price Contract, CCDC2.

Comparing different contracts is helpful to understanding contracts, and different countries sometimes deal with the same contractual matters in different ways.[4] The standard construction contracts of English-speaking countries have much in common, which makes their differences instructive. In changing times, no person and no industry can expect to remain isolated.

Amendments to Standard Contracts

There is a cardinal rule for amending standard forms of contracts: Do not amend an original copy for a project and then reproduce the amended contract by completely rewriting it so that the amendments are no longer obvious. Amendments done this way obscure the content and detract from the value of using a standard contract. Some readers cannot readily recognize the amendments, even though they may recognize that the contract in hand is from a standard form. A better way is to amend and use several printed copies. The best amendment method is to incorporate a standard contract by specific reference in a project's specifications; then set down in detail any needed amendments or supplements. In this way the amendments are clear, and if there is any perceived ambiguity the amendment governs. Later, parties to the contract may sign two printed standard contracts with the same amendments and supplements inserted.

The Parol-evidence Rule

In the matter of mutual agreement remember the important parol-evidence rule that says a written contract supersedes anything previously agreed to orally. (Parol = spoken word) That rule is proper, as allowing the significance of anything spoken in a written contract would make the written contract futile. Many are not aware of this.

CASE

A trade contractor discusses work with a general contractor. They agree that certain trade work shall be done under a subcontract for a certain price and with certain conditions, including one that the general contractor shall provide the scaffolding. Later, just before the work is started, the general contractor calls the trade contractor and tells him they should sign a subcontract that he, the general contractor, has prepared. The subcontract contains the contract sum previously agreed to, which reassures the subcontractor, and they sign the subcontract document.

Trusting, or unwilling to appear otherwise, the trade contractor does not read everything in the subcontract, and so does not discover until later that according to the written agreement he must provide the scaffolding. He confronts the general contractor who denies there was a previous agreement that the general contractor should provide the scaffolding.

The written contract represents the valid contract between them, and the parol-evidence rule excludes anything previously agreed to orally.

Seeking Legal Counsel. The law allows individuals to make contracts and requires only a few specifics. Of course, there is much more to contracts (e.g., the complications of a conditional acceptance that in fact becomes a counteroffer, and matters of mistake and misrepresentation). Once a construction contract exists, however, its performance is the concern of statutes and regulations, particularly in matters of public health and safety. Providing one acts legally, the law allows individuals to deal with each other unsupervised. When something involves the public at large, however, the law acts as a guardian.

Talk to a lawyer about specific projects and their contractual needs or problems. You cannot get an adequate understanding of contracts or the law by reading books. Particular cases and circumstances require a lawyer's knowledge, experience, and expertise.

1.2 THE MAIN KINDS OF CONSTRUCTION

In the broadest sense construction means the design and production of **improvements** erected on land. Construction work includes anything built on and permanently attached to land; including such diverse structures as buildings, bridges, roads, sewers, dams, and manufacturing plants. Given the diversity of construction and construction companies, one thing to look at is the kind of construction work done. Most construction work is in one of the following classes:

1. **Building construction work**
2. **Engineering construction work**
3. **Industrial construction work**
4. **Specialized construction work.**

There are many subclasses of construction work where classes overlap and intermix. House construction, especially when speculative, is in many ways different from other building construction.[5] By examining building and engineering construction work and the differences between them, their effect on construction companies can be understood. The primary characteristics and differences between the first two main classes follow.

- Building Construction Work

1. Includes the smallest construction jobs (e.g., custom-designed houses, stores, etc.)
2. Mostly done by private financing (as opposed to public financing)
3. Includes a greater variety of materials and methods, relative to project size
4. A minimal amount of the design is done by contractors
5. **Fixed-price contracts** for a stipulated sum are more common
6. Urban and suburban sites also are more common

- Engineering Construction Work

1. Includes the largest construction jobs (e.g., canals, dams)
2. Mostly done by public financing (as opposed to private)
3. Includes a lesser variety of materials and methods, relative to project size
4. A greater amount of design is done by contractors
5. **Unit-price contracts** are more common
6. Rural and remote sites are more common

Each of these features will be considered and compared in more detail as a means to better understanding the differences:

Smallest and Largest Construction Jobs

Project size means the total cost and complexity of a project. The main considerations in this comparison are the requirements of the work performed and the distribution of managerial skills. Proportionately, dollar for dollar, a small building project may require more attention than a large project. Yet, it is not economically possible to have several individuals with different specialized skills working on small projects, so they require generalists with several skills.

The risks on small projects often are proportionately greater, because the short time-span of the contracts does not allow for much correction and adjustment of methods; i.e., a work item may be half-finished before inefficiencies are obvious, and then it may be too late. Therefore, an adequate profit margin is needed to allow for such inefficiencies and contingencies. Consequently, the percentage **markup** on smaller projects typically is greater.

As more companies can do smaller projects, the competition for them often is greater. Therefore, smaller companies must keep overhead costs as low as possible to remain competitive. They do this by having a small but versatile staff and minimal equipment and facilities. Large construction contracts require the managerial functions and skills that only large construction companies can provide because (optimally) they can keep their specialists busy.

The basic unit of work management is an individual who cannot be divided. What can the estimator of a small construction company do when not estimating? Some smaller companies require estimators to also manage the work they obtain. In the smallest of companies the estimator may also be the principal, with a dozen things to do. In larger companies, there is a more-or-less constant demand for special skills. Computers enable an increase in the scope and efficiency of smaller companies by helping individuals to be more informed, versatile, and efficient.

Requiring a contractor to provide a **performance bond** relates capacity to project size. Surety companies only guarantee the performance of those companies that have the capacity to perform; therefore, they rate construction companies by "capacity, character, and capital." A company increases its bonding capacity as it increases its financial and technical capacity, which governs the size of its projects. The projects it performs affect and shape a company's organization and the systems and skills it needs and employs.

Private or Public Financing

In a publicly funded project there often are contractual terms and conditions that are not found in contracts for private work. Public works' contracts may require

- Lists of employment openings placed in government offices
- Environmental impact studies and controls at a site
- Utilization of minority and small business enterprises
- **Value engineering** by the contractor
- Examination of contractors' and subcontractors' records by the owner or project manager
- Inspection of work by government and other inspectors
- Wage standards and special payroll arrangements
- Special reporting procedures
- Identification of employees
- Employment of minorities
- Accident prevention plans and management

Such requirements make work and require additional staff. Routine inspection of public works may result in extra supervision, paperwork, and overhead costs. Generally, we recognize that government departments and public corporations demand more forms to be completed and more reports to be submitted than do private corporations. Therefore, we may expect that public works usually require more staff for their management and, therefore, higher costs.

Variety of Construction Materials and Methods

All building construction involves several trades, the work of which consists of handling and installing several different kinds of materials and products. Engineering projects, though often physically larger and for greater contract sums, typically require fewer trades and materials. (Some engineering projects are exceptional however and require a great variety of trades and materials.) It is only in engineering works (e.g., dams) that we find a combination of relative simplicity and large size and cost. What effect does this have on construction management?

Even in small building projects there are many subcontractors coming and going at different times. A hospital is one of the most vivid examples of large size and complexity. With mechanical work divided among plumbing, heating, air conditioning, sheet metalwork, gas fitting, and insulation, typically the amounts of individual subcontracts are no more than 10 percent of a hospital project's total costs, and most are much less.

Obviously, this number and diversity of trades make a demand on management and supervision and adds to the overhead burden. By comparison, a massive hydrodam (costing perhaps several thousand times more than some buildings) does not have anything like the same complexity of work and variety of trades—dollar for dollar. Engineering projects do have other costly characteristics; such as the high technology and precision often involved in the work and the high risks related to performance, and these too have their effect on management. However when compared with building construction, the complexity of engineering projects often is not commensurate with their large size.

Minimum or Maximum Design Done by Contractors

Once a building is out of the ground, the work usually can be completed without concern for subsurface conditions, although there may be other reasons why various parts of a building may be delayed. As a result, fixed-price contracts are more common in building construction, and fixed-price contracts require that the design be virtually completed before bids and a contract are made.

With engineering works often there are indeterminate conditions that affect the design and the work, its methods and solutions. Therefore an **owner–designer** of an engineering project usually prefers to leave many of the construction methods to be decided by the contractor; the contract prescribes only the final results and the performance of the work. Frequently a larger scope for inventiveness by a contractor exists in engineering projects. In building projects the methods usually are prescribed in the contract.

In engineering works the design often is only outlined by the owner–designer and the contractor designs the details. Consequently, contractors in engineering works frequently have to employ designers and drafters. In most building projects, a con-

tractor designs only the temporary works (e.g., falsework, and formwork). Some specialist trades must submit **shop drawings** for a designer's approval. These are prepared at the subcontractor's office or factory (i.e., shop) and usually show only production and installation details.[6] It is unusual to find designers and drafters working on-site on a building project in North America[7] and usually the amount of designing by a building contractor is small or nonexistent. In engineering projects the opposite frequently is true.

Fixed-price or Unit-price Contracts

Because of the indeterminate nature and scope of most engineering work, and the risks involved, **fixed-price contracts** for a stipulated sum are less common for engineering work. The opposite is true of building construction, for which the stipulated-sum contract is most common.

In some engineering contracts for which the design information is practically complete, but for which the precise quantities of work required are not known, a **unit-price contract** is common. Unit-price contracts are not common for building works in North America.[8] For some engineering works, it may be considered necessary to use a cost-plus-fee contract; perhaps with unit prices for certain parts of the work. The effect of either unit-price or cost-plus-fee engineering contracts is to require the contractors to employ site staff either to measure the work in progress for payment at the contract's unit prices, or for bookkeeping in cost-plus-fee contracts. Also, such contracts may require a contractor to have design and drafting staff on-site. Therefore, the kind of contract directly affects a contractor's site organization and project management.

Urban and Suburban or Rural and Remote Sites

Major engineering projects are more likely to be found outside urban and suburban areas. The reverse is true for building projects. Projects on urban sites often can be administered from a contractor's head office with a minimum of staff on-site. For projects at more remote sites, purchasing, payroll, and other management functions may have to be done on-site. Obviously, the location of a site affects a company's organization, administration, and **overhead costs**. The overhead costs related to expatriated staff and workers on overseas projects frequently are very high.

Some companies specialize in projects in remote locations and require only a small staff at their head office. They create a complete management organization on-site for each project. Key management staff, who would otherwise spend most of their time in an office, may move around from project to project and country to country. The structure and overhead costs of North American companies working overseas are quite different from those of companies at home.

Some projects are atypical and have characteristics different from those attributed to their class. Some building contracts are large in both size and cost, and some contain proportionately large elements of structural engineering and mechanical work. Some engineering contracts contain large portions of building work. Construction contracts also vary, and some building contracts are not fixed-price contracts. We have discussed and compared what is commonplace to illustrate an important point: The class of construction work has a great influence on a contract, a contractor's organization, and the management systems used.

As for the other construction classes identified earlier, industrial and specialized construction (e.g., highways and pipelines) have more in common with engineering construction. Also, many of these projects are driven by economic considerations that override the capital costs of construction; therefore, and because of site conditions, fixed-price contracts for industrial work are not common.

1.3　CONSTRUCTION MANAGEMENT, GENERALLY

There are two kinds of construction management objectives.

1. Specifically, to perform a construction contract according to its terms and conditions, minimizing risk and maximizing profit.
2. Generally, to acquire, record, and apply the experience and information gained to future cost estimates and projects; to reduce overhead costs, maximize productivity, and improve the opportunities and probabilities for success and corporate survival.

One set of objectives is short-term, and the other is long-term. Both are equally important since the construction business involves a series of contracts to be performed. The terms and conditions of a contract have a distinct effect on construction management and cannot be ignored. Therefore, ignorance of contracts, disregard for their contents, or a lack of information about them lead to poor management and performance. **Information** and *risk* are linked, since more information means less risk. If we knew all that would happen there would be little or no risk. Risk and profit are linked, and as risk of financial loss increases, so should potential profit. Survival of a company depends on an adequate cash flow and information. Management is difficult to define, and to give ourselves the largest scope we shall define it as

- Getting work done efficiently with the available resources
- Minimization of risk
- Perpetuation of the company
- Maximizing of productivity
- Maximizing of profits.

Given the need for an authoritative definition we might turn to Drucker: "[M]anagement by objectives and self-control may properly be called a philosophy of management." To define management further, Drucker offers an anecdote:

> An old story tells of three stonecutters who were asked what they were doing. The first replied, "I am making a living." The second kept on hammering while he said, "I am doing the best job of stonecutting in the entire country." The third one looked up with a visionary gleam in his eyes and said, "I am building a cathedral."[9]

Drucker describes management by self-control and by objectives. What are the objectives of construction management? They vary in importance, but those listed here are fundamental. Obviously, management in construction should include the management of the **design phase** that precedes production. Usually, in the English-speaking countries, construction and design are separate, and so construction management does not begin until after the design phase. Exceptions are **design-build** projects and to some extent those with **phased construction.** Design-build is becoming more com-

mon. Offshore companies already are selling design-build services in North America. A construction manager would do well to get an education in design principles and learn to communicate with designers.

The use of the term, "professional construction management" shows there may be some confusion about the term, "construction management." So we need to distinguish the so-called professional management from the management done by **general contractors.** There are now two distinct meanings:

1. "Construction Management" (here, *capitalized*), sometimes called "professional construction management" (frequently abbreviated to CM), and
2. "construction management" (here, *not capitalized*), used to refer to traditional construction management by a general contractor.

Capitalized CM refers to construction management in a contractual arrangement in which an **owner** has separate contracts for several parts of the work, all under the direction of a **construction manager,** or a **management contractor,** who may or may not undertake part of the work himself. In CM, an owner no longer has a single construction contract with a general contractor who has several subcontracts (see Figure 1.1). Alternatively, an owner may employ a management contractor who subcontracts all the work, but is fully responsible for performance.

The primary purposes of both CM and traditional construction management are the same: the proper and timely execution of construction work according to the contractual requirements. But some of the means are different. The text frequently compares the two methods. A contractor in

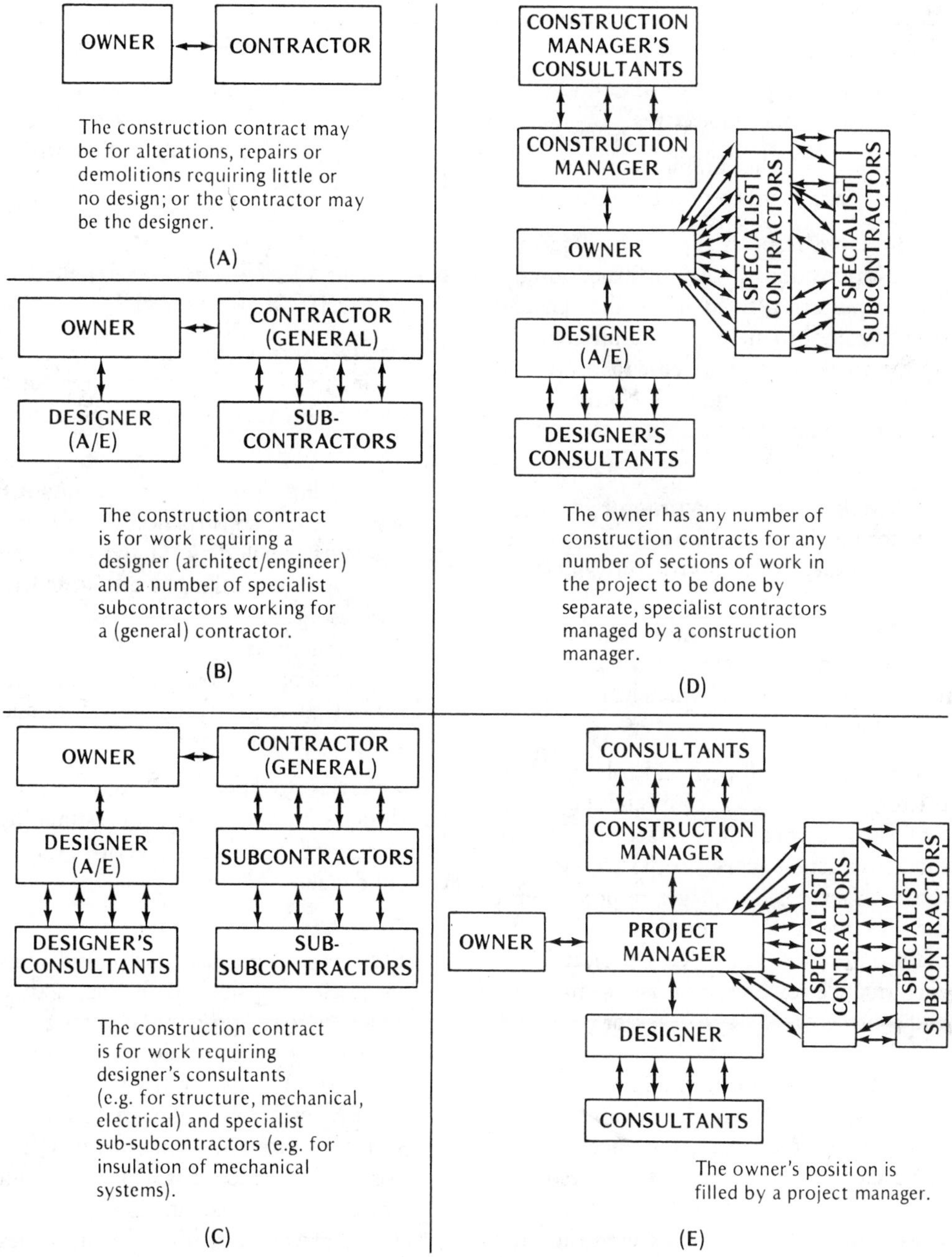

OWNER
CONTRACTOR
The construction contract may be for alterations, repairs or demolitions requiring little or no design; or the contractor may be the designer.
(A)
OWNER
CONTRACTOR (GENERAL)
DESIGNER (A/E)
SUB-CONTRACTORS
The construction contract is for work requiring a designer (architect/engineer) and a number of specialist subcontractors working for a (general) contractor.
(B)
OWNER
CONTRACTOR (GENERAL)
DESIGNER (A/E)
SUBCONTRACTORS
DESIGNER'S CONSULTANTS
SUB-SUBCONTRACTORS
The construction contract is for work requiring designer's consultants (e.g. for structure, mechanical, electrical) and specialist sub-subcontractors (e.g. for insulation of mechanical systems).
(C)
CONSTRUCTION MANAGER'S CONSULTANTS
CONSTRUCTION MANAGER
OWNER
DESIGNER (A/E)
DESIGNER'S CONSULTANTS
SPECIALIST CONTRACTORS
SPECIALIST SUBCONTRACTORS
The owner has any number of construction contracts for any number of sections of work in the project to be done by separate, specialist contractors managed by a construction manager.
(D)
CONSULTANTS
CONSTRUCTION MANAGER
OWNER
PROJECT MANAGER
DESIGNER
CONSULTANTS
SPECIALIST CONTRACTORS
SPECIALIST SUBCONTRACTORS
The owner's position is filled by a project manager.
(E)

NOTE
Double-headed arrows indicate *contractual relationships* (Privity of ↔ contract) in contracts of all kinds.

Figure 1.1 Some contractual arrangements for construction

a construction project in the traditional mode has two main objectives:

1. To perform the contract satisfactorily.
2. To make as much profit as possible.

In some respects these two objectives are in opposition. If the construction contract stipulates a fixed price, that enables the contractor to increase his profit if he can do the work for a lesser cost than the estimated cost. In traditional contracting a contractor plays the following two distinct roles:

1. **Specialist trade contractor** for a minor portion of the construction work of the project (e.g., substructure and structure)
2. **Construction manager** obliged to coordinate his work and the work of all the subcontractors for which he is responsible as contractor.

In the first and practical role, the contractor is one of a team of specialist contractors, each of whom does a particular part of the construction work; in the second role, the contractor is a manager responsible for the performance of the **prime contract.** The main difference with a CM project is the performance of the two roles—manager and contractor—by two different persons.[10]

Where does traditional construction management begin and end? For an owner it begins when the owner awards a construction contract to the contractor. For a contractor it begins earlier, with an estimate of the costs of the proposed construction work. For an owner it ends with the total performance of a construction contract and its subsequent **warranty period.** For a contractor it ends with his final analysis of the completed project to discover the actual **costs of the work,** and the reasons for any

losses, followed by the warranty period. But a contractor's liability for the work may extend much longer, and up to the statutory limitation period.

1.4 THE ESTIMATING–PLANNING–CONTROLLING CYCLE

Figure 1.2 shows the three phases of the estimating–planning–controlling cycle of construction management applicable to most construction.

1. **Estimating:** preceded by a **quantity survey** of the construction work[11]
2. **Planning:** including analyzing, planning, and scheduling **work activities** and resources
3. **Controlling:** using and applying schedules, estimates, cost accounts, and a budget to ensure proper performance and to maximize profit.

Referring to Figure 1.2, and its numbered parts in the phases of estimating, planning, and controlling, let us examine each in detail.

1. Cost data filing/retrieval: the information link between new and past projects. Data filing is the last activity of a completed project. The first activity of a new project (following the quantity survey) is data retrieval. Both are more efficient when done in a computer system. Information obtained by a final cost analysis (shown as item 11) is combined with similar information from earlier projects already in the data files. In this way, **information** becomes **data** and shows the levels of productivity that an estimator needs. Alone, specific information may be of little value, but when combined with information from

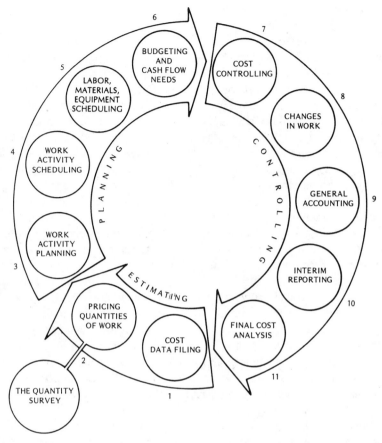

Estimating
(1) *Cost data filing:* an estimator draws on information obtained from other jobs in making an estimate
(2) *Price quantities of work:* this completes an estimate and bid and may lead to a construction contract
Planning
(3) *Work activity planning:* construction work is analyzed into parts (activities) which are then arranged in logical sequence
(4) *Work activity scheduling:* estimated times for activities are included in a schedule for the project
(5) *Labor, materials, and equipment scheduling:* amounts of resources required at different times throughout a project are estimated and scheduled
(6) Budgeting and cash flow needs: these are calculated and scheduled to find out the amounts of financing required throughout the project
Controlling
(7) *Cost controlling:* daily costs of major items are obtained and compared with the amounts of work performed; resultant unit rates are compared to those in the estimate; unsatisfactory production rates are discovered and corrections in work methods may be made
(8) *Changes in work:* these require costs to be negotiated and recorded
(9) *General accounting:* including payrolls and payments for materials and equipment rentals, etc., and for cost accounting requirements
(10) *Interim reporting:* on actual costs and progress periodically made and the schedule adjusted accordingly
(11) *Final cost analysis:* compares actual costs and times spent on work activities with those in the estimate and schedule to provide information for future projects.

Construction management is a cyclical process of input and feedback; a constant learning process; a process requiring continuous revision and adjustment as actual results vary from predictions and estimates; it is a steering process towards a goal.

Figure 1.2 The estimating–planning–controlling cycle of construction management.

other projects it shows levels of productivity and the costs of **items of work.**

2. Pricing quantities of work: includes estimating costs, and preparing a bid for a construction contract. This concludes the estimating phase. Pricing items is most efficient and reliable when using a spreadsheet. A cost estimate is a primary means to effective construction management.

3. Work activity analysis and planning: identifies work by different crews at different times and divides large work items into more than one activity. Planning arranges activities in logical sequence, and in parallel sequences if certain activities can be done simultaneously. Critical activities and work items then become apparent as a work schedule is prepared. Planning and scheduling software that can interact with a cost estimating program is available.[12]

4. Work activity scheduling: requires estimates of the time needed to complete each work activity. Adding calendar dates produces a schedule showing starting and finishing dates for activities. A schedule usually is in the graphic form of a **Gantt bar chart** or a **network.** Such a schedule is essential to management and to the creation of other schedules, including a **resource schedule** and a **cash-flow schedule.** All these can be created and used interactively in a computer system.

5. Resource scheduling: necessary to determine the extent and timing of required resources (i.e., labor, materials, and equipment). Not only should the total resources be not greater than those allowed in the project estimate, the correct amounts must be available when required. Delayed deliveries of materials and premature arrival on-site of equipment or labor may result in losses.

6. Budgeting and cash-flow projections: depend on periodic contract payments; the project duration and schedule; and the scheduled requirements for labor, materials, and equipment on a site. These are primary considerations in construction planning because construction projects depend on an adequate cash flow. Also, the need for cash is never entirely met by **progress payments** which are made in arrears for work completed. Interim short-term financing therefore is needed to ensure an adequate cash flow. Cash-flow projections can be made with a computer system using estimating and scheduling software.

7. Cost controlling: means monitoring work activities in progress, day by day. The actual costs and production rates are compared with those in the cost estimate. Cost controls should enable any production losses to be quickly identified so as to reduce or eliminate them before completion. Quick responses are essential, and a computer system helps make them possible.

8. Changes in contract and work: are commonplace and often require changes in the schedule. The effect of a change must be identified, measured, and incorporated into a modified project's schedule and budget.

9. General accounting: includes payroll and payments to suppliers, subcontractors, equipment rental companies, and others. Job costing allocates amounts of payables and payroll to work items and to job overhead, and corrects or verifies the project estimate. Accounting software is the most widely used and some interacts with estimating software.[13]

10. Interim job-cost accounting and reporting: provides the information and data required for management and estimating through monitoring the work in progress, assessing the values of work done, and preparing progress reports. It also provides the information needed to adjust methods, schedules, targets, and estimates.

11. Final job costing, cost analysis, and cost data filing: the review and correction of production rates and unit prices in a project's estimate in the light of actual results; the completion of job costing, the inquest to discover mistakes and losses in the estimate and in the work done, and the final feedback of information about actual costs and performance. This is the information for new cost estimates, and the planning and scheduling of new projects. Again, a computer system makes all this more feasible and economical and the results more useable.

Although for financial accounting purposes each project is seen as an independent cost center, construction management requires the feedback and recording of **experiential information** and data, and its use in future estimates, bids, and projects. Because construction projects consist of many **work items** that resemble items in other projects, each construction project has a resemblance to others through items such as:

- Site works in one project that are rarely identical with those in another, but some work items such as clearing and excavation may be similar.
- The foundations and structure designed for one site that may not be identical with those at another, but concrete materials and placing methods often are similar.

- The exterior wall cladding in one project may be of similar specification as that in another, and the material and labor costs may be similar.

So it is with other items of work: roofing, finishes, mechanical and electrical services, etc. The more utilitarian the work, the more it tends to be commonplace.[14]

As a whole, each construction project is uniquely different. That is the fundamental nature of sites and construction design. Because construction is complex and made up of many parts although the parts always are in a unique arrangement different projects often have similarities in their details and work items.

One fact stands out: *There is no better source than the experience of past projects from which to get information and data about new projects.* How else can the costs of future work be estimated if not from the facts and experience of past projects? Most contracting companies specialize in one kind of work; therefore, often there are similarities among the work undertaken on different projects. For example, most building projects contain the following:

- Concrete footings and foundation walls
- Concrete slabs (on ground and suspended)
- Concrete or steel columns and beams
- Steelwork, and miscellaneous metal products
- Carpentry work
- Plumbing and electrical work, etc.

We can identify hundreds of work items common to most building projects.[15] These work items make construction management a cyclical process whereby, of necessity, the experience gained in today's work provides information for tomorrow's cost estimate. Storing and manipulating large amounts of data such as construction produces can be done efficiently only by using a computer with suitable software.

1.5 PERSONS IN CONSTRUCTION MANAGEMENT

In one way or another, everybody in construction is, involved in, or affected by, its management. Only the front-line managers are identified and reviewed here. The standard construction contracts require a contractor to employ a **superintendent** as his or her representative. It is with a contractor's superintendent that an owner's employees, his or her agents, and their employees, have the most interaction in the field.

A superintendent is in the front line of construction management. It is the responsibility of the superintendant to receive and execute instructions and complete the work as shown in the contract. In a **CM project** the construction manager usually employs a **supervisor** whose duties are similar to those of a superintendent. A supervisor is often called a superintendent,[16] which can be confusing when it is necessary to make a distinction. Their respective duties are different.

On a CM project, all of the contractors' superintendents receive their instructions from a construction manager's supervisor; therefore, different titles are needed. Others referred to in contracts and involved in construction management include

- The construction manager, discussed in Chapters 2 and 3
- Owners and designers, discussed in Chapter 4
- Contractors and subcontractors, discussed in Chapter 5
- The owner's cost consultants (e.g., a cost engineer or quantity surveyor) mentioned in several chapters.

SUMMARY OF MAIN POINTS

- Contracts are fundamental to construction. Validity and enforceability require mutual agreement, genuine intention, legal capacity of the parties, consideration of some value, and a lawful object. Some construction contracts need not be written, but oral contracts often create problems.
- Standard contracts are useful, but must be read, understood, and amended or supplemented for a project. The standard agreement AIA Document A101 expresses the essential requirements of a contract.

- The parol-evidence rule says a written contract supersedes any prior oral agreement.
- Legal counsel is advisable for specific contractual questions and problems.
- Building and engineering construction are different in several respects: project size, financing, variety of materials and methods used, parts designed by a contractor, type of contract, and locations of sites.
- Traditional construction management has two general objectives: (1) to perform

a contract, to minimize risk, and to maximize profit, and (2) to record and apply experience to future cost estimates and projects, to improve opportunities for business success, and to ensure survival.

- Construction Management (CM) (capitalized) is by a construction manager or a management contractor. (The noncapitalized term refers to that done by a general contractor.)

- A general contractor has two roles: (1) specialist trade contractor performing certain parts of the work, and (2) construction manager for an entire project.

- A general contractor has two objectives: (1) to perform a contract satisfactorily, and (2) to make as much profit as possible (to some extent these objectives are mutually exclusive).

- The three phases of the estimating–planning–controlling cycle of construction management are

  1. Estimating costs of work, including data retrieval and pricing quantities

  2. Planning and scheduling work activities and resources, and budgeting and cash flow prediction
  3. Controlling work in progress according to an estimate and schedule.

- An estimator makes a quantity survey before pricing the work. In some cases, it is the work of a quantity surveyor employed by the owner. Then the schedule of quantities may be a bidding document.

- Experience of past projects is the most reliable source from which to get information and data about new projects.

- Similar work items are found in most building projects. This makes it possible to use past experience in estimating costs of future projects.

- Superintendents and supervisors on sites are in the front line of construction management. In a standard contract, a superintendent is the contractor's representative.

NOTES

[1]Lawrence M. Friedman, *A History of American Law*, (New York: Simon and Schuster, 1973), II, Chap. IV, *Contract*, p. 245–47 on "Contract."

[2]Including, AIA Document A101, *Owner-Contractor Agreement*, and AIA Document A201, *General Conditions of the Contract for Construction*; and the equivalent Canadian document, CCDC2, a *Stipulated Price Contract*, which combines both agreement and conditions.

[3]See Friedman on *Consideration*, pp. 245–46, 247.

[4]The Canadian CCDC2 (1982) contract conditions say, for example: "In the event of conflicts between Contract Documents" that certain documents shall govern others; e.g., "specifications shall govern over drawings." Some architects in the United States use a similar condition as a supplement to the AIA Document A201. For more on standard contracts in English, see: Keith Collier, *Construction Contracts*, 2d ed. (Englewoods Cliffs, N.J.: Prentice-Hall, 1987).

[5]Speculative house construction is different from other building construction because the builder–developer also is the owner–designer, and so is not governed by a construction contract with an owner. This affects both company structure and project management in speculative house construction.

[6]It has been found that building projects with only outline designs and specifications and requiring proposals and shop drawings from bidder/contractors can produce much cheaper building space than those fully designed by architects.

[7]On-site designers and drafters are not uncommon in some countries; especially on major building projects.

[8]Elsewhere however, and particularly in other English-speaking countries, contracts based on **bills of quantities** are not uncommon for building projects.

[9]Peter F. Drucker, *Management: Tasks, Responsibilities, Practices* (New York. Harper & Row, Publishers, 1973, 1974) Chapter 34, pp. 431, 442.

[10]A person may be an individual or a company, and in most CM projects the construction manager is, of necessity, a company. See more on CM in chapters 2 and 3.

[11]The quantity survey is shown outside the construction cycle because it is a translation of the design information and, in some contracts, may be made by a professional quantity surveyor or other cost consultant. Usually, however, a quantity survey is made by each estimator–bidder. If the bid is not successful, the result usually is wasted effort.

[12]Timberline Software's Precision™ Estimating Extended, for example, provides a **work breakdown structure** from the cost estimate.

[13]Timberline's Medallion Accounting and Job Cost software and Precision™ Estimating software are designed to interact. The Job Cost program is essentially a reporting program.

[14]Consider **M & E services** within different building types. Behind the plumbing fixtures, the systems in buildings of a type contain many common work items.

[15]For estimating and costing, the common items of building construction are identified as **basic items.** These are the basic content of master specifications, cost codes, data bases, and model estimates.

[16]Some construction managers are loathe to call their on-site representatives "superintendents" because this identifies them with general contracting. Many construction managers want to emphasize that they are not contractors, because of workers' compensation assessments and their position as an independent advisor.

QUESTIONS AND TOPICS FOR DISCUSSION

1. Explain concisely the following terms:
   - (a) quantity survey
   - (b) work activity
   - (c) planning
   - (d) scheduling
   - (e) cost controlling
   - (f) general accounting
   - (g) cost accounting
   - (h) interim report
   - (i) final cost analysis
   - (j) cost data file

2. Explain concisely the two primary meanings for the term construction management as used in the text.

3. Summarize the distinction made between two kinds of construction made in this chapter.

4. What are the five essential ingredients of a valid and enforceable contract?

5. Define the meaning of valid, and enforceable, as used in the text.

6. Which two contract ingredients have the greatest effect on a construction contract's character and its management, and why?

7. Identify and describe briefly all the main management functions of a contractor

in a lump-sum construction contract performed in the traditional mode.

8. Explain the primary objectives of construction management by a general contractor.

9. Draw a diagram illustrating the construction management cycle and annotate the diagram sufficiently to explain all the various management activities in the three major phases.

10. Explain the statement, "A quantity survey interprets the information given in the construction drawings."

11. State an owner's argument against entering a traditional contract with a contractor.

12. State a contractor's argument in favor of a traditional contract with an owner.

13. State an owner's argument in favor of a construction management project.

14. State an owner's argument against a construction management project.

15. Compare the primary objectives of a contractor with those of a construction manager.

16. How can construction management improve the chances for success of future construction projects?

17. Describe briefly the relationship between a project's cost estimate and the scheduling of its time and resources.

18. Explain the essential differences between general accounting (and its objectives) and job cost accounting (and its objectives).

2

CONSTRUCTION MANAGEMENT AND COMPUTERS: AN OVERVIEW

You are not a man, you're a machine.
George Bernard Shaw (1856-1950)

This chapter examines the fundamental nature of construction, main management functions, and possibilities for the use of computers in construction management. Management is both self-control and the systematic achievement of objectives, and management science has become a powerful instrument. In many business schools, however, **project management** is not a subject for study, capital budgeting is not learned, and most business teachers and writers ignore the construction industry.

2.1 CONSTRUCTION MANAGEMENT, GENERALLY

The Construction Industry

Why is the construction industry hardly ever mentioned in business schools and textbooks? Perhaps, it is because the construction industry is so different. Why mention the complications of a maverick industry like construction when examples can be taken from the better-known and understood manufacturing and retailing industries? Yet the products of the construction industry are the infrastructure of modern life. The differences between cost accounting in manufacturing and construction are significant. Industrial cost accountants deal with small units of production, e.g., trucks, hand tools, shirts: things that are mass-produced. In construction cost accountants deal with thousands of different and often incomplete work items that make up a custom-designed structure: a product that takes months, sometimes years, to complete.

In dealing with the construction it is necessary to understand the nature of construction and its sites: construction works of unique design, built on sites also with unique characteristics, under a unique set of conditions. Most manufacturing is of small units, and mass production is the norm. Accounting for the costs of mass production is simple. Over a certain period, the units produced are counted. The number produced is divided into the total production costs to arrive at the average cost per unit. Cost accounting for construction is called project cost accounting (or **job costing**) since almost all costs are related to a specific project. Certain **overhead costs** are directly related to being in business and not to a specific project.

In manufacturing, a number of units are produced in a given period. In construction, a project produces only one item, and the typical production period is much longer; typically, months or years. Cost accounting in manufacturing involves counting units of production. Project costing involves *the measurement of incomplete parts of a project* (i.e., the work items and components of a building). Therefore, unlike general cost accounting, the costing of construction work requires technical knowledge and skills similar to those need-

ed in cost estimating, which is the other side of the coin from job costing. Cost estimating is the head, and job costing the tail; you can't have one without the other. Other features of construction that are different from those of manufacturing include the following:

- An industry with a product that, as part of *real estate,* legally and physically becomes part of the site
- A mobile work force of journeymen and other workers, often with loyalties to a trade or union instead of an employer
- A large, complex, custom-designed, and immovable product integrated with a site to which most of the production resources are brought, and upon which the product is built
- A capital-intensive product that requires a big investment in a limited market
- A cyclical demand for work that rises and falls with the economic and political tides
- A conservative industry that has not radically changed in decades

These characteristics make construction and its management different from most other industries; often to the surprise of newcomers to property development and construction buyers.

Project Management

Despite the uniquely different features of the construction industry, it is interesting how often other industries use the terminology of design and construction. True, buildings were the first among major productions, but it suggests that construction and some other industries do have something in common. In his book of essays on software engineering, *The Mythical Man-month,*[1] Frederick P.

Brooks, Jr. (described as "the father of the IBM System/360" and named "the architect [*sic*] of the IBM Stretch and Harvest computers")[2] uses such terms as

> *architect*
> *architecture*
> *Reims Cathedral* (as an example)
> *estimating* [costs] (several references)
> *written proposals, the formality of specification, architectural*
> *Tacoma Narrows Bridge* (another example)
> *Tower of Babel* (described as the first engineering fiasco).

Presumably because buildings are the most common examples of complex systems, Brooks compares software engineering to building design and construction. The use of such metaphors relates something about design and construction as well as software engineering. For example:

> "How does one keep the architects from drifting off into the blue with unimplementable or costly specifications?"[3] asks Brooks. "Until estimating is on a sounder basis, individual managers will need to stiffen their backbones and defend their estimates with the assurance that their poor hunches are better than wish-derived estimates."[4]

2.2 OBJECTIVES OF CONSTRUCTION MANAGEMENT

What are the goals and objectives of construction management? The first objective for any company is to stay in business. Another is to make a profit that will satisfy the principals and shareholders, thus ensuring that the key people will keep their jobs.

Management must therefore seek ways to improve productivity. In construction, most management is project management: the monitoring, controlling, and recording of project costs and productivity. This is true of a one-man firm, a two-person partnership, or a private or public corporation. However, there are times when all that can be done is to hold a company together, to hold onto the primary assets (e.g., the key staff, the organization, the ability to get work, and the corporate reputation). These assets are essential to existence. It is fatal for a company to have overheads that cannot be met by income. It is almost as critical to lose key employees.

Next, a company's goals and objectives are management's primary concern: to decide, express, and achieve them. To paraphrase and quote Drucker: The result of a construction company is a well-built building. "Inside an enterprise [e.g., a construction company] there are only costs."[5] Throughout every project there is this need to know about and to control costs, and so there is the need for information, its use, and management. Computation is not the main strength of computers; it is information management.

2.3 FUNCTIONS OF CONSTRUCTION MANAGEMENT IN OUTLINE

Because of its diverse nature, it sometimes is difficult to say things that apply to the entire industry. Therefore, in describing management functions, sometimes it is necessary to look at companies larger than the typical one with less than 10 employees that make up most of the industry. This text will keep to a logical sequence of functions: from cost estimating and bidding to the completion of work.

The Cost Estimating Function

The combination of estimating and bidding is the primary means of getting work for most companies. It is, therefore, the first function of a project. As a means of getting work, it is first in importance (see Fig.1.2). However, in the use of computer systems, financial accounting seems to be ahead. Accounting, however, deals with history, while cost estimating is the means to future work.

An estimator must provide reliable quantities and estimates of **direct costs.** Decisions as to markup to be included in a cost estimate and bid for **indirect costs** belong to management. A cost estimate is the primary management instrument and information source, and therefore it must be made so as to provide the information needed: for planning, scheduling, budgeting, cost control, and job costing. It is not necessary, however, for all the information to be explicit and immediately available in a cost estimate. Certain information can be extracted later.

There are several programs for estimating, costing, and planning and scheduling, that interact in the creation and flow of information and data needed in construction management. (There is more information on estimating and job costing in Chapter 7.)

The Job Cost Accounting Function

This function creates the input from which a cost estimate is the output. Project costs occur; an invoice goes first to **job costing** (for coding) and then to accounts payable. From job costing, the information returns to estimating for reporting and comparison, and then into the data base for later use. With computer programs, information moves faster and is more readily accessible.

Reasons for indifferent job costing, or its virtual absence, include a view of estimating and bidding as a gamble, like betting on the horses; a lack of people who really understand job costing; the effort and the costs of setting up and using a job-costing system. Integrated estimating, job costing, and accounting programs make this easier, but a well-planned system is needed first. (There is more on this in Chapter 7).

The General Accounting Function

General accounting is concerned with the general ledger, accounts receivable, payroll, and accounts payable, and with preparing

- Balance sheets (company's financial status)
- Income statements (showing revenue and expenses)
- Financial management reports

There is a lot more to accounting in the construction business, and there are more references to it later, particularly as it relates to estimating and job costing. Computers are widely used for accounting. However, the accounting software must be able to work with that for estimating and job costing.

The Design Function

In most construction companies design is limited to formwork, falsework, and temporary facilities. Some companies provide building design services, as in **design-build projects** and **turnkey projects.** They employ designers, drafters, and other design-related people. Other design-build companies employ independent design firms (architects and engineers) when needed.

There always is a design function in construction, and probably one day integration of design and construction will be more common in North America. Some countries export design-build services and transnational construction companies are already working in the North American and European markets. Some general contracting companies are now better able to offer design-build services by using computer-aided drafting and design (CADD) integrated with computer-aided estimating, job costing, scheduling, and accounting.

Other sectors of construction in which design and graphic presentations are important and which need integrated information and management include: renovation and retrofitting, interior design and construction, and landscaping.

Companies that design and build falsework, forms, components, and complete structures, eventually will find CADD necessary. Linking between CADD and estimating programs, so that data from CADD drawings can be exported into an estimating program already is possible, although it is not yet widely used. Like many other innovations, eventually it will be required by the purchasers of construction. Owners will write contracts requiring designer-builders to provide project information in a digital format about their buildings (e.g., CADD as-built drawings, technical specifications, product information, and the operational manuals for a completed building, all on CD-ROM disks).

The Contracts Function

All contractors must be able to write and understand contracts and subcontracts. It is not enough for a **prime contractor** to base his subcontracts solely on the documents of the **prime contract**. Prime contracts often do not address all the requirements of the subcontracts, since usually the owner is not concerned with how work is allocated and organized. An owner's concern is only with the result, and this shows in the contract and specifications written by a design team.

A subcontract should deal with *all* matters peculiar to the relationship between contractor and subcontractor. The absence of a well-written subcontract is especially hazardous to a subcontractor.

Word-processing programs make it easy to produce documents, letters, and records from pro formas with amendments to suit particular requirements. Free-form data base management programs enable us to store, analyze, sort, search, compare, and retrieve every kind of textual and graphic information. Document management programs make it easier to handle many documents.[6] As accountants have led the way with computers for computation, so the legal profession has led the way with computers as systems for handling textual information.

The Field Engineering Function

Field engineering refers to that which can be done only on site. On each project, the superintendent is the key individual; on a large job, it is a general superintendent. In some companies, a general superintendent may have authority over several superintendents and travel from job to job. A superintendent has the distinction of being the only member of a contractor's staff recognized by explicit reference in published **standard contracts**, as in the AIA Document A201.

The fundamental purpose of field engineering and supervision is the successful performance of a contract and its work. As projects and management needs differ, some functions normally performed in the field may be done instead at a company's office, or vice versa. There are many things (e.g., certain **general requirements**) not mentioned in contract documents to which a contractor's superintendent must attend. For example, in a fixed-price contract, there may be no mention of the need for temporary heating, services, structures, and enclosures, formwork for concrete, and other things required for construction, because the documents specify only the required results—not the means of achieving them. At present, there are not many computer applications to field engineering. CADD programs and computer systems with modems can transport design information, records, and reports. As methods and programs for construction management develop, autonomy of on-site management will become increasingly feasible. Portable computers have been in use for over a decade, and in field work related to mining, forestry, and other industries. As yet, their impact on construction has been minor.

The Safety Function

The safety function is a part of field engineering that deserves special mention, since accident, injury, and fatalities seem to be a part of construction. For some cultures in the past it was common practice to bury a live person in the foundation of a new building.[7] It is disturbing to realize that today there often is a blood payment to be made for a structure, although not every project has serious accidents or deaths. Accidents of all kinds are disruptive and uneconomic. Reportedly, the use of computer programs that provide workers with biorhythm reports, to warn them when they are most susceptible to accidents, may be effective. (Safety is discussed further in Chapter 12.)

The Job Planning and Scheduling Function

If a bid is accepted and a contract is made, then there is a project to be performed. It is possible that those who do the **planning and scheduling** are first introduced to the job during the estimating and bidding. Often, costs cannot be properly estimated until at least the main **work activities** are planned:

EXAMPLE:

The total costs of formwork often are as much as a third of the total costs of a concrete structure. It may not be possible to decide the amount of formwork material required, or the number of times it can be used, until the job operations are planned, at least in outline.

In major **engineering construction work**, preliminary planning and scheduling are more essential and critical, because engineering construction methods often are decided by the contractor. Once a contract is made, planning and scheduling of work activities must be done so that no time is lost. Scheduling and resource-management programs are available that can be integrated with cost estimating and job costing programs. (See Chapters 10 and 11 for more on planning and scheduling.)

The Purchasing (Procurement) Function

The purchasing agent often has to obtain prices of materials, equipment, and services for the estimators during bidding; however, this may apply to relatively few major items whose costs are most significant. Firm prices for minor items usually are not sought until a bid becomes a contract. An expeditor is responsible for the economic and timely procurement and delivery of all materials, equipment, and supplies for the company's work and for the its own operations.

A purchasing agent may have several buyers and expeditors as assistants. Because of the opportunities for personal gain, these positions require a high degree of trust, especially in overseas projects. In smaller companies, a **superintendent** or a **contract manager** may do purchasing and job planning. (This is why we refer to functions and not to people.)

Computers have been in use for resource management, inventory control, and purchasing for years. Some estimating programs can automatically generate **bills of materials** prepared from the contract documents and the estimate.

The Personnel Function

Hiring and firing staff and tradesmen as required is normal in construction. Most companies usually keep only a small complement of key personnel, and these are the construction company. Beside the principals, key personnel may include managers, estimators, accountants, and purchasing officers. In the field, they may include superintendents and foremen, and some tradesmen who may have been with a company for years. Larger companies may employ a personnel manager and an expert in labor relations.[8]

2.4 CONSTRUCTION MANAGEMENT (CM) PROJECTS

Chapter 1 defined construction management and drew a distinction between traditional management in construction and Construction Management (CM). This chapter and Chapter 3 review the main features of a CM system. Later chapters examine how specific functions and features of construction management apply to CM projects.

Phased Construction

Examining phased construction leads directly to an understanding of a main reason for CM. Phased construction is best understood if one first examines what phased construction is not.

- Phased construction is not construction done in the traditional mode by using a general contractor who employs several subcontractors
- Phased construction is not waiting until every part of the work is designed before calling for bids (i.e., it is not calling for bids for all parts of the project's work simultaneously)

Phased construction is achieved in a project through the following:

- Performance of a project's work by several separate contracts between the owner and the **trade contractors** who start and finish their work at different times under the direction of a construction manager
- Compression of the design and production phases of construction so that they overlap (as illustrated in Figure 2.1)

Both time and timing are critical in phased construction. The objective is to reduce the total time spent in design and production and thereby to reduce an owner's costs. Time in property development is money; mostly through interest paid on loans. Time also is a major factor in the calculation of overhead costs. Timing lies in the selection of the best times to start and finish parts of a project. Timing is important, particularly the work of certain trades.

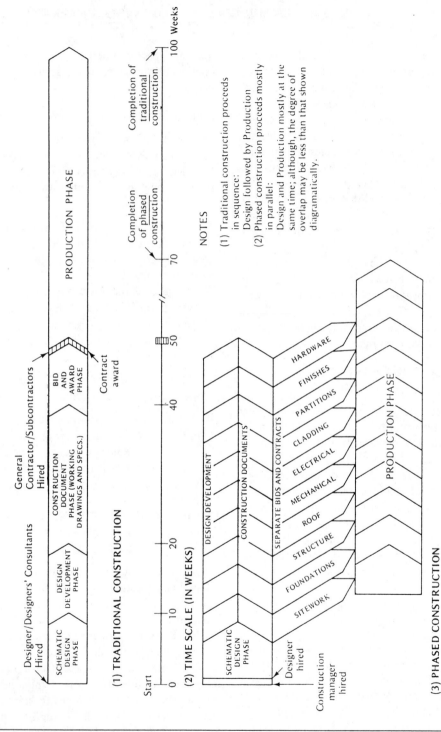

Figure 2.1 Traditional and phased construction compared

Other things for which timing may be important include the following:

- The supply and demand for construction work
- Availability of labor, materials, and equipment
- Availability of affordable financing
- Start and finish of labor agreements
- Major holidays and other seasonal events
- Political events (e.g., elections)
- Legal enactments (e.g., new legislation)
- Local considerations that affect work and productivity

By considering timing it may be possible to obtain certain materials or work at lower prices. Owners do not always realize the extent to which construction prices depend on market conditions; or that the costs of trade work do not always consist only of the **prime costs** of materials, labor, and equipment, but are affected by supply and demand.

Achieving the ideal timing for work is difficult in traditional projects, because of the designing and building sequence. It is possible to design a project and then wait before calling for bids and awarding the prime contract. Once a contract is awarded, however, the time and costs practically are fixed. To gain flexibility large projects sometimes are divided into two or more contracts (the CM concept). Usually an owner and designer can manage a project divided among two or three contracts. (That is the reason for the references in AIA Document A201 to **separate contractors** in Subpara. 1.1.4 and elsewhere.) When a project's work is split by many separate contracts, a full-time construction manager usually is needed.

By dividing a project among separate contracts with separate trade contractors,

an owner can let several parts of the work at different times (i.e., phase the work), and deal directly with them. That introduces some flexibility. Instead of one monolithic lump-sum contract, there are several separate and smaller contracts. Instead of subcontractors with whom an owner has no contractual privity, an owner can deal directly with the trade contractors doing the work. Instead of a general contractor engaged in work while managing subcontractors, an owner in a CM project employs a construction manager, who should be a specialist. Management of complex projects often is better done by a specialist, although many straightforward and ordinary projects can be done well by a general contractor.

The Construction Manager

Usually a construction manager is a corporation that provides the variety of skills and knowledge necessary. There are individuals who call themselves construction managers, just as there are individuals who call themselves contractors. There are some relevant questions to ask about this matter.

- Is incorporation important?
- Can an individual do everything needed for proper Construction Management (CM)?
- What happens if the key person is indisposed?

The requirements for CM on larger projects make it practically impossible for an individual to be an adequate construction manager. One individual cannot possess all of the necessary knowledge and skills, to say nothing of time and energy constraints. Consequently, construction managers usually are corporations.

Most of the key staff in a CM company already have experience in contracting companies. Also, design experience (or more precisely, experience in working with designers) is an important requirement for CM.

Some CM companies have been criticized for their lack of ability to deal effectively with designers. Construction management companies that originally were contracting companies have been criticized for their lack of ability to prepare and use **conceptual estimates**. These and other shortcomings appear related to the traditional separation of design and construction in English-speaking countries.

Skills Needed in a CM Company

The staff in a CM company should include people with some or all of the following skills and experience:

- Good oral and written communication skills
- Management with a general contractor
- Field engineering as a superintendent
- Knowledge of trades and **trade contractors**
- General cost estimating for bidding and contract negotiations
- Conceptual estimating for budgeting and cost control in the design phase
- Design and erection of temporary structures
- Design and installation of systems according to the class of work to be managed
- Understanding of architectural design (but not necessarily conceptual design ability)
- Project planning and scheduling using CPM/PERT and other related techniques
- Cost accounting (job costing) experience
- Accounting and finance for construction
- Experience in dealing with labor unions, particularly in matters of jurisdictional

disputes and disputes over the employment of nonunion companies
- Experience with contracts, claims, and disputes
- A working knowledge of computer systems and the more common application programs (e.g., word-processing, spreadsheets, data bases, scheduling)
- Some computer programming ability, at least with high-level languages applicable to data bases

This list is basic but incomplete because the variety and complexity of projects is so great. The items are in no particular order of importance, because what is critical in one project may not be in another. The nucleus of a CM team might be an experienced superintendent and a graduate with appropriate degrees in business management and architecture or engineering. Academic skill and experience alone are not enough. The following abilities also are needed:

- Leading and managing people
- Effective decision-making
- Effective language and communication skills
- Dealing with designers, public officials, and authorities with jurisdiction

The most valuable people in a CM company often are the generalists; those with varied experience in design, construction, development, and management, based on a specialist's technical education and training.

The Project Manager

A **project manager** may be an employee of an owner; as in the United States federal government's Public Buildings Service of the

General Services Administration (GSA/ PBS), which appoints public servants as project managers for CM projects. In such projects, the project manager acts for the government. Similarly, a project manager may be employed or hired by a private corporation. Since committees and boards are notoriously indecisive and slow, invariably it is better to have only one person with adequate knowledge and authority making decisions for an owner. Whether employee or hired agent, a project manager should have wide but clearly defined authority to make decisions for a project. A project manager also may be a construction manager. Or, he may have authority to appoint and direct the construction manager, or the designer and the **designer's consultants**.

The Development Manager

According to this text's definitions, a **development manager** has at least the same authority as a project manager. He also has the authority to act on the owner's behalf to obtain land, financing, and other prerequisites; including the approvals of all authorities with jurisdiction over the **work**. Also, following substantial completion of a project, a development manager may manage the property. In some projects, a development manager prepares financial feasibility studies, arranges early leases with blue-chip tenants, and places leases with other tenants as the project progresses. In other words, an investor in real estate development may rely on a development manager for everything except the cash to be invested. Therefore, we may speak of the following:

1. CM projects, with a construction manager as the **prime agent** of an owner
2. PM projects, with a project manager as the prime agent, and a construction manager, or with the CM function performed by the PM
3. DM projects, with a development manager as the prime agent, with a construction manager, and possibly a project manager; or with CM and PM functions performed by the DM or PM

Remember, it is possible that two or three functions might be carried out by one or more person(s).

2.5 COMPUTERS AND CONSTRUCTION MANAGEMENT

If a machine was designed for cost estimating, it would look like a personal computer. Computers can be used to do many things in design and construction. The accounting profession took the lead with personal computers in business, through good business sense and because financial accounting is required by law. However, despite the tax department's requirements, for contracting companies, cost estimating is much more immediate and critical than accounting. If using computers for accounting makes sense using them for cost estimating is even more logical.

Computer Communications

The ability to access hundreds of data bases for information will cause one of the greatest changes in design and construction. The means already exist. *CompuServe*[R] is the largest computer information service in North America at present, and there are others. Some services already provide information for specialists. This sector of computer use and this part of the information deluge is growing rapidly, and you need to keep in touch.[10]

SUMMARY OF MAIN POINTS

- Construction is a unique, project-oriented industry through its relationship with the land and is different from retailing and manufacturing.

- Primary objectives of construction management include: (1) keeping the company in business; (2) minimizing risks; and (3) making a profit by maintaining and increasing productivity, and by recording and using historic information and data (i.e., construction experience).

- Construction company assets primarily are its key personnel, organization, ability to get work, and reputation.

- Functions of construction management include:

  Cost estimating: to obtain work and provide information for management.

  Job cost accounting: the other side of estimating; different from cost accounting in manufacturing, as it requires quantitative information about incomplete work.

  Accounting: deals with the general ledger, accounts receivable, accounts payable (relates to job costing), and other typical business accounting practices.

  Design: most builders only design temporary work (e.g., formwork); some make shop drawings; some offer design-and-build services.

  Contracts and subcontracts: some must be written and understood by contractors. Subcontracts cannot be based entirely on the prime contract, since a subcontract's conditions go further.

  Field engineering: this is a superintendent's primary concern and embraces all that needs to be done on a project site.

  Safety: part of field engineering. Accidents, injuries, and deaths on construction projects are frequent, traumatic, and uneconomic.

  Job planning and scheduling: this begins during cost estimating and relies on an estimate for information.

  Purchasing: a separate department in larger companies. The essential functions include expediting to ensure materials are on site when required and inventory control.

  Personnel management: involves not only hiring and firing workers and staff and related problems, but also dealing with labor unions and keeping personnel records.

- Construction Management (CM): features include management of several separate prime contracts by a construction manager, and phased construction (i.e., the compression and overlapping of design and construction.)

- A construction manager: to possess all the skills required, this position usually must be a company.

- Project managers: may be an owner's agent or employee (or a contractor's contract administrator).

- Development manager: usually has most extensive authority on behalf of an owner.

- Computer applications in construction management are many. Programs exist for virtually every construction management function. Electronic information services will be important to construction.

NOTES

[1]Frederick P. Brooks, Jr., *The Mythical Man-month: Essays on Software Engineering* (Reading, Mass.: Addison-Wesley, 1982).

[2]Ibid., Frontispiece, "About the Author."

[3]Ibid., p. 43.

[4]Ibid., p. 21.

[5]Peter F. Drucker, *The New Realities*, (New York: Harper Collins Publications, 1989) p. 230.

[6]See, *BYTE*, 17:6, June 1992, titled "Managing Infoglut," pp. 244-86. Also, *BYTE*, 17:9, Sept. 1992, "Profiles in Document Managing," pp. 198-212. Also, see later chapters for specific computer programs.

[7]*Encylopaedia Britannica*, (1972), s. v. "sacrifice."

[8]The titles of managers in construction companies are numerous and often misleading (e.g., project manager). See, Carleton Coulter III and Jill Justice Coulter, *The Complete Standard Handbook of Construction Personnel Management* (Englewood Cliffs, N.J.: Prentice-Hall, 1989) for one authority's job descriptions.

[9]See, General Services Administration, Public Building Service, *The GSA System for Construction Management* (Washington, D.C.: 1975).

[10]The computer applications and management journal for design and construction, *A/E/C SYSTEMS: Computer Solutions,* is one way. See also, *Scientific American*, special issue on "Communications, Computers, and Networks," 265:3, Sept. 1991.

QUESTIONS AND TOPICS FOR DISCUSSION

1. Describe what is different about the construction industry when it is compared with most others.

2. Make a list of at least 10 college courses (both arts and sciences) to which principles and techniques of design and construction are applicable, and briefly explain how, why, and where.

3. Explain the few primary objectives of any business corporation.

4. Fully describe three of the several functions of construction management.

5. Describe in detail the fundamentals of Construction Management involving a construction manager.

6. List and briefly describe the main functions of CM.

7. Identify several programs used with computer systems that can be used in specific CM functions.

8. Explain concisely the differences between a construction manager and a general contractor.

9. Explain concisely the differences between a construction manager and a project manager.

10. Explain concisely the differences between a project manager and a development manager.

11. Explain nature and functions of phased construction.

12. Explain the statement: A cost estimate is the primary construction management instrument and information source.

13. Identify and list at least 10 specific skills needed in a construction management company.

CHAPTER

3

A CONSTRUCTION MANAGEMENT SYSTEM

There are only two qualities in the world:
efficiency and inefficiency;
and only two sorts of people:
the efficient and the inefficient.
George Bernard Shaw (1856–1950)

This chapter examines an integrated and comprehensive Construction Management system that employs a computer. Not all companies need such a comprehensive system, but the management functions it embraces are essential in some degree and in one form or another to all projects. Every builder needs to make cost estimates; therefore, every builder needs job costing, and business accounting is required by law. Making them all parts of an integrated and computerized management system makes each more efficient.

3.1 CONSTRUCTION MANAGEMENT PROJECTS

In the early 1960s, Construction Management (CM) appeared in North America as a new and different contracting method for large commercial development projects. The purposes of CM were (and still are):

- To employ the best managers available
- To reduce project time and financing costs
- To create a flexible method of building that leaves as much control as possible with the owner–developer

In real property development, financing costs are critical; so, time saved is money saved. Also, a commercial developer needs flexibility during construction to accommodate future tenants and their needs. Traditional design and general contracting procedures are protracted and rigid. In large part, commercial development is a matter of time and timing, and traditional contracting is not conducive to changes and interruptions. Commercial developers need hands-on control and the means to make adjustments economically, so they adopted CM.

At first there was resistance from some general contracting companies who viewed CM as a threat. It was not long, however, before many general contracting companies became construction managers, or set up CM companies. In the early 1970s, the United States General Services Administration's Public Buildings Service (GSA/PBS) adopted CM for major public works projects. Since then, CM has become common in North America, and in the last decade some British and European companies have employed it. Arguments in favor of CM for projects include:

- Savings of time through phased construction, and as a result:
  (1) Savings in financing costs
  (2) Earlier availability of the development and an early start to a new cash flow
  (3) Less risk from variations in construction costs during construction
- Owner–developers retain more control over CM projects in progress
- Fewer subcontracts and related problems
- A construction expert—a CM—is involved on an owner's behalf during both design and construction.

In summary, the effect of CM for government and private owners alike can be significant savings of time and money, provided an owner employs a competent CM company. As a concept and method, CM has been around for centuries, although not in the same form. In medieval Europe, master builders designed and built the large cathedrals, castles, and mansions (the title, *maitre d'oeuvre* is still used in France); possibly, they were the first civil construction managers on record.[1] Later, some architects (such as Alberti of Italy) made design a specialization separate from construction. In the nineteenth century, this dichotomy became established and formalized. Consequently, in English-speaking countries, architecture and building have developed separately. Large general contracting companies first appeared in the nineteenth century to finance and construct buildings that neither church nor state could support.

3.2 CONTRACTS FOR PROFESSIONAL CM SERVICES

Contracts for professional services generally are more difficult to write than contracts for construction work, because professional services (including construction management) are more difficult to define. Two standard contract forms available for CM services include:

1. The AIA Document B801, Owner-Construction Manager Agreement[2]
2. GSA/PBS Construction Management Contract format as published in the GSA System for Construction Management[3]

Comparing such documents from different sources is an effective way to understand the subject.

The AIA CM Document

The American Institute of Architects (AIA) Document B801 is an agreement with terms and conditions that embody the most important parts of a contract.

1. The date of the agreement
2. The names of the owner and construction manager
3. The title, location, and scope of the project
4. The name of the project's architect
5. A brief description of the nature of the professional CM services
6. The compensation, or professional fee, for the CM services to be paid by the owner:
   (a) A lump-sum fee, plus expenses
   (b) A multiple of all the expenses for time and consultants (excluding the lump-sum professional fee), or
   (c) A fixed fee, as a lump sum, or
   (d) A fee based on a percentage proportion of the construction cost, as defined[4]

The terms and conditions of this agreement contain the following articles:

Article 1   Construction manager's services
Article 2   The owner's responsibilities
Article 3   Construction cost
Article 4   Direct personnel expense
Article 5   Reimbursable expenses
Article 6   Payments to the construction manager
Article 7   Termination of agreement
Article 8   Successors and assigns
Article 9   Arbitration
Article 10 Insurance
Article 11 Extent of agreement
Article 12 Governing law
Article 13 Other conditions or services.

It should be observed that, in certain respects, the views of the AIA and the GSA/PBS on the subject of CM and reflected in their publications are different, and a comparison provides insight.

The GSA/PBS CM contract is much more detailed and extensive. Having designed its own system, the GSA/PBS can be more objective; whereas the AIA can only publish a standard but adaptable document for a variety of projects. Also, the AIA naturally considers the architect as the owner's prime agent and leader of the owner's team.

In AIA Document A201/CM-1980, General Conditions of the Contract for Construction, for CM, the architect retains all of his traditional prerogatives; the construction manager's position is solely advisory and administrative and subject to the authority of the architect. In the GSA/PBS document, the construction manager appears independent of the architect and has instructions to report directly to the owner's project manager (e.g., "any apparent defects in the design").

The GSA/PBS CM Contract

The federal government designed the GSA document for multimillion dollar projects and for a particular management structure. Much about the fundamentals of CM can be gained from its study. The GSA/PBS CM contract contains some 60 articles. The topics of some articles are peculiar to the United States federal government, including: "Equal opportunity," "Davis-Bacon wage rate decision," and "Buy American." The terms defined in this contract are illuminating. Some synopses follow.

1. Head of Agency: the Administrator of GSA [Owner]
2. Contracting Officer: the person executing the CM contract for the government; the project manager
3. Resident Engineer: the technical employee of the government assigned to the job site as representative of the Contracting Officer
4. Architect-Engineer: to be named for a project
5. Construction Executive: designated by a CM company as fully responsible for the CM of a project
6. Construction Superintendent: designated by the CM company to work for the construction manager on the job site, managing, directing, inspecting, and coordinating work
7. CMCS Supervisor: designated by the CM company to implement the GSA/PBS CM Control System, including planning, data collection, and control of computerized CM systems
8. Separate Contractors: those with contracts with the government for supply of **long lead items**
9. **General Condition Items:** items that do not lend themselves readily for inclusion in any of the separate construction contracts, such as guards, scaffolding, hoists, and signs (**job overhead costs**, rather than specific **items of work**)
10. Deliverables: all the professional CM services performed by the construction manager, for which the government pays a fee. The only terms that require additional explanation, because they are unique to this form of contract are
    (i) The GSA/PBS CM Control System (explained later in this chapter)
    (ii) Deliverables

Deliverables (Professional CM Services)

In its standard CM contract, GSA/PBS sets down in detail specific CM services as the basis of the fee payment to a construction manager. This is not a definitive description of professional CM services. It is almost impossible to describe fully any professional service in words because, by definition (at least historically), professional service requires something more than a specified, limited effort. It requires the earnest effort of a professional person to achieve some known goal for his client. There is no absolute guarantee of success because of the inherent nature of the goal strived for (e.g., a medical cure; an acquittal through due legal process; or the performance of a construction project by contractors within a stipulated budget of money and time). The deliverables of CM, however, do give tangible form to and a measurable basis for the services of a construction manager. They also create a measurable basis for progress payments of a CM's fee. A synopsis of the GSA/PBS CM deliverables follows:[5]

1. General management of design and production of the work
2. Narrative reports and job diary by key CM personnel
3. Schedule control, including preparation and updating
4. Cost control, including data provision and analysis
5. Financial control, including monitoring of cash flow, changes, payments, and claims
6. Design development and review by the construction manager, including recommendations and reduction of costs through value engineering

7. **Long-lead procurement** (advanced purchasing)
8. Planning of contracts for phased construction
9. Interfacing to guard against overlapping contracts
10. Establishment of construction requirements for temporary facilities and services and other general requirements arranged or provided for by the construction manager
11. Review of drawings and specifications, and reporting of deficiencies
12. Development of market analyses and stimulation of bidders' interest in providing materials and construction work
13. Soliciting bids, arranging pre-bid conferences, and reviewing and recommending bids for contracts
14. Management and inspection of construction work on-site
15. Management of general condition items (general requirements)
16. Preparation of a safety program to integrate the required safety programs of separate contractors
17. Conduct of labor relations, to obtain labor harmony on-site
18. Implementation of changes in work required by owner
19. Processing of claims by contractors and others, including making reports and giving evidence as required
20. **Value engineering** and management to achieve economy for the owner

In reviewing these deliverables, remember that the construction manager is a professional agent who provides management services for a fee. The deliverables do not limit the CM services to be provided. Each deliverable is priced separately by CM companies making proposals (bids) for CM services to GSA/PBS. This enables the owner to better evaluate proposals and forms a basis for progress payments of the CM fee as the construction work proceeds.

Summation of Requirements for CM Contracts

In terms of performance objectives, CM services must ensure that a CM project will be

1. Well designed (technically and economically) by the architect–engineer
2. Well performed according to all contractual requirements
3. Completed as soon as possible and not later than the stipulated date for completion
4. Completed at an economic cost not greater than the stipulated amount

These four items are the final summation of objectives for all CM contracts and CM projects.

Well-Designed Projects

This is the most difficult to monitor and to achieve. Unlike the other three objectives, it is not the subject of textual documentation; it does not fit easily into a verbal description. Many CM contracts between private owners and construction managers do not include this requirement of a construction manager. The General Services Administration is to be commended for its effort at objectivity. What use is it if a building is economic and completed on time if it is not well-designed?

Naturally, most designers would react to the sight of a contractual requirement that a construction manager should monitor his or her design. In its contract documents, the AIA insists that the architect have the final word on all matters pertaining to "artistic effect." Perhaps the AIA could publish guidelines for construction managers whose review and duties include the criticism of designs. It is difficult to separate economy and technology from artistic effect, especially by means of prescriptive writing and contractual terms, but who better to do it than the architectural profession?

The GSA/PBS stipulates that a construction manager will not be deemed to have failed in his contractual obligations and will not be held responsible if the following occur:

1. Costs exceeding the stipulated budget: provided the construction manager has furnished the services required to control costs as in the CM contract
2. Project time exceeding that stipulated: provided the construction manager has supplied the necessary services to control project time as in the CM contract
3. Design deficiencies: provided the construction manager has furnished the necessary services to identify defects in the design; advised as to defects, and has taken reasonable precautions to ensure that the separate construction contracts contain no duplication (overlapping requirements for work); and ensured that all the work required for the project is included in one contract or another
4. Defective construction: provided the construction manager has exercised proper supervision to ensure that the work was performed according to the construction contracts[6]

In its CM contract, GSA/PBS has tried to create a truly professional position for the construction manager, while stipulating specific deliverables. It has stipulated the required performance: a well-designed project properly completed within a specific budget of money and time. Realistically, it says that a construction manager cannot be held responsible for the design and construction work of others, providing the CM has done a professional job. Some will criticize this CM contract because it does not directly make a construction manager financially liable for failure of a CM project. Such criticism may be misplaced. When a person contracts to provide something tangible recognize that it always is possible to perform the contract without giving the best. A construction manager provides management services directed toward the proper and economical performance of a construction project by others. His presence does not limit their obligations to design well and to produce good quality construction.[7]

3.3   SELECTING A CONSTRUCTION MANAGER

Having reviewed CM contracts, how is a construction manager selected and appointed? GSA/PBS requires a competition for a CM contract, as do many private owners. GSA/PBS uses the following two-step procurement procedure:

1. Request for and evaluation of qualifications of CM companies
2. Request for and evaluation of priced proposals and a construction management plan for the specific project

After evaluating the submitted qualifications of CM companies and their key personnel, a CM evaluation committee scores each applicant. Those CM companies with the top scores (ideally, five companies or more) are then invited to submit:

1. *Priced proposals* to provide CM services with separate prices against each listed deliverable
2. *Management plans* for the specific CM project, with details for the three main phases of the project
3. *Resumés of key personnel* employed by the construction manager

There are discussions between the CM evaluation committee and the CM companies submitting proposals, both prior to and after submissions. Applicants can make written modifications to their proposals up to a specified time following the last discussion. The evaluation committee then gives numerical scores to each submission. Maximum scores are the same for a priced proposal and the resumés of key personnel; with a slightly higher maximum score for the management plan (30, 30, and 40 percent). In other words, price is not the only consideration. It is not even the most important consideration.

The many anecdotes about work done by the lowest bidder contain some truth. Awarding contracts to the lowest valid bidder assumes that all bidders are equally capable and will give equal value, and that price therefore is the only consideration. Since that is the law for public works, it is applied even when the price difference is only a few dollars, disregarding any differences in reputation or skill. By requiring "evidence of capability" through a management plan, evaluators of CM bids make it less likely that a lower level of competence will succeed simply by being cheaper.

In construction, the rule of "lowest bidder gets the job" has prevailed too long. Ironically, to omit something from an estimate and a bid has been a certain way to obtain work. Private purchasers of construction and services might consider this method of selection as an alternative. Also, the same method might be followed in the selection not only of construction managers, but also of designers (architects and engineers) and contractors. Since judgments must be made about the quality of plans and people, a computer program using fuzzy logic might be helpful.

3.4 A CONSTRUCTION MANAGEMENT CONTROL SYSTEM

In the GSA/PBS CM contract referred to herein, a *Construction Management Control System (CMCS)* is described in detail as an essential part of any CM contract with GSA/PBS. An analysis of this description reveals all the fundamentals of any CM system. There are four subsystems.

1. A narrative reporting subsystem
2. A schedule control subsystem
3. A cost control subsystem
4. A financial control subsystem

In these four subsystems, the main objectives of CM are recognized: to monitor a project closely and to control its

1. Quality (through reporting)
2. Time (through time schedule control)
3. Costs (through cost control), and
4. Cash flow (through financial control)

To monitor a construction project, each key person on the construction manager's staff writes a monthly report on a particular aspect of the project. These key people include the construction executive, the supervisor (CMCS), the construction superintendent, the chief estimator, and the project accountant. The reports include the project diary and a schedule analysis report.

Many individuals in construction instinctively revolt against writing reports, which is an obstacle to good management. The slavish recording of facts and events does not constitute management; paperwork is not a substitute for management. There must be action on events and information. For reporting to be worthwhile, something positive must be done with reported information.

The act of reporting merely helps to compel certain actions and results. First, it requires mental concentration and deliberation; just like putting a topic on a slide and examining it under a microscope. Next, through scrutiny of others, recording and reporting helps to clarify observations, thoughts, reactions, decisions, and actions now and in the future. Often a person thinks more before committing himself in writing. A report also attracts attention and action by exposing the need for action. Finally, a report makes reviews, inquiries, and analyses possible because written evidence exists. There is a risk that in an attempt to demonstrate performance, a construction manager may try to drown an owner or the contractors in paper. The content of the monthly reports and the subsequent results in the project work on-site must be monitored and proven.

To complete a construction project within a specified time requires not only planning and scheduling of activities, but also schedule control (i.e., the necessary adjustments to both the schedule and project as they progress). It is not enough to say, "We shall get the job done in the shortest possible time. Nobody can do better than that." What is the shortest possible time? Only a schedule can determine that. Similar to reporting, scheduling requires a commitment to paper that can be reviewed and criticized. It demands deliberation, mental concentration, and commitment; these always are more effective than merely reacting.

To complete a construction project with a specified expenditure requires not only estimates of cost, but also cost controls to adjust expenditures. Cost control and financial control are two different things. Cost control is for expenditures, and financial control is for income and cash flow. It is necessary to ensure that financing is available when needed. (See Chapter 20 for more on financing and payments.)

Keep these fundamentals in mind to design a CM system to suit any particular project. Obviously, smaller projects need less personnel and less reporting than larger projects. A smaller, complex project, however, requires more attention than a larger, simple project. Creative project design is not enough. A project also needs creative contract design and creative management. Construction includes both design and production, and an effective CM system must apply to the entire process, from conception through design to occupation.

A construction manager often is as valuable in the design phase as he is after construction starts. The traditional system is to design, produce working documents, call for bids, and get the work done by a general contractor. So, during the design phase an owner has only the designer as adviser. Design and construction, however, cannot be separated without causing deficiencies in both. Most designers consider the construction details while designing; however, many designers' knowledge of *construction economics* is limited, and some are not familiar with all practical aspects of construction. Therefore, a construction manager can contribute much toward a design. Many designers recognize the value of a construction manager in a project's design phase and welcome the contribution. Others find a construction manager's concern with costs inhibiting.

3.5 OTHER ASPECTS OF CM AND TRADITIONAL PROJECTS

Some comments about CM and construction management in traditional contracts follow. They are presented in no special order.

Construction Manager

A construction manager should be an expert in construction with a primary obligation to think and act solely on behalf of a client—the owner. In traditional construction, an owner employs a contractor for construction only, but often a contractor's experience would be useful in making a design. In a CM project with a construction manager the owner has a construction expert throughout.

Planning and Scheduling

A CM project with phased construction depends for its success on compressed time and accurate timing. Planning and scheduling must therefore be an integral part of CM. Purchasers of certain types of construction should be able to demonstrate that savings in time and money are gained from CM projects. Owners of a single project, however, usually cannot do that because

they have little or no historic data for comparison. A detailed estimate of costs is, therefore, the first, and sometimes the only yardstick.

Project Manager

Those corporations that often purchase construction find the employment of project managers beneficial. Project managers become experienced in dealing with construction managers and designers, and in the use of a CM system, and that increases efficiency. Project managers get to know their employers' needs and to understand the persons with whom they regularly deal. Project managers should be vested with adequate authority to make decisions on behalf of their employer, the owner.

Specialization

Specialization fosters efficiency. A construction manager is a specialist in the management of construction, whereas a prime contractor is a specialist in the construction of certain parts of buildings (e.g., the structure) who takes on the management of subcontractors because his work supports their work. Most contractors cannot afford to employ experts in all the specialized fields of construction management. (N.B. It is characteristic of the construction industry that, apart from a few very large contractors, most companies are small and with limited management skills and resources.)

Responsibility

A general contractor practically takes on all the risks involved in construction work. This leaves the owner almost risk-free, but at a cost. Some owners and designers believe that construction managers should have to carry some of the risks carried by a contractor. Otherwise, they argue, a construction manager has little incentive to perform effectively on his client's behalf. Historically, the nature of professional services has been that a professional commited herself to do her best for her client, but she could not guarantee success because of the nature of the undertaking. It seems that a CM project comes within this definition, and that a construction manager's position is comparable to that of a designer, or any other professional. However, the nature of professions is changing, and professionals now must take a less detached position and accept more responsibility for results.

Freedom From Financial Involvement and Risk

A construction manager's freedom from financial involvement and risk in projects allows him to advise the owner more effectively. The provision of job overhead (general condition) items by a construction manager, however, may limit that freedom and reduce his or her effectiveness as an impartial adviser. It is not unusual in a CM project for a contract to be made with a separate contractor for the provision of job overhead items, including such things as temporary services and facilities, certain kinds of equipment, and site clean-up. If CM projects become more common, this need may bring forth a new kind of specialist contractor.

Fees

Fees for construction managers may vary from 1 to 10 percent of construction costs. About 5 percent appears typical, but such figures mean little without specific details

about the expenses paid by an owner. CM contracts must precisely define the scope of fees and expenses of all kinds. Site supervision is a big item; its costs must be defined and allocated.

Owner's Risk

By entering a CM project, an owner takes on greater risks than in a traditional project. He also stands to gain more. Typically, an owner has no guarantee of the ultimate, total cost in a CM project, but the CM services should include good estimates and cost control. In a traditional project, the owner knows his commitment from the outset of production, but extras are the norm, not the exception. Beyond the actual costs of work the owner also pays the general contractor to carry most of the risk.

Management Contractors

Management contractors are different. Like many construction managers, they perform no construction work, but they do undertake to guarantee performance of a project within the limits of time and cost. In fact, many general contractors are really management contractors in that they do none of the work.

Designers

Designers' duties and the overlap of design and production in CM involve designers more in construction. This involvement by designers can only enhance their capabilities. Similarly, the involvement of a construction manager in the design process suggests the artificiality of separating design and construction.

Construction Costs

Construction costs are adversely affected by

- Lack of communication among designers, contractors, and subcontractors leading to misunderstandings and flawed contracts
- Misunderstanding of bidding documents
- Fear and risk of unknown requirements when bidding for work in a fixed-price contract
- The need for allowances to cover contingencies, omissions, and errors
- The constraints of bid depositories that can reduce competition among bidders
- Unnecessary inspections that add to costs
- Over-robust contractors who take advantage of subcontractors
- Subcontractors who should have remained as tradesmen
- Superintendents who should be foremen
- Construction managers who should be contractors

The list is endless, but many causes can be minimized or avoided entirely by using a CM system with such features as

- Direct selection of specialist contractors and suppliers by an owner's **A/E/CM** team
- Objective and accurate construction documents
- Direct payments by owner to specialist contractors and suppliers, and therefore reduced risk of problems with payments

CM is not Only for Large Projects

Owner–designers have successfully used CM on building projects such as custom-designed residences costing approximately $500,000 (1992 dollars).

CASE

An early CM project (1963–1964) was managed from the architect's office. Local general contractors tried to obstruct the project by privately threatening to deprive local trade contractors of cost-plus insurance work. The CM project succeeded because the trade contractors saw advantages in the new method.

Contract

Contract documents even for small CM projects should be specially written. If the AIA standard form of CM contract appears unsuitable, a CM company should create its own standard contract. Agreements should contain all the provisions essential to CM. This may require extensive amendments and supplements to the contents of standard CM contracts, as indicated later.

Cost Consulting

CM services can be the result of cost consulting services provided to owners. Some CM companies are **cost consultants** and provide cost feasibility studies, conceptual estimates, and economic studies based on preliminary design drawings. Costs drive most projects, and cost consultants can show where savings are possible. Because of cost studies and the savings they indicate, a cost consultant often can convince an owner that he would benefit from a CM project.

Building Renovation

Construction Management is especially suitable for building renovation work in which information is sparse and risks high.

If an owner seeks a fixed-price contract for renovation work, he must pay a contractor to take the risks. Yet, not all the risks may materialize. Bidders generally have to assume the worst and allow for all perceived risks in their bids. If the purpose of a CM project is renovation work, the owner takes most of the risks, but he pays for nothing he does not receive. Small renovation jobs, however, usually cannot justify the costs of a construction manager, and may be more economically done by a general contractor.

Price-Book Secrecy

Contractors make a mystery of construction costs, often to their advantage. Some make an issue of price-book secrecy, but any experienced cost consultant (cost engineer, quantity surveyor, or construction manager) can analyze and synthesize the costs of construction work in the same way as contractors and their estimators. The only secret is a construction company's markup for overhead costs and profit. Even that figure can be measured by analyzing bids and comparing them with a consultant's estimate of costs.

Many owners, bankers, financial managers, and some designers seem mystified by construction costs and cost estimates; yet not all will seek the help of cost consultants.

The Need for a Cost Consultants' Organization

There is no profession established in the United States that specializes in the costs and economics of building construction on behalf of owners and developers. There are competent cost consultants, but owners must first recognize the need for their services. **Cost consultants** need an effective professional organization.[8] Construction managers need better skills in making accurate conceptual estimates of costs, because with them a construction manager is better able to control a project and its budget.

Required Skills and Experience

There is no reason why contractors and designers (architects and engineers) cannot be successful construction managers, provided they have the required skills and experience. Other aspects of CM and specific construction management procedures and techniques are included in subsequent chapters.

3.6 ALTERNATIVES TO CM PROJECTS

For various reasons, some owners are not candidates for a CM project. Other ways for an owner to obtain some of CM's advantages without hiring a construction manager include

1. Separate fixed-price contracts for the different parts of a project employing **separate contractors**
2. **Cost-plus-fee contracts** with a contractor employing subcontractors
3. A fixed-price contract in the traditional mode, but with most of the work done using **cash allowances** and subcontractors

Let us examine these alternative methods and note some of their advantages and disadvantages.

Contracts with Several Separate Contractors

Separate contractors for a project are provided for by the standard forms of fixed-price contracts. The general conditions of AIA Document A201-1987, Subparas. 1.1.4, 3.14.2, and 4.2.4, refer to "separate contractors." (In CCDC2 it is "other contractors.") Contracts with separate contractors are common for such work as

- Preparatory site work, such as clearing, demolitions, and landscaping
- Substructure work, such as piling
- Specialized work, such as the installation of special machinery and equipment in buildings

Standard contracts recognize and define separate contractors and refer to their mutual obligations in the interests of a project's owner. If there are many separate contractors on a project, it becomes similar to a CM project. Traditionally, the designer coordinates separate contractors, but if a project is complex and has many separate contracts a full-time construction manager or management contractor is needed.

Cost-Plus-Fee Contracts

Cost-plus-fee contracts give an owner almost unlimited flexibility, but at what price? With a tried and proven contractor, cost-plus-fee contracts can be effective, but many appear to result in financial loss or even disaster for their owners. A better alternative is a **maximum cost-plus-fee contract** in which a maximum cost is stipulated. These contracts are a hybrid with features of both parents: fixed-price and cost-plus. Unlike a mule, however, this hybrid is neither inflexible nor sterile. As before, a project's owner may need a construction manager if the work is complex and if there are several contractors on-site.

Contracts with Cash Allowances

Another alternative to a CM project is a fixed-price contract in the traditional mode, but with one major difference: the extensive use of **cash allowances** stipulated to be expended as the owner–designer directs as set out in standard contracts. In other words, **nominated subcontractors and suppliers** do most of the work. In this method of contracting, an owner selects a single contractor through competitive bidding in the usual manner. The contractor estimates the direct costs for and bids on those items for which he would normally bid—typically, work in Divisions 1, 2, and 3 of the *Masterformat* (i.e., general requirements, site works, concrete). Instead of calling for subbids for the remaining trade work, bidders simply include all the cash allowances stipulated in the bidding documents. In addition the bidders stipulate a percentage markup for overhead and profit (including all the costs of management) in the usual manner.

Everything in such a contract is bid for competitively. The so-called "general contractor's work" is bid for at the time of initial selection of the contractor. The remaining work by the nominated subcontractors and suppliers is bid for later as directed by the owner–designer. In this way, an owner–designer achieves a measure of phased construction and retains considerable control.

Contractually, there is no difference between this method and the traditional mode of contracting. The significant difference is the proportion of project work contracted and paid for by cash allowances. In traditional contracts, the proportion in cash allowances might be from 10 to 20 percent of total costs. In this alternative method, the proportion of cash allowances might be as high as 80 percent. This gives an owner–designer more flexibility and control and the opportunity of employing phased construction (most of the advantages of a CM project, previously described).

One shortfall of this method may be the absence of a construction manager, particularly in the design phase. Nevertheless, this method of contracting has advantages. Typically, it is used in countries in which professional **quantity surveyors** practice. Quantity surveyors are similar to construction managers in North America, and their work and methods are described in more detail elsewhere.[9] As agents of owners, it is normal for quantity surveyors to work with designers during the design phase of projects to make conceptual estimates of costs; advise on contracting methods and procedures; prepare contract documents, including **schedules of quantities** of work, and arrange for bids based on these documents and the unit prices they contain; administer contracts; and generally act in their clients' interests.

The quantity surveyors' familiarity with construction costs and contracts, their participation in a project from its inception, their use of **contracts with quantities** and unit prices, and their experience in construction administration make the use of extensive cash allowances in a traditional fixed-price contract an effective method of contracting. There is no reason the method cannot be adopted and used by owners and designers elsewhere, but accurate preliminary estimates of costs must be made early in the design phase.

3.7 COMPUTER APPLICATIONS IN PROJECTS

A computer system enables a manager to handle large quantities of information and data that otherwise would be unavailable or never used. This information includes payroll costs, bills of material for purchasing, purchase orders, invoices, and the accounts payables' ledger; all these and more are made and used for routine purposes. All data can be instantly transferred and manipulated by computer and used for other purposes such as job costing, schedule updating, making **applications for payment**, interim and final cost and progress reports, financial statements, and so forth.

Another feature of a computer system is that every person involved in a project can be connected, including owners' and contractors' representatives. Verification of facts about costs and progress can be made part of a system devised for sharing project information. Simultaneously, the privacy and security of such information as fees and markup can be provided by the makeup and format of prices, by programmed features of information handling, and through the scope of the information made available to specific persons. Today, there is much talk of smaller, leaner, and more efficient businesses. Selected wisely and used properly, computer systems can help to create them.

REFERENCES

1. Keith Collier, *Construction Contracts,* 2d ed. (Reston, VA: Reston Publishing Co., 1987).

2. General Services Administration, Public Buildings Service, *The GSA System for Construction Management* (Washington, D.C.: 1975).

SUMMARY OF MAIN POINTS

■ Construction Management (CM) began with commercial developments in the 1960s. Reasons for CM include: (1) more flexibility and control for owner; (2) saving of project time and financing costs by phased construction; (3) earlier acquisition and use of new buildings.

■ Standard contracts for CM services are published by AIA, the federal GSA/PBS, and by CCDC in Canada. AIA Document B801, *Owner-Construction Manager Agreement*, keeps the architect as an owner's prime agent, while the construction manager is primarily an advisor and supervisor of the work.

■ Deliverables in a CGSB/PBS CM contract include 20 items, beginning with (1) General management of design and production of the work and ending up with (20) Value engineering. CM services are required to ensure that a CM project will be: (1) well designed and economical; (2) performed according to contract requirements; (3) completed by or before stipulated date; (4) completed for not more than stipulated amount. A CM will not be deemed to have failed if the following occur: (1) design deficiencies—if CM has advised owner of defects in design; (2) defects in construction—if CM has provided proper supervision of the work; (3) project time exceeding that stipulated—if CM has provided proper services to control project time; (4) costs exceeding the stipulated amount—if CM has provided proper services to control costs of the work.

■ GSA/PBS has made CM a professional service and does not hold CM responsible for any faults of designer and contractors.

■ Competitions for supply of CM services to GSA/PBS are in two parts: (1) evaluation of competing CM companies; (2) evaluation of priced fee proposals and a CM plan.

■ A GSA/PBS CM control system is specified and required by GSA/PBS that consists of four main parts: (1) a narrative reporting system (quality control); (2) A schedule-control system (time control); (3) A cost-control system (cost control); (4) A financial-control system (cash-flow control). Key CM staff write these monthly reports for GSA/PBS.

■ Aspects of both CM projects and traditional projects include: a CM acts on behalf of the owner in both phases, design and production; a CM project uses phased construction and compressed project time; a PM represents the owner and makes decisions for him; a CM should be a professional expert, and act as such; freedom from financial involvement should enable a CM to give the owner unbiased advice; an owner takes on more risk in a CM project, but stands to gain in flexibility, time, and costs.

■ Important features of CM projects include:
1. Direct selection of contractors and suppliers
2. Direct payments to contractors and suppliers
3. Fewer subcontracts (only with major trades)
4. Better reporting and documentation is required

- CM can be effectively used on small projects, such as custom residential construction costing less than $1 million.

- A CM can guarantee the final cost of a project, under certain conditions.

- CM is suitable for such as building renovations and other projects in which it is better for an owner to accept some risks and have more control of the work.

- Contractors' costs are better understood by a CM.

- No profession specializes in building construction costs on behalf of owners and developers.

- Contractors and designers can be CMs if they have the necessary skilled staff.

- Alternatives to CM projects that enable an owner to retain more control of a project include

  1. Separate fixed-price contracts for parts of a project employing separate contractors
  2. Cost-plus-fee contracts with a contractor employing subcontractors
  3. A fixed-price contract with a general contractor and all the work covered by cash allowances and by nominated subcontractors

NOTES

[1]Before *civil engineering* there was *military engineering,* which had its construction managers in the officer corps of ancient armies. It is said, the Roman army's victories often were as much due to the shovel as the sword.

[2]AIA Document B801, *Owner-Construction Manager Agreement* (Washington, D.C.. American Institute of Architects).

[3]General Services Administration, Public Buildings Service, *The GSA System for Construction Management* (Washington, D.C.: 1975).

[4]See the original Document B801 for the many details of professional payment.

[5]See The *GSA System for Construction Management* for a complete description of deliverables.

[6]See *The GSA System for Construction Management* for complete details. The design, construction, costs, and time of a project are all the substance of contracts made by an owner with others; not with his construction manager. However, a construction manager could be held at least partly responsible for any of the deficiencies named in the GSA/PBS contract if his services were shown to be inadequate, or if the construction manager was proven negligent.

[7]Compare the construction manager's position with that of a management contractor, who subcontracts all the work, for which he is responsible.

[8]The American Association of Cost Engineers appears to specialize more in engineering and industrial than building construction and its costs.

[9]Keith Collier, *Construction Contracts*, 2d ed.; (Reston, VA.: Reston Publishing Co., 1987) Section 1.2.11 and Chapter 1.6.

QUESTIONS AND TOPICS FOR DISCUSSION

1. Why was Construction Management introduced, by whom, and when?

2. Define the following terms, as used:
   (a) Management (generally)
   (b) construction management (not capitalized)
   (c) Construction Management (capitalized).

3. List and briefly explain the main purposes and functions of Construction Management.

4. Explain in detail, with a diagram as an aid, the term "phased construction."

5. Describe three benefits from saving project time through phased construction.

6. Describe the essential differences between the functions of (a) an architect, (b) a construction manager, as described in the AIA Documents A201/CM and B801, *Owner-Construction Manager Agreement.*

7. Explain briefly the essential differences between the functions of (a) a construction-management-control-system supervisor, (b) a construction superintendent.

8. Describe in outline form a system for the selection of design or construction management companies to provide professional services in construction in which the cost of the services is not the sole criterion.

9. Discuss the pros and cons of making a construction manager responsible to an owner for the total costs of a project.

10. Discuss from the owner's point of view the pros and cons of CM when compared with construction in the traditional mode.

11. Discuss in detail the statement: Those who often purchase construction find the employment of project managers as agents has several benefits.

12. Discuss in detail the statement: Construction Management (CM) is (is not) only for large projects.

13. Explain the statement: By entering a CM project, an owner takes greater risk than he would in a traditional project.

14. Explain in detail the statement that: In CM projects, designers are obliged to become more involved in construction.

15. Describe in outline two different contractual alternatives to a CM project as outlined in this chapter.

CHAPTER

4

OWNERS AND DESIGNERS

The end is to build well. Well building hath three Conditions. Commodity,
Firmness, and Delight. Elements of Architecture (1624) pt. I.
Sir Henry Wotton (1568–1639)

In Chapter 3 the construction manager's relations with the owner and designer were examined. In this chapter there is a closer study of the owner and the designer, an owner's need for advice, and how an owner can obtain that advice. The owner is considered as a developer. Finally, the designer is considered as owner's agent and manager of construction work.

4.1 OWNERS, GENERALLY

Owners have rights to land, initiate construction, employ **designers** and **contractors**, and pay for the construction work, which is an owner's first obligation in a contract. In the past, owners had little direct involvement in construction. After an owner had provided access to the site and certain information, an architect or engineer usually acted on his behalf. An owner's only

significant involvement was to pay the contractor periodically on presentation of the designer's certificates. Today, many owners are more involved in their contracts and projects. They are more likely to be business corporations or government departments; often with at least as much business experience as the builder, and sometimes represented by an employee who is a qualified project manager. As evidence, consider two items: the advent and development of professional Construction Management (CM), and the changes in standard forms of construction contracts that now give greater responsibility to the owner.

Professional CM was started by owner–developers. As a result, there are now fewer projects with general contractors and administered by architects. As for standard contracts, the shift in responsibility is apparent when comparing the earliest and latest editions of the AIA's standard contracts (e.g., owners are now required to make more unilateral decisions).[1]

In the past, designers made most of the contractual decisions. Today, through the standard contracts, the architects say that owners must make decisions and assume the risks and responsibilities arising from them. Owners, therefore, must fully understand their relationship with designers and contractors, and their obligations;[2] particularly those of a designer as an administrator, arbiter, and judge of performance in a construction contract.

Some owners believe that, after creating the design, a designer's primary function is to ensure that the work is performed according to the construction contract. The specific wording of a particular contract is paramount, but the latest standard contracts now specifically limit a designer's responsibility for construction work. The primary responsibility for the proper performance of work lies with the contractor.

Construction owners should be dissuaded from the idea that it is always right to accept the lowest bid for work because the designer is obligated to see that the work will be done properly. Obviously, periodic supervision by a designer is not sufficient to ensure that all work will meet a contract's requirements. It is the contractor who undertakes, as a primary obligation, to do the work according to the terms and conditions of the construction contract.

Some owners go into a building project without an independent consultant (designer or construction manager) and may spend thousands of dollars on work while dealing with only one construction company. Sometimes, an owner hires a designer to make a design and nothing more. The owner then proceeds to construction by dealing only with a builder. It is a reasonable contention that even a regular purchaser of construction should not enter into a construction contract without first seeking independent advice, especially about contracts, quality, and costs.

In the 1960s, for example, reinforced concrete tilt-up walls replaced masonry walls in many new warehouse buildings. How can owners decide on the relative merits of buildings of different designs and specifications? Owners need expert and independent advice on technology, contracts, construction costs, and the **costs in use.** As a prospective owner, it is one thing to have a clear idea as to what a commercial store or an apartment building should be like; it is another to communicate those ideas and the specific methods of implementing them to a contractor. It is one thing to select a contractor by means of bids made for the same work; it is another to select the best design-build proposal for buildings of equal size or capacity, but of different designs using different materials and construction methods. It is even more difficult and hazardous for an owner to select and enter into a sound construction contract.

Many have tried to do construction development alone, and many have suffered losses, trouble, and the costs of acrimonious disputes and a great waste of time. Even business and professional people who know the wisdom of the saying, "Each to his own trade," and who would not attempt to service their own cars, or to invest in stock without professional advice, will invest the equivalent of several years' income in a building project and deal with only one contractor, sometimes without a written contract. In the long term, contracting companies will benefit if they advise an owner who wants to build to first obtain independent advice. Performing a construction contract in a project with a competent designer or manager is more straightforward for a contractor than dealing directly with an owner who knows little about the construction industry.

CASE

In a fixed-price contract for the building of a brick-masonry church building, when the contractor ordered the facing bricks he also ordered some of the same bricks for another contract. His intention was to make a saving by combining two orders. All the bricks were delivered to the church site. Later, when the contractor sent a truck and two men to pick up bricks, the parish priest protested vigorously that the contractor was stealing them.

It was an effort for a representative of the designer to explain to the priest how a fixed-price contract works and that the contractor was not dishonest. Some owners with not much more understanding of construction contracts than that of the priest try to manage a project alone.

CASE

A lawyer in a law firm with contractors and construction managers as clients bought a parcel of land on which to build a house. The lawyer hired an architect to design the house, and that was the extent of the architect's services. The lawyer then negotiated a cost-plus-fee building contract with a house builder. Before the house framing was complete,

the lawyer had approached a construction-manager client and asked him to act as an expert witness in a court action against the contractor.

The cause of the lawyer's dispute with the builder is not important. The point is, had he sought and taken expert advice on construction contracting at the outset, probably the dispute would never have happened. Should you think that those cases involving individuals are not representative of corporate owners who undertake major construction projects, remember that all corporations are represented by individuals. Many are lawyers, and both priests and lawyers spend a lot of their time giving advice.

4.2   OWNERS AND THEIR ADVISERS

Common sense and experience tell us that the best advice usually is that obtained from an independent expert who is paid. Yet, some people spend hundreds of thousands of dollars on constructing a building without getting independent advice; either because they don't know how, or because they think they can buy furnishings and equipment with the money saved. When selecting a design, many people know what they like. The attitude regarding costs and risks is that, "Competitive bidding will tell me what the costs should be. Risks are the builder's problem. That's what I pay him for."

If an owner insists on dealing directly with a builder, he should at least hire a cost consultant. For a comparatively small fee, a cost consultant can provide advice and information that ultimately may save a lot more. An owner should have a suitable contract;

preferably, one based on a standard contract, minimally amended, and supplemented to suit a project's particular needs and circumstances. Many cost consultants can offer expert advice about contracts. If the site and the construction work are not exceptional, a standard fixed-price contract may be suitable. Otherwise, a construction contract should be custom-designed. This can be as important as designing the building.[3]

Is the layman aware enough of building design and contracting procedure to build without professional advice? Apparently many believe this is true. However, consider the evidence to the contrary. Most houses are neither well-designed nor well-oriented. Most are built speculatively from stock designs. Most houses designed by professional designers publicize that fact. In designing and building a house, why consider first the mailman and locate the main entrance facing the street? What about noise, the sun, the prevailing wind and weather—and privacy? Why consider only one structural system for a warehouse? A builder may offer only a system for which he has a franchise; another system may be cheaper or more suitable. Even a construction company's reputation is not always a reliable guide. The capability of a project's superintendent is important to good performance, but even a well-reputed construction company may hire a poor superintendent.

An outline of procedure for a prospective owner seeking a designer's services follows.

1. Building-space requirements: Write down your requirements. List the areas required for different uses. Use existing buildings as a guide.
2. Make a proposed plan: Use graph paper cut to size (at a scale of 1/8-inch or 1/4-inch to one foot) for each separate space required (e.g., storage area, offices, etc.). Make a workable arrangement that suits your needs, and which fits into a simple, overall shape of suitable proportions. (A square plan is the most economical, but square plans do not suit most buildings. Also, long, narrow plans with large perimeters are not economical.)
3. Building elevations: Decide on the building's height and sketch the elevations. Show doors and windows. Note any special requirements or dimensions. If you cannot draw, include a written description with the space requirements; attach a copy of a surveyor's plan of your site.
4. Describe the proposed building: Start with the elevations (north, south, east, and west) and describe each exterior and interior view: walls, floors, ceilings, and fittings. This is better done in a schedule. Describe by exception; i.e., make a general description, and then state the exceptions (e.g., 1/2-inch gypsum wallboard on all walls and ceilings, except in Room Nos. #10, 12, and 23; ceilings to be suspended systems).
5. Fixtures and machinery: Make a descriptive list of everything needed inside the building. State dimensions where possible.
6. Finding a designer: Look at some recently built and similar buildings and talk to the designer.
7. Contracts and costs: Ask about the probable costs of the proposed building, and about the basis of the cost estimate. (Costs per square foot often are not reliable.) Ask about the most suitable kind of construction contract and how it should be made (e.g., selective bidding for a fixed-price contract). Ask about the need for and the advan-

tages, costs, and value of engaging a construction manager, a cost consultant, or other consultants.

8. Fees: Ask about design fees and the fees of other consultants. Ask for written proposals with full descriptions of the design services offered, the total fees you will have to pay, and their basis. Get all the important information in writing and study and compare it before making a commitment.

9. Proposals: If you deal with a construction company that offers design-build or a package deal, follow the same general procedure. Get firm proposals for design or design-build in writing on the understanding that they are open for acceptance for a specified period of time. Tell the design-build companies that you intend to get an independent opinion as to the cost, terms, and conditions of the proposed package. Hire a construction consultant and a lawyer to examine proposals and give you written reports. You will have to pay for this advice, but it will be worthwhile if you go to the proper individuals.

10. Quality standards: Do not assume that construction work that meets the local building code requirements is necessarily adequate for your purposes. Building codes require only certain minimum standards for safety and health; these standards are not always adequate for other purposes. Insist on complete, written specifications of the construction work to accompany the drawings, even in a package deal.

11. Legal advice: Have all documents (for both construction and professional services) reviewed by a lawyer who is familiar with construction contracts and procedures, especially if the amounts involved are large.

Simple CAD programs[4] can be used by the layman to make such preliminary drawings with a computer. Drafting services are available at hourly rates. If an owner is looking for design-build services, the same information and initial approach is required.

One of the first problems for an owner is finding professionals who are qualified and experienced in construction matters. Some designers do not have accurate information on up-to-date construction costs. Some construction companies that offer package deals like to keep the terms of contracts as loose as possible. Sometimes, it is not easy to get everything in writing so that you can take a detailed proposal away and get an independent opinion. Every lawyer knows contract law, but not all of them are familiar with construction and its particular contracts.

If a company is not helpful, find another. Usually there is another firm glad to go the extra distance. Remember that almost anybody can call himself a contractor or a construction manager. The best way to check experience is to request the names of completed projects and call the owners. Ask about the work and services they received. Take the same approach with an architect, professional engineer, or builder. Generally a professional organization will not recommend a particular firm or member.

4.3 DEVELOPER–OWNERS

There is a distinction between those owners who have construction work done for their own use, and those who have it done in order to sell a developed property. A corporate or individual owner who contracts for work to develop property for his own use obviously has a long-term interest in the property and in its costs in use while occupying or leasing and maintaining the building. A **developer** who is primarily interested in selling will have little or no interest in a property once it is sold.

The amount of profit a developer makes depends on the original cost, total costs of the development (the **hard** and **soft costs**), and the selling price. It is worth noting that the costs of construction (the hard costs) often are less than half of the total costs of a development; the costs of land and the soft costs comprise the remainder. Some developments are sold before construction work starts or is completed. For example, a developer may, purchase an option to buy undeveloped property, and then obtain from the **authorities with jurisdiction** the necessary approvals for a change in zoning, followed by a development plan, design, and building permit. The developer then is ready to seek bids for the construction work. At that point the developer may decide to sell the property as it stands, or he may start construction and sell the development while work is still in progress.

Development is a high-risk business that has created fortunes and caused many bankruptcies. Rights to properties are bought and sold at all stages of development. In many developments, the major part of the profit comes not from building, but from a quasi-political act: a change in zoning (e.g., from agricultural to commercial use). A vote in favor of rezoning may increase a property's value many times. Because of the complexities of zoning, development, contracts, law, and construction projects, few fields are more suitable for chicanery than that of real property development.

There are many ways to cut construction costs, and there can be a large difference between work's high and low costs. Inspections by those representing the interests of mortgagees (who lend the money to build) may be only perfunctory or simply an endorsement of inspections done by the building inspector's staff. Much work is done with inadequate contract documents and with oral and unrecorded changes. As a result, some benefit from the losses of others.

CASE

Owner–developer A has a CM project under way to develop a parcel of land for commercial use. So that the development can be sold before construction work is finished, it is provided that the construction contracts can be assigned. Owner A also has agreed orally with some contractors and in letters to others to certain changes in work that effectively lower the standards and costs. With construction work under way, Owner A sells the development to Owner B, who knows nothing of A's oral agreements with some of the contractors. Soon, the new owner is at odds with those contractors because he wants things done according to contract specifications that conflict with the oral agreements they made with Owner A.

By nature, developers are different from technicians. Some see only the big picture and read only the bottom line. Often, they are not concerned with construction details or other things that concern technicians. In describing the development business, a developer said that ultimately all contracts are worthless, and that there is only one significant fact: Who holds the money and has the clout?

In other words, the developer said a contract is as good as the intent behind it, that enforcing a contract through the courts is not economical, and that to control the cash is to hold the real power and authority. Without developers and entrepreneurs, the private enterprise system will not work. Somebody must take the initiative and risks in getting a development under way and completed.[5] Governments, for example, have been singularly unsuccessful in providing housing, and the demand for housing will not be met except by developers who see an opportunity for profit.

4.4 THE DESIGNER AS MANAGER IN TRADITIONAL PROJECTS

The role of the **designer** as interpreter of construction contracts and the judge of their performance has evolved over decades. Study the differences between AIA Document A201-1987 and the earlier editions, particularly that of 1976. Whereas AIA Document A201-1976 said, "The Architect will be the interpreter of the requirements of the Contract Documents and the judge of the performance thereunder by both the Owner and the Contractor" (Subpara. 2.2.7.), the later edition, AIA Document A201-1987, lowers the import of the wording and says, "The Architect will interpret and decide on matters concerning performance under and requirements of the Contract Documents on written request of either the Owner or the Contractor" (Subpara. 4.2.11) and, "When making such interpretations and decisions, *the Architect will endeavour to secure faithful performance by both Owner and Contractor, will not show partiality to either and will not be liable for results of interpretations or decisions so rendered in good faith*" (Subpara. 4.2.12). [Emphasis added.]

This comparison shows a marked change in the AIA's view of the **architect** and his relationships with owner and contractor in the standard stipulated-sum contract. It is suggested by the new order and titles of the articles. In the 1976 edition, the significant article was *Article 2, Architect*. In the 1987 edition *no* article is so titled, and the primary reference to Architect is under Article 4, *Administration of the Contract*.[6]

Standard contracts require an owner who discharges the architect–consultant to replace him or her with another in the same capacity. Their presumed intention is to protect the contractor against the absence of an arbiter between contractor and owner.

Briefly, a contractor is responsible for the work he contracts to do. According to the standard construction contracts, a designer is obliged only to see "*in a general way*"[7] that the work is performed in accordance with the contract documents. Therefore, a designer is required to make only periodic site inspections. In fact, once work has started, some owners elect to have the designer not involved in a project at all. Conversely, some owners believe it is necessary to have somebody on-site on their behalf to oversee the work, otherwise they believe the quality of work will suffer.

In Britain and many other English-speaking countries, many owners engage a **quantity surveyor** as an agent (or employee) to perform project administration, which includes checking a **schedule of values** and the **applications for payment,** negotiating **changes in the work,** and settling the final account. In France, the quantity surveyor's equivalent is the *economiste de la construction* (self-explanatory), and at a lower level the *metreur-verificateur* (measurer-checker). In the other European countries that employ bills of quantities in building contracts, the services and functions typical of a quantity surveyor are performed by the designer.

In a cost-plus-fee contract, the designer may be obliged to undertake management functions that in a fixed-price contract would normally be done by the contractor (or, in a CM project, by a construction manager). Similarly, in a fixed-price contract in which a larger-than-normal portion of the work is done through cash allowances, a designer must be more involved than usual in the construction management. Both these arrangements already have been described as alternatives to a CM project.

4.5   THE DESIGNER IN CM PROJECTS

In a CM project, both the **designer** and the **construction manager** are agents of the owner. In the **design phase**, the designer usually is the owner's prime agent, aided by the construction manager. In the production phase the roles may be reversed. This apparent symmetry in the division of authority and responsibility is seen, however, as an oversimplification when we consider phased construction, as illustrated in Figure 2.1, and see the overlapping of design and construction. What, then, of the relative positions of the designer and construction manager? Obviously, the utmost cooperation is needed in the interests of their mutual client, the owner. In construction, with its intricate and overlaying networks of contractual obligations, authority and communications responsibility always has been difficult to allocate. As a result, hoping for a hit and a score, a plaintiff in construction often sues everyone involved.

The AIA and other professional institutions have modified their standard construction contracts to reduce the exposure of professional members to legal actions by third parties. CM projects, with the duties and obligations divided between designer and construction manager, may increase a designer's exposure to legal actions. A CM system creates more benefits and more risks for owners and, therefore, more risks for their agents.

The avoidance and settlement of misunderstandings and disputes in contracts always is desirable, especially in CM projects with their emphasis on time and its effect on the economics of construction. To this end, therefore, it is important to consider the need for one person as an interpreter and judge of the performance of the construction contracts in a CM project, and who that person should be. Should it be an **architect** or an **engineer** (a designer), as in most projects? Or, should it be a person more directly involved production and dealing with contractors (i.e., a construction manager)?

The AIA standard contract documents for CM contracts set out the traditional situation in which the architect is identified as interpreter and judge of a contract's performance. Is this simply the perpetuation of a tradition, or is it considered by all concerned to be in the owner's best interests? It should be acknowledged that it is professional tradition that helps to develop and sustain knowledge and expertise and to pass it on. Every textbook on architectural practice refers to the architect as an impartial referee between the parties in a construction contract. In the AIA standard document, *General Conditions of the Contract for Construction–Construction Management Edition (A201/CM)* (as in its predecessor, A201), the architect is described as the interpreter and judge of a contract's performance by both parties. At the same time, both the architect and the construction manager are to administer the contract.

This appears to be an adaptation of the original AIA document A201 designed to keep the architect as the team leader. Is this always in an owner's best interests? Do most owners have the knowledge and opportunity to decide for themselves?

Argument can be made for the construction manager as interpreter and judge in the contracts of a CM project. Generally, a construction manager has more on-site experience. It is therefore reasonable to assume that most CM companies have more experience with the kinds of problems that commonly arise on construction sites. Disputes frequently arise from contract documents, and although writing them should give a designer insight into their meaning and intention, it is not necessarily a more objective insight.

Another argument claims that as a past member of the contracting fraternity a construction manager could be biased toward a contractor. In the end, probably it comes down to the abilities of certain individuals, and owners are left without a simple solution.

4.6 THE DESIGNER AS CONSTRUCTION MANAGER

Can a designer be an effective construction manager? To find an answer the meaning of construction manager must be understood. An owner, designer, contractor, or construction manager, usually is considered as a company or firm, not an individual. (It is in that sense that these titles are used herein.) Whether a person is an individual or a corporation makes a difference. As discussed previously, an individual usually cannot be an effective construction manager on a large project, because no individual has sufficient skill, knowledge, experience, or energy. Except in a small project, it takes a

team to be an effective construction manager. Therefore, a more realistic question is, Can a design firm be an effective construction manager? The answer is yes—providing the design firm employs persons with the necessary skills and experience. The people most likely to be missing in a design firm are those related to on-site construction; i.e., superintendents and project managers in construction companies who have the ability to organize a large construction site, can deal with many subtrades, can use the stick as well as a carrot in getting work done, can select the proper construction equipment, make conceptual estimates, and understand construction as a builder and a contractor. Therefore, to be effective construction managers, design firms need to employ those typically not found in designers' offices, including

1. Cost engineers, quantity surveyors, or construction economists, (the terms are more or less synonymous), and
2. Construction supervisors or superintendents (the titles may indicate different backgrounds, but similar functions).

These individuals are essential to a construction management firm that must make conceptual estimates, control costs, do on-site supervision, and perform other management functions. Entry into CM need not disrupt the organization of a design firm. Most of the extra personnel needed work on sites most of the time and often can be hired for a project's duration.

Provided all the necessary skills are present, there are obvious advantages when designer and construction manager are found together in one company. Then an owner only needs one contract to get the services to design and manage. Integration of both functions should lead to greater efficiency, and much of the potential friction between designer and construction manager can be avoided. However, since an owner often benefits from the independent design criticism by a construction manager, this may be an offsetting loss.

As construction managers, designers once again can become master builders without abandoning their role as agents of and independent advisers to the owners of con-

struction projects. If there exists potential conflict with any statutory regulation (e.g., workers' compensation) or rule of conduct (e.g., one regarding designers' commercial involvement), a design firm can avoid it by not acting as a contractor. As designers/ managers, however, they can participate to the fullest extent in construction, its innovation, organization, and management.

SUMMARY OF MAIN POINTS

- Owners' primary obligations are to provide the requisite information and to pay for services and work; the advent of construction management (CM) and the wording of standard contracts indicate a greater involvement of owners in construction.

- Owners need a designer (architect or engineer) and often other agent-consultants (e.g., a CM or a cost consultant).

- Any owner who proposes to deal directly with a builder or to enter into a design-build contract needs a cost consultant.

- A procedure for an owner seeking design services:
  1. Make a space schedule
  2. List other building requirements
  3. Describe building, by elevations
  4. Make a graphic plan of building
  5. Sketch elevations, with openings
  6. Take this information to a selected designer
  7. Ask designer about building costs, bidding, and construction documents, and a need for a construction manager and other consultants
  8. Ask for fee quotations, and get written proposals
  9. If dealing for a package deal (design-

build), get a firm proposal in writing open for acceptance for a suitable period, and an independent expert's opinion
  10. Do not assume that a building inspector's supervision is sufficient: require written specifications in a contract
  11. Get advice from a lawyer who knows about construction.

- Development is a high-risk and complex business; developers look for the overall picture and the bottom line, but not always at the details of construction. Developments for sell or lease may affect quality.

- Designers usually provide limited supervision of owner's construction work; therefore some owners employ a project manager, a construction manager, or a construction economist (quantity surveyor), for contract administration or supervision, or both.

- Designers with the necessary skills may be construction managers. There is a need for "an interpreter, a judge of performance," but who should it be: designer or construction manager?

NOTES

[1]Study the references under "Owner" in the Index of AIA Document A201-1987.

[2]Contractual obligations involve both rights and duties. My duty is your right, and your right is my duty.

[3]Most building projects are driven by economics. Therefore, anything (such as a construction contract) that affects costs and value is critical.

[4]*AutoSketch*[R] by Autodesk, Inc., the makers of AutoCAD, can be used with little difficulty on a personal computer. Some such programs provide libraries of drawing symbols to make computer sketching (CAD) even easier.

[5]For more on developers and their views, see Chapter 20.

[6]The Canadian Document CCDC2-1982 says, under general condition GC3 *Consultant*, "The Consultant [designer] will be, in the first instance, the interpreter of the requirements of the Contract Documents and the judge of the performance thereunder by both parties to the Contract" (Para. 3.6).

[7]AIA Document A201-1987, subpara. 4.2.2.

QUESTIONS AND TOPICS FOR DISCUSSION

1. Describe the recent increased involvement of owners in their construction projects, and explain briefly why this has occurred.

2. If an owner intends to accept a package deal, what criteria should be used to judge its worth?

3. Regarding the case involving Owners A and B, what should have been done to ensure that contractual irregularities could not occur.

4. A developer has an option on a parcel of land and has prepared a preliminary design for its development. He also has a development permit. Precisely what has the developer available for sale, and how would you determine its worth?

5. Explain what may be wrong in an owner's acceptance of a very low bid because he assumes the architect and the local building inspector both have an obligation to see that the construction will be properly performed.

6. Find a construction cost consultant and report on the services he provides, and to whom.

7. Present arguments for and against architects acting as construction managers on the building works they have designed.

8. Why should an architect not design and produce construction work for owner–clients?

9. Describe the contractual duties which both a designer and a construction manager do and do not have in common.

10. From a published standard contract's conditions, make a synoptic list of the duties of the architect, owner, and contractor.

11. Write an essay on the history of the development of the architecture profession in your own state or province (not less than 400 words).

12. Write a concise report on the obligations of an architect to (1) a client–owner, and (2) a contractor, as expressed in a pub-

lished national standard form of construction contract.

13. As an owner, and following the guidelines provided for owners, prepare written and graphic information for an actual or hypothetical building to give to a designer who may be commissioned to prepare the working drawings and specifications.

14. Discuss the effect on a building project for a developer who will lease the space compared with one who will try to sell the developed property as soon as possible.

15. Discuss the architect as arbiter in a construction contract based on the AIA standard documents, A101 and A201.

16. From the point of view of an owner and a contractor in a CM project, discuss the appointment of a construction manager as prime agent of the owner and judge of the performance of the construction work.

CHAPTER

5

CONTRACTORS AND SUBCONTRACTORS

All sensible people are selfish, and nature is tugging
at every contract to make the terms of it fair.
Ralph Waldo Emerson (1803–1882)

This chapter examines more of what shapes construction companies. A research study into construction management and productivity is reviewed, and there is examination of the contractors and superintendents who perform and supervise construction work. Supervision in both traditional and CM projects is discussed, as is management of subcontracts and subcontractors.

5.1 CONSTRUCTION COMPANIES

Many people do not recognize the construction industry as an entity. How, they ask, can you compare a house builder who builds a few houses each year with an international company that builds hotels? Such

disparate companies, however, do have things in common: they use many of the same materials, employ many of the same kinds of tradesmen, and do many of the same items of work. Their work is of a different scale, however, and it is size, as well as type of project, that makes the differences among construction companies. Even in residential construction, there is an obvious difference between high-rise and other construction. A contractor or superintendent who specializes in high-rise construction is considered to be in a different league.

A carpenter who has worked in house building may get a job with a civil engineering construction company, and instead of erecting forms for a basement he might build them for the raceway of a dam. Since there appears to be a relationship between the size of a company and its projects, let us first consider company size.

Small Construction Companies

Small companies may consist of a principal and one other person who works as book-keeper, secretary, office manager, and assistant estimator. Sometimes he is the principal's spouse. Without other staff, the principal of a small company performs all the other functions: president, company secretary-treasurer, general manager, estimator, general superintendent, field engineer, and any other function for which she has the time and skill. Other than a pickup truck, this company may own no plant or equipment. The company's office could be in the principal's residence.

Such companies fill a need in performing certain kinds of work. Many are house builders who subcontract most or all of the work; some are also developers. Others do renovations and additions, and some do a surprisingly large volume of work.

EXAMPLE I:

One builder-development company builds about 50 homes a year, has two principals, but no regular employees. One principal is a business graduate and the other an ex-superintendent. They buy cheaper land, hire designers, do all their office work from their homes and cars, and build a good product that sells quickly.

EXAMPLE II:

A one-man company has a mechanical engineer as president and manager, and builds thousands of square feet of warehouse space each year. All the work is subcontracted, except the mechanical work that the engineer/principal does in conjunction with one journeyman-helper. There are no other employees; there is no office other than a truck, and all purchasing and other administration is done on-site. Cost estimating and accounting is done in the evenings and weekends at home.

These are real examples of small companies in which the principals perform several functions and for which the operating overheads are minimal—one reason for their survival. The principal of a small design-build company now can do everything in the office or on-site with a computer, including:

- Design and drafting
- Making subcontracts
- Correspondence and document preparation
- Accounting (payables, receivables, payroll)
- Cost estimating (and bills of materials)
- Purchasing and expediting
- Job costing and cost control
- Data filing and retrieval
- Planning and scheduling
- Resource planning and control
- Client, job, and personnel records

Specific examples of certain programs are offered in later chapters.

Medium-size Construction Companies

With an office staff of only three or four (e.g., a receptionist-typist, secretary-bookkeeper, an estimator, and with one or more project managers in the field) many such companies perform multimillion dollar contracts. They employ subcontractors for practically all the work, which typically may include housing estates, commercial buildings, stores, apartments, and smaller institutional buildings. Some specialize in industrial or commercial work of certain kinds. With such medium-size companies, each company's principal is a full-time manager and promoter. When management demands nearly all of a principal-manager's time, so that other staff must be employed to do estimating and supervision, the company no longer is small.

Large Construction Companies

These companies require a team of managers specializing in the major branches of finance, marketing, project management, engineering, labor, and so forth, depending on the kind of work performed. One source describes a large company as doing work worth over $50 million a year; a medium company, from $5 million to $50 million; and a small company as under $5 million a year gross.[1] The size of projects and the volume of work done may depend on a company's ability to get **performance bonds** and *interim financing*.

The shift toward management instead of building enables smaller companies to take on larger projects. Many contractors today are more like construction management companies than the traditional general contracting company that used to employ journeymen of several trades. Some are management contractors. Specialization and computer systems increasingly make this feasible. There are other characteristics that affect company organization and administration, including the following:

- Employing union (or nonunion) workers
- Employing a variety of tradesmen
- Owning construction equipment
- Specializing in certain classes of work:
  1. building work in remote locations
  2. building work of unusual design
  3. uncommon engineering work, such as sea defenses, drainage systems, etc.

There is no such thing as a typical construction company with a typical organizational structure, although many have common features and functions. The trend is to smaller and leaner staffs. It is sometimes surprising to find that a modest-looking company does so much work. Perhaps there would be a different view of construction companies if they were examined from the bottom up rather than at from the top down.

The Fundamental Work Crew

All construction companies have one thing in common—the work crew. It is the basic labor unit in estimating, work planning and scheduling, and in organizing labor. Work crews are fundamental to construction, and an annual publication on construction cost data contains several pages showing the composition of standard crews and the costs per day as the basis of labor costs.[2] For example, consider the following two crews:

Crew D-2
3 bricklayers
2 bricklayers, helpers
1/2 carpenter (scaffolding)

Crew F-5
1 foreman, outside
3 carpenters
(power tools)

Work crews are defined by the kind of work they perform. Crew D-2, for example, constructs masonry veneer and walls. Crew F-5 installs wood structural joists with bridging and blocking panels. Different kinds of work require different kinds of crews, the basic unit of labor. (This does not mean that a worker never works alone: sometimes a crew consists of one man.)

It is impossible to estimate the costs of construction accurately without considering the proper crew for specific work. It is equally impossible to talk of planning work and on-site organization without mentioning work crews. The greater the number and variety of work crews required, the greater the number of foremen. More foremen means more general foremen, and if there are several general foremen on a project more than one superintendent may be necessary (probably one for labor and another for administrative duties). As already noted, there also is some relationship between the administration on site and the staff required in a contracting company's office.

The Inverted Hierarchy

To understand construction company organization, it is helpful to turn the typical hierarchy upside down, as shown in Figure 5.1., and to place the work crews and foremen at the top. The general foremen, the superintendents, and the staff in the head office that administer (minister to) the workers are more appropriately shown at the base of the pyramid, correctly indicating

that they are the "masters through service."[3]

The Basis of Construction Organization

To understand the organization of a construction company and the relationships among the individual members and their functions we should ask about

- The general class of work (i.e., building or engineering) and the specific kinds performed
- The sizes of projects performed in terms of total value and duration within a specific period
- The annual gross volume of business
- The total number of management staff
- The limit for performance bonding

As for the staff and organization on specific projects, we should consider

- The owner; i.e., public or private
- The nature, design, and complexity of the work, and the mix of trades required
- The design team's makeup and experience
- The scope and quality of the design information
- The kind of prime contract involved
- The location of the site and resources
- The availability of skilled labor, experienced trade contractors, and other resources.

These factors detail a company's constitution, organization, and management, which may vary over time and from project to project. Construction is conservative and likes the chain-of-command structure, but the traditionally hierarchical organization is starting to look more like a matrix.

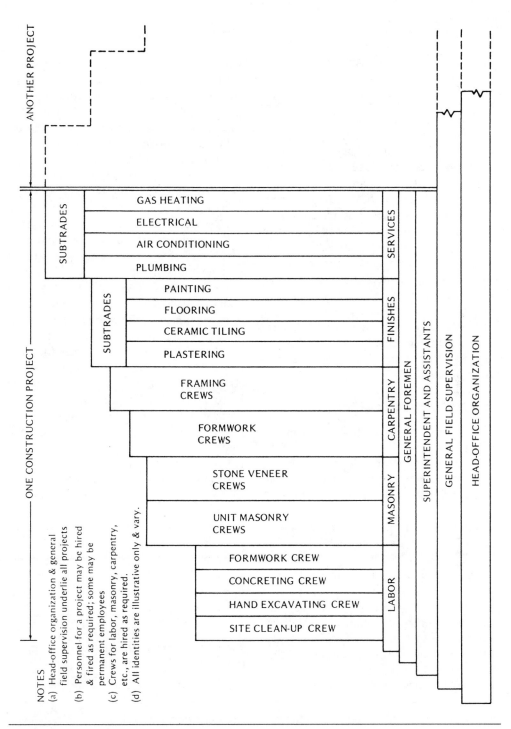

Figure 5.1 Typical arrangement of construction functions.

5.2   MANAGEMENT BY CONTRACTORS

It is significant that construction companies have one of the highest rates of bankruptcy. Reportedly, the main reason is poor management and lack of management experience.[4] In number, the biggest proportion of construction companies are specialists that employ one or two trades. A large part of their work is done in subcontracts for prime contractors. Prime contractors also are managers; they not only manage their own companies, they also manage the projects in which they employ subcontractors.

There has been a shower of books on construction management published in the past few decades, but few real studies have been done to learn about construction management. An outline of the methods and results of one such study follow.

A Study of Construction Management

A pilot study[5] made in 1963 was intended to break ground for future studies that would refine the first study's findings, but it seems no such follow-up was made. The results of this study may again be contested as they were when it was first published. Nevertheless, the results, which generally appear sound, are too significant to be disregarded because of minor criticisms of the assumptions made and the methods employed.

The study has been cited by at least one other writer on construction management[6] and analyzed by hundreds of students. This writer interviewed Aird, the leader of the study team, some years after the study's publication, and he described the strong initial reaction to the study's perceived criticism of labor. As Aird pointed out, the study's findings are mostly a criticism of management in construction. The purposes of the study were to establish authenticated facts about the construction industry and to suggest directions for further studies in the field. (Cost estimating and job cost accounting were not included.)

The research methods used in the study included *work sampling* by direct observation of work on site by the study teams, and the recording and analysis of interviews with people in the construction industry. The theory of work sampling is the same as that of the sampling techniques used in many industries: The number of times a man or a machine is observed idle, working, or in any other condition equals the percentage of the total time spent in that state.

As in all sampling, the larger the sample, the more accurate the results. Work sampling, like all sampling, is based on the law of probability. The manual technique of work sampling is similar to observation by time-lapse photography, but instead of a camera, human observers immediately record on charts the activity they have just observed. There was no attempt in the study to do time-and-motion studies, which acquired something of a bad reputation in industry in the first decades of the twentieth century.

The primary purpose of the site observations in the study was to learn the proportion of work time spent in different activities, or work elements.

The Work Elements Studied. After doing a trial study to establish the best procedures, the study team selected the following classifications of work elements:

1. Receiving instructions

2. Reaching/searching for tools, materials, equipment
3. Walking with tools, materials, equipment
4. Doing trade work (carpentry, bricklaying)
5. Doing work of another trade (a carpenter using a spade)
6. Held up by other tradesmen
7. Waiting for materials, tools, equipment
8. Walking unloaded
9. Being idle for no apparent reason
10. Talking, other than about work[7]
11. Personal delays (toilet, breaks, weather delays)
12. Planning, discussion, layout

The published report of the study contains a detailed analysis of the meaning and content of these 12 different work elements, and it describes their strengths and weaknesses. It recognizes, for example, that direct observation could not decide whether certain work elements were necessary to the actual work in hand. "Walking with tools, materials, equipment," for example, might or might not be necessary. To determine this would require further studies with different objectives.

Scope of the Study. The scope of the study extended to four sites in one city and to 12 sites in another. Of these 16 projects, all except one were building projects; there was one road construction project. In addition, the researchers interviewed more than 40 people in the design and construction industry. Two premises of the study were

1. That a construction company's methods of operation and its utilization of labor are fundamental to company success, and

2. That the control of labor costs and the costs of overhead on site are the most problematic. (These two types of costs also are the most difficult to estimate.)

Some Results of the Study. Some results of the study follow:

Carpenters (based on 2,981 observations)	Percent of Total time
1. Held up by other tradesmen	2.9
2. Waiting for materials, tools, equipment	1.9
3. Walking unloaded	8.0
4. Being idle for no apparent reason	17.4
5. Personal delays	2.7
Total idle time	32.9%
6. Walking with tools, materials, equipment	5.3
7. Doing trade work	33.7
8. Doing work of another trade	2.9
Total productive time	41.9%
9. Receiving instructions	3.5
10. Reaching/searching for tools, materials, equipment	5.8
11. Planning, discussion, layout	15.9
Total productive/ nonproductive time	25.2%

One could argue that "walking unloaded" may be a necessary part of working, but it cannot be denied that it also is unproductive. Similarly, "walking with tools" could be called unproductive, but often it is necessary in completing a job. On could disagree with the third intermediate classification, "Productive/nonproductive time," and say that all of those elements are essential to doing work. Nevertheless, the following facts remain:

1. Almost one-third of the total working time was spent idle and waiting
2. One-third of the time was spent actually working (if you exclude walking with tools as work)
3. Approximately one-third of the time was spent doing other things; some of which were essential to work (planning, discussion, and layout); some of which probably could be curtailed or eliminated (searching for tools).

Obviously, as previously stated, more studies are necessary to establish optimum efficiency. A preliminary study such as this is essential to find out exactly what does occur. It is interesting that the results for laborers were much the same as for carpenters. From 2,630 observations of laborers, it was recorded that "Total idle time" was more than 50 percent. If you exclude "walking unloaded," which might be a valid activity for a laborer, the idle time is still more than 25 percent. The total time spent actually working, including walking with tools, materials, and equipment, was 57.2 percent. Being "idle for no apparent reason" was practically identical for both carpenters and laborers: 17.5 and 17.3 percent, respectively.

For bricklayers, of whom 1,812 observations were made, the actual working time was 58.5 percent and the idle time was much less, 10.1 percent; the balance of 31.5 percent was spent in partially productive activities, including receiving instructions; reaching and searching for tools, materials,

and equipment; and planning and layout. The bricklayers' lower proportion for idle time, particularly being "idle for no apparent reason," fits the style of bricklaying work. There is not much reason for bricklayers to move around and do nothing as long as the bricks and mortar keep coming. Differences in the results such as these suggest the validity of the results.

The Study's Conclusions. A synopsis of the study's conclusions shows that construction management needs three essential things:

1. Information and data
2. Planning and scheduling
3. Well-trained supervision

Of all the conclusions listed in the study's final report, the primary conclusion was: "There is a lack of detailed cost information available to most contractors." Talking to the study group's leader, this writer asked if that conclusion was listed first for any special reason. The reply was that it is listed first because it is the most important.

As we have seen, contracting is largely a matter of information and risk—more information means less risk. Experiential information is necessary for cost estimating and construction management. Few companies, however, do much job cost accounting; consequently there is a lack of detailed cost information available to most contractors. We know that is true, and contractors know it best. Contractors also know that time and its cost are the main obstacles to collecting information. Part of the solution is the use of computer systems that make the collection and processing of information more efficient and, therefore, more economically feasible.

5.3 CONTRACTORS' ORGANIZATIONS IN CM PROJECTS

In a CM project there is no general contractor. So, contractors on a CM project and their organizations are mainly specialist trade contractors with only a few subcontractors.

On a CM project, a contractor erecting a reinforced concrete structure, for example, may subcontract the formwork and the reinforcing steel; or alternatively each trade might have a prime contract directly with the owner. Similarly, a mechanical contractor on a CM project (who would be a subcontractor on a traditional building project) may have subcontracts for the ductwork and insulation.

Normally, a contractor in a CM project will never have as many subcontractors as a general contractor in a traditional project. A few CM contractors may have two or three subcontractors, and many will have none. This obviously shapes the organizations of the specialist contractors as well as that of the construction management company or management contractor.

Specialist trade contractors are work-oriented and self-managing. Those with subcontractors also manage their subcontracts, and to that extent they are similar to a general contractor. Construction managers are management-oriented and have little or no need for functions such as purchasing, personnel management, and handling equipment. In both instances, functions decide management structure.

Fees for Construction Management

On CM projects, owners pay a fee to the construction manager of from 1 to 10 percent of total project costs, and typically about 5 percent, depending on project size and complexity. Theoretically, this fee is partly or wholly offset by a reduction in the total markup for overhead and profit of the contractors on a CM project, in part because of the lesser risk of losses that otherwise arise from a traditional prime contract and its many subcontracts: lower costs and lessen contingency allowances that should be reflected in lower bid figures and contract amounts. It is impossible to be more specific than that, since management fees and contractors' overheads vary so much and depend on so many things; particularly on the supply and demand in the construction market. Also, although we may compare the costs of work items among projects, comparing the overhead costs and fees of different projects is more difficult.

Based on a general and loose comparison of construction managers and their fees with contractors and subcontractors and their overhead costs, it is likely that construction managers' fees are offset by the overhead costs saved. If, as is usually intended by CM, total time is reduced through **phased construction**, not only will overhead costs related to time be reduced, the owner also will get use of the constructed facilities earlier, resulting in earlier revenue and other cost savings not directly related to the site. Interim (short-term) financing costs also are reduced if project time is reduced. More important are the possible savings made in the early stages by the CM monitoring design details and controlling the future costs.

It is certain that the contractual requirements typical of CM projects, such as tight scheduling and more detailed **applications for payment**, must have a salutary effect on the organization of trade contractors and their operations; particularly since many of them had worked before as subcontractors and were patronized by prime contractors.

5.4 CONTRACTORS' MANAGEMENT

Objectives and Goals

Before all else, managers must establish certain goals, and define the objectives to be reached on the way to those goals. A practical case in point: To make a cost estimate and a bid requires estimation of **operating** (office) **overhead costs** and the amount of the markup. This cannot be considered objectively without first estimating the total amount of overhead expense for a given period and to project a total value of work to be done over the same period. In turn, this requires the planning of other objectives to reach that goal. Anything less is shooting in the dark. To add to this conundrum, the result (markup) will partly decide the success of the bid about to be made: an objective in reaching the goal of the total work needed in a given period.

Why are people in business? What is the market? How do companies obtain work? How much work, how much overhead, cash flow, and profit? These are some questions to be answered in deciding objectives. Like a project plan and schedule, a business plan and a schedule must be reviewed and adjusted periodically according to information obtained. To answer questions information is needed.

Information and Data

The need for **information** and **data** touches all aspects of construction. It begins with cost estimating and bidding for work, and it goes on through the planning phases of management, including planning and scheduling work, budgeting costs, planning the cash flow, and ordering materials; to the controlling phase: controlling costs, costing, and business accounting, as shown in Figure 1.2.

Information is the primary resource for construction management, and data is essential to all cost estimating and planning: the parts of management that require the prediction of future events based on the past. Cost estimating and job costing, and planning and scheduling, are subjects enlarged on in later chapters, as their principles and subject matter are considerations in the quantitative aspects of planning and managing contracts and projects.

Estimating and Job Cost Accounting

Even if cost estimates were not needed to make bids, they still would be needed for project management. A cost estimate is a translation of the design information embodied in the bidding documents into the quantitative parts of an estimate (the measured quantities of work and their costs).

Measured quantities of work typically are converted into costs by pricing the materials and the crew-hours to install them. From the crew-hours required for different work, the times required for the work activities of a project can be calculated. That is the information needed for planning and scheduling.

Planning and Scheduling

From the study by Aird referred to earlier, a lack of planning and scheduling of work apparently results in inefficiency and lower productivity. A general conclusion of reading Aird's study and examining its results is that labor generally spends about half its time working at that for which it is employed, and approximately one-quarter of the time in related activities. The remainder of the time is wasted. Some will disagree, but nobody can deny that inefficiencies exist, and that everybody would benefit from increased efficiency.

It has long been a general rule of estimating costs of work done by equipment that an efficiency factor—or more precisely, an inefficiency factor—of 0.75 must be applied to theoretical productivity figures (i.e., a reduction of 25 percent). Perhaps this is unavoidable, perhaps not. In all work there is room for improvement and one way is through planning. It is interesting to note that the results of Aird's study seem to prove this rule of thumb: about one-quarter of all working time is spent in idleness for one reason or another.

Well-trained Supervision

Surveys have shown that only a minority of building superintendents does more detailed planning and scheduling than is involved in a simple bar chart, and only a minority of building companies regularly practices job costing. Visits to site offices frequently show that once drawn and pinned up a job schedule remains unchanged for the duration, because of ineffective management. One reason for the widespread lack of management is a scarcity of well-trained supervision. In part, that deficiency is the result of the industry's attitude to any cost that cannot be directly charged to a project.

Construction reportedly spends less on research and development and on training than any other industry. The usual way of getting skilled personnel is to hire them pretrained from college, or to take them from the competition.[8] An excess of overhead costs is a common cause of business failure. Many construction companies, however,

can hardly bring themselves to pay for anything the costs of which cannot be charged directly to a job. This is commendable up to a point. In good times when there is plenty of work, it may apply even to personal luxuries.

CASE

One cost estimate included under General Requirements the cost of a new Cadillac for the construction company's president. This was the year for a new car, and therefore this was the project to pay for it.[9]

Even those companies that recognize the need for training often are not able to provide it, while others, after a small investment in training, unreasonably expect too much too soon from their staff.

CASE

Mature students in construction courses described their duties. Some superintendents were simply told to run their jobs so as to make as much money as possible—and little more. Some were not given copies of project estimates, apparently for fear that with such information and knowledge a superintendent might give way to Murphy's Law and permit the work to fill the time available. For others, the list of on-site duties covered almost every aspect of construction management, all to be accomplished by taking a course at night school.

Their employers saw training as desirable, but their perceptions of training, its results and returns, and the economics involved were quite unrealistic. From such cases we can identify those with certain attitudes toward training for management:

- Those who do not know what should be done
- Those who know what should be done, but are not prepared to pay for it
- Those who know what should be done and do it

No corelationship was demonstrable from such a small and informal survey of instances over a period of years. It is likely that the second group's attitude toward training would reflect their attitude toward job costing: that it would be a good thing— if they could afford it. There is a distinct reluctance to make any investment that could not show the beneficial results within the life of a specific project. To paraphrase Drucker: Outside, only a company's performance is seen, while inside the company there are only costs to be paid. Training must be economic, and according to the experts in management training pays off.[10]

5.5   STAFF AND EDUCATION FOR MANAGEMENT

Apart from some cost consultants and accountants, and a few individuals from other fields, the effect on construction of separating architecture from the business of building has been to limit the entry of university graduates to professional engineers. Apart from immigration, graduates from college programs in construction management (or similar) are the main source of trained construction personnel. Many of these programs, however, have no extension to the university level, and this effectively stops advancement and hobbles the industry.

Cooperative education, by which a construction employee takes construction courses either at night or during short periods away from his or her employment, or both, is probably the better way to train middle managers and technicians. The industry needs more training and education, particularly in contracts, economics, marketing, and in all aspects of management.[11]

An ideal background for construction management would begin with a trade apprenticeship. This should be followed by a few years spent working with the tools to develop trade skills and site experience; followed by three or four years in a degree-level construction management program. Ideally, superintendents would have at least a first degree, and those with greater responsibility a suitable master's degree. Degrees, however, are not always significant, although well-directed degree programs with suitable internships probably are the best way to obtain a construction education. Designers could follow the same route and then study architectural or engineering design. This would serve to mend the separation of design from construction and would produce designers worthy of the title, master builder.

An Ideal Construction Superintendent/Supervisor

A nominal distinction has been made between superintendents employed by contractors and supervisors employed by construction managers, and we use those titles to distinguish between them. We have also adopted the generic title of super' so that we may refer to them both simultaneously.

A super' is a key figure in management on a site. Apart from his employer (the contractor) the superintendent is the only person in the construction team identified in a standard fixed-price contract (AIA Document A201-1987, Para. 3.9). Consider the following qualities most needed by a super':

- Apprenticeship training and at least two years' subsequent experience in a structural trade (masonry, carpentry, or steelwork), or mechanical or electrical work, as appropriate
- Some higher education, preferably leading to an appropriate first degree (not necessarily technical)
- Education and training in cost estimating, job costing, bookkeeping, planning and scheduling, supervision, construction management
- Ability to use a transit, level, other survey instruments, and a computer
- Abilities to type, write for business and contractual purposes, communicate well verbally, and to make sketches and drawings of details and diagrams
- Understanding of all kinds of bidding, contract, and other related legal, financial, and technical documents, including test reports, surety bonds, financial statements, lien claims, and affidavits
- Practical understanding of civil law as it applies to real property and construction; particularly in codes, regulations, contracts, purchasing, commerce, employment, and labor agreements
- A general understanding of the idiosyncrasies, training and functions of others in construction, including: architects, engineers, construction managers, and their staff
- A working knowledge of finances, cash flow, budgeting, job cost accounting, general accounting (especially payables and statements), purchasing, and the other management functions
- Expertise in layout, and planning and scheduling work
- A working knowledge of structures and their design
- An ability to give and receive instructions
- An ability to analyze and solve problems
- An ability to manage people, to delegate authority, and to take and use responsibility
- An ability to make decisions quickly, most of which should prove to be good decisions
- An ability to deal with individual idiosyncrasies, and simultaneously to see both the contractual person and the individual and his views
- A sense of humor and a cool head in a crisis

It always is possible to add to such a list, but the skills and features listed are fundamental and realistic. Meanwhile, certain personal characteristics and experience may be equally important, including leadership and diplomatic qualities. A superintendent should be able to manage a construction job at a distance from his company's office, including all hiring, firing, payroll, and purchasing, as necessary.

5.6 CONSTRUCTION SUPERVISION

Construction supervision first requires knowledge and then its application. To supervise means to oversee. "Supervisor" means overseer, which also is the original meaning of the word "surveyor" (from Old French). "Superintendent" originally meant much the same thing, although the root *in-*

tendere also gives the meaning, to plan. All these words have the prefix super-, meaning "over," which later became sur-. Supervision, meaning to oversee, therefore requires detachment because he who oversees must be over that which he sees, and over those who do that which he oversees. Clearly, one cannot properly oversee that which one does oneself, because the necessary element of being over, or above and detached, is absent. One cannot judge one's own case. One cannot oversee one's own work. Separateness is necessary. In part, it should be that separateness that comes with authority and the greater knowledge that should precede authority. Despite the frequent use here of the male pronoun, management and supervision is not limited to men. Although a woman who is a superintendent with a construction trade background at present is not common, it is only a matter of time. Already a few women are contractors, construction managers, quantity surveyors, and estimators.

CASE

In 1956, in Karachi, Pakistan, a Muslim businesswoman managing a concrete pipe plant was easier to deal with than any of her competition's male managers.

Supervision, by definition, requires inspection to determine that what is done is properly done. Inspection not only seeks out that task improperly done, it also is a deterrent. It is not uncommon for an owner to require the full-time supervision of construction work. Some owners employ a full-time supervisor, contract manager, or representative with a different title (such as **clerk of the works**) to ensure that work is completed according to contract and to partici-

pate in a project's administration. Alternatively, this kind of supervision may be provided by either a project's designer or a construction manager. In any event, the costs of supervision are paid by the owner.

The AIA standard contracts say that the architect will not have control of construction, and that the contractor shall supervise and direct the work. They do not mention full-time supervision on the owner's behalf, except for representatives of the architect (A201-1987, Subpara. 4.2.10.). There are, however, other AIA documents that provide for an architect's project representative to act on site on behalf of an owner (see AIA Document B352).

To what extent is a full-time representative necessary to an owner on a project? If one must generalize, it can only be said that usually a full-time representative is desirable; not only for communication between the owner–designer and contractor, but often a necessary presence to ensure that the owner receives what he pays for; except on smaller projects with fixed-price contracts, or a project performed by a contractor in whom the owner has complete confidence. The economics of supervision, however, must be considered: the risk of loss versus costs.

On projects, there are too many people and too many valuable things for dishonest acts not to occur. A question arises when estimating the costs of site security. On a large project, or one of long duration, full-time inspectors or security guards will cost a lot. Is security worth the costs? Will the costs be less than the indefinable savings? What does an insurance agreement require? It all depends, but a decision must be made.

In a fixed-price contract, the contractor must produce the completed work according to the contract's requirements, and in some projects it may be possible to ascertain the quality of the work by inspection after completion. Even with the simplest construction (such as a warehouse building) much work that requires inspection soon is covered by other work. (See Chapter 14.)

5.7 SUPERVISION IN CM PROJECTS

As stated in standard contract conditions, a contractor must employ a competent **superintendent** on the project's site as the contractor's representative. It is a superintendent's duty to see that the work is performed according to the contract, and to receive communications (from the owner and the designer) on the contractor's behalf. The work of a CM's **supervisor**[12] consists of facilitating and overseeing the work of others. A supervisor works for the owner, as a counterpart of the superintendents (in a CM project there are several contractors). Consequently, a superintendent who previously worked for a general contractor and then works for a construction manager needs a different point of view—that of the owner.

The test of a superintendent is whether his supervision and the project are satisfactory, and will a project at least bring in the expected profit? For a CM supervisor, the test is different. Was the owner's project completed on time and within budget? If not, who was at fault? There lies the potential weakness of CM: If a project is unsuccessful, who or what was responsible? As a construction manager's on-site representative a supervisor must think as his employer thinks. The supervisor should act always in the best interests of his employer and his employer's client—the owner. A supervisor is on site to see that the work is performed according to contractual requirements of quantity, quality, time, and costs. In many ways, the work of a supervisor is the same as that of a superintendent. However, usually a CM supervisor is not responsible economically for any work, assuming his employer (the construction manager) has not contracted to perform work as a contractor; though an owner may follow the GSA/PBS practice (Chapter 3) and requires certain general condition items[13] to be provided by the construction manager.

A superintendent often can overcome certain obstacles because he has clout; the contractor controls a subcontractor's payments, and the possibility of future work. A CM supervisor lacks the same clout and therefore must be a better manager. A CM supervisor must deal with not only contractors and their superintendents, but all the others on the owner's team, particularly the designer, the consultants, and their representatives. For good working relations and efficiency, a supervisor must know and understand each person's function and how it relates to the functions of others. A CM supervisor may occasionally find it difficult to assert authority, particularly with those not experienced in CM projects. Contractors and their employees, for example, may try making end runs around the supervisor and go directly to the designer instead. This must be avoided by seeking the cooperation and support of the designer and by keeping in constant touch with all contractors and their superintendents. In a CM project there are many more lines of authority and communication to be properly used.

All instructions and notices should be in writing, or later confirmed in writing, with copies sent to all parties involved. Memoranda, letters, reports, and records are a large part of a CM supervisor's work that requires special mention. Largely, people prefer talking to writing. Yet in projects, it is necessary to put things in writing. The standard forms of contract emphasize the fact. All notices, instructions, and modifications are required to be in writing. Many supers do not write enough. Diaries are neglected and important instructions often are not confirmed in writing. If a superintendent makes money, often such shortcomings are overlooked. For a CM supervisor writing and communications are even more critical.

Saving Time

Phased construction is common in CM projects. Time and the timing of events are therefore critical and require precise planning and scheduling and careful management. These begin with the terms and conditions of the contracts in which contract time and the periods for giving notice, etc., must be realistically stated in calendar days. Often the periods stipulated in the standard contracts are excessive if contract time is critical, and the immediate communication of notices is part of the solution. Therefore, if standard contracts are used, the appropriate conditions should be made precise. Other practical means of saving time through faster communications include:

- Courier services
- Fax or fax-modem machines
- Shortwave radio, CB radio, and cellular telephones
- Low-powered vehicles for site use (e.g., mountain bikes, motorcycles, golf carts, etc.).

On major CM projects, a CM supervisor may find it useful to have a shortwave radio to talk with the construction manager in the office, or to use a CB radio. If a shortwave radio is employed, check its efficiency and monitor its use. Some people appear to undergo a change of personality when using shortwave radio and other powerful technology.

Supervision Without Responsibility

Finally, be aware of the supervisor or superintendent who develops the art of supervision without responsibility. A CM supervisor may find it easier to be nothing more than an intermediary, and to never make a unilateral decision. Instead, questions and problems always are referred to somebody else and decision-making and responsibility are avoided.

A supervisor's authority is limited, but within certain established limits he must exercise that authority, otherwise he is not doing his job. The measure of effective supervision is the number of decisions made and the proportion that proves to be sound, not the number of mistakes avoided.

5.8   SUBCONTRACTORS

By definition, a subcontractor is party to a subcontract that, in turn, is subsidiary to a prime contract. A subcontractor, at law, is an "independent contractor" and not an employee. Suppliers are not subcontractors; the distinction is important.[14] In the traditional building contracting mode, subcontractors do the major proportion of the work of a project with the balance performed by the prime contractor. Most of those contracting companies that would in traditional projects be subcontractors are contractors in CM projects.

Although there is no *privity of contract* between a subcontractor and an owner, and the subcontractor payments for work performed come from the owner through the contractor, a subcontractor and an owner have certain mutual obligations. For example, if a subcontractor's work is defective, an owner's first recourse is through the prime contract and the prime contractor.

Should that prove ineffective, an owner ultimately can take legal action for damages against a subcontractor; this should be done only following legal counsel.

Subcontracting often is governed more by local custom and widely held standard practices than by contracts. In part, this is due to the nature of traditional bidding practices, the pressure of time, and the informal methods of contractors. As a result, subcontracts often are loose (if they are in writing), unwritten, and potentially full of misunderstanding and disputes.[15] Although the management of subcontracts and subcontractors undoubtedly is made easier by well-written and equitable subcontracts, it is improbable that the construction industry will improve subcontracting practices soon. The coming of CM projects, however, has improved the position and practices of many trade contractors who found new life and challenges by becoming contractors and dealing directly with owners and designers. Therefore, we must address subcontracting as it exists, and primarily from the subcontractor's viewpoint.

Too many subcontracts are either oral or inadequate reflections of the prime contract. They do not contain those additional provisions and conditions needed for a subcontractor's work and for their dealings with prime contractors. As a result, subcontractors often find themselves subjected to **back-charges** by contractors; charges that give a contractor and his superintendent leverage, or clout, in their dealings with a subcontractor. One reason subtrade contractors have welcomed the arrival of CM projects is the freedom they provide for them to work as contractors. Their payments then are directly from an owner, as certified by his agent. As a large and significant group, subcontractors can improve

their lot by insisting on and maintaining certain minimum standards of practice in contracting that include

- Clear and unequivocal sub-bids to prime contractors with adequate descriptions of scope of work
- Procedures to control the submission of sub-bids prior to the submission of a prime bid (e.g., adequate bidding time; bid depositories or filed bids with rules equitable for all concerned, including owners, subcontractors, and contractors)
- Full access to and understanding of the prime contracts to which subcontracts are subsidiary
- Properly written subcontracts that go beyond the **flow-down conditions** of prime contracts to deal with those things peculiar to a particular subcontract
- Provisions in subcontracts for those things of concern to subcontractors not normally mentioned in prime contracts (e.g., provision and use of equipment, facilities, and services on site)

Let us examine these in more detail. Access to and understanding of a prime contract is essential. So much of a subcontract (written or not) is governed by the prime contract between the contractor and the owner, and prime contracts usually contain requirements for its subcontracts to be so governed. Yet, it is not uncommon for **subtrade contractors** to submit sub-bids without having seen the prime contract documents. This is a faltering first step. Also, sub-bids are offers that must be accepted before a subcontract is made; meanwhile a prime bidder/contractor has no legal obligation to accept any offer. Much goes on in the period between the awarding of a prime contract and the awarding of all the subcontracts; often to the disadvantage of sub-bidders.

Properly written subcontracts are best made by using a national standard (e.g., AIA Document A401) with the necessary amendments for a particular site and project. Such documents, however, do not deal with a specific contract's scope, and scope of work is an area of frequent contention in subcontracts. Particular attention should be paid to the particular requirements in subcontracts:

- Scope of work should be given in detail, with (if necessary) a schedule as a contract document
- Details of payment procedures, dates of progress payments, basis of payments, and whether payments are to be made for materials delivered to site but not yet installed; dates for release of **retainage** (especially if prior to completion of prime contract's work), and details of final payment
- Bonding requirements; even if not required by the prime contract, a contractor may require bonding from a subcontractor for performance of work and payments for labor and materials
- Provision and use of and any charges for use of facilities and services provided by the prime contractor
- Provision and use of temporary facilities and services to be provided by the subcontractor
- Insurance provisions and requirements, stated in detail, and any payments to be made
- Statements in the contract agreement as to working conditions on-site, labor agreements in force, and any other conditions affecting the work, contract time, and contract amount
- Claims by the subcontractor for extra time or extra costs, damages for delay, and other causes

- Remedies available to the subcontractor for late payments and for payments believed to be in error
- Supervision of subtrade work (i.e., by full-time superintendent, or foreman, as the work requires)

To the extent that they are relevant, all the terms and conditions required by a prime contract should exist in a subcontract. That an aspect of subcontracting is not listed herein does not mean it is unimportant.

Scheduling Work and Subcontracts

Any provisions affecting contract time and performance (among other things) in a prime contract should flow down to a subcontract. On major projects with a master schedule, the work of a particular subtrade might appear as one or more activities in the master schedule. Coordination and progress of subtrade work is a major responsibility of a prime contractor, and constant monitoring and updating of schedules is essential.

Supervision of Subtrade Work

Not only is a prime contractor obligated to supervise subtrade work, but also he should ensure that, like himself, a subcontractor has on-site a competent superintendent or foreman as required by the scope and complexity of the subtrade work.

Payment of Subcontractors

The main point in need of agreement is whether final payment of a subcontractor is to be on completion of the subcontractor's work or on completion of the prime contract's work. Either procedure is valid and enforceable, provided the wording of the subcontract is explicit. If a subcontract says nothing on this matter, the prime contract's wording may decide the time of final payment to a subcontractor.

Subcontractors' Warranties

As with payments, an important point about subcontractors' warranties is the time at which they begin: on completion of the subtrade work or of the work of the prime contract. Prime contractors want all their subcontractors warranties to be in place for the same period as the prime contractor's warranty to the owner is in place. Therefore, the prime contractor should ensure that all the subcontracts are explicit about this condition.

5.9 SUPPLIERS AND SUBCONTRACTORS

The distinction between subcontractors and suppliers is made in the standard contracts. A subcontractor has a contract to do part of the work of the prime contract at the site.

The distinction is a traditional one that used to be clear, but now often is blurred by the changing nature of construction work. Suppliers are paid according to terms applicable to the sale of goods governed by the Uniform Commercial Code. Suppliers' warranties often are problematic for a prime contractor because of the standard (prescribed) terms of sales used by suppliers. Often the standard terms do not meet the requirements of the specifications of a prime contract. Meanwhile, a prime contractor's purchase order probably will quote or refer to the warranty requirements for products in the specifications. This situation often remains unresolved and is a potential source of dispute and litigation. Prime contractors should try to get agreement on the warranties they require by making explicit and specific references to their requirements at the time of first contacting a supplier for quotations. To do this for every small order, however, is time-consuming.

SUMMARY OF MAIN POINTS

- Construction companies vary greatly, but also have things in common in the work they do; e.g., the trades, materials, work items.

- Small construction companies have a principal who does more than only management (e.g., estimating, supervision, etc.). Some are developer–builders while others are contractors and management contractors.

- Medium-size construction companies have a small office staff, including one or more full-time estimators, and a full-time principal-manager; this distinguishes them from the small company.

- Large companies need a team of specialized managers dealing with such sectors as finance, marketing, engineering, etc., depending on their operations.

- Company size may be connected to gross value of work done annually: small, less than $5 million; medium, up to $50 million; large over $50 million, according to one expert opinion. Bonding limits are another indication.

- General contractors today are more managers than builders.

- Work crews are the basic unit of production and costs and the smallest unit of organization in construction.

- Hierarchical charts of a construction company's organization mean little; instead consider the kind of construction and the annual gross volume of business to understand a company's structure.

- Management of construction is largely influenced by the kind of construction contract and the class of work performed.

- The high rate of bankruptcy among contracting companies reportedly is due to poor management.

- A study of construction management (Aird) concluded that the inefficiency of construction labor is due to deficiencies in management and supervision; particularly, a lack of cost information, planning and scheduling.

- Aird's study said that the three main needs in construction management are (1) information and data, (2) planning and scheduling, and (3) well-trained supervision.

- Construction Management (CM) projects are managed by a construction manager specializing in management, and usually only some of the separate contractors have subcontractors.

- Phased construction is common in CM projects and this demands better management through tight planning and scheduling and controls.

- Construction management generally requires
  1. Stated goals and objectives (i.e., to plan work volume, staff, and overhead costs)
  2. Information and data to estimate and manage
  3. Planning and scheduling of work
  4. Well-trained supervisory staff

- Training has a cost, but creates profitability.

- Staff for supervision and management with higher education are needed; cooperative education is a partial solution.

- An ideal construction super' must have a wide range of knowledge and skills—from tradesman to manager.

- Supervision requires knowledge, presence, and inspection. Designers usually only provide partial supervision of work, and an owner may require full-time inspection.

- Supervision in a CM project gives an owner continuous supervision for a fee.

- A CM supervisor requires even more knowledge and skills than a contractor's superintendent.

- Beware of the superintendent, supervisor, or manager who will not make a decision.

NOTES

[1]Carleton Coulter III and Jill Justice Coulter, *The Complete Standard Handbook of Construction Personnel Management* (Englewood Cliffs, N.J.: Prentice-Hall, 1989) Chapter 3.

[2]*Building Construction Cost Data* (Duxbury, Mass.: Robert Snow Means Co., annual publication).

[3]As described by Peter F. Drucker, "founding father of the science of management."

[4]See reports by Dun & Bradstreet reports and ratings, and a synopsis of these in *The McGraw-Hill Construction Business Handbook*, 2d ed. (New York: McGraw-Hill, 1985), Chapter 11.

[5]David Aird, *Manpower Utilization in the Canadian Construction Industry*, Technical Paper No. 156 (Ottawa, Canada: National Research Council, Division of Building Research, 1963).

[6]George E. Deatherage, P. E., *Construction Estimating and Job Preplanning* (New York: McGraw-Hill, 1965), p. 63.

[7]This work element was subsequently omitted from the study.

[8]For another opinion about this, read Coulter and Coulter, *The Complete Standard Handbook of Construction Personnel Management* (Englewood Cliffs, N.J.: Prentice-Hall, 1969), Chapter 6.

[9]The company and the president were Canadian. Perhaps presidents of American companies are more fastidious.

[10]Ibid., *Training Builds Profits;* also, Dun & Bradstreet, cited therein; and many others.

[11]See Coulter and Coulter, *Construction Personnel Management,* pp.70–76. The authors refer to the paucity of training in construction, and the "shortage of skilled workers and competent supervisors."

[12]The GSA/PBS Construction Management program refers to a CM supervisor as management (at the level of a project manager); and to on-site supervision by a superintendent. We use supervisor to make a distinction with superintendent, although their positions are roughly equal.

[13]"General condition items" is an imprecise term, as many such items are required by a contract's general requirements.

[14]See Collier, *Construction Contracts,* 2d ed. (Englewood Cliffs, N.J.: Prentice-Hall, 1987), pp. 31, 172–73.

[15]See Collier, *Construction Contracts,* 2d ed. in which the nature and making of subcontracts is dealt with at length. This text is mainly concerned with their management.

QUESTIONS AND TOPICS FOR DISCUSSION

1. Describe the main differences between building construction and engineering construction that affect the organization of construction companies.

2. Among the differences between building and engineering construction, which do you believe have the greatest effect on construction company organization? Explain in detail.

3. What are the main differences between the work of superintendents on low-rise buildings and that of those on high-rise buildings?

4. On the premise that the work crew is the basic unit of organization, how does this affect construction costs and organization? Give illustrative examples.

5. Describe in detail both the main organizational and contractual differences between traditional construction projects and CM projects.

6. Explain one scale of measurement of the size of construction companies.

7. Explain the sizes of construction companies according to their key staff.

8. Consider each work element for carpenters listed in this chapter and briefly explain how and why it occurs. Suggest what could be done to improve productivity.

9. Explain why a contractor's superintendent needs a good working knowledge of estimating construction costs.

10. Describe in detail the primary differences between the duties of a contractor's superintendent and those of a construction manager's supervisor.

11. Discover and plot the organizations of two construction companies of similar size, and make a verbal comparison. Explain their differences.

12. Why is it significant to differentiate between persons and functions in construction?

13. Why is the annual gross turnover (in dollars) of a construction company not a precise gauge of a company's size? What are the other factors?

14. Why is contract amount not necessarily an accurate indication of a project's complexity and of a project's need for management effort.

15. List 12 of the most important skills or abilities required by a construction superintendent.

16. Explain the contractual difference between a subcontractor and a supplier.

17. Why cannot a written subcontract be a subset of the prime contract?

18. Describe the advantages for a specialist trade in being a contractor on a CM project instead of a subcontractor in a traditional-type project.

6

BIDDING AND CONTRACT DOCUMENTS

The hand that signed the paper felled a city.
(Dylan Thomas (1914—1953)

A fter selecting the right kind of contract, the next steps toward proper management and performance are the **bidding documents** and the **contract documents**. What is or is not in them is significant to construction management, and sometimes there may be grounds for a claim. The subject of contracts is too big for one book, but it certainly cannot be overlooked in a text about construction management; especially here, where construction management is dealt with from a contractual viewpoint.

6.1 TYPES OF CONSTRUCTION CONTRACTS

The type of contract selected by an **owner-designer** decides much about how a project is managed and who manages it. This text examines the main types of contracts, although any contract can be a combination of several types.

Fixed-Price Contracts

Fixed-price contracts, also known as stipulated-sum and lump-sum contracts, are the most common and the best understood. Essentially, a **bidder** for one of these contracts says in a bid:

> We hereby offer to do the work shown on the drawings and described in the specifications for the sum of $XXXXXXXXX (a stipulated number of dollars)....

In a fixed-price contract, the contractor takes almost all the *risks* by offering to do the work for a stipulated sum (i.e., that stipulated in the bid). Since a fixed-price contract is for a complete structure, the **work** includes that reasonably inferable from the contract documents.[1] For an owner there is a risk of default in performance of the work by the contractor. This risk can be reduced by requiring and paying for a performance bond. In this kind of contract a contractor can minimize his risks and maximize his profit by

- Making the best possible estimate of costs
- Bidding for the work at an amount based on the cost estimate; i.e., not below the estimated direct costs of the work, to which is added an adequate markup
- Performing the work for not more than the estimated direct costs by
  1. Getting competitive prices for sub-trade work, materials, equipment rental, etc.
  2. Maximizing the productivity of own work force
  3. Minimizing overhead costs by completing the work as soon as possible

To make the "best possible estimate of costs," a construction company needs two different kinds of information:

1. **Design Information** from the owner and the designer supplied through the bidding documents prepared by the designer
2. **Experiential Information** (i.e., that gained from experience) about the kind of work and its costs, and about the project's site.

Only the owner and designer can provide the design information "shown on drawings and described in the specifica-

tions," but that information is never sufficient to complete the work. Examining construction drawings critically shows they actually omit a lot.[2] In addition to the design information, experiential information must be provided by the contractor.

EXAMPLE:

An owner–designer usually does not tell bidders the types of equipment to use in excavating for the foundations and in placing the concrete. The drawings do not show how to construct the formwork for the concrete foundations.

This information is part of the experiential information that a bidder (and the contractor) must bring to the cost estimate and later to the performance of the work. You may think it academic to distinguish between design and experiential information. Reasons soon will become clear.

A fixed-price contract requires an owner–designer to make practically all the design decisions before calling for bids. Decisions about the specifics of work that do not affect the direct costs of that work, and of that work covered by cash allowances need not be made by the owner–designer before going to bid for this kind of contract. For example, usually, it is not necessary for an owner–designer to specify the colors of paint: only the type, quality, and number of coats. Colors usually do not affect costs and so may be selected later.

Bidders must stipulate the sum of money for which they will contract to do the entire work "shown on the drawings and described in the specifications." Therefore, bidders must know exactly what an owner requires in the work. Otherwise, a bidder must make assumptions. Sometimes, the details of a minor part of the work of a project cannot be decided by an owner–designer before calling for bids for a fixed-price contract. This minor part may be described and isolated in the bidding documents and covered by a **cash allowance**, the specified amount of which must be included by all the bidders in their bids. Thus, the bidders do not have to estimate the costs of that part of the work. The designer estimates the costs and specifies it as a cash allowance.[3]

EXAMPLE:

Specifications may say: "Make an Allowance of $10,000.00 (ten thousand dollars) for the prime cost of Finish Hardware supplied and delivered to the site by a company selected by the architect...."

Although the minor parts of the work are not yet designed or otherwise decided upon, with such allowances, a project's work can be bid for and performed through a fixed-price contract.

A good cost estimate[4] for a fixed-price contract requires a bidder to have adequate experiential information to enable him to estimate the costs and to perform the work at a cost not more than the estimated direct costs. As noted, design information usually does not include information about the kinds of equipment a contractor should use. If a bidder's experience is inadequate and he over estimates the costs of work by selecting the wrong equipment, his estimated costs may be too high, and his bid not competitive. Or the estimated costs may be too low. If he subsequently gets the contract (perhaps by default), he may lose money.

Cost-Plus-Fee Contracts

Regarding information and risk, and a contractor's primary obligations, cost-plus-fee contracts are the opposite of fixed-price contracts. In the most simple kind of cost-plus-fee contract, no design information of any kind may be available, though in reality that is rarely the case. Nevertheless, we may consider a theoretical case for purposes of comparison and as an aid to understanding. In such a contract, the contractor might have bid for the work by saying:

> We offer to do construction work [of any kind] for the actual costs of the work, as defined, plus a fee of [say] 10 percent of the actual costs [to cover the overhead costs and profit]..."

In this kind of contract, definition of "costs of the work" and "fee" is critical. The fee is for **operating overhead** and profit (i.e., the **indirect costs**). The owner pays the **direct costs**, whatever they are. Operating overhead costs and a project's overhead costs depend on organization and procedure.[5] The distinction must be defined by every contract because there must be complete understanding—a meeting of the minds of the contracting parties.

In a cost-plus-percentage-fee contract, the owner carries practically all the risk. The contractor's only risk is whether the fee is adequate to cover his operating overhead cost and profit. The owner however must pay for all other (direct) costs. Therein lies the owner's risk. The owner's primary obligation is to pay the direct costs (as shown by invoices, timesheets, etc.) and the stipulated fee. The reason the fee in this kind of contract typically includes the operating overhead costs is that they are costs that a contractor cannot accurately allocate to specific projects. That is why, like the profit, they are included in a cost estimate as a percentage of the direct costs.

In most cost-plus-fee contracts, some design information usually is known at the outset, prior to making a contract. It is the amount of design information known that should decide the exact nature of the cost-plus-fee contract. Suppose that at the time of bidding the amount of information is small and includes only a general description of the building and location of the building site. The size and details of the building to be constructed are not yet known. Such limited design information would not be adequate for a bidder to bid at cost-plus-fixed-fee; since no bidder could accurately estimate the amount of the overhead costs, which largely depend on the amount and duration of a contract. As always, it is a matter of information and risk. In this case the type of contract should be selected accordingly, as a cost-plus-percentage-fee contract.

If, however, the amount of design information available to bidders (though still incomplete), is large, and includes almost complete working drawings, large-scale details, and specifications, then bidders could accurately bid for a cost-plus-fixed-fee. Given almost all of the design information, it is possible that bidders might be able to estimate and bid for a maximum cost-plus-fee contract as will be described below.

Target-Figure Contracts

A modified type of cost-plus-fee contract contains a stipulated target figure; that is, a realistic total estimated cost arrived at by the bidder from the design information provided. Through a **sharing clause** in the contract, the contractor agrees to pay a percentage of any costs above the target figure. Similarly, the owner may agree to pay to the contractor a percentage of any saving resulting from a total cost below the target figure besides an agreed fee. Variations in sharing clauses provide large scope for variations in the terms of such contracts, which can be designed to reflect the variations in the risks carried by both parties.

A target-figure contract is like a maximum cost-plus-fee contract, except that in the latter the stipulated cost is the maximum cost the owner will be obliged to pay. A target-figure contract means the contractor tries to hit the target. To the extent that he misses it, that amount (either a loss or gain) is shared as agreed by both parties.

Maximum Cost-Plus-Fee Contracts

Maximum cost-plus-fee contracts are a hybrid contract; that is, a cross between the basic fixed-price and the cost-plus-fee contracts. Some hybrids are more like one parent or the other. With contracts it depends mostly on the amount of design information provided. It also depends on owner–designers and whether they select the kind of contract best suited to a particular project. Some maximum cost-plus-fee contracts are practically the same as a fixed-price contract. The only fundamental difference is that in a cost-plus-fee contract the cost to the owner is split in two:

1. The maximum cost: more than which the owner does not pay the contractor, no matter what the actual costs are (as in a lump-sum contract), and
2. A fixed lump-sum fee.

Some maximum cost-plus-fee contracts are practically the same as cost-plus-fixed-fee contracts. Usually, maximum cost-plus contracts do not have percentage fees because owners prefer fixed fees. Fixed fees are reasonable for this type of contract because the design information available should be sufficient to estimate an accurate enough maximum cost for the work and enough to estimate the duration of the work.

In some contracts, any savings (i.e., the difference between a contract's maximum cost and the actual costs incurred) are shared in the proportions of 75 percent to an owner and 25 percent to the contractor. However, a sharing clause can provide for the sharing of savings equally, or in any other proportions that suit the conditions and risks of a project and the requirements of the contracting parties.

Unit-Price Contracts

Unit-price contracts are not always a separate kind of contract. Often, they are a form of fixed-price contract, but with separate **unit prices** and separate sums stipulated for each item of work required. The format of this kind of contract agreement is similar to that of a fixed-price contract. In addition to submitting a bid stipulating the sum, bidders also submit a completed **schedule of quantities**, provided as a bidding document by the owner–designer. The schedule shows the descriptions and quantities of the items of work and the items of overhead required by the project. Bidders complete a schedule of quantities by entering against each item their estimate of the unit price and the estimated cost (quantity × unit price). By totalling the costs of each item of work and overhead, the bidder arrives at the total estimated cost for the project.

The main difference between a unit-price contract and a stipulated-sum contract is the schedule of quantities provided by the owner–designer and completed by the bidders. There is a schedule of quantities because an owner–designer does not know exactly how much work is needed. Approximate quantities of work are the basis for bidding. As work proceeds, the owner's agent and the contractor measure the actual quantities of each item and the contractor is paid accordingly (quantity × unit price = cost). If the owner requires work not included in the contract's schedule, the owner–designer and the contractor negotiate unit prices for that work. Negotiated unit prices are based on the unit prices for any similar work in the schedule.

Most unit-price contracts contain a condition dealing with changes in the quantities of items of work. If the change is within certain limits (typically ±15 percent) no change is made in the unit price. Beyond the limits, a new unit price is required to be negotiated. Usually if the quantity increases greatly, the unit price may be expected to decrease, and vice versa. This is because every unit price contains a fixed-cost element and a variable-cost element.

In a unit-price contract, the owner pays the contractor according to the amount of work he does. The primary reason for selecting this kind of contract is a lack of design information (i.e., the precise amount of work required to be done). In a unit-price contract, the owner–designer knows the kind of work required, but not the exact quantities. Rather than enter a cost-plus-fee contract, the owner seeks to minimize the risk by entering a unit-price contract.

In the United States and Canada, unit-price contracts are used mostly for engineering construction projects in which there are few items of work relative to total project costs when compared with most building projects. Typically, in such projects exact quantities cannot be determined during the design or bidding stages because of site conditions that remain unknown until after the work is under way. Engineering projects such as dams are a good example of those that require a unit-price contract.[6]

Contracts-with-Quantities

In some countries, particularly those of the British Commonwealth and other countries such as Europe, Asia, the Middle East, and Africa, a form of unit-price contract is used for many major building projects. These are called contracts-with-quantities. The main difference between contracts-with-quantities and unit-price contracts is primarily in the quantities of work provided in a contract-with-quantities. For the most part, contracts-with-quantities have quantities that are not approximate. They are accurate quantities measured by an agent of the owner known as a **quantity surveyor**. Also, a professional quantity surveyor may handle the financial adminstration of a building project, from the initial conceptual estimates to the settlement of the final account. In contracts-with-quantities the quantity surveyor is responsible to the owner for the accuracy of the quantities provided to bidders in the bidding documents. If there is any subsequent variation from those quantities in the contract, the owner pays the contractor according to the actual quantities of work done. If a quantity surveyor is negligent in measuring work from the drawings, he is liable to the owner. Quantities of some work, such as that in a substructure, may be labelled "provisional." The contract then says that this provisional work is subject to

remeasurement. Some arguments in favor of contracts-with-quantities are

- All bidders used the same quantities as a basis for bidding, and those quantities are part of the contract
- A shorter time is required for bidding because bidders do not have to measure quantities of work
- The costs of bidding are thereby kept lower
- A quantity surveyor is an expert in construction costs and cost estimates, especially in conceptual estimates, and is employed throughout a project on the owner's behalf to manage the costs and finances

Some arguments against the use of contracts-with-quantities and quantity surveyors are

- **Bills of quantities** are prepared according to a national **standard method of measurement**, which may require too much detail (e.g., **labor items**)
- The presence of another agent of an owner, a quantity surveyor, may cause delays in the administration and final settlement of a contract
- An owner pays fees to a professional quantity surveyor

There are many pros and cons; nevertheless, contracts-with-quantities for both buildings and other kinds of construction are a part of the construction industry in many countries. Professional quantity surveyors are similar to construction managers. The responsibility of a construction manager in a CM project, however, usually is greater than that of a quantity surveyor in a contract-with-quantities. Contractors vary in their opinions about the employment of professional quantity surveyors and contracts-with-quantities by owners. Many see bills of quantities (as bidding documents) as a practical means to reduce the time and costs of bidding and regularize the estimating and bidding process. Some contractors see disadvantages in an owner having an adviser-agent with a knowledge of costs. Others, having worked on projects on which the owner employed quantity surveyors, complain that sometimes they slow down a contract's administration and final payment with their concern for detail. Understandably, more owners than contractors seem to favor the employment of quantity surveyors and contracts-with-quantities. Architects generally appear to favor the involvement of a quantity surveyor in a project providing

- The owner pays the quantity surveyor's fees, and
- The quantity surveyor's efforts to control costs do not jeopardize a particular design

On the other hand, professional engineers appear less enthusiastic about quantity surveyors hired by owners; apparently they prefer to make their own schedules of quantities and administer engineering contracts themselves.

Mixed Contracts

Examining the standard form of stipulated-sum contract published by the American Institute of Architects (AIA Document A201) shows that it contains, under Changes in the Work, provisions for deciding the cost or credit of changes in the work.[7] Briefly, these provisions are

1. By a lump sum (for additions or deletions)

2. By unit prices (for additions or deletions)
3. By costs (as agreed) plus a fixed or percentage fee (for additions)
4. By actual costs (as defined in the contract), recorded by the contractor, and checked by the architect, and with certain allowances; or, in credits for work deleted, by net costs as decided by the architect.

You will notice that the first three methods represent the three basic kinds of contracts:

1. Fixed-price
2. Unit-price
3. Cost-plus-fee

(The fourth method (in A201) is similar to cost-plus, but with the definition of costs set out in the contract.) In other words, changes in a fixed-price contract require the introduction of elements of other kinds of contracts into the fixed-price contract to make it work. From this, an important fact about construction contracts becomes apparent: They do not have to be simple and of one type. Practical needs make it necessary or desirable that most contracts contain elements of more than one kind of contract; such as with the standard form of fixed-price contract.

A unit-price contract, for example (or any other contract), might contain cash allowances for work that ultimately could be done by another kind of contract (i.e., as a fixed-price subcontract, or separate contract). In a simple cost-plus-fee contract (with no maximum cost), often trade contractors who have subcontracts with the general contractor do certain parts of the work. These subcontracts can be any kind of contract but typically are, if possible, to minimize the owner's risk, for a fixed price.

In building contracts-with-quantities, which are essentially fixed-price contracts, it is common practice to keep separate the provisional work in a building's substructure. Later, the quantity surveyor measures the work done, and the owner pays the contractor at the unit prices in the contract. The substructure work is effectively in a unit-price contract. The same use of unit prices for other indeterminate work can be made in any other kind of contract.

6.2   DESIGN OF CONSTRUCTION CONTRACTS

Since we can combine in a contract the elements of other types of contracts to deal with particular parts of a project, it means that a contract can be custom-designed. Every project is unique, and every project can and should have a uniquely designed contract. In practice, this need does not mean that every time we write a contract we have to start again from the beginning. It does mean we should always consider what there is about this site and this project that may require special consideration.

The fixed-price contract is *not* the best kind of contract for every project; therefore, it is a mistake to believe that an owner is always best served by such a contract. It also is a mistake to believe that an owner always knows where he stands financially with a fixed-price contract; or that only with a fixed-price contract can an owner be sure of paying the lowest price for work. A lack of design information may be no one's fault. It may be the result of indeterminate site conditions, of undecided tenants' requirements, or the result of an owner's procrastination. A lack of design information in

a fixed-price contract, however, can create inordinate risks for a contractor. Or there may be unnecessary risks for an owner if certain contract provisions are not made. Specification clauses such as those which follow illustrate the kinds of risk a contractor sometimes has to accept in a fixed-price contract:

EXAMPLE I:

"The contractor shall allow for excavating in any and all kinds of materials to such depths as are necessary to attain the minimum soil-bearing capacities required and indicated."

EXAMPLE: II

"The intention of the Documents is to include all labor and materials necessary for the proper execution of the Work …and the Contractor will be deemed to have included in the Contract Sum for all things necessary and for all contingencies that may arise in the execution of the Work."

It is not in an owner's best interests to have a fixed-price contract containing such **weasel clauses**. What does a bidder do when he reads such a clause? Usually one of the following two things:

1. Make an allowance in the cost estimate large enough to cover all the costs of the excavation work, whatever they might be; or

2. To remain competitive, the bidder takes a chance and puts into the cost

estimate an inadequate allowance (or none at all) for unknown conditions and unknown amounts of work with the intention of making later any possible claims for additional costs.

In the first instance, if need for all of the work allowed for in the contract does not appear, the owner will have paid something for nothing. In the second case, if the contractor's estimated allowance is inadequate for all the excavation work required, the owner probably will be faced with a claim. The best contract is one in which both benefit because it is a fair contract and a bargain to both parties. We all know of contracts in which one party has benefited at the expense of the other because of the wording in the contract documents. But no one can make contracting a gamble and expect to always win. A gambler in construction never really can learn the game because the rules are never the same. The better alternative is to make contracts that minimize the risks for both parties, and in which

- The owner pays for what he gets
- The contractor is paid for the work he does, and according to the risks he takes
- The owner carries the risks arising out of a lack of design information and the conditions of the site
- The party with the greater ability to minimize a risk is required to take that risk to the extent the risk cannot be otherwise avoided
- Adequate provisions are made for foreseeable risks to be minimized by bonds, insurance, or other means

Above all, to be effective a contract must be a bargain for both parties. Often this can be achieved by selecting a suitable type of contract, and by including in it the elements of other types of contracts to deal with specific contingencies.

6.3 TYPES OF CONTRACTS IN CM PROJECTS

Construction management (CM) projects may include contracts of all kinds. No particular kind of contract is peculiar to CM projects, except the CM contract itself between the owner and construction manager. The signal feature of the contracts in a CM project is that all are made with the owner (except any subcontracts); and there is a construction manager instead of a prime contractor.

If CM projects are more conducive to any one kind of contract it is the fixed-price contract because, in CM, contracts are made as needed. This means that more time and therefore more design information is available prior to calling for bids. As has already been shown, an owner carries less risk in a fixed-price contract, providing the contract was made with virtually complete design information. Because of **fast-tracking**[8] in CM projects, and because of the several trade contractors on site, it is critical that bidding/contract documents be accurate, comprehensive, and readable. (As to special terms and conditions, such as those respecting periods for notices and specific actions, there are examples later in this chapter.)

There may be an erroneous tendency by a CM or a designer in writing documents for a contract in a CM project to refer to a bidder/contractor as if he were the only contractor. Every bidder and contractor on a CM project must be given all the available information about the entire project. A bidder then may consider all the conditions of all contracts, the site, and the work, when making a cost estimate and bid, and every contractor may organize and perform his work accordingly. Depriving bidders/contractors of available information may bring claims for extra costs or extra time. For example, **M & E contractors** need to know about the work of an excavation contractor and about the concrete formwork.[9] There is a risk to assume otherwise.

6.4 READING BIDDING AND CONTRACT DOCUMENTS

The difference between bidding documents and contract documents is a contract. Without a contract there can be no contract documents. This is not a split-hair distinction, but a genuine and important one. Not all bidding documents become contract documents even when a contract is made. The following bidding documents, for example, do not become contract documents:

1. Notice to Bidders
2. Instructions to Bidders
3. Bid Bond
4. Bid Form, unless otherwise stated

In some projects, some **bidding authorities** stipulate that the completed bid submitted by the contractor shall become a contract document. This is a good practice, especially if a bid contains information such as a list of sub-bidders or a list of unit prices to be used in the contract. Otherwise, under common law a bid is not a contract document. Therefore, a contractor might not be bound by information (e.g., unit prices) provided in a bid. The contract documents—and a project's cost estimate—are the primary sources of information for construction management, whatever the project, and whatever the kind of contract; therefore, the players must understand them fully, and know how to use them effectively.

Instructions to Bidders

The best instructions to bidders are clear, concise, and contain all the important facts of bidding and nothing more. Read them carefully. Some may contain contractual matters. Many are ineffectual in communicating such matters as contract time and completion dates, and the reasons for liquidated damages. Often such things are negotiated later. It better suits the idea of competitive bidding, however, if an owner communicates all the requirements before bidding occurs.

Meetings between Owner–Designer and Bidders

The ideal supplement to even the best instructions to bidders is a meeting between bidders and the designer, with the owner present if appropriate. Given the usually limited contacts with a bidding authority, some may find the idea improbable. Why should it be? Is it because bidders would then know each other? That might serve to heighten competition. It is because oral questions from bidders might be many and incisive? Negotiations after bidding are not necessarily the best way for an owner to make an agreement. In later discussions involving costs, a builder usually has the advantage. Often the reason for such negotiations is that bids are higher than expected.

Reading Documents for Estimating and Bidding

Specification writers should address the specifications they write to one person: the contractor. Most contractors are companies; corporations cannot read or write, and documents must be read and understood by individual persons, including:

- Estimators who prepare estimates and bids
- Company officers who sign the documents
- Superintendents and foremen who use the documents
- Others who use the documents, including public officials, inspectors, consultant-monitors of lending institutions, insurance brokers, sureties, and more

Different reading materials and different purposes require different reading techniques. You should not read certain text material in the same manner you read a newspaper or a magazine. Ideally, we should read all documents word by word, but this is not always practical and in practice we need to vary our reading techniques. When reading documents the main considerations are

- The time available for reading
- The purpose in reading the documents (i.e., for estimating, bidding, making a contract, or a claim for an extra, or preparing for a legal action)
- The format of the documents
- The documents' hierarchy of precedence

Time and purpose in reading documents should decide how a document is read. Prior to bidding, one cannot read every word of a bidding document, nor is it necessary. Unfortunately, this causes some individual's not to read carefully enough. This especially applies to the general conditions of a contract, and whether they are in a standard format, such as AIA Document A201 or CCDC2. Everybody who regularly deals with construction documents should take a reading course, not only to increase reading speed and comprehension, but also to learn how to read different kinds of material in different ways.

A detailed knowledge of the content and format of the standard contract documents is essential; especially before reading a contract based on a standard document. Unusual and nonstandard wording should be easily recognized and read with greater care. Similarly, the atypical, nonstandard parts of specifications must be recognized, marked, read carefully, and applied in any cost estimate and bid. If more than one person is involved in estimating and bidding, the documents can be read and analyzed while the quantities of work are measured. The way to read bidding documents for an estimate and bid follows.

Read the Agreement. If it is not a standard agreement, read every word. Probably it is brief (like the standard agreement form, AIA Document A101). If it is not, take extra care in reading it, especially if it is from a bidding authority with whom you are not acquainted. An agreement document is the heart of a written contract and it sets down a contract's fundamental terms, including:

1. Names of the contractor, the owners of the project, and the names of the architect, or engineer, or construction manager, or both
2. A list of the other contract documents
3. The contract time (and dates, ideally)
4. The contract sum (if it is a fixed-price contract), and the contract fee (if it is a maximum cost, or simple cost-plus-fee contract)
5. The method of payment and **retainage** if any
6. Other terms, as needed, including references to governing laws, assignment of the contract, and other miscellaneous provisions

An agreement may contain the unexpected, so read it carefully. If it is long, or complex, or contains unreasonable requirements, consider the need for a lawyer's advice, and consider whether you should bid for the job. If you decide to bid, give enough time to reading the documents. Otherwise, do not bid.

Reread. Reread the notice to bidders and the instructions to bidders, assuming you read these before deciding to bid the project. See if they contain any contract requirements (which should not be there unless repeated in the bidding documents). Do not be misled by titles of documents as they are not always correct; e.g., Instructions to Bidders may include contractual requirements not mentioned elsewhere.

Read the Bid Form (Proposal). See if the proposal contains anything that should be in the agreement (e.g., anything affecting contract time or contract sum). Determine if it contains any other contractual provisions not included elsewhere in the documents. Some bidding authorities add to bid forms important requirements that are significant.

Read the Contract's Conditions (general, supplementary, and special). If the conditions are not standard conditions incorporated by reference, or physically present (i.e., copies of published standard conditions), you must read every word. If you think any words need clarification, consult a lawyer. If the conditions are standard conditions and incorporated by reference, read carefully every word of any amendments and supplements. (If you do not know the standard conditions referred to, you must study them.) If at first sight the conditions appear original (i.e., not standard), but subsequently you find the conditions have been copied in whole or in part from standard documents and reprinted in the bidding

documents, then be especially careful. You must determine whether any changes in the standard wording were made, which can be difficult and time-consuming.

Consider then whether you really want to bid for the job. If you do, *read every word of all nonstandard conditions, even if large parts are from standard documents.* Unfortunately, that is the only way to find out if a word, a sentence, or even a punctuation mark has been omitted or changed. You have to read and compare every word with an original copy of the standard document. Reproduced standard documents are a possible minefield and an abomination. Rarely are they necessary because, in almost all cases, standard documents can be incorporated in bidding documents by a simple and concise reference. Only amendments and supplements need publishing in full.

Reading Selectively. This is an important technique, but it should be used only when appropriate. First read titles and headings while selecting those parts to be read with care and scanning the rest. Scanning is how many people read a newspaper. If you have not learned to scan, do so. It is essential in the reading of standard construction documents, standard specifications, and so forth. Scanning essentially is checking and confirming the contents of a standard document with which you are already familiar. However, there are risks in scanning. Critical words may be overlooked, or their absence not noticed.

Read or Scan. Read, or scan, all remaining documents including any bonds and samples of documents to be used in the project.

Incorporate and Read Addenda. Addenda, if any, require special attention. By definition, they point to an omission or an amendment.

Because they usually are conceived in haste, they too may be flawed. Addenda should be physically interposed in the original documents affected, or written into a copy of the original. This puts each addendum in its proper context and makes it more understandable. This also will make it useful and easier for future reference. Addenda may be fruitful ground for a contractor when searching for claims. (Computer systems are helpful in dealing with addenda as with all other documentation, as explained in Chapter 17.)

Highlight Selected Parts of Bidding Documents. Make copies of the documents for highlighting or underlining for convenience and better understanding and for the attention and information of estimators and others involved with the bid. If bidding documents are not returnable (or if the returnable deposit is small and less than the cost of a bidder's time) copies are not necessary. The originals can be marked.

Checklist/Query List. Make a checklist/query list of important and unusual points and queries arising from the bidding documents. Make the list clear and well-organized so that it can be used by others. Put down the project title, the date, and a suitable heading. Each point should be enumerated, written as a question, and later answered on the same sheet with sources and dates noted next to the answers. This list, as with all similar papers, must be filed and kept.

Maintain a Project Estimate File. Every bit of information should be written down and filed. Before finishing an estimate, examine all checklists and query lists to be sure that all questions were answered satisfactorily and that the necessary action was taken. Anything less may result in errors.

Read the Project Specifications. Reading the specifications can be formidable because so much of project specifications is a form of owner's insurance. Therefore, specifications often are long. Even well-written specifications contain material that usually need not be read closely. Much of the content is for future reference and use, should it be needed by the owner–designer. Part of a bidder's knowledge and skill is in knowing what is and what is not immediately critical in bidding documents. There are times when it is critical to know and understand a standard specification (ASTM, CSA, etc.) in all its detail. Everything in a **project manual** must at least be scanned, otherwise the reader will not know what must be read carefully and what can be passed over.

EXAMPLE:

Practically all concrete specifications contain a clause specifying the quality of portland cement, usually with reference to a standard such as an ASTM or CSA specification. It is unlikely that any contractor will want to use portland cement that is not according to a standard specification, and probably it could not be found.

Nevertheless, complete project specifications must contain a suitable clause specifying portland cement, so that, when scanning concrete specifications, a reader can see that nothing there is unusual. It should be listed as "Portland cement, Normal, Type 1," and not as an obscure brand of cement made in Transylvania and imported into the United States in Liberian freighters. On the other hand, if he comes to a clause entitled, "Concrete to be placed under Water," the reader should either mark the clause for future study, or immediately read it with care and make notes.

Find Out from the Contract Whether Some Documents Govern Others. In the event some documents do not agree, if the contract does not say which governs, an interpretation will be needed. Actively seek out such discrepancies. For the contractor, they may prove problematic or profitable. Some contract conditions stipulate the hierarchy of precedence of the documents.[10] The AIA documents do not.

Time Available for Bidding

Time usually is critical in bidding. If hard pressed, or if the documents are standard and long, you may take the risk and read them selectively. It is better, however, to use competent help and to make and use check-lists and querylists. A computer system that includes a scanner (to input electronically the contents of documents) and a free-form information base[11] (to enable information to be searched and otherwise manipulated) can reduce the time to comprehend bidding documents. Further advantages will arise after bidding. If a contract is gained, the value of such an information base is immediate and obvious. Even if a bid is unsuccessful, the information still has value in making future bid strategy.

Project Manual Format

The format of **project manual** and the documents within it often suggest the difference between a project that can be bid for without serious risk and one better avoided. If contracting companies accept bad documentation without protest, they become part of the problem. By rejecting offers to bid for projects with inferior documentation, contracting companies demonstrate their awareness and concern with quality. On the other side, poor documentation and many addenda may suggest opportunities for claims.

6.5 READING DOCUMENTS FOR SIGNING

The initial reading of bidding documents for cost estimating and bidding should be done to understand a contract and to enter it properly prepared. Only a minority of estimates and bids lead to a contract, and simple economics require limited time and effort on bidding. That has to be balanced against the risks in bidding in ignorance of facts and requirements. If something is to be done, it is better to do it properly, and to make what economies one can by applying the maxim that refers to two birds and one stone.

Read the documents once again and even more carefully before you sign them. Signing a contract signifies understanding and mutual agreement, and a commitment to the contract and its obligations. A checklist should be made earlier by the estimator of all matters to be reviewed by the signing officer or by an adviser. Some of these may come from an earlier checklist made during estimating and bidding. Copies of the bidding documents should be thoroughly checked against the contract documents (including any addenda) before signing. There should be no differences between bidding and contract documents, except for those bidding documents excluded from a contract, as previously mentioned.

Addenda as Contract Documents

Particular attention must be paid to the manner of correlating addenda with other contract documents, both prior to bidding and again, prior to signing a contract. One procedure makes notes on the original contract documents (drawings, specifications, and conditions) in the appropriate locations, identifying an addendum that affects the documents at that point. Such annotations must be signed (or initialled), by the signing authorities.

If, however, the designer chooses to amend original drawings to incorporate addenda and to issue amended drawings different from those used in bidding, the contractor must retain copies of the original bid drawings. Before signing, the contractor should carefully compare the revised contract drawings with the earlier (pre-addenda) bid drawings to ensure that there are no inconsistencies. Sometimes, this is difficult. The contractor should keep original bidding drawings on file until after a project's completion. The better procedure for handling addenda is not to change the original drawings, but instead to put on the drawings a note referring to an addendum. The pertinent principle is that there should be no effective difference between bidding documents and contract documents. This should be ascertained by both parties before signing a contract. Deliberate and deceitful changes in contract documents are possible, if unlikely. However, not everybody in a design office always fully understands the significance of a change in a document, or the effect that a change may have on the costs of work. Similarly, it should never be assumed that a change in contract documents is unnecessary because the costs of work are (supposedly) not affected. **Modifications** (e.g., changes in contract and work) are dealt with further in Chapter 16.

6.6 READING DOCUMENTS FOR CLAIMS AND ACTIONS

Changes in the work of a fixed-price contract are normal and in some projects, frequent. Some contractors complain about them, while others view them as an opportunity to increase profits. Claims and actions that lead to interpretations of contracts (by the designer), arbitration (by an arbitrator), and court cases (by a judge) are less frequent, but often they are critical.

Claims and actions may be considered together for an important reason: all changes in work, claims for extra time or for extra work, and all modifications, (especially those affecting contract time and amount) should be dealt with as if leading to a judicial action. The related documents should be handled accordingly, although only a few claims will ever end up in arbitration or a court. The most effective method of dealing with claims is to assume that each is a potential judicial case. This attitude should not be seen as merely pessimistic, but as a practical posture and procedure for doing things properly. This means

- Every record and communication must be in writing
- Telephone calls and oral statements and instructions must be confirmed in writing, or at least noted in a journal
- All writings should be clear, understandable, dated, filed, and readily retrievable, otherwise other efforts in making a claim may be futile.

Claims are often substantial and may go to the root of contract. Therefore, their treatment deserves all the care and attention of a bid. (There is more on claims in Chapter 17.)

6.7 DOCUMENTS FOR CM PROJECTS

In a CM arrangement of contracts administered and supervised by a construction manager, the bidding and contract documents in certain important respects should be different from those of a traditional project. An example is the AIA Document A201/CM, *General Conditions of the Contract for Construction–Construction Management Edition*, first published in 1980. This useful document differs from the similar, but earlier, AIA document A201 (for construction with a prime contractor) in that it includes references to the construction manager as an agent of the owner working with the architect to administer a project for the owner, their mutual client. Some typical CM project documents will be examined to see how they differ from the documents prepared for a traditional contractual arrangement with a single prime contractor.

An Invitation to Bid for a CM Project

This document, or an equivalent notice to contractors for public works, probably is the first document to be seen by prospective contractors. Therefore, it is important that an invitation (or notice) conveys the fact that the project is a CM project, and not a project with a prime contractor. This is especially important since specialist contracting companies (trade contractors) who have never worked on a CM project may require guidance. Appropriate wording in an invitation to bid for a contract in CM might be as follows:

You are invited to bid for a stipulated sum contract for.... [Here give a brief description of the work; e.g., Unit masonry work, including concrete blockwork and clay brick veneer] "One of the several contracts for work in the Project entitled... [Here state the standard title of the project] designed by [Here state the name of the designer], to be managed by The XYZ Consultants, Inc., acting as Construction Man-

agers for the Owner... [Here state the name and address of the owner] that consists of... [Here give a brief description of the project's physical character; e.g., Two hundred townhouse dwelling units in three separate blocks, each of three stories, and of wood-frame construction with stucco plaster and brick-veneer exteriors and with electric heating...]. The Owner and his agents, the Architect and the Construction Manager, will receive sealed bids from selected bidders until..." [Here state the time and date for the latest receipt of bids].

Additional wording referring to the instructions to bidders, the bid Form, and other documents, and to any other instructions, will be as for traditional projects.

Take note that the examples are for illustrative purposes only and should not be used without the advice of a lawyer.

Also, note that the examples contain only wording appropriate to CM projects. The preceding sample shows three ways in which CM contracting differs from the traditional contracting.

1. The scope of work in each contract is limited to one trade, or in a few instances (e.g., mechanical work) to a small group of trades (e.g., plumbing, heating, sheet metalwork)
2. There are several such contracts in a CM project
3. There are two agents of the owner, a construction manager and a designer, in a CM project

By the invitation to bid, the bidding authority intends to tell each trade contractor that this is a CM project in which each will be a separate contractor (not a subcontractor), and that each will bid directly to the owner–designer.

Instructions to Bidders for a CM Project

Again, typical wording extracted from a document written for a CM project, with only the critical parts of the document that are peculiar to CM projects, makes it obvious. Appropriate wording in instructions to bidders for a CM project might include the following:

> Examination of Bidding Documents and the Site of the Work of the Project: Before submitting a Bid, each Bidder shall carefully examine all the Bidding Documents, particularly the Drawings and the Specifications that show the Work of the Contract and the Work of Other Contracts that together constitute the entire Work of the Project, and each Bidder shall visit and examine the Site of the Work and of the Project and shall fully inform himself as to the scope, requirements, and conditions of the Work of the Contract to be performed as set out in the Bidding Documents....

All other wording in instructions to bidders may be the same as for a traditional project. For emphasis, or for precautionary or contractual reasons, some such wording may be repeated in documents that later will become contract documents.

A Bid Form for a CM Project

As in instructions to bidders for a CM project, the only wording different from wording in a bid Form for a traditional

project is the wording that emphasizes that the work of the contract will be only part of the total work of the CM project; also, that the bidder (should he obtain a contract in the CM project) will be working on a site with several other separate contractors also doing some work of the project. (A guide can be found in AIA Document A201 and its references to "separate contractors," and in the CM version A201/CM.) Appropriate wording in a bid form for work in a CM project might include the following:

> Having examined the Bidding Documents for the Work of the Contract and the Drawings for the entire Project,
> WE HEREBY OFFER to do the Work as indicated and described in the Bidding Documents (including: The Agreement, the General Conditions, the Supplementary Conditions, the specifications, the Drawings, the Master Schedule, and the following Addenda _____), including all contingency sums, cash allowances, sales taxes and all other taxes in force at this date (but not including any additional taxes that may be imposed after this date that shall be payable by the Owner, according to the Bidding Documents), for the Stipulated Sum of: _____.

An Agreement between Owner and Contractor for a CM Project

The AIA Document A201/CM, *General Conditions–Construction Management Edition* already has been mentioned. There is an equivalent AIA Document A101/CM, *Owner-Contractor Agreement–Construction Management Edition,* that reflects the contents of AIA Document A201/CM. The standard document A101/CM refers to the construction manager and the architect and to some of their respective duties connected with payments and applications for payment. These references to duties may need amending if, in a particular CM project, the duties of the construction manager and the designer are not the same as those described in the AIA documents. There also are references to "Miscellaneous Provisions," including temporary facilities and services and working conditions.

A Master Schedule for a CM Project

Because planning and scheduling of the work of several contracts in the phased construction of a CM project is so important, it is advisable to make a master schedule for a CM project, a bidding and a contract document. The master schedule should be identified in the agreement and the general conditions, and may, if legally advisable, be defined as a contract document.[12]

A Schedule of All Project Drawings for a CM Project

It is helpful to include in CM contract agreements a schedule of all project drawings, listing every drawing for a project, including those drawings that do not directly apply to the work of the contract in which the schedule appears. It is advisable to do this in all contracts in a CM project. Although the work of a particular contract may be limited to only a few drawings, it is important that every contractor in a CM project is aware of all the project drawings that show the full scope of all the project's work and how the work of a contract re-

lates to all other work in the project. Contractors also must be afforded the opportunity to look at any drawing or specification at any time.

Completion of Work, or of Project?

In the matter of progress payments to a contractor in a CM project, it is necessary to refer to the "Substantial Completion (Performance) of the Project," instead of "Substantial Completion (Performance) of the Work," if it is not the owner's intention to make final payment to contractors when they substantially complete the work of their own contracts, but instead to make final payments when the entire project is substantially completed. (There is more about substantial completion of work in Chapter 11.)

Conditions of a Contract in a CM Project

It is better to use published, standard general conditions for contracts in a CM project, even if there is no special edition of general conditions for use in CM projects. The standard form for traditional stipulated-sum contracts usually can be adapted by making a few changes. Also, some owners in the United States may choose not to use AIA Documents A101/CM and A201/CM. For example, they may wish to give greater authority in the administration of contracts to the construction manager.

Amendments of standard contracts and all terms and conditions drafted for a specific project should be checked by a lawyer.

6.8 ADEQUATE SUBCONTRACTS AND SUPPLY CONTRACTS

Virtually every prime contract requires that subcontracts contain all of its terms and conditions relevant to a subcontract. Many prime contractors consider that requirement sufficient, and as a result their subcontracts are simply an exchange of letters with the prime contract's general terms either implied or expressed, if they are written about at all. Many subcontracts have requirements that, because they arise from the organization and management of the work (which in most prime fixed-price contracts is the sole prerogative of the contractor) are not in any way expressed or implied in the terms and conditions of the prime contract; they are peculiar to a particular subcontract.

Therefore, a prime contractor who relies on the prime contract as the sole basis for his subcontracts' requirements and conditions probably is omitting important things from his subcontracts that may directly touch on critical matters (e.g., of scope of work, changes, and timely completion). Thus, a prime contractor without adequate and written subcontracts may find himself in a serious position in which he bears an onerous and unnecessary risk as a result of a subcontractor's default.

6.9 COMPUTER APPLICATIONS

We may expect further developments in computer systems that simplify the reading and understanding of long and complex documents. Even with current technology, a contract document can be scanned and stored in digital format on a disk and in a computer where it can be searched for key words, analyzed, and compared.[13] Developments in artificial intelligence, expert systems, and in the integration of design and experiential information will produce systems that can effectively deal with bidding and contract documents and other recorded information, so that all the information needed by everybody involved in a project can be found in one place. This should mean better and more efficient communication, assimilation, understanding, and use of information by bidders and contractors so that, ideally, fewer unexpected conditions and requirements will appear, and misunderstandings will not occur. Such ideals, however, are rarely ever completely attained. Knowledge and care always will be essential, and written instruments signed by contracting parties probably will be around for a long time.

Bidding/contract documents are both graphic and textual. Too often, drawings suffer from the creative-artist syndrome, from the idea of architecture as a fine art (which it can be), and by frustrated designers who became drafters of others' designs. There is a reluctance in some design offices to turn to **CAD** for the making of drawings, and therefore the ability to convey combined graphic and textual design information electronically is frustrated. However, today developments indicate the integration of electronic information for construction, which, in turn, should help to encourage reintegration of design and building.

SUMMARY OF MAIN POINTS

- Fixed-price (stipulated or lump sum) contracts are the most common; usually they are for a completed structure, and include work reasonably inferable from the contract documents. Ideally, they require complete design information, and adequate experiential information. Most risks are borne by the contractor.

- Cash allowances are stipulated (in fixed-price contracts) by an owner–designer to provide for identified work or materials that are not specified in detail.

- Cost-plus-fee contracts are properly used when adequate design information is not yet available. Cost usually is defined as direct costs; fee, as indirect costs. The actual definitions are critical. Most risk is carried by the owner since he pays all direct costs incurred, plus a fee.

- Target-figure contracts are something like a cost-plus-fee contract, but because more design information is available a bidder can estimate a target figure of total direct costs. Through a sharing clause, both contractor and owner share in excess costs, or savings, relative to the target amount.

- Maximum cost-plus-fee contracts are similar to target-figure contracts, but because sufficient design information is available, a maximum cost can be estimated and bid. To this extent they are similar to a fixed-price contract, but are administered like a cost-plus-fee contract. Any savings (below the maximum cost) are shared, as agreed.

- Unit-price contracts are similar to fixed-price contracts, except that, in some only the unit prices are fixed, and the total cost to the owner depends on the quantities of work items done and measured. Usually in North America only for engineering work. Other unit-price contracts may be for a total fixed price and the unit prices are significant only when changes are made.

- Contracts-with-quantities are similar to unit-price contracts, but the bills (schedules) of quantities are prepared by a consultant quantity surveyor employed by the owner.

- Mixed contracts are one of the main types; they contain features of other types of contracts. Mixed contracts can be designed to suit particular projects.

- A specially designed contract should be produced for each project to suit its requirements.

- Weasel clauses in contracts may cause bidders to make unreasoned cost allowances, or take a risk; the results may be detrimental.

- Risks for both parties are minimized if the owner pays for what he gets, the contractor is paid for what work he does, the owner carries risks due to a lack of design information and the site, the party with greater control over a risk bears that risk if necessary, and contract provisions for insurance and other means are made to reduce risk.

- CM project contracts can be of any kind, but fixed-price contracts are preferred by an owner.

- Bidding documents generally become contract documents when a contract is made, but not those dealing only with bidding, nor the bid itself, except when a contract says the bid shall be a contract document.

- Reading bidding and contract documents is critical, and their understanding requires a knowledge of contract law and standard contracts; different reading techniques should be used for different documents.

- Readers of specifications should mark for special attention those parts that are not typical or standard.

- Reading contract documents before signing is critical. Except for addenda, there should be no difference between the bidding documents and the contract documents. Ensure that a comparison between them always can be made.

- Addenda require particular attention; ensure they all are taken into account. Many addenda may suggest inferior documentation and opportunities for claims.

- Before signing contract documents careful reading is required. Review addenda and their incorporation.

- Read documents and collect evidence for claims as if expecting to take a case to adjudication.

- Consult a lawyer with specific questions and interpretations of documents.

- Documents involved with changes in work (and all other modifications to contracts) should be written and read as contract documents.

- Documents for CM projects should be written to properly convey the full information about a CM project, its nature, and work.

- CM projects and their documents require particular conditions, some of which include explanations and special conditions. Time periods in standard conditions may be too long or indefinite for a CM project.

- In all cases, amendments of standard contracts and all terms and conditions drafted for a specific project should be checked by a lawyer.

NOTES

[1]See AIA Document A201-1987, Subpara. 1.2.3, which contains the phrase "reasonably inferable from them [the contract documents]." CCDC2-1982, says "properly inferable." See Collier, *Construction Contracts*, 2d ed., 1987, pp. 60–78; and see references in the Index to "Stipulated sum contract" for more on their nature. That fixed-price contracts require a complete job, and that work can be inferred, should be understood for its important implications.

[2]Excavation usually is not shown at all on drawings. Neither is most concrete formwork.

Rebar often is only partly shown. Structural framing is outlined. Most finishes are only described. Mechanical and electrical work is outlined. Drawings are arrangements of quasi conventional symbols that leave much to be filled in by the experienced builder.

[3]See, A201-1987, Para. 3.8, *Allowances*.

[4]By a "good estimate" we mean one that by its results is subsequently shown to be accurate to within an acceptable degree; one that results in a contract sum that is fair and beneficial to both contracting parties and has the potential to produce a satisfactory profit.

[5]Whether purchasing, for example, is done on-site, or at a contractor's permanent office, decides whether the costs of purchasing are a job overheard (direct cost), or an operating overhead (an indirect cost).

[6]Often in unit-price contracts for engineering works large portions of the work are described and priced as lump-sum items (i.e., as fixed-price portions of the whole) that require measurement and pricing by the estimators.

[7]AIA Document A201, *General Conditions of the Contract for Construction* (Washington, D.C.: American Institute of Architects, 1987). The Canadian standard construction document CCDC2, has similar provisions.

[8]In a CM project that is on a fast track and in which project time is compressed, however, contracts may be of those types most expedient under the circumstances, as described earlier.

[9]In some instances, it is possible to avoid inter-reliance among separate contractors by technical means; e.g., by drilling concrete for pipes and conduits instead of installing cans in form-work.

[10]For example, CCDC2, in which the order of governing documents (in the event of differences among them) is the standard agreement, supplementary (nonstandard) conditions, the standard general conditions, the specifications, and the drawings. The agreement governs all.

[11]Not the usual data-base manager, but a free-form, verbal information manager that can handle text, numbers, and graphics, whether structured of unstructured; such as *askSam* by askSam Systems.

[12]Some lawyers advise against listing a schedule as a contract document.

[13]See Raymond G.A. Cote & Ben Smith, "Profiles in Document Management," *BYTE*, 17:9, Sept. 1992; also, Raymond G.A. Cote & Stanford Diehl, "Searching for Common Threads," *BYTE*, 17:6, June 1992, for information on text managers such as *askSam*.

QUESTIONS AND TOPICS FOR DISCUSSION

1. Briefly describe the essential nature of each of the two most fundamental kinds of construction contracts and point out their main differences.

2. What is meant by a "mixed contract," as used in this text?

3. Using an actual trade specification written for a construction project, underline those parts which you believe to be uncommon and of particular significance (i.e., not standard wording). Explain the reasons for your selections.

4. Describe how addenda to bidding documents should be treated by: (a) bidders, before submitting bids, and (b) a contractor, before signing a contract's documents.

5. Why in a unit-price contract for a building might work in the substructure be described in the contract as "provisional"?

6. In bidding documents for a CM project, what are two of the main points of information to be communicated to all bidders? How can this be achieved? Give specific examples.

7. Describe a particular topic of importance related to a contract's documents that should be attended to in a contract agreement for a CM project.

8. Describe a general condition that should be especially written for contracts in CM projects.

9. In view of the importance of phased construction in most CM projects, what might be included in the conditions of a contract regarding requirements for the timely execution and completion of work? Give specific examples.

10. If adequate bidding and contract documents are the second most important step toward a fair and properly performed construction project, what is the first decision and step? Explain your answer.

11. Explain a potential contractual risk to an owner in a typical fixed-price contract made through competitive bidding, and suggest a safeguard.

12. Discuss the fundamental difference between (a) design information, and (b) experiential information, relative to cost estimating and bidding.

13. Explain the significant difference between a target-figure contract and a maximum cost-plus-fee contract.

14. Explain the primary reason for a unit-price contract.

15. Explain briefly the relationship in cost estimating and bidding between Risk and Information.

7

ESTIMATING AND COST ACCOUNTING

Take calculated risks.
That is quite different from being rash.
General George Patton (1885–1945)

To understand their importance to construction management, this chapter examines the nature and results of cost estimating and job costing rather than how they are done. The fundamentals of their practice have been explained elsewhere.[1]

7.1 ESTIMATING CONSTRUCTION COSTS

The objective of construction management is to get construction work performed within certain limits of time and cost. As already seen, a primary prerequisite for construction management is adequate information and data: estimating and cost accounting provides a large part of it. Few will buy something unless they know the price; however, the price of proposed construction work is initially unknown because each project is unique. So, to make a fixed-price construction contract a project's total cost must be estimated. That is the first purpose of cost estimating.

Information for Cost Estimating

Information about construction work is of two kinds and comes from two sources:

1. **Design information** from the owner/ designer in specifications and drawings and other bidding documents and contract documents

2. **Experiential information** from the bidder and contractor, which complements and supplements the design information.

Only with both kinds of information combined can a proper cost estimate be made that will indicate the probable costs of construction and provide the needed information for management. In the speculative housing market, a house is much like any other product offered for sale. Most construction work, however, is done to order; it is custom-designed and unique—if only because of its location. The only way a price can be established before the work is done is by estimating the costs. A novice might ask: If a product is unique how can its costs be estimated? The answer is revealing and lies in the fact that most construction work can be analyzed into many **items of work**. Estimating, therefore, consists of two main parts: (1) measuring the quantities of work items, and (2) pricing work and overhead costs. This text will examine these more closely.

Measurement of Work

To measure work we must be able to identify and describe it. Measurement is fundamental and the beginning of any analytical process. Construction work already has been divided into several classes:

- Building construction work
- Engineering construction work
- Industrial construction work
- Specialized construction work

Building construction provides shelter structures. Engineering construction includes every other structure, from bridges to dams. Industrial construction work consists mainly of plants for manufacturing and processing. Often its structures are a minor part of a project, and their construction is similar to that of other classes. Specialized construction work includes highways and pipelines.

In most structures there are **basic items of work** (e.g., concrete foundations, structural steelwork, carpentry, and painting). All these and many others are common to building, engineering and other construction work. Therefore, not only are the principles of estimating and cost accounting (or, job costing) the same for all work, many of the work items also are common.

During a project, the contractor does job costing to account for the costs. The purpose is to know the costs of each element of each part of the work: the costs of labor; materials; and of tools, plant, and equipment. The contractor also accounts for the job overhead costs at the site: supervision, temporary facilities (sheds, pumps, etc.) and other such costs. By dividing the costs of different work items by the amounts of work done we can find the **unit costs** for the various items of work and their constituents.

EXAMPLE:

If the concrete work in a project consists of 150 cubic yards (CY) of concrete footings, and the total cost of concrete work (excluding formwork and reinforcement) is $15,000, the average cost per cubic yard is $100 per CY. The item of work is "cast-in-place concrete footings," and the unit cost of this item of work for this project is $100 per cubic yard. Of this unit price, $70 might be for materials, $20 for labor, and $10 for equipment rental.

Cost accounting on projects is the only way to know the actual costs of work. Only with such information can other estimates of costs be made. This kind of information allows production of bills of materials, a work breakdown and plan, a schedule of work activities, and provides all the other information needed for management. There is no other way. The use of price books, intuition, and so-called hunches really are nothing more than crude forms of costing. This is the only trade secret for cost estimating: job costing is the guide to measurement and the main source of information for pricing, except the quoted costs of materials.

EXAMPLE:

We have built an 8-inch thick concrete-block wall 50 feet long by 8 feet high: a total area of 400 square feet. The wall contains 450 whole and part blocks. We purchased 470 hollow blocks (face-size, 16 in. × 8 in.), and some were later broken or cut. We also purchased a cubic yard of ready-mixed masonry mortar. The total direct costs were:

470 blocks @$1.00 each	$470.00
1 cubic yard mortar	70.00
Scaffolding costs	100.00
	$640.00
Blocklayers, 25 hrs @$16.00	400.00
Helpers, 10 hrs @$12.00	120.00
Total direct costs	$1160.00

This simple cost account tells the cost accountant and the estimator several things about concrete blockwork that will be useful in estimating and in construction management

- **Waste** of material (blocks) amounted to 4-1/2 percent (470 − 450 = 20; 20/450 × 100 = 4.444) of the total number of blocks installed. This allowance (more or less) must be made in other estimates.

- Approximately one cubic yard of masonry mortar, including waste, is needed to lay approximately 500 blocks. As waste of mortar is always high, it is of no use to attempt to be more accurate.
- Scaffolding rental costs approximately 22 cents per block, or 25 cents per square foot of wall. (All unit costs are direct costs.)
- Total material and equipment costs are approximately 55 percent of total direct costs. Labor costs are approximately 45 percent of direct costs for this blockwork.
- Concrete blockwork requires approximately one hour of helper's time to 2 1/2 hours of blocklayer's time, or, subject to conditions, two helpers to five blocklayers.
- Blocklayers can lay approximately 18 blocks an hour in this kind of work.

These bits of information (which are for illustration only) are incomplete and more details are needed (e.g., the kind of blocks, location of the wall, and other things that may affect construction costs). Nevertheless, the example shows the kinds of information required. The nature of work determines how its costs can be accounted. Obviously, there are only two ways to measure and price concrete block walls: (1) by the superficial (surface) area of the wall, or (2) by the number of units installed. One is a function of the other, except for a possible minor arithmetic discrepancy resulting from part-blocks. It would be fruitless to price a block wall by its volume. Area, however, has a large influence on the costs of all kinds of walls, including those of masonry units and concrete placed in formwork.

The costing of work items establishes both the actual costs and the methods of pricing, and the method of pricing work establishes the units of measurement. Estimating methods are determined by costing, and estimating without costing soon becomes guesswork—or highly theoretical.

Costs of Work

Instead of a cost estimate, some talk of a "material take-off" or a "schedule of materials" and the labor element of work is only implied. Construction contracts define work as that which a contractor performs for payment. That which requires estimating is the total **costs of work**, as defined. It is true that some trade contractors (e.g., plumbers) estimate costs by measuring only the materials (e.g., piping). After the materials are priced, then the labor costs may be calculated as a proportion of the material costs.[2] This is common in estimates for plumbing and electrical work, in part because of the relatively low proportion of site labor costs. A better method, however, is to relate labor costs to pipe lengths and joints, or to wiring circuits, and to the installation of fixtures. Measurement is then a matter of simple counting and description.

A published **standard method of measurement** is an aid in estimating because it serves as a common standard, as a checklist, and as a live repository of experience. Many estimators are aware of deficiencies in their estimates, but do not know how to make them more accurate, or how to make estimating more efficient. It is not our present purpose to examine in detail how construction work should be measured, but to point out those things about the measurement of work that affect estimates, estimated costs,

contract sums, and consequently the management of construction.

A cost estimate is the primary source of information for planning and scheduling, controlling and costing a construction project; if the estimate is deficient, the quality of management may be affected. To measure something is to be able to understand it. This axiom of science also applies to estimating the costs of construction work. Inadequate measurement means an inadequate understanding of the work.

EXAMPLE I:

The measurement of concrete work by volume, irrespective of the quality, size, shape, form, and purpose of the concrete work often is inaccurate measurement.

EXAMPLE II:

The inclusion of formwork with the concrete, so that the two items are priced together, is even more inaccurate.

These are extreme but actual examples of inaccurate measurement: inaccurate, because it does not represent the work in a quantitative form that can be accurately priced. It is not in a form that can be converted to discrete work activities for work planning and scheduling.

To measure work so that the quantitative information can be used for cost estimating, job costing, and for other management purposes like scheduling, all construction work should be measured as simply as possible. The measurement of work in the same units in which the material is purchased—like the view of a cost estimate as a bill of materials—comes from the past when labor costs were less significant. (The method still is used effectively by some estimators for certain projects located in places where labor costs are very low.)

EXAMPLE:

Formwork to concrete walls often is measured by the superficial contact area. The better way to measure formwork to concrete walls is by length, describing the height and other details.

Measurement by length retains the critical height dimension in a concrete wall's description, whereas measurement by area is likely to cause the height to be overlooked, and the formwork to walls of different heights (and unit costs) to be collected together as one item.

Simplified Measurement of Work

Measurement of work includes not only setting down dimensions and calculating quantities, it also includes the accurate coding and description of the work so it can be properly understood, identified, and priced. In fact, an item's description and dimensions cannot be separated since they are parts of a whole; one is meaningless without the other. Incomplete descriptions deprive an estimate of information, and to that extent the estimate is deficient. Existing measurement methods owe their format to

- Traditional trade measurement and pricing[3]
- Traditional quantity surveying practices[4]
- Manual (pre-electronic) calculating and information-handling techniques

These methods limit the number of items that can be handled in a cost estimate (and in a schedule of quantities). Similar work items are grouped together, therefore differences in their location and size are often ignored in pricing. Now, computer systems make it possible to handle vast numbers of work items and perform the calculations efficiently. An increase in the number of work items in a project estimate need not cause difficulties or inefficiency. Not only does the computer allow working with more bits of information more efficiently, it also enables conversion of information from one form into another with little time and effort. For an example of this, study Figure 7.1.

An input of design information from a drawing (manually, by instrument, or by electronic transfer) about the perimeter foundations produces from a data base the required information for

- Cost estimating for bidding
- Bill of materials for ordering
- Work activities for planning and scheduling
- Equipment times for scheduling and hiring

Working with a data base, one can apply a new principle of measurement: Measure work items and calculate their quantities with the least possible number of dimensions.

If feasible, it is better to simply count work items and fully describe them using all three dimensions; failing that, measure by

DESIGN INFORMATION: Concrete footings on drawing:
24 in. × 12 in. × 360.0 lf.

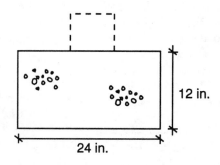

TYPICAL FOOTING SECTION

QUANTITY INFORMATION: Concrete footings in estimate:

Concrete footings (2000 psi/1-½ in.) 24 in. × 12 in.	360 lf.
Place concrete footings from truck	27 cy.

QUANTITY ANALYSIS:

Concrete (2000 psi/1-½ in.)	27 cy.
Form rental × 12 in. (2 - sides measured)	720 lf.
Form oil	2 gl.
Form stays	120 pc.
Form nails	25 lb.
Crew #17 Layout and install forms	1 × 8 hr.
Crew # 19 Remove and clean forms	1 × 2 hr.
Crew #22 Placing concrete	1 × 8 hr.
#2 Barrow	2 × 8 hr.
#1 Shovel	4 × 8 hr.

Figure 7.1 Design and quantity information

length and describe by including two dimensions in the description; failing that, measure by area and describe using the average, minimum and maximum depths (e.g., for over-site excavation); failing that, measure by volume, but still describe the work by referring to its critical dimensions since they often affect the method and costs of work (e.g., excavations).

This new rule of measurement creates more work items in a cost estimate, something avoided in the past, but no longer a problem; it also produces more information that otherwise would be obscured. This method of measurement introduces a new way of estimating: a method that relies less on traditionally measured quantities and more on information and data in data bases and costs allocated to construction components (aggregations of work items). Using a computer system, work can be analyzed and examined at any level of detail and complexity for all aspects of management.

Pricing Measured Quantities of Work

Pricing work is different from measurement as it requires experiential information from several sources:

- Costs of materials, labor, tools and equipment
- Information from past jobs about material waste, labor productivity, overhead costs, and other cost information and data obtainable by job costing.

The 80/20 Rule of Cost Estimating

This rule says that about 80 percent of the total costs of a project come from about 20 percent of the *number of items* in the cost estimate, and studies have confirmed this.[5] Therefore, it seems reasonable that only the

costs of that critical minority of major items need to be based on current quotations and bids and on detailed analysis. The costs of the remaining items (about 80 percent) can be taken from an estimator's database, or otherwise derived. This is an important consideration in estimating costs and deserves more research: something that an estimator using a computer system should consider.

EXAMPLE:

Cast-in-place concrete work in a building complex: An estimator obtains firm quotations for the prices of ready-mixed concrete of different mixes delivered to a site. From experience the estimator estimates crew sizes, selects equipment, and designs methods for placing concrete in the several major parts: e.g., perimeter footings and foundation walls, isolated footings, columns, suspended slabs.

When this work is priced as (say) 10 different major work items, the estimator is left with about 40 related minor work items to be priced (e.g., concrete stairs, steps, planters, minor retaining walls, miscellaneous footings, machine beds, sumps, etc.), all of which can be priced on the basis of the 10 unit prices for the major items, plus estimated premiums for location, small quantity, difficulty in placing, complexity of forms, excessive waste in placing, forms not removed, etc.

The major items (the 20 percent) are carefully estimated by the best available methods and data. The minor items (the 80 percent) are priced on the basis of the costs of the major items with premiums added as needed and intuitively estimated for specific characteristics and job conditions, as follows:

EXAMPLE:

C-I-P Concrete placed below grade:
Major work item: Continuous strip footings, max width, 24 in., max depth 18 in., placed directly from a ready-mix truck into forms in surface trenches:

Minor work items:	Material	Labor
Small isolated footings max 24 in. × 24 in.	× 1.10	× 2.50

Periodically tested, and proven, such cost factors (here, only illustrative) can be used to cost minor items automatically from the unit costs of major items. Job costing, however, must be used to derive and test them. Using a computer, an estimator should analyze all project costs (estimated and actual) to establish other relationships and rules such as that expressed by the 80/20 Rule.

Those who estimate costs know from experience how accurate estimates can and cannot be. Studies indicate that a margin of ± 7 percent is a limit to practical accuracy.[6] Beyond that limit there is fuzziness. Yet even fuzziness has its logic.[7] The 7 percent margin is always open to question, as are all estimates and statistics. Seven percent of what? Of the average of all the estimates made for bids? Or 7 percent of the actual costs established by cost accounting after the work is completed? One can say the total costs of construction projects cannot be absolutely and finally determined even after work is completed. What does "completed" mean? Substantially completed? Finally completed? Or completed as at the termination of the warranty period follow-

ing substantial completion? Before completing a project's costing one first must determine when the project is complete. The only valid information is that which is discovered within a known set of conditions.

What are cost estimates? They are expert opinions about fuzzy images seen through a glass darkly and never understood absolutely. Often, they are seen clearly enough for practical purposes if made and used by people with knowledge, experience, and common sense. Sometimes they are proven so distorted they are abandoned by the contractor who has just received a contract. Cost estimates and financial statements are not hard facts. At any time, an estimated cost for any item of work in any estimate can be questioned and shown to be only relatively accurate. All estimates and all estimators rely on the roundabouts and swings whereby the differences (the pluses and minuses) between estimated costs and actual costs tend to cancel each other out. A well-made estimate is, nevertheless, essential to many purposes. In any event, there is no alternative. Owners require bids; negotiators, a starting point; and managers, detailed information expressed in terms of costs, time, and resources.

Estimates are a source of information. When a bid is not successful, do not say it was a waste of time. Keep the estimate and all its information. Use it in another way. Find out all you can about the other bids and the subsequent contract. Check your own bid and cost estimate to discover why your bid was not the lowest. (Your estimate and bid may yet prove to have been the better one.) The more information about the bids, the contract and the project that you can uncover the more valuable your own estimate becomes. Subsequently, take whatever useful information you can from your estimate and add it to your data bases where it will become valuable data to be used in making other estimates. In this way, you effectively do cost accounting—even on the jobs you do not get. The effort you put into making a cost estimate need not be wasted, even if it does not directly produce a job. It may do so eventually; and, perhaps, the new estimate will be more profitable because it is made with data enhanced by earlier estimates. Computer systems can make cost estimating more effective and economic in more ways than one.

7.2 COSTING SYSTEMS AND COST CODES

The basis of a job costing system is a cost code: a series of alphabetic, or numeric, or alphanumeric symbols representing items of work that can be used in cost estimates, cost accounts, and general accounting. Such a system is offered in outline by the North American standard *Masterformat*. This, however, is a closed system and therefore limited.[8] Often only some of the 16 standard divisions are useful to a particular contracting company. By reviewing and criticizing this format one can gain a better understanding of cost codes, their purposes, and functions.

Many say that a mixture of numbers and alphabetical letters is easier to remember; especially if the letters are mnemonic (an aid to memory). Seven digits seem to be a practical maximum for both human memory and for computer printouts. *Masterformat* uses only numbers. It also contains Broadscope headings such as 03300 CAST-IN-PLACE CONCRETE, and subsidiary Mediumscope headings that use the last two digits for the final identification (e.g., 03310 Structural Concrete). Many Mediumscope items of work already are identified and standardized by the *Masterformat* while

other numbers are left blank in the published list to provide flexibility.

The arrangement of items (and the unassigned spaces) is such that a general contractor in building construction who does, for example, a lot of concrete work might find it difficult to use the standard format and simultaneously have sufficient codes to do detailed costing of a variety of work. Some therefore have found it easier to develop their own cost codes. However, there is the advantage of familiarity and limited compatibility with other similarly coded documents in using at least the Broadscope headings of *Masterformat* as the framework of a cost code for general contracting.

If one does not object to using five (out of a practical maximum of seven or eight) digits to identify the Mediumscope of, say, Structural Concrete (03310), then perhaps one can adapt and use the *Masterformat's* Mediumscope headings for detailed costing. Remember, the object is to identify basic items of work. This means that with cast-in-place concrete, for example, many items of "placing concrete" are necessary:

EXAMPLE:

Placing heavyweight concrete in:

- Footings continuous or isolated, according to size
- Footings of piers attached to walls
- Foundations walls of varying thicknesses and heights
- Walls above grade of varying thicknesses and heights
- Piers attached to walls
- Columns
- Beams, slabs, and slabs-on-ground
- Isolated beams and lintels, etc.

With so many items, a potential problem with the *Masterformat* soon becomes apparent. Structural concrete is represented by 03330, and it may be necessary to have at least 10 identifications for placing concrete. But *Masterformat* allocates only nine unassigned digits under 03310–Structural Concrete (from 03311 to 03319, with 03320 Concrete Topping). No more numbers are available. More digits or alphabetical letters might be added, but then the codes may prove too long.

The classifications should be as many as one needs. Some cost codes begin with too many. Remembering the 80/20 Rule, it is better to start by using codes for only the major items (the 20 percent) and to increase the coded items as the system and format is proven.

Concrete formwork usually needs a lot of attention because it involves mostly labor and is relatively expensive. Under Division 3, Concrete, the *Masterformat* allocates few numbers to Structural Cast-in-place Concrete Formwork (03100–CONCRETE FORMWORK is the Broadscope, and the unassigned numbers are 03101-03119, with 03120–Architectural Cast-in-place Concrete Formwork as the next Mediumscope heading). This may not be enough for complex work. There are three fundamental processes with almost all formwork:

1. Making forms
2. Erecting forms
3. Stripping and removing forms.

Alphabetical letters could be used to represent these three processes. All stripping could be represented by the letter **S**. Similarly, **M** for making forms, and **E** for erecting them, would be easier to remember than individual numbers.

Creating a cost code is not to be undertaken lightly, or without much thought about its structure and use, and about a company's requirements. The more specialized the work, the easier it is to make an effective cost code. General building construction companies have the biggest problem with cost codes because of the variety of work and the large numbers of items.

There is at present much discussion about architects/engineers/contractors' systems (AEC systems) and project integration (using object-oriented project data bases). Many acronyms have been coined and registered for the application of computers to every aspect of design and construction. One proposal would have the CSI *Masterformat*[9] combined with *Uniformat* in "a hierarchical structure, such that (1) *Uniformat* provides the link to drawings and Cad, and *Masterformat*, the link to specifications, and (2) estimating systems can use *Uniformat* for initial and *Masterformat* for later estimates."[10]

The best advice for students is to keep up with developments, keep an open mind, wait for a consensus to appear, and learn everything possible about the fundamentals. Do not hesitate, however, to question even the fundamentals. This is an era of radical change, and only by questioning will the inadequacies of existing systems be exposed. Meanwhile, do not overlook what is happening in places other than North America. Worldwide changes include the globalization of finance, technology, and even culture. Today, the word "international" means global—not just the United States and Canada. Sooner or later, whatever standard for the integration of project information is chosen, the next step will be to link it with the European equivalent of *Masterformat*: the Swedish-developed *SfB system*.[11]

Therefore, to be well prepared, today's students of construction should have the broadest possible view.

General Project Costing

It is not easy to introduce and establish a costing system. Probably the biggest difficulties will be on-site, especially with foremen. Yet, the success of a cost accounting system mostly depends on the foremen, because foremen direct crews and fill in or check the timesheets. The initial requirements of a new cost accounting system, therefore, should not be too onerous. Workdays are best divided into quarters (by breaks), and these are allocated to major work items. Job overheads is the last category to which costs should be allocated. Even overhead-crane time can be roughly allocated to work items.

At the outset, only selected projects and items should have cost accounting. Small and unusual projects, such as alteration work and renovations, should not have cost accounting until the company is comfortable with the system. Above all, a costing system must be kept simple, and on-site personnel especially must be convinced of its worth. Refinements and greater detail and coverage can be introduced later. The purposes of costing need to be made clear to all, and the view of costing as a policing system for uncovering mistakes must be dispelled.

A costing system must be integrated with existing procedures for accounts payable and payroll. Few object to filling in timesheets. Construction superintendents ultimately are responsible for the proper costing of the projects they supervise, and they must ensure that the foremen do their part. Costing can be a benefit to a superintendent since it helps to uncover deficiencies in cost estimates. A young computer-wise technologist may be the best person to work on-site at costing and assisting the superintendent.

7.3 CLASSIFICATIONS AND USES OF INFORMATION AND DATA

As defined here, **data** means **information** that has been integrated with other information and related to a common reference, or datum. (An analogy is a datum or reference level used in layout and surveying.) As a common term, data means any information stored in a computer system. Since the distinction is useful, however, many choose to use it as defined herein. Information about the costs of basic items of work is useful only when analyzed and converted (e.g., when labor costs are converted to **production rates**) and integrated with data collected at different times or from different sources.

Data are essential to estimating and construction management, but not all data are of equal quality and value; therefore, we classify them according to source.

First-class information and data are obtained from known sources by means under the collector's control (e.g., information obtained from a project by cost accounting). The cost accountant is aware of the work conditions at the site from which the information is obtained and is able to analyze the information and relate it to other data.

Second-class information and data are obtained under the same conditions as first-class data, but are passed on to another system or organization for analysis and integration (e.g., first-class information and data integrated with data from sources not known at firsthand).

Third-class information and data are that which cannot be classified as first- or second-class, as defined, and of which little is known about their origins.

From the 80/20 Rule, it follows that the major items should be given most attention and that only first-class data should be used to estimate their costs.

Second-class data can be used in estimating the costs of less critical items. Third-class data should be used only for noncritical items, and only when it is uneconomic or impractical to use other data. The use of third-class data always should be the exception. Therefore, it is necessary to be able to identify those critical major items in a project before a cost estimate is made. In the case of an ordinary building, usually this can be done from experience. Alternatively, a preliminary cost estimate (quickly made using a computer) will show the distribution of costs and indicate the critical items. Such identification should become progressively more easy as data bases are developed.

REFERENCES

1. Keith Collier, *Fundamentals of Construction Estimating and Cost Accounting with Computer Applications*, 2d ed. (Englewood Cliffs, N.J.: Prentice-Hall, 1987).

SUMMARY OF MAIN POINTS

- Construction cost estimating depends on information from (1) bidding/contract documents, and (2) experience of past projects.

- Cost estimating is comprised of two main parts: (1) measurement of work, and (2) pricing. Job costing influences how they are done.

- There are several classes of construction, including building construction, and engineering construction. These classes and others share common principles of estimating and cost accounting, and many common work items.

- Job cost (account)ing analyzes actual costs and demonstrates how work should be measured and priced.

- Simplified measurement is better, and with computers it is practical. A new measurement principle says: Measure work items and calculate their quantities with the least possible number of dimensions, and fully describe them using the other dimensions.

- Pricing in estimating depends on information obtained by job costing from past projects. Otherwise, it is gambling.

- The 80/20 Rule says about 20 percent of the items in an estimate require first-class data for pricing. The other 80 percent of the items can be priced from the estimated costs of the former, and from experience and data.

- Cost estimates are expert opinions as to the actual future costs of a project. There is no such thing as an absolutely final, total cost.

- Estimating effort should not be wasted. By using a computer, estimates can be made more efficiently and the information can be used from every estimate.

■ A cost code is the basis of job costing and estimating (and is used in scheduling); it may be based on *Masterformat*, which has limitations and benefits. A new cost code requires much effort.

■ Foremen direct and allocate time to work items using 1/4-day periods (separated by breaks).

■ Job overhead cost is the last category in which to allocate costs; it is not a catch-all category.

■ Information and data are different things; they should be classified according to reliability and value, since not all are equal.

NOTES

[1]Keith Collier, *Fundamentals of Construction Estimating and Cost Accounting with Computer Applications*, 2d ed. (Englewood Cliffs, N.J.: Prentice-Hall, 1987).

[2]If for certain plumbing systems the division of costs is usually about 75 percent for materials and 25 percent for labor, some contractors will estimate labor costs as a percentage of material costs (i.e., about 33 percent, in this example). More sophisticated cost estimating for plumbing systems are based on labor costs related to the number of joints in piping of different sizes and types.

[3]Starting with the trade guilds in the Middle Ages, when measurers were tradesmen who specialized in measuring trade work for payment at unit prices, measurers later became quantity surveyors (nineteenth century), and then construction economists and managers (twentieth century).

[4]Professional quantity surveyors developed and publish standard methods of measurement originally based on traditional trade measurement. See Collier, *Fundamentals of Construction Estimating and Cost Accounting with Computers Applications*, 2d ed., 1987. Also, F. M. L. Thompson, *Chartered Surveyors: the Growth of a Profession* (London: Routledge & Kegan Paul, 1968).

[5]Allman, "Significant Items in Estimating," *CQS–Chartered Quantity Surveyor*, Sept. 1988; (London, Royal Institution of Chartered Surveyors).

[6]Reported in the *Chartered Quantity Surveyor*.

[7]Fuzzy logic and fuzzy sets is a recent development in the field of mathematics and probability.

"In many fields of science, problems having an element of uncertainty and imprecision are conventionally treated according to the concepts and methods of probablity theory. However, there are also situations in which imprecision stems not from randomness but from the presence of a class or classes (that is, fuzzy sets) that do not possess sharply defined boundaries."
Thomas L. Saaty, "Operations Research: Some Contributions to Mathematics," *Science*, Dec. 8, 1972, p. 1069.

[8]Only by increasing the number of characters in a code identity can the number of items be increased in a closed system such as *Masterformat*.

[9]Developed by GSA, AIA, and Hanscomb Associates, an international firm of quantity surveyors.

[10]"A/E/C Systems Computer Solutions," (journal, Autumn 1991, p. 7.

[11]Project information systems for computers were developed in Sweden in the early 1960s. See Collier, *Fundamentals of Construction Estimating and Cost Accounting*, 1st ed. 1974, pp. 21–30.

QUESTIONS AND TOPICS FOR DISCUSSION

1. Define the following terms:
   a. Work item
   b. Engineering work
   c. Item of work
   d. Direct costs
   e. Indirect costs

2. Explain what determines how work shall be (a) measured, and (b) priced, and why.

3. What does "waste" mean? Explain in detail with examples of different kinds.

4. Explain why formwork for poured concrete walls is better measured linearly.

5. State and explain the new general principle for the measurement of work, using examples.

6. Explain the two basic kinds of information used in cost estimating.

7. State and explain the 80/20 Rule of Estimating.

8. Design in detail a cost code suitable for one of the following: (1) cast-in-place concrete, (2) formwork, and (3) concrete reinforcement.

9. If you find a major difference between the quantities of yard lumber in a job estimate and the actual quantities charged to the job (substantiated by invoices and delivery tickets), what would you do to avoid such discrepancies in the future?

10. a. Explain how you would deal with equipment idle-time in a cost account
    b. Determine where in cost classifications, and how, the costs of the following items of equipment should be charged: a masonry saw, a water pump, a tower crane

11. What are the main uses of information obtained by cost accounting?

12. What are the advantages of a standard method of measurement? To what extent is a standard method of measurement essential? Explain in detail.

13. How should waste be dealt with in a cost estimate? Give examples of two methods.

14. What usually has a significant effect on job overhead costs? Explain how and why.

15. What is significant about: (1) the distinction made between data and information, and (2) the given classifications of information?

16. Why classify information and data?

8

MANAGING CONTRUCTION RESOURCES

Give us the tools, and we will finish the job.
Winston Churchill (1874–1965); addressing President Roosevelt
by radio broadcast, 1941.

The resources used in construction work are materials, labor, tools, plant, and equipment, and information. With job overhead expenses, their costs are the direct costs of construction, and the need to manage these is paramount.

8.1 CONSTRUCTION MATERIALS

Materials are everything tangible incorporated into construction work and include the following:

1. Raw materials: those without particular form or shape (e.g., sand and gravel)
2. Products: manufactured from raw materials away from the construction site,

and without specific design (e.g., gypsum wallboard, yard lumber)
3. Components: manufactured from raw materials or products, usually away from the site, to a specific design, and often identified as prefabricated (e.g., roof trusses, precast exterior panels)
4. Machinery and equipment: similar to components, but power-driven and installed for uses related to the occupancy and use of the building or structure (e.g., motors, fans, elevators, processing equipment); not to be confused with **construction equipment**.

The distinctions among these is increasingly important, although not yet explicitly recognized in standard contracts. Long ago, all construction was with raw materials, and simpler buildings were built with materials taken directly from the land. As construction evolved, there were fewer raw materials and more products and components. This development continues and has great significance to the future of construction. Also, as a result, the distinction between **subcontractor** and **supplier** is disappearing[1] along with the traditional trades, and the amount of machinery installed in buildings is increasing.[2]

Bills of Materials

Bills of materials is an old term for lists or schedules of materials. In some projects, a bill of materials in the documents tells bidders which materials will be provided by the owner. The difference between **bills of materials** and **bills (schedules) of quantities** is explained in Chapter 7. With schedules of quantities, bidders do not have to measure the quantities of work. Quantities of work in a cost estimate are the main source of information for bills of materials.

EXAMPLE:

A concrete-block wall is 50 feet long × 8 feet high, with a total area of 400 square feet. The wall contains 450 whole and part-blocks. The description in the cost estimate is as shown in Figure 8.1.

If we make an estimate with an estimating program and a computer, the bill of materials can be generated by the program, and the scaffolding equipment analyzed into its parts (i.e., metal tubing and fittings).

Waste of Materials

A careful estimator measures construction work net, as installed, and includes an allowance for **waste** (e.g., an estimated factor, usually a percentage) in an item's description to tell how much to allow in the unit price for *waste*, or for *laps*, or for the *shrinkage and swell* of the material. In some instances of standard products for which waste usually is small, a stated allowance can be included for waste in the measured quantity. Keeping quantities net (and free of waste) generally makes accounting for waste much easier. Waste, or the risk of waste, can be calculated and allowed for in a cost estimate in several ways

- As a measured or calculated quantity of the material, shown as a *separate* waste item; i.e., for items with significant and measurable waste
- As a percentage addition to the net quantity; i.e., for items with small but predictable waste
- As a percentage addition to the cost: for the calculated risk of waste through breakage or other such cause

Some waste is quite predictable (e.g., offcuts), and some is less so (e.g., breakages and theft). We have to assume that all construction materials, even products and components, are potentially subject to waste. (The definition of waste here is comprehensive.) Some waste (e.g., theft or breakage) may be covered by insurance: either by mutual insurance or by self-insurance, by the builder taking the risk.

If a product is standard and easily reordered and replaced, it is not necessary to over-order to allow for unpredictable waste. If reordering will cause a serious delay, extra material might be initially ordered. For

```
                        ESTIMATE


JOB J. Willis School    LOCATION   204th Ave, Brisby, NJ

OWNER New County S B    ARCHITECT  James & Brown

ESTIMATOR kc            CHECKED    dm   DATE 93-04-01



DIV 04   SEC 40  WORK   Hollow Concrete Blockwork

SPEC-REF 04.2.1-4                              page 1/3


                            MATERIAL        LABOR
0440                       $       $       $       $
8in EXTR WALL X 8ft  50.0lf 11.00 = 550   10.50 = 525

0440
Masonry Scaffold, erect/remv (LS) = 100      -       -
```

```
                   BILL OF MATERIALS


0440-1
8x8x16in Hllw Blck type 401 . . . . . . . . . . units    470

0449-0
Mnry Mrtr type A . . . . . . . . . . . . . . . . . . . . cuyds    1
```

Figure 8.1 Masonry work—in an estimate and a bill of materials.

this purpose, and as a guide in making decisions, materials might be rated in a data base as standard, special, or highly special. Also, a diary record of unusual waste should be made. Waste calculations are easier with estimating and job costing programs.

Shrinkage and Swell

Compaction causes *shrinkage*: a cubic yard of natural material, as purchased, may be only two-thirds of a cubic yard after compaction. *Swell* (sometimes called bulking) is the opposite of shrinkage, and also creates a cost. A cubic yard of excavation may result in 1-1/4 cubic yards of excavated material to be handled or removed. Both swell and shrinkage can be more significant than waste. In an estimate they can be handled in the same way as waste.

Laps in Materials

We mention *laps* to avoid confusion with waste. Some measure laps with the quantities of work by adding a percentage; e.g., to a net area covered with wood panelling. Others leave measured quantities net, and make an allowance for laps in the unit price.[3] With many materials laps are a constant factor, but for some work, such as steel rebar, laps vary depending on design requirements, and therefore need to be described and counted. A **standard method of measurement**[4] should define what should be measured. Also, an estimator should state in an item's description whether laps are measured and included. If laps are not measured, the description should include a note as to the allowance for laps to be made in the unit price.

Serious errors have occurred when ordering materials such as shiplap, siding, and roofing materials because of confusion over laps. Some trade contractors claim that wrong measurements of materials and related errors in costs are a primary reason for differences among bids. Clear descriptions and standard practices are the solution.

A super' needs to know of these things because they are often the stuff of misunderstandings and disputes. In a fixed-price contract, the super' should first check the original cost estimate. If discrepancies appear among cost estimates, bills of materials, purchase orders, delivery slips, invoices, and quantities delivered, a super' should find out the reason.

Purchasing Materials

Purchasing is important in the economics of construction. Materials amount to roughly one-third to one-half of its direct costs, and smart buying can save money. In larger contracting companies, there are purchasing officers, but in smaller companies purchasing often is another function of the principal or a superintendent.

Some may ask: What is there to purchasing? Is it more than shopping around for materials? Unlike purchasing groceries, purchasing materials requires knowledge of the materials, a complex market, and of negotiating prices. A wide knowledge of specifications, sources, markets, manufacturers, and suppliers, is essential. To be known in the market also is important. A purchaser may get opportunities to buy at favorable prices because a salesman needs to move products, or because he wants to keep in touch.

EXAMPLE:

A purchasing officer of a construction company receives a telephone call from a lumber merchant who offers him 20,000 board feet of 2×6 Douglas fir tongue-and-groove decking at an attractive price. The merchant knows that the company often builds warehouses with wood roof-decks. He says a mill has too much decking. The construction company has no immediate need for decking. What should the purchasing officer do?

The purchasing officer will consider the costs of the decking, and of delivery, handling, and storage. Handling will occur at least twice. Storage has a cost. Purchasing involves more than just buying. A purchaser often deals with subcontractors as well as suppliers. Purchasing therefore requires technical and legal and contractual knowledge and skills, including:

- Preparation of lists of materials from cost estimates and contract documents
- Getting prices of and quotations for materials during estimating and bidding
- Selecting bidders for supply and work contracts
- Preparing purchase orders and contracts
- Negotiating prices for major materials
- Informing superintendents and storekeepers of orders and delivery dates
- Expediting orders to ensure timely deliveries
- Working with a resource-scheduling program[5]
- Checking, correcting, and confirming deliveries

- Making claims for delays and damages
- Approving invoices and bills for payment by accounting, using an accounts-payable program
- Interviewing salespersons and manufacturers' representatives and updating an information data base
- Maintaining price lists, catalogs, instructions, lists of contacts, and other information related to purchasing, materials, and costs in data bases
- Maintaining inventories of materials, equipment, and supplies, using an inventory data base program
- Maintaining information about prices, market conditions, trends, fluctuations, and other conditions affecting costs and purchasing
- Maintaining information about carriers and their services, rates, and schedules
- Editing and approving requisitions and purchase orders made by others (e.g., superintendents)
- Coordinating and cooperating with all other departments and with superintendents on job sites
- Obtaining and checking warranties and manuals
- Obtaining the approval of owner–designers with regard to alternative materials
- Reporting to accounting and management about resources and inventories

The list is not exhaustive, but it illustrates the scope. Effective purchasing requires a broad general knowledge of materials and methods, estimating, cost accounting and construction documents, codes and regulations,[6] business skills, and computer expertise. Purchasing also requires honesty. Other aspects involve all the legal complexities of warranties, insurances, damages caused by delays, indemnification from the effects of liens, defects, patents, and other causes, mentioned and unmentioned, arising out of material supply contracts and subcontracts for work.[7]

Misappropriation of Materials

Because purchasing involves large sums, it offers opportunities for inventive dishonesty. A purchaser is in a position of fiduciary trust, but experience shows that dishonesty does occur. Because of the complex nature of construction and the value of the materials used, some are misappropriated or converted.

EXAMPLES:

- Materials are delivered short, sometimes with connivance and kickbacks
- Materials, supplies and **consumable items** are wrongly charged to projects
- Construction materials are diverted to other projects
- Suppliers and contractors conspire to cheat owners in cost-plus-fee contracts and use false invoices
- Purchasers get kickbacks or favors from suppliers or contractors
- Workers have to kickback part of their wages to a labor contractor or foreman

The possibilities for dishonesty and chicanery are unlimited; especially in offshore projects where the markets, culture, and customs are unfamiliar. Dishonesty, however, knows no limits. One salesperson resigned when instructed to ensure that orders of yard lumber were shipped from 1 to 2 percent short.

It is reasonable that employees of a construction company engaged in construction for their own purposes should tell their employers. Once someone diverts and unloads a load of yard lumber or ready-mixed concrete, it is difficult to identify it.

Overseas Purchasing

Purchasing of local resources overseas by local purchasers employed for their knowledge of the language, culture, and the markets can be costly, but so too can be the alternative. Other than knowledge and constant awareness, there is little protection against dishonesty. The ignorance and naivete of some expatriates is an opportunity for graft and fraud. The histories of some projects read like the fabulous stories of wartime black markets. Some contractors supplying materials and labor to companies working overseas have traditional systems for price-fixing and overcharging foreigners. Their success in part is due to purchasers who are careless and ignorant of local costs, or who are conniving.

Knowledge of local markets and practices should be obtained from local consultants by an advance party, then tested, confirmed, and progressively developed. Premiums and other expenses generally are at least lower when recognized and understood. Real costs are then easier to estimate. In some countries there are two economies, each with its own separate set of accounts. The older the culture, the greater the accumulated experience, and the more ingrained the customs. In some countries, illicit dealing is a way of life. What is customary and acceptable in one may be unethical or even criminal in another. Although tempted, you might be surprised to find that sticking to the rules may be admired even by the tempters.

Advanced Purchasing

Advanced purchasing is an effort by owners to avoid delays resulting from late delivery of critical materials (e.g., imported machinery). It means identifying critical materials in a project as early as possible in the design phase and ordering them by certain scheduled dates. Although in CM projects advanced purchasing is commonly a part of fast tracking, it is not necessarily limited to CM projects.

Advanced purchasing crystallizes a part of the design, and unless the materials can otherwise be diverted, or the owner will accept a loss, the purchased materials must be installed. A commitment to advanced purchasing therefore should not be made without careful consideration. An advanced purchase might be described as a pre-contract cash allowance used by an owner before making the construction contract for the main body of work. Since several contractors may be involved in receiving, handling, storing, positioning, and installation of an advance-purchased item, project documents should clearly define the scope of an advanced purchase. There should be no contractual gaps or loose ends between an advance purchase and the installation. Every step in the process should be part of a contract. To avoid claims, all involved contractors should be fully informed about their obligations.

8.2   CONSTRUCTION LABOR

Labor is the application of manpower to materials, using **tools**, and **equipment** to produce construction work. Almost all labor involves the use of tools or equipment. Labor, tools, and equipment are so closely interrelated that in cost estimating they

should always be considered together. Their productivity and costs are accounted similarly, but separately.

Construction Labor Requirements

Usually, the supply of good workers is more problematic than that of materials. Materials can be stored until needed: labor cannot be stored; it must be on-site when needed, but not before. It must be of the right kind and in the right amounts. There is an optimum crew size and, often, an optimum number of crews.

A project may incur extra costs from delayed deliveries of materials and equipment. With labor, any extra costs mainly arise from undersupply, oversupply, and low productivity. In a fixed-price contract limited by costs and time, labor management requires

- Assessment of crew sizes for the work of different trades
- Assessment of crew productivity rates
- Planning and scheduling of labor requirements
- Supervising, monitoring, and controlling labor to attain optimum productivity and time objectives

Since one objective is to smooth out the valleys and peaks of the labor histograms, the diagrammatic representations of labor requirements, as illustrated in **Figure 10.1**, is called smoothing (or levelling) the demand for labor.

Construction Labor Rates and Costs

The formula for **labor costs** is: *time × charge-out rate*; when "time" is crew time, and "charge-out rate" includes wages, holidays, fringe benefits, compensation assessments, and payments for unemployment and Social Security made to or on behalf of workers. Charge-out rates also may include premiums for overtime and the costs arising from special conditions (sometimes specified in labor-management agreements and working rules, or otherwise agreed with workers), and the costs of tools associated with a specific crew. Such costs that arise from employing labor, as a rule should not be classified as an overhead cost. When the costs of workers can be allocated to specific work items, they are part of **direct labor costs**. Some labor costs can be properly attributed only to specific job overhead items (such as temporary facilities), and are then a valid part of job overhead costs. Beside the direct costs, sometimes there are other costs of employing labor:

- Transportation to and from or on a site
- Travel time and expenses to and from a site
- Camp facilities and services
- Bonuses and gratuities
- Medical and other personnel services
- Recreation and recuperation, vacations, etc.

Uncommon locations and conditions may cause other costs, and some projects need

- Security guards for protection
- Support from local people of influence
- Premium time for holidays, feasts, and fasts
- Local drivers, facilitators, and guides
- Payments to ease authorizations and imports
- Special payments to acquire proscribed items
- Gifts and favors for certain persons
- Self-insurance against losses related to expatriate staff[8]

The list might be longer; its content varies according to contracts, conditions, and cultures.[9]

Construction Labor Contracts

In some projects, the owner or prime contractor supplies the materials (e.g., lumber, gypsum wallboard), and a *labor contractor* provides labor and tools. The reasons for **labor contracts** include

- A trade contractor's desire to avoid the need for credit, financing, handling, and storage of materials
- An owner's or prime contractor's ability to buy materials at lower prices

Potential problems in labor contracts include

- Excessive material waste
- Other abuses of the materials supplied
- A lack of care for the work of others and in cleaning up

The main objective of a labor contractor with a fixed-price contract is to complete the work as quickly as possible. Often, the workers are paid for piecework. Incentive bonuses may be offered. As a result, less care and attention may be given to the materials supplied and their conservation. Labor contractors with a small investment and a smaller reputation—and the lowest bid—may cause problems with other trades and their work. There may be disagreements over wages that result in liens filed against the site. In a labor contract, care should be taken (by means of contract conditions and supervision) to control the quantities of materials supplied and the amounts of waste that result.

On some overseas projects, contracts for the supply of labor are offered by local contractors. The alternative is for an expatriate contractor to hire workers at the site, but in some places this may be problematic. Some pros and cons of labor contracts follow.

Pros of Labor Contracts.

- There is only one person to deal with: the labor contractor
- Costs for labor hired through a local contractor may be more competitive
- Local conditions are a less direct problem
- Labor might not be obtainable by other means
- Certain labor problems may be avoided (e.g., disputes with workers, government officials)

Cons of Labor Contracts.

- A labor contractor's practices may be unethical
- Labor contractor may not pay the agreed wages
- Workers may be impressed, underpaid, and dissatisfied with wages and conditions
- Workers' dissatisfaction may effect the work or the contractor's reputation
- Hidden costs may arise from a labor contractor's hiring practices (e.g., from cited problems)

Labor productivity

The other ingredient of the labor-cost formula is **productivity**, the estimating and control of which makes job costing so necessary. We discussed some aspects of productivity in Chapter 5, but this is a large subject with many aspects beyond the scope of this book. The primary concern of resource man-

agement and of monitoring and controlling work is productivity. As the report by Aird showed (Chapter 5), low productivity is primarily a management problem. Higher productivity is the result of better management, and better management requires information about costs and productivity (from job costing), planning and scheduling, and well-trained supervision.

8.3 EQUIPMENT, PLANT, AND TOOLS

The differences among **tools**, **plant** and **equipment** are explained in the Glossary. Small tools may be the workers', or an employer's responsibility. Usually, tools are considered as incidental, and equipment may be thought of first with the operator incidental. Yet, economically, tools and equipment are the same; the difference is only in size.

The costs of plant and equipment are kept in separate categories. With a company's owned equipment (as opposed to rented), if the information is available, an estimator should consider operator's efficiency. Plant is no longer common on building sites, especially since introduction of ready-mixed concrete, but plant is still in use on some overseas projects. Construction equipment, however, is increasingly important everywhere.

Because workers operate equipment, most of what has been said about labor also applies to equipment, but there are other considerations. *Idle time* was mentioned. Unlike sick workers, equipment that stops working often stays on-site. During this idle time, equipment still causes expense. Not only using equipment costs money, it also costs money just to own it. Calculate the expenses: depreciation, interest on payments (or the equivalent loss of interest on capital not invested), and the costs of storage (essentially of the same kind). Put equipment up for sale, and in constant dollars you will get less than you paid for it, even if it was never used. Put equipment on-site, and the depreciation increases, even if it remains idle.

Each piece of equipment on a site should be accompanied by a maintenance kit containing certain spare parts, tools, and the consumable items required. Kits must be maintained and replenished regularly. For rented equipment, the lease-contract should precisely set out the terms dealing with rates for idle time, repair and maintenance responsibilities, transportation to and from the workplace, insurances, and breakdowns.

Chapter 5 examined aspects of labor productivity and idle time. By way of comparison, it is interesting to note that some authorities also consider the productivity of excavating equipment to be about half the theoretical potential productivity. Traditional guides to equipment productivity commonly assumed 75 percent efficiency: one authority suggests 50 percent of the theoretical figures that already allow for a 50-minute hour and an 83-percent job efficiency.[10] Presumably, these are actual productivity rates obtained by work studies. There is plenty of room to be more productive and more competitive.

To Own or Rent Equipment

This is a perennial question: Is it better to buy construction equipment or to rent it? A generalization is meaningless, as the answer depends on many things, including

- The amount of expected use by the owner
- The possibilities for hiring-out the equipment

- The availability of capital and the cost of credit
- The availability of similar equipment for hire as and when needed, and the rates charged
- The location of future projects and the availability of economic transportation for the equipment
- The availability of access, storage, and security for equipment on-site
- The availability of skilled operators

The consensus seems to be: rent it if you can, providing you can get suitable terms. If you purchase equipment, use it economically and as if it belonged to another company. This means charging owned equipment out to your own jobs at realistic rates. If you do not make proper charges, what appears as profit from a contract will be part of the equipment's value. Some simple bookkeeping will help to avoid the delusion, by finding out the real costs of items of work done by the equipment. To rent equipment or to subcontract the work may prove cheaper.

The Costs of Small Tools

Include small tools with the crews that use them, as part of the crew rates. Their costs are then easier to estimate and account. For small tools on a large job, charge the job with their full cost. Using a percentage of labor costs to estimate the costs of small tools can be unreliable, unless cost accounting confirms the percentage. Do not charge out small tools as an overhead cost. They are part of labor costs.

8.4 COMPUTER SYSTEMS FOR RESOURCE MANAGEMENT

Almost all the management operations described in this chapter are more efficient when using a computer with appropriate software programs, including:

- A cost estimating program that generates bills of materials with allowances for waste, laps, shrinkage and such, and that can interact with the other programs listed below
- A project planning and scheduling program that includes features to deal with resource scheduling and levelling, and costs
- Data-base and accounting programs to store and provide information about
  1. Material inventories
  2. Purchase orders, invoices
  3. Manufacturers and suppliers
  4. Representatives and salespersons
  5. Carriers and the routes and schedules
  6. Project records and critical date reminders
- A spreadsheet program that enables data from other programs to be manipulated to make what-if analyses.

In a planning and scheduling computer program, resource management should be completely integrated with the cost planning and with the work planning and scheduling. The primary information source for all these must be the cost estimate because the cost estimate determined the fixed-price of the contract that also contains the cost and time constraints. Therefore, it is senseless to use information for planning or scheduling not derived from the cost estimate that led to the bid and contract. However, for other kinds of contracts lacking in design or experiential information, it may be necessary to introduce information obtained after the contract is made. Whatever we plan and schedule for a fixed-price contract's performance, the primary information source must be the cost estimate. It is through a cost estimate and a contract's time and costs that all plans and schedules are interrelated. When choosing a planning and scheduling program, this interrelationship is the first thing to look for, as anything else will lack common sense. (There is more on this topic in Chapter 10.)

SUMMARY OF MAIN POINTS

- Construction materials include (in order of complexity): (1) raw materials, (2) products, (3) components, and (4) machinery. As building evolves, more complex materials are used and site labor is reduced.
- Bills of materials (for ordering) are not bills of quantities (of work). Both should contain appropriate allowances for waste, shrinkage, or laps.
- Purchasing materials is more than just buying, and includes knowing the markets, and being known. Expediting material purchases often is critical. Misappropriation often is a hazard. Overseas purchasing has its own hazards.
- Advanced purchasing by an owner is one way to ensure materials on-site on time. Contractual provisions must be made.
- Construction labor uses tools and equipment: economically they are the same, but equipment cannot always be sent away, and costs of idle time must be paid.
- Labor requirements are critical and must match the cost estimate, which must be

made according to the nature of labor (i.e., in crews).

■ Resources for a project need balancing (i.e., levelling or smoothing of the histogram).

■ Labor costs includes all costs incurred because labor is employed, including those of: travelling; board and lodging; premiums and bonuses; R and R, etc. Unusual locations may cause other costs (e.g., for security, local support and workers, special payments, etc.).

■ Labor productivity is the primary subject of resource management, and monitoring and controlling work. Low produc-

tivity is a management problem (Aird) requiring: information, planning and scheduling, and good supervision.

■ Equipment (such as tools) matches labor in its economic characteristics, except equipment's idle time must be paid for, usually at a lower rate.

■ Small tools should be costed with the crews that use them; not as a job overhead.

■ Computer systems. Almost all the management operations described in this chapter can be facilitated by using a computer system. A cost estimate is the primary information source.

NOTES

[1]The traditional differences between subcontractor and supplier were: (1) subcontractor's work was done at a site, (2) subcontractor's work was custom-designed. Increasingly, custom work is done elsewhere (i.e., prefabricated). Unlike a supplier's products, custom work cannot be used elsewhere.

[2]Prefabrication of buildings was long prophesied but came only gradually. As with automobiles, radical changes in material and methods of construction are occurring. Already, better quality wood is a luxury, and the use of metals and plastics in ordinary housing increases.

[3]See Collier, *Fundamentals of Construction Estimating and Cost Accounting with Computer Applications*, 2d ed., 1987.

[4]In the absence of a national standard method of measurement, construction companies or their associations should create their own but seek a wider standard.

[5]Resource scheduling may be a function of a planning and scheduling program in which the resources (material, labor, and equipment) needed are extracted from a cost estimate and allocated to scheduled work activities.

[6]A purchaser needs to know the requirements of pertinent building codes and regulations, and of the Uniform Commercial Code governing the sale of goods.

[7]For more on this extensive topic, see Richard M. Hollar, "Procurement in the Construction Industry," in *The McGraw-Hill Construction Business Handbook*, 2d ed. (New York: McGraw-Hill, 1985) Part IV, Chapter 15.

[8]Some expatriates succumb to exotic influences and develop abnormal habits and excesses, doing things that they would never do in their own countries.

[9]In one Asian country, a European international construction company found that 40 percent of expatriate staff did not complete their first employment contract of 18 months' duration. Alcoholism, sickness, and low morale were among the causes.

[10]"Actual production costs...average about 50 percent of the theoretical values listed..." *Building Construction Cost Data–1980* (Duxbury, Mass.: Robert Snow Means Co., 1980), p. 298.

QUESTIONS AND TOPICS FOR DISCUSSION

1. List and define the four classes of materials.

2. Explain the nature and purpose of (1) a bill of materials, and (2) a bill of quantities.

3. Describe four methods of dealing with material waste. Give an appropriate example of the use of each in a cost estimate.

4. Define shrinkage and swell, and explain how to deal with them in a cost estimate and in a bill of materials.

5. How should laps in installed materials be handled in an estimate, and in a bill of materials? Give examples.

6. List and briefly describe at least 12 functions of a purchasing department in a contracting company.

7. Describe five examples of misappropriation of materials and a way to prevent each.

8. Describe advanced purchasing and its main purposes and contractual requirements.

9. Identify and briefly describe as many constituents of labor rates as you can.

10. Write a short essay on labor productivity in construction; its shortcomings, and possible ways of overcoming them.

11. Describe the major potential problems with labor-only contracts and suggest remedies.

12. Explain the difference between tools and equipment, and how this affects cost estimating and work scheduling.

13. Discuss the relationship between labor productivity and equipment efficiency rates.

14. What is the preferred way to deal with the costs of small tools? Explain your response.

15. What are the primary objectives in using a computer system for construction management, and how is that to be achieved?

9

CONTRACT TIME AND SCHEDULING

To choose time is to save time.
Francis Bacon (1561–1626)

Time is one of four major elements of fixed-price contracts. Others are: quantity, quality, and the contract sum. We examine in this chapter how a contractor can establish and manage contract time. Here is one of the most obvious examples of the effect of contract type on a project's management.

9.1 CONTRACT TIME, GENERALLY

In bidding and contracting, the time for performance of a fixed-price contract may be established in one of two ways:

1. By the owner–designer, and prescribed in the bidding documents
2. By the bidder–contractor (**precontractor**), and subsequently stated in his bid, if required

Even if bidding documents stipulate a contract time, bidders still have to verify or modify it after making their own time estimate. If the time stipulated appears too short, bidders then have to allow in their cost estimates and bids for the extra costs of completing the work on time and for accepting certain risks, such as

- Costs of overtime work
- Costs of additional supervision
- Costs of incentive payments
- The risk of having to pay damages should late completion occur without extension of the contract time

Therefore, if a stipulated contract time is considered inadequate, the contract sum will increase accordingly. What if bidders believe a stipulated contract time is too long? In that case, bidders should still establish their own time,—and expect to complete the work before the completion date. There remains, however, the possibility that the time for completion is stipulated for a particular purpose, such as to

- Have a project completed to coincide with the start of a business season, or of financing
- Fit in with other projects, or other requirements, or other obligations of the owner (e.g., in leases).

Bidders should not assume that an owner always will be pleased by an earlier completion. A meeting of minds is essential. Here is good reason to have more than the usual communication between owner–designer and bidders. Too often it is limited to terse instructions to bidders perhaps followed by some telephone calls and hastily prepared **addenda.** As explained in Chapter 6, meetings between bidders and a bidding authority are the better way to an agreement about complex contractual matters. Some of the reasons related to contract time that cause bidders to make allowances and increase their bid amounts should be reviewed.

- Parts of the work appear overspecified
- Requirements in the documents are vague
- *Design information* seems to be lacking
- Some detail drawings show unusual construction
- There are requirements for many samples, shop drawings, inspections, and tests[1]
- There are many requirements, or complicated requirements, for alternative prices in bids for different, or additional, or omitted, parts of the work, requiring much extra work for bidders[2]

The list could be longer. Any of these problems can affect a contract's duration. If bidding documents are not clear and precise, there may be reasons or doubts that may cause a bidder to allow for extra contract time and costs. Some may prove false; others may be due to misunderstandings. Open discussions help make better contracts.

Contract Time As Reason for a Contract Awarded

Since a shorter construction time often might be to an owner's advantage, its stipulation in a bid might be a consideration in awarding a contract. If this is so, it should be expressed in the bidding documents. Some bidders and some contractors' associations do not approve of owners awarding contracts for any reason but the lowest bid, because (they say) an award for another reason may

- Lead to irresponsible offers as to completion
- Make an owner's decision complicated (i.e., the weighing of contract time against costs)
- Result in dissatisfaction among the unsuccessful bidders

Other than for public-funded contracts, an owner may accept or reject any bid, for any reason, or for no reason at all. An owner can do as he likes provided it is legal. For most owners, dissatisfaction among bidders is not significant enough to demur. Negotiating the terms and conditions of a contract is discussed elsewhere.[3]

Time in Fixed-Price Contracts

In any fixed-price contract, time is important to the contractor because to a large extent it governs the job overhead costs.

Therefore assume in all fixed-price contracts, and all other contracts containing a fixed-price element (i.e., unit-price, maximum cost-plus-fixed-fee, and even the cost-plus-fixed-fee), that time is important to a contractor and affects costs. The AIA Document A101-1987, Article 3, *Date of Commencement and Substantial Completion*, shows the importance of time; it is stated in the agreement. If so stipulated in a contract, contract time is something that "is of the essence" and "goes to the root of the contract" (i.e., is vital to its existence). Time is not considered of the essence of a construction contract unless the contract says so.

The AIA Document A201-1987 says, in Subpara. 8.2.1: "Time limits stated in the Contract Documents *are of the essence* of the Contract" [emphasis added]. It then goes on to say (in Subpara. 8.3.1), "If the Contractor is delayed at any time... [by] causes beyond the Contractor's control...then the Contract Time shall be extended by Change Order for such reasonable time as the Architect may determine." This seems to contradict the previous statement that time is of the essence. Although time is critical to contractors because of its direct effect on overhead costs, the fact is not always made obvious. If time affects costs, why do some contractors have so many delays? Causes may include

- The seasonal nature of much construction work
- An unexpected confluence of several jobs
- A shortage of skilled workers and supervisors
- A lack of preparation, planning, and scheduling
- Generally inadequate construction management

Such causes are avoidable, or at least foreseeable. There are others, some of which are accepted by owner–designers as valid causes for extensions of time.[4] Some other contracts, however, allow time extensions only for an **act of God** or a **force majeure.**

A fixed-price contract may contain provisions for **liquidated damages** should the work be substantially incomplete by the stipulated completion date. However, it does not follow that early completion would entitle a contractor to a monetary reward.[5] (See Chapter 17 for more on claims.)

Job Overhead Costs and Time

Many claim that job overhead costs are the most difficult to estimate, and those are the costs most directly related to contract time. Direct costs of work are related mostly to quantity and quality; however, on job overhead costs, time has the greatest effect. Similarly, time also affects operating overhead costs, but less directly.

The method of estimating the duration of a project depends on the nature of the work. Because the time allowed for bidding is short, often bidders estimate time intuitively by the so-called seat of the pants method; i.e., by how one feels about a project's duration after discussing ideas and opinions. From experience, some estimators and supervisors are able to estimate time accurately; e.g., to within a month out of a 12- or 15-month period, although that is not always accurate enough. If proposed work is complex or unusual, to estimate the required time more precisely it may be necessary to make a preliminary **work plan** and **work schedule.**

9.2   FIRST ESTIMATES OF CONTRACT TIME

The earliest estimates of contract time are made by bidders for a fixed-price contract to estimate the costs of job overhead and other costs dependent on time; e.g., supervision, and the costs of major plant and equipment (such as a crane or an excavator) that may be on-site for most of a project's duration. It may be necessary to first make a schedule: either a **Gantt bar chart,** or a network diagram showing a **critical path**. After estimating the direct costs of work, only the time required for all the work on a critical path is estimated.

One method of approximate planning and scheduling work depends on a relationship between costs and time. The missing factor is optimum degree of *mobilization*. For example, suppose we have to place concrete in a large slab. The estimate may show the following:

Placing Concrete in Slab and Beams using an Overhead crane:

Slab demensions, 200 ft × 72 ft =
$$14,400 \text{ sf} \times 9 \text{ in. avg} = 400 \text{ cy}.$$

(At 0.5 man-hrs per cy = 200 man-hrs allowed; therefore, a crew of 5 laborers has 40 crew-hrs, or 5 working days (8 hrs per day), to place 400 cy of concrete in the slab and beams).

In this example, the best degree of mobilization is a crew of five laborers; if increased to two crews we might expect the concrete to be placed in half the time: in two-and-one-half days. But possibly it would require three days; the work expanding to fill the time available. So, for our preliminary time estimate we allow either five days or three days for pouring the slab: a major item of work on the critical path.

The main point of this simple example is that task and project time to be scheduled is largely determined by the cost estimate and the practical degree of mobilization.

To ignore the cost estimate in a fixed-price contract would be foolish. When the labor costs of a major work item are estimated, an estimator relies mostly on the data of **productivity rates** (obtained by job costing), with adjustments according to perceived conditions; e.g., the rate of 0.5 man-hours per cubic yard in the example.

In most projects, certain work is critical to the total time while other work is not. First, from the cost estimate we make a **work breakdown structure** (WBS) for a project. Even if it consists of only a few phases or items, a work breakdown is easier to deal with than an entire project. For example, phases of work for a warehouse project might include

- Certain site works (i.e., those essential to the work that follows)
- Foundations and other work in the substructure (rough-in of mechanical and electrical services)
- Block-masonry exterior walls
- Structural steelwork (roof supports)
- Wood roof deck
- Roof membrane
- Openings (e.g., windows, exterior doors)
- Rough-in of mechanical and electrical services
- Concrete floor slab
- Equipment installation (dock levellers)
- Fixture installations (plumbing and electrical)
- Finishes (e.g., painting)

These phases and certain subphases are shown diagrammatically in Figure 9.1. The form and content of a WBS depends on the type and design of the building. For exam-

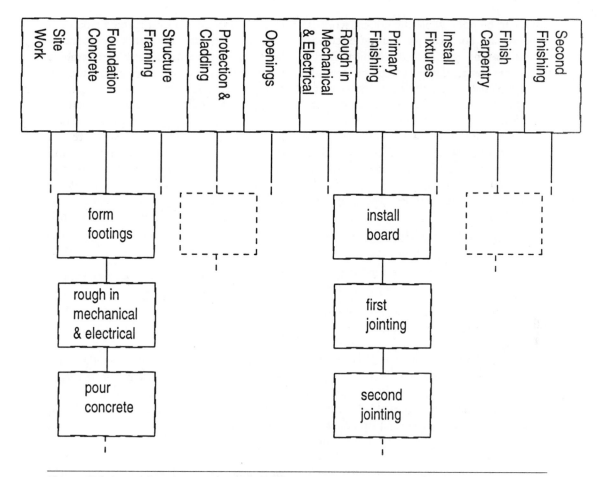

Figure 9.1 A work-breakdown-structure diagram

ple, for a multistory building, the work above the substructure should be separated and identified by floors. At the lowest level of analysis, each phase of the work is broken down into work items.

The term phase is common to estimating, job costing, and project management programs, manuals, and texts. A phase, however, is whatever one wants it to be, depending on the project, the types of work involved, and the system or program used.

In an integrated construction management system, in which a cost code is used for estimating and job costing, the definition of a phase and a work item should be found in the cost code, and would apply to related planning and scheduling. A cost code and its definitions, therefore, is fundamental to an integrated system.

Next, critical work activities should be defined (those on the critical path of activities) as distinct from the rest of the work that can be done while the critical work is under way. For example, certain electrical work may be critical to mechanical work, but other electrical work can be substantially completed within the time necessary to complete the mechanical work. It takes little effort to allocate major work items in a cost estimate to the phases in a WBS (especially if using an estimating program that interfaces with one for planning and scheduling)[6] and to calculate the number of days needed for major activities. The simplified formula is:

$$Time = \frac{Estimated\ labor\ costs}{Crew\ rate}$$

When, Crew rate = The total cost of a crew per hour/day

In the labor equation, workers and time are not interchangeable. In the slab example one would not expect two crews to do the job in 2.5 days. Neither would one expect to pour the concrete slab in one day by employing five five-men crews. One crane would be inadequate even if the 25 men of five crews did not get in each other's way. Selecting suitable crews and suitable numbers of crews for different work is critical. Also allow extra time for the *resource levelling* of labor and equipment requirements, and make allowances for probable contingencies (e.g., for equipment delays, inclement weather, etc.). This method of estimating time converts estimated labor costs to estimated labor time, based on crews.[7] With this information it is possible to make a fairly accurate estimate of the completion time for each phase.

Next, the phases on a **bar chart** and any possible overlapping will be shown. Then the chart will show the project's approximate duration. Check the total estimated project time in the chart against independent and intuitive estimates made by a superintendent and the estimator. Remember that most preliminary estimates tend to be optimistic, and that later events usually tend to delay a project.

With a preliminary cost estimate, a designer can also use this method to establish a contract's time to be stipulated in instructions to bidders. Consultants and contractors for mechanical, electrical, and other important parts of the work should be called upon to advise and independently estimate the time needed for their own work phases.

9.3 PLANNING AND SCHEDULING CONTRACT TIME

Project Scheduling and Management, Generally

Estimating, planning, and scheduling are necessary for proper construction management to control time, resources, and the costs of work, and to ensure completion within both the contract time and the contract sum, or budget.

Planning work consists of arranging work activities in a logical and economical order. Scheduling work sets dates for the start and completion of activities. The work and its costs must then be managed to attain completion within the budget by the scheduled date. It is necessary to monitor the schedule and the work regularly, to compare the results with the schedule and with the cost estimate, or budget, and to adjust work methods as needed. This is the function of controlling work that follows estimating and planning, as shown in Figure 1.2, the construction-management cycle.

This brief explanation is an oversimplification of a sometimes complex and dynamic process. In summary, assuming a project with a fixed-price contract, at the outset the contractor has only the drawings and specifications, and then a cost estimate. Almost all of the design information is in the contract documents. The cost estimate is a translation with the contractor's cost and experiential information added. The objective is to perform the work according to the contract within the constraints of the contract time and contract sum. Therefore, it follows that any information used in planning, scheduling, and managing the project must be consistent with the cost estimate. There are, however, activities in a project that often are not mentioned in a cost estimate (because they are part of the project management, supervision, or of subcontracted work) that can affect a project's duration. Examples of these activities include preparation, submission, and approval of shop drawings; project mobilization; resource mobilization; and obtaining several kinds of permits and licenses.

Bar Charts

Gantt bar charts are simple to understand and to make. They are the most commonly used diagrams for project planning and scheduling. They are linear diagrams with (1) a horizontal axis showing project time (usually in days or weeks), and (2) a vertical axis listing work phases (as in the WBS). The horizontal bars are scaled according to duration, as in Figure 9.2. A bar chart can be made with a spreadsheet program.

Because they are simple, bar charts are incapable of showing all the logic and relationships of a work plan. Also, they often are of little use because they show insufficient detail; e.g., certain major trades, such as *M&E work*, often are represented by bars that extend throughout a project's duration—and so tell nothing. Also, for an extended and complex project, bar charts can be very long and unwieldy. As they are easily understood, however, bar charts may be made for use on-site from information obtained by various methods including the **critical path method** (CPM).

The Critical Path Method

A **critical path** in a network (logic) diagram is a sequence of activities that determines the total length of a project; i.e., the longest irreducible sequence of activities that cannot be made shorter except by special means, or crashing, such as working overtime.

A project's critical path can be found by making a logic or network diagram, of which there are two basic kinds: (1) Activity-on-Arrow (AOA), and (2) Activity-on-Node (AON), as illustrated in Figure 9.3. The AOA diagram usually is employed for the CPM. The AON diagram is commonly used in the Precedence Method (PM) of planning and scheduling described later. Both methods can be applied to any project. An AOA-CPM network logic diagram includes

- **Activities** shown as arrows, sometimes time-scaled, and annotated to show duration
- **Events** shown as numbered nodes (polygon figures) separating and identifying the activities

The ruling logical relationship is: Activity Y cannot start until Activity X ends. The AOA-CPM logic diagram probably is more widely known and used in construction than any other logic diagram. Unlike the bars on a bar chart, the arrows of an AOA

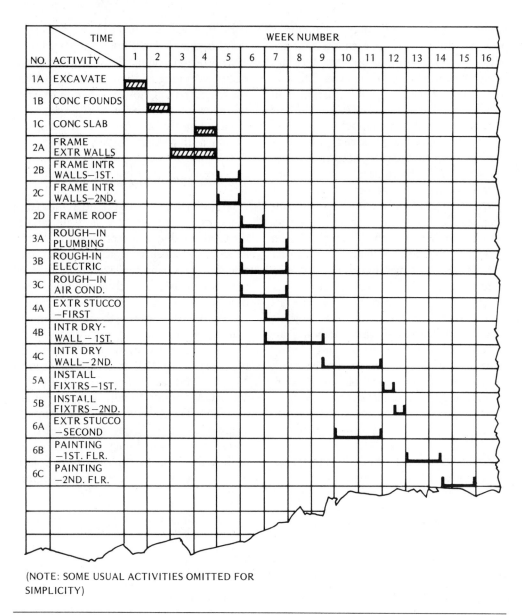

NO.	TIME / ACTIVITY	WEEK NUMBER															
		1	2	3	4	5	6	7	8	9	10	11	12	13	14	15	16
1A	EXCAVATE	▨															
1B	CONC FOUNDS		▨														
1C	CONC SLAB				▨												
2A	FRAME EXTR WALLS			▨▨													
2B	FRAME INTR WALLS—1ST.																
2C	FRAME INTR WALLS—2ND.																
2D	FRAME ROOF																
3A	ROUGH—IN PLUMBING																
3B	ROUGH-IN ELECTRIC																
3C	ROUGH—IN AIR COND.																
4A	EXTR STUCCO —FIRST																
4B	INTR DRY-WALL — 1ST.																
4C	INTR DRY WALL—2ND.																
5A	INSTALL FIXTRS—1ST.																
5B	INSTALL FIXTRS—2ND.																
6A	EXTR STUCCO —SECOND																
6B	PAINTING —1ST. FLR.																
6C	PAINTING —2ND. FLR.																

(NOTE: SOME USUAL ACTIVITIES OMITTED FOR SIMPLICITY)

Figure 9.2 A gantt bar chart.

diagram are not necessarily drawn to a time scale, but they can be. Dummy-activity arrows are used to show a restraint of one activity on another, and to maintain the network rule that all activities begin and end with uniquely identifiable events.

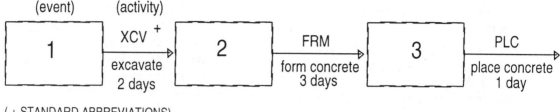

ACTIVITY - ON - ARROW (A - O - A)

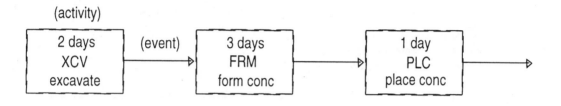

ACTIVITY - ON -NODE (A - O - N)

Figure 9.3 A-O-A & A-O-N network diagrams.

The Precedence Method (PM)

An AON-PM network logic diagram reverses the meaning of the arrow symbols so that:

- Activities are shown as nodes
- Relationships are shown as arrows

These are illustrated in Figure 9.3. The relationship arrows in AON diagrams indicate only the logical relationships between activities and so are never to scale. Activity lag, or delay, is indicated by numbers placed near the arrows. In the CPM only one kind of relationship—complete-start or start-complete—can be shown. In the PM, four logical relationships can be indicated as matters of precedence between early start, early finish, late start, late finish. This enables a logic diagram to show a relationship between part of one activity and part of another.

Opinions differ about the use and value of the AON and AOA diagrams and techniques. The AOA technique is simpler and easier to learn. In some cases, it is less capable of expressing complex relationships among activities; in other cases, it is more capable. The AON-PM technique is common in project management programs for computers, and better represents more complex relationships among activities.

Program Evaluation and Review Technique (PERT)

In 1958, a technique was developed to deal with uncertainty due to a lack of information or data for estimating activity durations. It was called the Program Evaluation and Review Technique (PERT). Its distinctive feature is the following formula used to estimate uncertain activity times.

$$\frac{(a + 4m + b)}{6} = \text{activity duration}$$

When,

a = The most pessimistic time estimate
m = The most probable time estimate
b = The most optimistic time estimate.

A later development of the PERT is known as the PERT/COST, as it contains cost-tracking techniques. Resource allocation to activities then followed. When task durations are for the most part already decided by the costs in a fixed-price contract, the value of the PERT formula is limited. In some projects, however, a separate and independent work schedule made with the PERT may prove useful. Also, in projects with work for which there is no experience or data to use as a guide in estimating, the three-times formula (above) may help in estimating work-activity time.

REFERENCES

1. Edward M. Willis, *Scheduling Construction Projects* (New York: John Wiley and Sons, 1986).
2. Keith Collier, *Fundamentals of Construction Estimating and Cost Accounting with Computer Applications,* 2d ed. (Englewood Cliffs, N.J.: Prentice-Hall, 1978).

SUMMARY OF MAIN POINTS

- Contract time, even if stipulated by an owner–designer for a fixed-price contract, has to be confirmed by the bidders for use in a cost estimate and bid.

- If a stipulated contract time appears too short, a bidder for a fixed-price contract must allow for extra costs to complete within the time.

- If the stipulated contract time in a bidding document appears too long, a bidder must work with his own estimated project time.

- Prebid meetings facilitate understanding and make for better bids and a better contract as published instructions to bidders often are inadequate.

- Reasons in bidding documents for higher bids include: apparent overspecification; vague or lacking information; unusual construction details; excessive requirements for inspections, tests, shop drawings, and samples; alternative prices required with bids.

- Bidding documents should state if a shorter contract time will be a consideration in awarding a contract.

- Job overhead costs are largely governed by contract time (e.g., costs of supervision, rentals, etc.); therefore contract time is important in any contract with a fixed-price feature (including, unit-price, cost-plus-fixed-fee).

■ Contract delays often are due to seasonal work, too many projects, shortage of skills, lack of planning, and inadequate management.

■ Estimates of contract time can be made using a work breakdown structure (WBS), by establishing the critical trades and using crew time = crew costs divided by crew rate, and allowing extra time for levelling labor demands and for contingencies. Compare such time estimates with others made intuitively.

■ Crews and Time in the productivity equation are not interchangeable; e.g., what can be done by one crew in five days probably cannot be done by five crews in one day.

■ Task and project time is largely determined by the cost estimate and the degree of mobilization.

■ A work breakdown structure is derived from a cost estimate, with certain work items rearranged in a practical sequence of phases, subphases, and work items.

■ Planning work consists of arranging work activities in a practical order: scheduling is applying dates to start and finish of activities; controlling work means monitoring a project, its schedule, and its costs, and making needed adjustments.

■ Bar charts are simple, easily understood, of limited use, and often lacking in detail.

■ A critical path in a logic network diagram is that sequence of activities that determines the total length of a project; i.e., the longest irreducible sequence of activities that cannot be made shorter except by special means (e.g., crashing).

■ Activities are represented in network diagrams by either arrows (activity-on-arrow, AOA), or nodes (activity-on-node, AON). The AOA diagram is simpler and often less versatile. The AON is often more capable, and more common in PM programs.

■ CPM-AON network diagram concepts include activities shown as nodes (circles, hexagrams); duration and lag, as numbers of days or weeks; events shown as arrows to separate the activities.

■ The AOA shows only one kind of precedence (end-start/start-end): the AON can show four different ones among early or late, start or end.

■ The program evaluation and review technique (PERT) also uses an AOA network diagram; its distinctive feature is the uncertain activity (three) time formula: $(a + 4m + b) \div 6 =$ time, useful when no data is available.

NOTES

[1]These are valid requirements; but an abundance may indicate to bidders that either the design is not complete, or that the designer will prove to be unusually demanding.

[2]The requirement for alternative prices with bids often indicates an owner-designer lacks reliable cost information about the project.

[3]Collier, *Construction Contracts*, 2d ed. (Prentice-Hall, 1987), Chapter 2.3.

[4]See A201-1987, Para. 8.3, *Delays and Extensions of Time*.

[5]See, Collier, *Construction Contracts*, 2d ed., 1987, pp. 150–153.

[6]Such as Timberline Software's Precision[R] Extended.

[7]The importance of crews was explained in Chapter 5.

QUESTIONS AND TOPICS FOR DISCUSSION

1. Explain this statement: Even if contract time is stipulated in bidding documents, bidders must establish it for themselves.

2. What does a bidder do if the stipulated contract time is too short? Explain in detail.

3. Briefly describe a method of arriving at an approximate estimate of a project's time using the cost estimate. Explain the key formula.

4. Fully explain the following terms and abbreviations:
   a. Gantt chart
   b. AOA
   c. AON
   d. The longest irreducible sequence of activities
   e. An event (in scheduling)

5. Select a common sequence of activities (such as changing a tire, baking a pie, or building a shed) and prepare a network diagram of the planned activities. Assume activity durations. Show the critical path and the least time needed to perform the work.

6. Explain why dummy activities are necessary in some network diagrams?

7. Write a 200-word (minimum) essay on the fundamentals of PERT and explain its uses and limitations in construction.

8. Explain how a bar chart can be derived from a cost estimate for use in construction, using a detailed and illustrative example.

9. Explain the following terms:
   a. Degree of mobilization (in a project)
   b. The intuitive approach to scheduling
   c. Crashing to save time

10. Discuss the advantages and disadvantages of activity- and event-oriented logic networks for planning and scheduling in construction.

11. In a construction project (a) on what is *time* mostly dependent, and (b) which group of costs is mostly dependent on time? Explain your answers.

12. Describe in outline the process of planning and scheduling and how it critically relates to a fixed-price project's cost estimate.

13. In a bar chart schedule with the time shown in days, should a week be shown as five or as seven working days? Explain your answer, and discuss the pros and cons.

14. Respond to the statement: It is not worth the time and effort to plan and schedule a project, since invariably the plan will change.

10

PLANNING, SCHEDULING, AND MONITORING WORK

Nothing in progression can rest on its original plan.
Edmund Burke (1729–1797)

The purpose of a cost estimate is a bid and a contract. Once a fixed-price contract is made, the estimated costs must be broken down again into those of the elements from which they were derived: materials, labor, equipment, and overheads. The objectives are to plan and schedule the work, to quantify and manage the needed resources, to monitor and control the contract time and costs.

10.1 COMPUTER PROGRAMS FOR SCHEDULING

Computers make planning and scheduling much easier. Perhaps the general absence of schedules made with a logic network diagram from so many projects can be explained in part by a lack of computers. They are necessary to avoid the drudgery of

calculating the earliest and latest times of work activities (perhaps several times over) to arrive at a suitable work schedule. Without a computer, the monitoring of work and its costs also takes more time. Many computer programs are available for project planning and scheduling. This is a brief introduction to the basic features of mid-level programs.[1]

Project Management Programs Reviewed

For computer users, an important source of product information is computer magazines. A recent computer magazine's review of several project management programs[2] listed the following criteria:

    Capacity
        Tasks per project
        Resources per task

Subprojects
Scheduling and Resource Control
    CPM calculations
    Selective resource levelling
    Manual or automatic levelling
    Split resource assignments
    Time-limited scheduling
    Resource-limited scheduling
    Partial resource allocation
    Lag time
    Prioritizes (projects/tasks)
    Task relationships
Planning and Tracking Capabilities
    Outliner
    WBS codes
    Histogram view
Editing Capabilities
    Table data entries
    Search and sort filtering
    Custom views/custom fields
Reporting
    Earned value analysis
    Variance reports
    Customize symbols
    Cost charting
    Chart annotation
    Import and export formats

The reviewer placed each program in one of three classes or levels of sophistication: (1) low-end, (2) mid-range, and (3) high-end. Program prices went from less than $300 to over $5000. The editor's choice of a high-end program was not the most expensive and cost about $2000. For most construction projects, network calculations, task sequencing relationships, and resource management and levelling are necessary features. Generally, these were only available among the mid-range and high-end programs.

Articles by experts in software applications[3] are a buyer's first step to selecting a program. The next step is to use the advertisers' request-cards to get product information. Software programs are upgraded frequently, and the computer magazines are the best source to watch; not only for upgrades, but also product comparisons, ratings, and advice for users, often by other users.[4]

Consider the several advantages of using a project management program that interacts with a cost estimating program.[5] Interaction with general accounting and job costing programs also is useful.

There is a general movement in design and construction toward integrated information systems using desktop computers. Project information created for one purpose (e.g., by estimating, for bidding) is useful for many other purposes (e.g., work scheduling, a schedule of values, applications for payment, etc.). A computer system converts information into other formats quickly and accurately and all the data is consistent. This is especially important for projects with a fixed budget, such as a construction project with a fixed-price contract. If, however, a project is to be performed within a cost-plus-fee contract, there may be more scope for ingenuity, and work planning may give rise to alternatives for which various solutions are possible. Most midlevel programs include the following salient features:

- Sequential and concurrent task relationships
- Baseline scheduling: to permit progress tracking and comparisons with a current schedule
- Resource allocation and levelling: to handle materials, labor, and equipment requirements
- Fixed and variable costs (planned and actual): for cost monitoring and control

■ Work breakdown structure (WBS) charts, PERT charts, Gantt charts, and task and resource summaries for report generation

Sequential and Concurrent Task Relationships

In Activity-on-Arrow (AOA) diagrams, only one relationship is possible: finish-to-start. The precedence diagram method introduced other relationships (see Chapter 9).

Baseline Scheduling

Some early versions of scheduling programs did not have the capacity for both an original and a current schedule and comparisons were difficult. A baseline schedule is for tracking time by comparing a current schedule with the baseline, or original schedule.

Resource Allocation and Levelling

The programs provide **Gantt charts** and histograms for resources (e.g., labor, materials, and equipment, or whatever resources are assigned). Resources are assigned to tasks (i.e., resource assignments). A resource bar chart shows the duration and nature of each resource assignment. A resource histogram shows a summary of each resource's assignments and the overall load, as shown for labor in Figure 10.1.

Fixed and Variable Costs (Planned and Actual)

Fixed costs are for material costs or lump-sum charges (e.g., building permits). Variable costs of tasks are those of labor and equipment, calculated by rate × hours. The total costs of each activity ideally should equal those in the estimate, but sometimes it is necessary to redistribute costs among several items.

10.2 COORDINATING AND CONTROLLING WORK

Coordinating work means managing it in a practical sequence and with a degree of simultaneity to produce the desired results: namely, the timely and economic performance of a project. Coordination is done first in the initial planning, but since construction is affected by so many variables, often a schedule requires adjustment. Coordination also means maintaining a system (a work plan and schedule) until all the work activities (the project) are completed. The guide to coordination usually is a schedule network diagram showing activities and the events that separate them. It also can be a table of activities with start and finish dates.

Controlling work means monitoring it, measuring it, adjusting the start and finish dates of activities, reallocating resources, and **crashing**, if necessary, so that the schedule is maintained. The adjustment of start and finish dates may be accomplished by several means. Sometimes, however, an activity's scheduled finish date cannot be met. If the project's completion is not to be delayed, lost time will have to be made up in later activities.

Cost controlling means the monitoring of productivity and costs to maximize one and to minimize the other. Sometimes, this means making changes, and robbing Peter to pay Paul; that is, reallocating costs (resources) from one task (work item) that in the cost estimate has more than enough of the costs of resources to another that does not. Coordination and controls are essential in all projects, even in the unlikely case of an apparently unlimited budget.

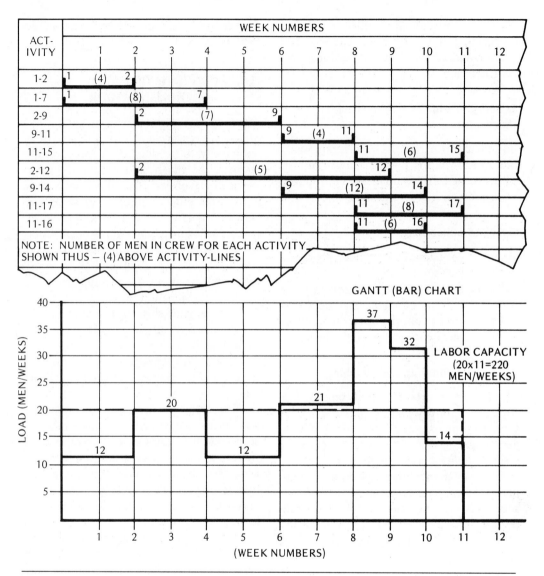

Figure 10.1 A histogram of manpower requirements.

CASE

A specialist firm dealing in the supply, installation, and servicing of controls for mechanical systems found that since the company was handed as much work as it could undertake there was no need to bid for work. As a result, they made no proper cost estimates, and did work at cost-plus or for quoted lump-sums. Although their prices contained a large markup for overhead costs and profit, after a few years the firm found it was losing money; it was failing because it did not know its real costs. Seeing that competitive bids were not needed, the staff and workers believed there was no need to be productive. Since there were no cost estimates, there was also no proper planning and scheduling of work, and no job costing.[6]

10.3 A SCHEDULE-CONTROL SYSTEM

When referring to a schedule this text refers implicitly to the plan of activities that underlies it. Scheduling should not be done in isolation, but together with budgeting, purchasing, controlling costs, general accounting, project cost accounting (job costing), and the other functions of construction management shown in Figure 2.1.

The main substance of scheduling and controlling is time and productivity and their variable costs. In order, however, to examine and discuss a function such as scheduling, it is necessary to refer to it in isolation, which can be misleading. Every management function must be studied and carried out in a relationship with the other related functions. A schedule-control system has several parts and functions:

- A plan of **work activities** based on a WBS
- A schedule calendar showing dates and durations
- A graphic representation of the plan and schedule, such as a **bar chart** or a **logic diagram**, showing scheduled activity times
- Monitoring and measurement of actual activity times
- Reporting and recording activity times and comparing with those in the baseline schedule
- A calendar for each resource
- Resource scheduling, reporting, and management
- Modification of the work and resource schedules, and, if necessary, the **work plan**
- Coordination of scheduling with cost controls
- Progress and cost reports in several formats.

Also, we should not overlook the need for coordination among subprojects, with which most project management programs can deal. A review of these functions of a schedule-control system follows.

The Plan of Work Activities (a Work Breakdown Structure)

Project management (PM) programs use the terms, **outline chart** and **work breakdown structure** (WBS). (see Figure 9.1). An outline chart contains a list of phases and tasks with information about the work from a project's cost estimate. In its most detailed form, a WBS is a list of **work items** from the cost estimate, although for scheduling purposes some items may be combined or relocated. (That depends on the detail in the estimate and the proposed schedule.) Time and effort can be saved by using a cost estimating program that can be linked with a PM program to transfer information. Also, the code numbers of work items used in an estimate should be used in a PM program. Unlike a building plan, a work-activity plan and a schedule often must be changed during the work. Bad is the plan that admits no change, said the Roman, Publilius Syrus, in the first century B.C. The Romans were great engineers and builders. As circumstances and conditions change, so must a work plan. That does not mean, as so many believe, that planning is of no use. It means that a plan and its updating are more necessary than ever to reach the goal of a timely and economic completion.

The Work Schedule

The previous remarks about a WBS and a work plan apply equally to a schedule, and to the start and finish dates. When a plan is changed, the schedule based upon it also is changed. A schedule may be changed without changing the plan, but never vice versa.

A project schedule may be a contract document, either from the outset, or after the schedule has been agreed, but this is not always recommended. In a CM project, the construction manager may make a master schedule, with the trade contractors' schedules as **subprojects** (activities) within the master schedule. To make a schedule, the following must be available:

1. A cost estimate, which fixed the project's duration and the total costs; also, the time allowed for each activity (through allocated labor and equipment

costs), and the amounts of materials and other resources required.[7]
2. Calendars that show the start and finish dates, the workweeks, and the holidays.
3. A work breakdown structure (WBS) in tabular form that identifies each task (under phases or headings) and uses a cost code.

Later, if the WBS lists their start and finish times, it becomes an alphanumeric schedule: it may show precedences, links, any **lag**, any constraints (e.g., anticipated delays in deliveries, inclement weather, subsurface conditions, etc.), and cost information.

Schedule information has to be distributed to all affected by it. Therefore, the format of a schedule must readily lend itself to reproduction and modification; although extensive modifications may require a new edition. In its most readable form, a schedule consists of a chart or diagram with notes. Many PM programs also make printouts of a schedule in an alphabetical–numerical format, which are not easy to read. Having run the first printout of a schedule to see the whole thing, pay special attention to the critical path and to the activities on it. Look also for **float** time in the schedule. There is no float on a critical path. To see float shown on screen, you may have to ask the program. If the first schedule produced is not satisfactory, it may be necessary to make a new schedule and

- Start the project earlier
- Revise one or more must-start dates
- Shorten task durations by **crashing** (e.g., work longer days and pay overtime)
- Allocate more resources (e.g., labor), or different resources (e.g., equipment)
- Do some tasks concurrently, instead of in sequence

The PM program used for construction also should provide a list of scheduled tasks with

- Activity numbers
- Code numbers and/or descriptions
- Durations (hours, days, weeks)
- Early start and early finish dates
- Resource allocations (assignments)
- Cost information.

Other information for a time schedule includes must-start dates (fixed dates that the user inputs) that are not scheduled by the PM program.

Monitoring and Measurement of Actual Work Times

Work activities on a critical path require more attention than activities with float (i.e., with spare time), but noncritical activities cannot be ignored. If they are, according to the law that "all work expands to fill the time available," noncritical activities may expand to use the available time (or more) and so become critical. Therefore, all activities need monitoring. Critical activities, however, need more careful monitoring and measurement of their actual times and the work done (the productivity). Monitoring also includes estimating the times needed for completion of activities.

In some projects, critical activities need daily monitoring. Noncritical activities may need monitoring only once a week, depending on their relative magnitude, float, uncertainty, and nature. It is largely a matter of common sense and vigilance. Also, as a project approaches completion, time usually becomes more critical and monitoring more necessary. As mentioned, it is characteristic of construction projects to begin with a bang and to end with a whimper. Typically they slow down toward the end.

Noncritical activities with plenty of float may be neglected; instead they need careful and regular monitoring. A change in the status of an activity from noncritical to critical sometimes seems to happen overnight. One day, an activity seems normal, the next day, it is falling behind.

Reporting and Comparing Results with the Schedule

In the description of a CM system in Chapter 3, reporting was shown as a major part. With the right program, updating a schedule and comparing it with the baseline schedule is simple. When a nongraphic format is used for a schedule, comparing is less simple. The value of an alphabetical–numerical format shows up in complex projects with too many activities to display in a graphic schedule. In typical building construction projects the graphic format is preferred.

When comparing schedules, the first things to compare are the times of the critical activities. Look first at the latest times because they are more critical. This helps to keep comparisons simple (see Figure 10.1). Actual times replace the scheduled times of completed activities, and the schedule is recalculated to give a new set of dates. Changes in float show that actual times no longer match those in the schedule. The general tendency is for float times to decrease and for noncritical activities to become more critical; that is, for tasks (and projects) to take longer than scheduled.

Modification of the Work Schedule

Modifications may be needed only to the schedule, or to both the plan and the schedule. If it is necessary to replan the work, deal only with activities not yet started. Another way to modify a schedule and avoid redrawing a network diagram is to use **negative float**. By inserting actual times and revised dates, the float for some activities may be reduced to below zero. This negative float shows the necessary reduction in time for those activities to complete the project by date originally scheduled. A computer program, will redraw a diagram almost instantly.

Coordination of Scheduling with Cost Controls

Activity times in schedules are based on estimated costs,[8] which are based on estimated crew sizes and productivity. As we modify a schedule, modifications may be necessary to the budget and to the projected cash flow. Also, delays and efforts to make up lost time (slippage) by crashing mean extra costs. Time and costs are inseparable, and one always affects the other. Control of a schedule and control of project costs should be done in conjunction. As each scheduled activity is completed, estimated and actual costs must be compared. When a plan and schedule have to be modified, the costs of alternatives must be considered to see which is more economical. Revised cash flow requirements also should be calculated, as they may affect decisions.

If there is any truth to the old saying that time is money, it is here that it becomes significant. To ignore the relationship between scheduled time and budgeted costs is patently foolish. The worth of an estimate is tested first by bidding. It is tested again when changes in construction methods are needed.[9] **Overhead costs** accumulate constantly and often are approximately equal to the anticipated profit. A day wasted is, in effect, a day's profit lost. Contractors always have the same objectives:

1. To complete the work not later than the stipulated contract time, as scheduled
2. To complete the work for not more than the estimated costs, and to make not less than the estimated profit
3. To perform the work according to the contract.

To achieve these objectives, coordination and control are essential. Driving a car, steering a boat, or erecting a building, each is a continuous process of receiving information, immediate analysis, making decisions, and acting upon them. Driving and sailing and construction are, in essence, similar processes.

The Resource Schedule

The resource most in need of management is labor: labor time and labor costs. A work schedule is a schedule of labor's tasks and their durations. The other two tangible resources in construction are equipment and materials. As we have seen, labor and equipment are essentially the same, and time and productivity measure their costs. Materials, however, are different as their costs were fixed in the cost estimate (though cost tradeoffs are possible). A cost estimating program should produce **bills of materials** for purchasing. From these, materials can be assigned to different tasks for resource scheduling. Depending on the type of project, only certain material deliveries may require scheduling (e.g., the concrete for a large structure). If there may be a supply problem (e.g., the limited output of a concrete mixing plant), then it is necessary to make a resource histogram showing the scheduled requirements, and resource levelling may be necessary. This probably will affect the project's need for labor, and so the two will need coordinating.

10.4 MONITORING, MEASURING, & REPORTING ACTIVITIES

Having briefly surveyed the essential parts of a schedule-control system, we shall now examine some parts in more detail. Monitoring, measuring and reporting activities are best done on a Progress Report at the end of each day's work.

A Daily Progress Report Form

The essential information in the section-headings is shown in Figure 10.2. as follows:

1. Activities completed that day
2. Activities started that day
3. Activities that will start after seven days (or any other selected period)

Like a countdown, the purpose of the report's third section is to remind the super' to plan upcoming work. Details of the information required in the Progress Report are described next:

Activity Code Numbers Activities in the AOA method (as in Figure 9.3) are on arrows, and activities are indentified by their i and j (start and finish) node numbers. Code numbers are those for work as in the cost estimate. (The number of digits allowed by a PM program for activity identification may be critical in printing reports.)

Description of Activity As in an estimate, some verbal description to go with a code number is needed for easy and accurate identification.

Total Float Days [Available] These are taken from the work schedule; i.e., the number of surplus days scheduled as available after an activity's completion.

[Identifying] Numbers of the Latest Starting/ Finishing Days. Each day of a project's time is numbered consecutively in the schedule, beginning with day No. 1, the day the work started. Time duration is measured by deducting earlier day numbers from later day numbers. A starting day or a finishing day is entered for an activity in the appropriate part of the form under the appropriate heading.

[Counted Number of] Days Before Latest Starting/Finishing Days. The counted number of days before the starting or finishing day of an activity is entered here. It is obtained by comparing the number of the starting or finishing day in the previous column with the day number entered at the top of the report. (Obviously, there will be no entries in this column under the heading "Activities Completed Today.")

Critical Days Lost. This is perhaps the most important figure. Comparing days remaining and needed, if no critical days are listed as lost, a task's progress may be satisfactory, but it is not a guarantee. One difficulty in reporting work progress is the assessment of the amount of work actually done and that remaining. We need to know how much of an activity is complete when a certain fraction of its allocated time has passed (and of its allocated costs have been spent). This requires inspection and possibly even measurement of the work done. Some daily progress reports provide for an entry of the quantity of work completed. This information is essential to a complete picture of an activity's progress. It also is essential to job

DAILY PROGRESS REPORT

PROJECT TITLE ....PROJECT NO. ....
PROJECT DAY NO. ....   DATE ....

Activity Node Numbers		Code Numbers	Description of Activity	Total Float Days	Numbers of the Latest Start/Fin. Days	Days Before Latest Start/Finish Day Number	Critical Days Lost
I	J						

1. Activities completed today

2. Activities started today

3. Activities 7 days (or less) before latest starting date

Signature ....
Title ....

Figure 10.2 Format of a progress report.

costing (another example of the multiple uses of information).

We consider the latest starting and finishing dates of activities to see whether they are on schedule, but that does not help us partway through an activity to know how it is progressing. Later, when we find that an activity has not finished on time, then we know that we have lost time, but then it is too late. One way of dealing with this is to divide each major critical activity into several part-activities in a plan and schedule:

EXAMPLE I:

If a work item requires an estimated 30 workdays for completion, maybe this item should be represented by three subactivities, so that no activity has a duration of more than 10 days. This will reduce the risk of losing time before noticing a loss. (Actual numbers of days selected will depend on the work.)

EXAMPLE II:

If a project consists of only a few work items, such as a sewer consisting of excavating trench, laying pipe, and backfilling trench, then the work of each item should be divided into equal parts (e.g., an average day's production) as separate subactivities.

Monitoring of Project Costs

Another way of monitoring and controlling major activities is to measure the amounts of work done each day. Some may consider this expensive, but the cost need not be high. Working on-site from the drawings and a cost estimate, a technologist can quickly measure most work. Several persons would benefit from this kind of monitoring for several different reasons:[10]

1. The owner: for accurate periodic payments
2. The first mortgagee: for equity protection
3. The contractor's lender: for equity protection
4. The mortgage insurer: for equity protection
5. The designer: for accurate certificates for payment
6. The construction manager: as for owner and designer
7. The prime contractors: for proper payment, cost controls, and other management purposes
8. The subcontractors: as for prime contractors
9. Those suppliers who advance substantial credit to contractors and subcontractors and who, therefore, have a significant equity in a project.

There is an argument for the employment on major construction projects of an independent cost consultant paid for by the owner: one who can provide all the needed information, such as a **quantity surveyor,** or **cost engineer.** The need for monitoring is obvious. Monitoring by one independent consultant, for all purposes and interests makes practical and economic sense. Mortgagees and mortgage insurers already require project monitoring, and when others realize the benefits, the cost-benefit ratio becomes even more economic and realistic.

10.5 REPORTING AND RECORDING RESULTS

Decision-making needs information. Some do not believe that a schedule-control and monitoring system is worthwhile, and the main reason is the cost. Overhead costs are among the easiest to increase without getting commensurate benefits. It is natural that unless we are certain of the value of doing something, we do not want to pay for it. It is not possible to prove conclusively that any project directly benefits from better management; or that cost accounting produces better estimates. The main conclusion of David Aird in his study of manpower utilization in the construction industry was that there is a lack of information with most contractors.[11] The truth of this statement can be easily demonstrated by asking questions. The difficulty lies in showing a connection between a lack of information and the management that is the result.

As described in Chapter 3, management by a construction manager requires much information-handling and reporting, but that is not necessarily evidence of better management. It may sometimes be only a paper blizzard—designed to blind. Reporting and recording information is not in itself a useful thing. The information collected has to be processed and acted upon before it is of value. It is a means to an end.

The Costs of Reporting on Construction Work

The reluctance to pay for something not really needed, the fear of increasing overheads, and the fear of becoming uncompetitive: all these inhibit construction companies from finding out and reporting information for scheduling, controlling, and costing. Overhead costs are passed on to the customers, but there have to be enough customers—and enough construction work at the right prices. If construction companies need more information, and if all paid more to obtain it, none would be at a disadvantage. The existing system, however, does not work like that. To make it more economic, gathering information has to be done for more than one reason so that the costs are distributed.

Experience shows that all information collection, reporting, and recording for management and for costing can be done by junior technologists with two to four years of training in construction management. One or two technicians can handle all the project information for a medium- to large-size construction company.

EXAMPLE:

One graduate-technologist with approximately six months of postgraduate, on-the-job training handled all the reports and costing on several large projects simultaneously.

Because it provides an insight into construction and its costs and the work of construction managers, this kind of field work is good training for future estimators, superintendents, and construction managers.

The Skills for Reporting

Above all, a general knowledge of construction materials, methods, and terminology is essential. The technologist must be able to look at construction and know exactly what is happening. This does not require the skill or knowledge of an artisan, although trade knowledge and experience is an asset. Reporting requires an analytical mind, and the ability to see the whole and its many parts: the same faculty needed for cost estimating. That is why cost accounting is good training for estimating. Reporting also requires a better-than-average ability to use words and figures. In CM projects, for which regular reports are especially important, above-average writing ability is required. To carry out cost accounting and reporting effectively, it is necessary to understand why the information is needed, and how it will be used.

10.6 DISTRIBUTION OF INFORMATION AND SITE MEETINGS

Not only must all contractors and subcontractors receive copies of the baseline schedule, they also must receive information about changes. The best way to distribute this information is at periodic site meetings. Attendance at site meetings should not be optional. Suppliers of major items also should be asked to attend some meetings. All representatives attending should have the necessary knowledge and experience to take part.

Running a Site Meeting

Most complaints about meetings are that they are a waste of time. There must be paperwork, but it should be minimal: copies of an agenda, minutes, and basic records. These should be concise (e.g., written in the staccato style) and with numbered paragraphs. Site meetings should be conducted by the construction manager (CM), prime contractor, or a representative. Rules of order should apply, but informally. Minutes of meetings should state briefly the outcome, point by point. List the action need-

ed, the names of those required to act, and the latest dates for action. The purpose of project site meetings is to distribute information and instructions and to discuss them. Meetings also provide an opportunity for making objections, proposals, pointing out discrepancies and omissions, and letting off steam. The CM may ask for opinions, but also makes the decisions. Construction is not a democratic process, but one in which authority flows from the contracts.

Agenda and minutes (including instructions and requirements for action) should be distributed within 24 hours after each meeting. A standard format should be developed and maintained (preferably on a word-processing program). All papers should be prepunched with the standard three holes for insertion in binders bearing the project's name. The objective is to achieve uniformity of acceptance, use, and application. Construction is a team effort. Therefore, it is advantageous at meetings to discuss such things as new instructions, modifications, and problems such as the loss of time—and possible remedies.

10.7 SCHEDULING IN CM PROJECTS

Effective scheduling is an important part of CM; especially for projects with phased construction, as explained in Chapter 3. CM may be limited to multimillion dollar projects by government. In the private sector CM has been used to advantage on projects costing less than $1 million. In a large CM project, each major contract requires a work schedule. Each of these is a subproject, or activity, in a master schedule. In large projects with repetitive units and work, it is helpful to have the computer rerun a schedule's activities using the actual times of completed activities and units.

Recognize, however, that not all problems can be solved by logic or mathematical techniques that may have no bearing on the illogical complexities and paradoxes of everyday life that cannot be fitted to a line on a graph or discovered by extrapolation. Beyond certain limits, most relationships are inconstant. The most important part of planning and scheduling is the analytical thought it requires. Measurement translates design information (from drawings and specifications) into quantities of work. Pricing converts the quantities into dollar amounts. Planning and scheduling converts work expressed as dollars into activities and times. Yet, often not enough time or thought is given to work before starting. This is the primary value of planning and scheduling.

REFERENCES

1. Mike Heck, "Keeping Jobs On Course," *MACWORLD*, April 1992.
2. Harvey A. Levine, *Project Management, Using Microcomputers* (Berkeley, Calif.: Osborne McGraw-Hill, 1986).
3. Lamont Wood, "The Promise of Project Management," *BYTE*, Nov. 1988.
4. Program Manual, *SuperProject Expert* (San Jose, Calif.; Vancouver, B.C.: Computer Associates).

SUMMARY OF MAIN POINTS

- Project management programs for most construction need to be mid- to high-level and at least include: adequate task capacity (>1000) and unlimited relationships, work breakdown structures, baseline scheduling, variance tracking, barcharts, network diagrams, resource histograms, variable cost handling, resource levelling, and comprehensive report printing.

- Task relationships include early or late start and finish, start-to-start, finish-to-finish, and with provision for lag.

- Baseline scheduling enables original to be compared with later amended schedules.

- Fixed and variable costs are the costs of materials (fixed), and labor and equipment (variable), to be assigned and monitored as work progresses.

- Resource histograms and levelling enable several resources to be allocated (assigned) to work activities (tasks). Levelling removes peaks and valleys in the histograms.

- Coordinating and controlling work means managing it in sequence to produce the desired result: on time and within budget; monitoring, measuring, and adjusting start and finish dates; reassigning resources; and crashing (if needed), to stay on schedule.

- Controlling costs means monitoring costs and productivity and making changes so as to minimize one and maximize the other.

- A schedule-control system includes a work breakdown structure (WBS); a schedule calendar; a calendar for each resource; bar chart and network diagrams; monitoring tasks; recording and reporting, and comparing results with baseline schedule; modifications of work and resource schedules; coordination of schedules with cost controls.

- A work breakdown structure (WBS) has an outline chart of phases and tasks; the most detailed contains work items from the cost estimate.

- A work schedule first requires a cost estimate, a WBS and a calendar of start and finish dates of tasks.

- Activity (task) times need monitoring and measuring to keep schedule up-to-date; especially those on critical path. Noncritical tasks can become critical.

- Coordination of schedule and cost controls is essential, as task times and labor costs are related.

- Resource scheduling is mostly of labor; some major materials may require re-scheduling (e.g., ready-mixed concrete): labor and material resources are interrelated.

- Reporting progress is part of management: one format includes three parts: (1) activities completed today (2) activities started today, and (3) activities to start in so many days, or less.

- Cost monitoring and reporting is needed to provide information to several sectors, including: owner, mortgagee, short-term lenders, mortgage insurer, designer, construction manager, contractors, subcontractors, and suppliers. This is done better by a cost consultant paid by owner.

- Contractors lack information about actual **costs** and productivity (Aird); this can be collected by a junior technologist.

- Site meetings are necessary for proper management and to distribute information to the construction team.

NOTES

[1]"Mid-level programs" refers primarily to program cost, and although price and capability generally go together, there are exceptions. There is a wide selection of project management programs available, and consumer research is recommended. None appear to be specifically designed for construction projects, although some use construction examples.

[2]"Keeping Jobs on Course," by Mike Heck, *MACWORLD*, April 1992.

[3]"Mike Heck is manager of electronic promotions for Unysis Corporation. He oversees large marketing plans and manages the company's electronic publications operations." *MACWORLD*, April 1992.

[4]The other main information source is computer bulletin boards, many of which are dedicated to special interests.

[5]*Primavera* project management program and *Precision Estimating Plus*, for example.

[6]Comparing this situation to the general situation on several construction sites described by Aird's report (in Chapter 5), we see similarities in what was lacking.

[7]As mentioned before, sometimes it is possible and necessary to reallocate resources or costs from one work item to another.

[8]Again we talk in terms of a fixed-price contract, or a fixed budget: the most demanding

cases. Otherwise, there is much more latitude for variation in work plans and schedules.

[9]Experiences shows that often in construction something can be achieved by another method at about the same cost.

[10]David Aird, *Manpower Utilization in the Canadian Construction Industry*, Technical Paper No. 156 (Ottawa, Canada: National Research Council, Division of Building Research, 1963). Aird's report said that poor management was the cause of inefficient "manpower utilization in construction"; and that the primary reason for poor management was a lack of information.

[11]David Aird, *Manpower Utilization in the Canadian Construction Industry*, Section 4.20.

QUESTIONS AND TOPICS FOR DISCUSSION

1. Define and explain the following terms:
    a.   Task relationships
    b.   Baseline schedule
    c.   Resource levelling
    d.   Work breakdown structure
    e.   Fixed and variable costs of work
    f.   A schedule calendar

2. Describe in detail the forms a work breakdown structure can take.

3. What is the purpose of a calendar in a project management program?

4. Identify and describe briefly the three main things needed to make a work schedule.

5. If the first computer-run of a work schedule shows an unsuitable schedule and completion date, suggest what can be done to make a suitable and workable schedule?

6. What specific information about activities (tasks) is needed to make a work schedule?

7. Define "a critical task" in a schedule.

8. In a work schedule, what does a non-critical task have that a critical task does not? Explain your answer.

9. In a project with a fixed budget, with what must the actual durations of tasks be consistent?

10. Identify and describe the specific kinds of information needed in a daily progress report. What other useful information should be included?

11. Describe how the type of construction contract used in a project affects that project's management.

12. Who needs to have project costs regularly monitored and reported, and why?

13. Describe who might economically monitor and report project cost information.

14. Describe the essential features of a construction project management program for use on desktop computers.

15. Explain other computer programs that should interface with a project management program, and explain why.

11

CONTRACT STARTUP AND COMPLETION

The end starts at the beginning.
Anon.

This chapter examines the special requirements for starting and completing a project. Startup requires much organizing and initial spending. Completion requires a special effort to get things done. Two contractual stages of a contract's completion: substantial and final completion are also studied. Additionally, this chapter discusses some obstacles to timely completion, and ways to overcome them.

11.1 CONTRACT STARTUP

As mentioned in Chapter 1, certain preliminaries are necessary for the startup of a project:

- Analyzing and planning the work
- Scheduling the work (i.e., setting dates)

- Ordering major materials and machinery
- Hiring staff, supervision, and labor
- Mobilizing plant and equipment
- Budgeting cash-flow requirements
- Obtaining all permits and licenses
- Setting up the project organization and systems
- Setting up the site for work, including all the temporary services and facilities needed

Combined, these steps may be called *project mobilization*, and they require initial expenditures that a contractor expects to recover from the first one or two progress payments. If a site is remote and isolated, or overseas, there will be even more to do before actual construction work can start, including:

- Setting up camp facilities for staff and workers
- Finding local suppliers of materials and labor
- Importing staff, materials, and equipment
- Arranging for temporary main services (e.g., water pipelines, temporary electric powerlines, temporary roads, etc.)
- Setting up workshops to manufacture items that cannot readily be imported or obtained from suppliers
- Meeting local personalities to enlist their influence and help

The purpose of field engineering is the performance of work, and there are many things (e.g., certain general requirements) often not mentioned in a contract's documents to which a field engineer or a contractor's superintendent must attend. In a fixed-price contract, for example, there may be no mention of the need for camp facilities to accommodate workers because they do not concern an owner; there may be no mention of temporary heating, temporary enclosures, or other common requirements for construction. A contract often specifies only the required results, not the specific means.

The outset of a project is a most critical period during which the superintendent puts his mark on the project and starts to influence its outcome. Again, at the end, when leadership and energy are especially needed to maintain velocity and to finish on time, there is another critical period. How a project starts will influence how it proceeds and finishes. The seeds of delay often are sown in the design phase—or even earlier, when a flawed policy or an inadequate budget is made. As a result, later there are contract **modifications** and extensions of time. Or, poor project planning or insufficient care with the first things may cause delays later. Because of entropy, a delay in completion is more likely than an early or timely completion. One aspect of this is referred to as Murphy's Law. The only remedy is energy in action. A good start is the first sure step to a timely completion. A fumbled start may cause the opposite—or at least expensive corrections.

Before startup on a site, one of the first requirements is a **notice to proceed** from the owner–designer. This is important as it may determine the completion date and other dates or time periods. A superintendent also must be prepared with a knowledge of the project and the positive attitude of a leader who will manage and bring the work to proper completion. Before starting, even though every project and site is unique, the superintendent's comprehension of the work should be close to that of the designer. A superintendent should develop checklists. Outlines for several follow:

General Contractual Requirements

The following should be in place on-site before the start of work:

- A true copy of the executed prime contract
- True copies of most (if not all) executed major subcontracts
- Copies of any environmental impact studies or similar documents relevant to the project work
- Copies of all relevant codes and regulations
- Copies of any issued purchase orders
- A copy of the cost estimate and the estimate file
- Company manuals for cost code, operations, etc.

- Performance bond, payment bond (if required)
- Builder's risk, liability, automobile, equipment, and other kinds of insurance required for special and unusual items or work, with copies of the policies
- Permits for building, zoning, plumbing, electrical, parking, storage of dangerous compounds, hoardings, street and bridge use, and others as required by law and regulation
- Business license (if required for the location)
- Safety program and first-aid equipment
- List of telephone and FAX numbers of officials of all authorities with jurisdiction over the work, including: building department, fire department, streets and traffic, city engineering, telephone, water, gas, and other public utilities, safety, police, and others
- List of emergency and other commonly required telephone and FAX numbers (police, ambulance, fire)
- Any approved samples with designer's written approvals

Before a project gets under way, the following things should be done:

- Open local bank account (if needed)
- Establish credit with local suppliers
- Arrange for the early testing and inspections
- Contact local unions, labor contractors, agencies, as required
- Go over the cost estimate and contract documents with the estimator, to acquire as much of the estimator's knowledge of the project as possible
- Study the contract documents and highlight and annotate them as required for special attention

- Review the contract agreement and all supplementary and special conditions of the contract, and note any unusual conditions or requirements (e.g., liquidated damages for late completion, materials supplied by owner, special labor requirements, and anything else that is not standard or commonplace)
- Make a list of queries about the contract and work
- Make a work schedule, and resource schedules
- Make a schedule of prime contractor's labor requirements
- Make a schedule of deliveries of major materials and machinery to be installed
- Make a schedule of equipment work and requirement
- Make an inventory of small tools and equipment to be maintained on-site
- Prepare a schedule of values and a job cost breakdown of the work (they are similar)
- Set up the job-costing system on site
- Prepare a cash-flow schedule using the cost estimate and the work schedule
- Locate special parts of work, including:
  1. Mechanical rooms
  2. Electrical rooms
  3. Elevators and conveyors
  4. Special equipment rooms
  5. Special construction work
- Anticipate any early requirements for special work or installations (e.g., drill-hole for hydraulic elevator, services' conduits in foundations, etc.)
- Contact M & E subcontractors to arrange for temporary services' installations and other early and preliminary installations
- Get major plant and equipment on-site before fencing-in, or otherwise blocking access

- Locate all existing underground services (sewers, water lines, gas lines, power lines, etc.)
- Install all temporary services (pumps, drainage, toilets, water, lighting, power, telephone, computer, FAX, etc.)
- Erect temporary fences, hoardings, walkways
- Put up identification and warning signs
- Set up temporary site accommodations (office, secured storage, first-aid, lunchroom, plan kiosks, etc.)
- Arrange for disposal sites, and negotiate fees
- Stabilize ground next adjoining property, as required
- Review staff requirements, and hire or arrange subcontracts for assistants, trade foremen, timekeepers, storekeepers, clerks, traffic controllers, cleaners, etc.

These lists are indicative, not exhaustive. Different projects for different kinds of work have different requirements.

General Site Requirements

- Visit the site several times and make notes
- Study the building's design and the site together, looking out for features that may affect work and access (e.g., deep excavations, adjoining property, existing overhead and underground service lines, bridges, watercourses, fishing waters, existing street use and access, existing schools, high-density populations, etc.)
- Try to foresee possible difficulties by imagining the building under construction at stages
- Get weather and earthquake records for the locality covering the last few decades
- Consider possible natural phenomena (e.g., extreme temperatures, rainfall, snowfall, high winds, tempest, flood, monsoon, earthquake, and review their frequency) and make preparations
- Look for road, bridge, and other restrictions to access and travel
- Look for road, air, water, and rail access centers; also, tolls, duties, taxes, and other related costs
- Get timetables for all local transportation
- Discover calendar dates of local holidays, feast days, and other cultural events, and enter in project diary and schedule, keep records
- Discover local customs, rituals, attitudes, superstitions, prejudices, expectations, unusual laws and regulations; especially those related to workers, their religions, construction, sites, and the public at large; schedule dates, make reminders, keep records
- Find information on any affected local wildlife
- Visit and examine any ongoing construction projects in the vicinity, look at their materials and methods, and make and keep records
- Talk to knowledgeable local people: officials, builders, suppliers, farmers, truck drivers, taxicab drivers, etc., and make records
- Designate on-site areas for parking, open storage, spoil heaps, rubbish dumps, and other areas required
- Find and record locations of the nearest hospital, pharmacy, medical, and other local services

When working in a remote or foreign location, take nothing for granted. People in North America, living in a large and modern continent, sometimes assume knowhow. Elsewhere, however, cultures and customs often are quite the opposite to what we believe is normal. Yet, their cultures often are older and more tested by time. Read about the place and its people. Awareness and humility are appropriate.

Site Works (Preparation)

- Do soil tests on-site and find the water table levels at several locations on a site
- Do sample excavations (trenches, holes) and examine them periodically for changes in soil and moisture conditions
- Get quotations for any site works originally estimated to be done by own forces
- Get information about site and soil conditions from local sources (e.g., engineers, building inspectors, excavation contractors, land surveyors, etc.)
- Find out and comply with all laws, regulations, and customs involving burning and otherwise disposing of debris, soil, vegetation, etc.
- Mark any trees, other vegetation, and other natural features to be retained and set up necessary protections
- Find and mark locations of all existing underground and overhead services on or near the site
- Review drawings, specifications, other contract documents, and schedules in light of any new information and actual site conditions; discuss any modifications with contractor and designer
- Review insurance policies regarding site works, especially excavations and other subsurface work (sometimes excluded from liability insurance coverage)
- Talk to local contractors and workers about the work and its effect and impact in the vicinity

Site work may have a significant impact on the surroundings and local inhabitants.

This may cause repercussions. It is better that the local people should be informed and prepared. Because you have permits and a contract, do not assume that your presence and the work is seen by everyone as a boon. Thoughtlessness and carelessness may cause serious reactions. Consider the effects of and remedies for

- Blowing dust from site stripping and excavations
- Vermin fleeing from operating equipment and demolitions
- Smoke from the burning of debris and rubbish
- Equipment vibration disturbance, etc.
- Working equipment disturbing people and livestock
- Water runoff from pumping, or new ground levels
- Watercourse pollution by site work
- Noise and disturbance on holidays and holy days

Such lists can be practically endless, depending on the work and the site.

Substructure Work (Preparation)

Concrete

- Design concrete formwork and other falsework
- Discover local forming methods, rentals, and subcontractors
- Visit local aggregate pits, ready-mixed concrete plants, testing companies, etc.
- Get quotations from local firms for any appropriate work originally estimated to be done by own forces
- Discuss the work with building inspector and find out any special requirements or possible alternatives
- Review contract documents and insurances (as for site works)

Preparatory to Trade Work, Generally

- Find out local trade methods and preferences
- Consider desirable changes in work details
- Design temporary supports, falsework, etc.
- Visit materials' sources and plants (e.g., pits, quarries, kilns, mills, factories, etc.)
- Get quotations for any work originally estimated as done by own forces; consider advantages and disadvantages, and make suitable subcontracts
- Discuss work with building inspector, suppliers, subcontractors, and local workers
- Review contract documents and schedules, and any possible alternatives and modifications with the contractor and designer
- Look for interfacings between trades and their work[1]
- Review insurances in light of special work or conditions
- Confirm timely deliveries of materials and equipment
- Confirm availability of workers
- Assess workers' productivity for different classes of work

The requirements listed are basic. Special requirements in contracts require special attention. If a construction company is in a locality for the first time, attention should be paid to making contacts and gathering and recording fresh information. Means include: cameras, recorders, computer system, and a laptop/portable computer with the superintendent or other staff members. As a cost estimate is part of a cycle that feeds back information for future cost estimates, so a project too is an information source for future work.

Computer System As an Aid to Startup

Estimators must make some decisions that affect costs with incomplete information. At the earliest opportunity, the superintendent should gather information on a new project. The cost estimate and contract documents are basic. Flatbed scanners can transpose printed documents onto computer disks and enable information to be handled in various ways. With a cost estimate and the contract documents on disk, a user can quickly find key words and phrases.

Also, a superintendent should get as much background information as possible from the estimator. Were there any parts of the work about which the estimator felt less than confident? Has the estimator since remembered any errors or omissions? Has he any doubts? Has he left any ends loose? Was any other information not recorded? Was anything revealed at the opening of bids? Any such information may prove valuable.

If the cost estimate and all the documents are on disk, a superintendent's tasks are much easier. Data bases make it easy to store and retrieve information and data. They may disclose trends and interrelationships not otherwise seen. As electronic information sources proliferate, project managers and superintendents should make all possible connections to get information about weather patterns, markets, and other things that touch on a project and its work.

11.2 SUBSTANTIAL COMPLETION AND FINAL COMPLETION

Most construction contracts follow national standard forms in defining **substantial completion** as something before and different from full, final, or **total completion**.[2]

Though the details may vary, the fundamental purpose always is the same: substantial completion exists to simplify the total completion of project work. The law defines and recognizes substantial completion as something less than absolute or total completion.

Generally, in a **fixed-price contract**, an owner cannot refuse to pay the contractor simply because there are minor defects or minor deficiencies in the work. If any exist, an owner may deduct from money due the contractor the estimated amount of the costs of making them good, but he cannot withhold payment beyond that amount. Amounts to be paid or withheld are, under most standard construction contracts, determined by the owner's agent (designer or construction manager) whose duty it also is to certify both stages of completion.

Substantial completion in a contract is recognition of the common-law perception of completion: that it is practical completion, and that a contractor is not in breach of contract if the work is deficient in minor ways. With an imperfect coat of paint or a missing screw, the contractor cannot claim total completion, but the work may be substantially complete, nevertheless. Also, a contractor can be paid what is due less the cost of making good any deficiencies. It is possible, however, for a contract to require absolute and total completion of all work before any payment, but except for small works such **entire contracts** are unusual.

Since an entire contract's intent is to achieve a specific result, failure to perform absolutely (e.g., to make the roof watertight, or a machine operable) would be a breach of contract. The owner would be allowed to withhold all payment, as entire completion is a condition precedent to any payment. In a standard fixed-price contract

(i.e., not an entire contract) in which payments are as work progresses, completion of the work is only a term of the contract and not a condition of payment. At substantial completion, an owner must pay the contract sum, less any amounts validly deducted for specific defects or deficiencies. Most national standard construction contracts make this kind of deduction for deficiencies part of their conditions. See AIA Document A201-1987, Article 9, *Payments and Completion*, Subparas. 9.5.1 (.1), 9.5.2, 9.8.2, 9.10.3.[3]

A practical definition of substantial completion of a building is completion that makes possible the occupancy and use of the building for the purpose for which it was designed. A similar definition appears in AIA Document A201-1987, Para. 9.8.1, and that document (like many others) requires that the architect certify substantial completion. This is common to contracts because the date of substantial completion is important to several aspects of performance, and an arbiter's opinion is preferred.

Determination of substantial completion is another example of an architect, engineer, or construction manager (as an agent of the owner), acting in a capacity as the judge of a contract's performance, as in the conditions of standard contracts. (See A201-1987, Article 4, *Administration of the Contract*, Subpara. 4.2.9; also Article 9, *Payments and Completion*, Para. 9.8, *Substantial Completion*.[4]

On certifying substantial completion, an owner's agent makes up a punch list of defects, deficiencies, and omissions from the work, for the contractor to correct before achieving full completion of the work. Document A201 calls it "a comprehensive list of items to be completed or corrected." Final payment follows final completion, as explained in Chapter 20. Substantial completion is the first contractual step toward total or final completion of a construction contract. It is a definitive step by which we decide and record those things necessary for full completion, so that a contractor knows specifically what remains to be done according to the opinion of the arbiter and judge of the contract's performance.

11.3 ACHIEVING COMPLETION

Construction management of a certain kind becomes increasingly essential as a building project progresses from the foundations and structural frame to finish carpentry and painting. Part of the reason for the typical slowdown is simply that most of the work on a structure and the major installations are done in the first half of a building project; while the second half consists of the installation of much concealed work (e.g., mechanical and electrical systems), and of trade work that consists of a high proportion of labor (e.g., painting and decorating, the costs of which may consist of about 75 percent labor).

As a matter of survival, trade contractors are more active whenever and wherever the cash flow is greater. Even without profit, a business may survive to operate another day; without cash flow it soon withers and dies. There has to be money available to pay wages, bills, and taxes. Consequently, a contractor concentrates on those projects that generate the greater cash flow. An almost completed job requires mostly labor, and while the work to be done requires cash outlay for wages it may produce little cash flow. Therefore, that job is at the bottom of the list when pressure is on a contractor's resources.

A general contractor's superintendent must make a special effort in the later stages of a project to overcome entropy and inertia. He must not allow the organization to break down or progress to slow down. Instead, he must convince subcontractors that they have both an obligation and a need to complete their work on time. Obligation is inherent in a contract. The need comes from the value of a reputation for performance, and for the remaining monies due. A superintendent must sustain the team spirit and motivation that he instilled at the outset. He must do this by the force of personality, authority, knowledge, goodwill, and clout.

Neglected Schedules

A neglected schedule is seen by workers and subtrades alike as a sign of permissiveness and carelessness by a superintendent: an indication that he is not really concerned with completing on time. This impression must be avoided not only in the later stages, but throughout a job since it detracts from authority and works against the drive needed to maintain progress. Part of the solution is an up-to-date schedule.

Losses of time and the results of a careless attitude are cumulative, and often compounding. Schedules must be continuously reviewed and updated right from the outset of a project. The old saw about the uselessness of schedules because people always change them is not valid. People make schedules so they can change and update them, like the flight plans of aircraft. If conditions change, so must the plan.

As explained in Chapter 10, a large part of the benefit of planning and scheduling comes from the knowledge gained by making a work breakdown and then planning the work. A schedule makes it possible to monitor and control parts of the work and to measure its progress. Subsequent adjustment is normal. No adjustments signal carelessness and neglect. For a superintendent to abandon or neglect a schedule just because the work has fallen behind is similar to a sea captain throwing away his charts when he finds he is not in the expected position. Without charts how will he know how to find his position and make good the error?

Schedules on construction jobs conform to a general law. Because they are intrinsically good they also can be bad. A good schedule, properly maintained, is a guide, a route map, and a challenge to complete the work on time. A neglected schedule may be taken by workers, subcontractors, and suppliers, as a sign that time is not of the essence in performance of the contract. Better to have no schedule than a neglected schedule that is a blatant expression of carelessness; and far, far better to have an amended and updated schedule than an unchanged one, or no schedule at all.

From the outset, a super' must ensure that work progresses at a sufficient rate. If a super' does not apply himself to timely completion from the beginning, he will find it difficult to do so when the work is more than halfway to completion and his efforts are most needed. From the start, he must instill in the trade contractors the need to keep up with their schedules. To this end, contracts must contain the necessary terms and conditions dealing with contract times and schedules. It is not sufficient to rely on a **flow-down condition** in a **prime contract** as a condition in a subcontract. Often, a condition in a prime contract is not immediate enough to have the required impact, since it may never be read by a subcontractor.

Subcontracts, even if based on a standard form, should be specially written. Generally, in standard forms of contracts the terms and conditions dealing with contract time and schedules are loose and may need amending. These can be changed by supplementary conditions. Some argue that a schedule cannot be a contract document because it is invariably subject to amendment and cannot, therefore, be enforced. This is misleading. Although there is a difference in degree, this is the same as saying that a fixed-price contract is not possible because changes can be made in the scope of the work and the contract sum.[5]

In some contracts, contract time is as important, or more important than the contract sum. A contract not completed may result in financial losses from lost markets and revenue. Financing costs may be the single largest cost directly related to contract time. For a $1 million construction job, interim financing might cost several thousand dollars per week. Delays cannot be treated casually, and everyone involved must be aware of the real costs of contract time.

Incentives for Maintaining Progress of Work

Several different incentives exist to maintain progress, though most are negative in nature. Inherent in all fixed-price contracts is the incentive for a contractor to complete early so as to minimize overhead costs and optimize profits. Also, there is the opportunity to undertake more contracts and more work. Sometimes, where early completion is a distinct advantage to an owner (e.g., a hotel completed early and just before a holiday season), cash bonuses to the contractor and his superintendent may be worthwhile.

The idea of offering financial incentives for timely completion or for earlier completion does not appear widely popular. It may be worthwhile to compare the costs of incentives for early completion with savings in the costs of financing a project. Incentives should be calculated in the same way that liquidated damages are calculated, according to the actual economic effect.

Liquidated Damages As an Incentive

There seem to be several reasons why owners do not incorporate liquidated damages in their contracts, including:

- Belief (or advice) that liquidated damages are not enforceable or supported by courts
- A reluctance by owner–designers to include provisions for liquidated damages in contracts because of their own possible actions or inactions that may cause delays; or the probability that liquidated damages will be voided by delays caused by changes in the contract
- A reluctance to write and enforce conditions for such as liquidated damages for fear of retaliation by a contractor who might take advantage of any deficiencies in a contract's documents
- An owner–designer may prefer a looser contractual situation in which informal tradeoffs can be made as work proceeds

Instead of the often biased contract, particular conditions (such as the following) are overdue:

- Tighter requirements for timely performance of contractual obligations by both parties.
- More negotiations for contract terms and conditions (including liquidated damages) so that construction contracts really represent a meeting of the minds of both parties.

The term, liquidated damages, means damages settled in advance, which in turn should mean that the parties discussed and agreed to possible damages resulting from late completion. However, most liquidated damages in contracts are put there by owner–designers before calling for bids: hardly a mutual settlement. If liquidated damages are really settled in advance, they will be more defensible.

Holdback As an Incentive

Another possible incentive for the timely completion of contract work is the holdback, or **retainage**: the retention by the owner of some stipulated portion of a contractor's progress payments to encourage him not to neglect an almost completed job by transferring key staff and tradesmen to another, new job site. The value of a holdback as an incentive may be dubious.

Certain lien statutes require retainage. Other, additional retainage sometimes is required as an assurance of performance: providing construction companies will bid for work under such terms, since monies held back create additional costs.

Nonstatutory retainage should not be prescribed without careful consideration of its effects on construction costs, and possibly on bidding. The cost to an owner of additional holdback, however, is not always a reason not to apply it. As an incentive to timely completion, additional retainage might be selectively applied to certain (sub)contractors and their work should they fall behind. The intended effect would be to reduce the profits of those who do not perform on time. Sometimes, however, it might compound whatever is causing the delay.

Avoiding Delays Caused by an Owner or Designer

Either an owner or a designer, or both, may be the cause of a delay and extra expense for a contractor; especially if the owner has no reason to desire prompt completion of a project. Standard contracts attempt to address this matter, but do not do so decisively; they leave it up to a designer to introduce precontract amendments or supplementary conditions; or to a contractor to seek enforcement of existing conditions; or to negotiate other conditions before executing the contract (usually not an easy thing to do). Nevertheless, before signing a contract, both parties (owner and contractor) should pay attention to a contract's conditions dealing with delays, and realizing shortcomings and their mutual advantages, try to negotiate better conditions.

The AIA Document A201-1987, Article 9, *Owner*, uses the term "with reasonable promptness" to describe an owner's duties. To remove the vagueness, this phrase might be changed to "within twenty-four hours," or something similar and reasonable—preferably by the designer drafting the bidding documents. Failing this, a contractor faced the first time with what he considers unreasonable delay, might seek an interpretation from the designer in hope of having reasonable promptness defined as it should have been in the beginning. Alternatively, a contractor might claim extra time and costs the first time the owner or designer unreasonably causes a delay. Better still, however, if a designer understands that

delays cost a fully mobilized contractor money, and that contract conditions (and the owner) should address the fact decisively in the first instance.

Higher Productivity Through Design and Management

More than some, the construction industry needs to increase productivity. This can be achieved in part by wider use of proven management tools and techniques: computer systems, fast-track projects, incentives, and more effective administration and management. Projects require better planning and scheduling, tighter monitoring and controls, and better supervision.[6] However, there are demands on both builders and designers. Productivity and economy must influence design. Contract documents should not be taken off the shelf any more than a designer would take off the shelf a building's design.[7]

Consistent and Specialized Supervision

Experience shows that changing a superintendent in the later stages of a project causes disruption and delay. Some standard contracts attempt to discourage this, whereas others say nothing. AIA Document A201-1987 says nothing about it, while CCDC2-1982 says that the superintendent shall be satisfactory to the designer "and shall not be changed except for good reason and only then after consultation with the [Architect]." This, however, is ineffectual because the contract does not define "good reason," which could be almost anything a contractor decides is good. A more suitable condition might read:

EXAMPLE:

"The Contractor's Superintendent shall be identified in the Contract and approved by the Designer before the start of the Work. The Contractor shall provide such evidence as may be required to show the competency of the Superintendent. In the event that approval of the proposed Superintendent is not given or, is withdrawn for cause by the Designer, the Contractor shall propose another Superintendent for approval. Approval shall not be unreasonably withheld. The Superintendent shall not be changed by the Contractor without prior approval and the establishment of an approved substitute. On no account shall the progress of the Work be impaired nor shall the contract time be extended because of a change of Superintendent."

Why should a contractor want to change a superintendent in mid-job? Often it seems that a replacement has less experience, and therein may lie the answer. Good staff of all kinds is scarce, and especially good super's. The best are always in demand to start new projects. When a job is more than halfway to completion, often the contractor wants to remove the super' to start a new job and to create a new cash flow. This is particularly true of general contractors, with their dual role of trade contractor and construction manager.

Superintendents employed by general contractors often are experts in concrete placing, masonry, or structural steelwork; however, when a traditional fixed-price contract is half-completed, the remainder is almost all subtrade work. A general contractor needs structural expertise at the start of new projects and believes (or, wants to believe) that the supervision of subcontractors can be done by a less-experienced substitute. As a result, a project suffers from inferior supervision and a slowing of progress in the later stages. This is a reason for superintendents especially trained in project completion and closeout, i.e., super's with more experience in a variety of trade work, particularly in the finishing trades, and more experience in dealing with subcontractors.

Specialized Supervision for Completion

Is it unreasonable to expect a superintendent to be an expert in substructural and structural work (site works, concrete, masonry, steelwork) and an expert in the work of many subtrades (protection, finishes, fixtures) as well? Given the level of specialization in construction work, is it not reasonable to match technical specialization with specialization in management and supervision? Are not building projects sometimes flawed, and their progress slowed—especially in the last quarter of the contract time—by ineffective supervision and management?

It appears common enough for a superintendent to leave subtrades pretty much to themselves, providing certain requirements are met (mainly, that their work is found acceptable by the owner, her agents, and the inspectors). It appears common enough for a superintendent to suggest that a designer's representative or an inspector should talk directly to a subtrade's foreman about quality or performance of trade work. It is probable that building projects would benefit from a regulated change of superintendent at some point in the middle half of a project's duration: from a structurally oriented super' to a finishes-and-services super'; each an expert in either startup or completion.

Equitable Contracts for Timely Completion

A good way to ensure completion on time is to make a good, equitable contract in the first place, to avoid changes in the work, and not to modify a contract during its execution. Of course, this means care and attention in designing both the work and the contract, and in creating the best possible conditions for bidding. Care and attention to detail in the early stages always are important formatives sometimes neglected in a rush to get a project started. Often, deficiencies in a project's budget and contract are caused at the beginning. For example, public works often start with an insufficient appropriation of funds, and without the guidance of a cost consultant.

Particular attention should be given to the scope of fixed-price contracts and to avoiding: (1) requirements for priced alternatives in bids, (2) excessive changes in the work, and (3) other modifications to the contract. With a well-designed project and contract, usually major changes should not be necessary. Only exceptional and essential changes should be ordered. Sometimes, additional work can be done later under a minor and separate contract. Because provisions for changes in fixed-price contracts are standard practice and often made and accepted as a matter of course, some may scoff at this suggestion.

Changes in fixed-price contracts are not allowable except by mutual agreement; either arrived at in the original contract, or subsequently. A change in a fixed-price contract is contrary to its fundamental nature,

even though it may be allowed by a contract's conditions. Often a change creates a disruption and a delay far beyond what is commensurate with its importance. Often, it is difficult to assess the real effect of change on a contract sum and contract time. Therefore, the valuation of a change often is unequitable to one party. Further, if contract time is important in a contract—and this question should be carefully considered and quantified—let it be apparent in the manner in which the owner–designer writes and administers the contract.

Timely occupancy is an important aspect of the economics of shelter construction. An owner needs housing units occupied and the cash to flow as soon as possible. Proper and timely completion of a sequence of units and the immediate issuance of official occupancy permits (and other required documents from the authorities having jurisdiction) are critical. In other kinds of development, such as office buildings, often the progressive completion and occupancy of portions of the work (e.g., by floors) is critical for the same reason: cash flow to the owner. In projects such as these, an effective superintendent may become a bonused hero. However, a superintendent who cannot deliver a building as scheduled may cause a significant financial loss. Management then may become a 16-hour-a-day job in which the contractor will do almost anything to meet scheduled completion dates, and because work is done frenetically, eventually it may prove uneconomic.

Management of People

It is helpful for a project superintendent to discover which individual in a subtrade or supply company is key and has the greatest effect on the trade work and its completion, or on the time of deliveries. Different companies have various organizations and methods, and different individuals have assorted degrees of effectiveness. It helps to know about such things. During a project, the superintendent (or a CM supervisor) should find out the facts about each company on site, with whom it is best to deal, and how best to deal with each individual. Some respond better to reasonableness and generally adhere to contractual obligations and follow proper procedures. Others respond better to humor or cajoling. Still others, unfortunately, respond better to threats before fulfilling their obligations. Do not threaten unless willing to follow through; this means a threatened action must be legally valid and enforceable.

EXAMPLE:

Most standard contracts provide for an owner to terminate a contract and to do the work himself if the contractor does not supply enough labor or materials. (N.B. In all subcontracts, a prime contractor should have the same provisions that exist in the prime contract.)

Termination of a subcontract may be troublesome and slow down a project. Nevertheless, in a bad situation it may be worthwhile to select the most dilatory of subcontractors and to terminate his subcontract for cause as an example to others. In such a case, the trouble of termination may be worthwhile.

CM Projects for Faster Completion

CM projects already have been described as a means to attaining earlier completion. To recapitulate, the means include fast-track-ing, and that requires compression of design and construction phases, so that they overlap: with several separate contracts starting at different times, and the employment of a construction manager.

General Precepts to Attain Timely Completion

Some precepts for superintendents to get timely and proper completion of work by others include

- Knowing the prime contract and its subcontracts, the subcontractors and their suppliers, and endeavouring to establish a good relationship with key personnel
- If necessary, choosing different means for expediting work for different subcontractors and suppliers, and using those that suit particular companies and individuals (as described previously)
- Being energetic, consistent, and persevering in applying contract provisions. Use all the necessary means of persuasion, including effective communications, decision-making, and clout

Underlying these precepts is a fundamental principle: Have an effective and written contract, understand it, and apply it. Without this document, a superintendent has little authority or clout. An effective contract requires properly written subcontracts.

Adequate Subcontracts and Supply Contracts

Virtually every prime contract requires that subcontracts contain all of its terms and conditions that are relevant to a subcontract. Those are the flow-down conditions. Many prime contractors consider them sufficient. As a result, their subcontracts are

CONTRACT STARTUP AND COMPLETION

simply an exchange of letters with the prime contract's terms either implied or expressed generally—if at all. Many subcontracts have requirements that, because they arise from the organization and management of the work (which in prime fixed-price contracts is the sole prerogative of the contractor), are not in any way expressed (or sometimes even implied), in the terms and conditions of the prime contract, they are peculiar to a particular subcontract and trade. Therefore, a prime contractor who relies on the prime contract as the sole basis for his subcontracts' requirements is surely omitting important requirements from his subcontracts—requirements that may touch directly on the matter of timely completion.

A prime contractor without adequate subcontracts may find himself in a position in which he bears an onerous and unnecessary risk because of late completion of work by his subcontractors. Even more probable, a subcontractor may suffer from an inadequate subcontract, as explained in Chapter 5.

11.4 PROJECT CLOSEOUT AND COMPLETION

Superintendents need special training and skills for the closeout and completion of projects. Momentum carries many construction jobs in the middle-half while the enthusiasm still is there. It is in the later stages (in the last quarter) that things slow down and supervision becomes more critical. An axiom for closeout and completion says: Do not to start to closeout a job too late. Since total performance and completion are primary objectives, start the completion of a job as soon as it begins.

As it is necessary to make an early and continued effort to maintain schedules, so it is necessary to apply all the terms and con-

ditions of a contract from the outset, because they all have the same objectives: proper performance and timely completion.

Cleaning Up

Cleanup of the work and its site is a good example of the need for initial and continuing application of a contract's requirements. If left until the last weeks, proper cleanup is unlikely. By cleaning up regularly from the outset of a project, the final cleanup will not be extraordinary and the benefits of a clean site will be felt throughout. The value of a clean site should not be underestimated, as it includes

- A safer site, because it is a cleaner site
- An economic site, with less waste and lost material
- An efficient site, easier to move around
- An impression made on the subtrades that the management is efficient and that proper performance is expected.

The fact that cleaning up is the subject of a general condition in standard construction contracts shows that it is important. See A201-1987, Para. 3.15, *Cleaning Up*.[8] As a **general condition**, however, and without specific requirements for cleaning up in the trade sections of specifications it may be misplaced, as standards of cleanliness differ for different trades.

Many (sub)contractors, foremen, and workers do not think cleanup requirements are important. Clearly it is not their intention to cleanup if they can avoid it. Many do a minimum of cleaning, and then they argue that they have done everything required, no matter what the (sub)contract says. This is especially true when requirements for cleaning up are stated only in a prime contract's general conditions.

Every **trade section** in a specification needs a practical definition of clean for different work and different trades, since clean is a word that means different things to different people. A general definition of clean and cleaning up is impossible. What is right for an excavation contractor is not appropriate for a flooring contractor. Cleaning up debris and dirt outside a site also should be a requirement.

Offcuts, waste, and other unwanted materials and empty containers are not acceptable fill material; they may prove a nuisance long after a contractor has left a site. It takes time and money to pick up and truck away rubbish. If proper cleanup is avoided, costs are saved at someone else's expense. Improper cleanup is as much a deficiency in work as the use of wrong materials or poor workmanship. From gypsum-wallboard waste and certain other materials, chemical pollution may occur for years afterward.

The only remedy for inadequate cleanup is an adequate contractual provision written and agreed to for each trade and to enforce it from the outset. The longer cleanup is neglected, the more difficult it is to insist on it later. After giving notice at the first signs of neglect, a super' should have others cleanup and charge the costs to the defaulter.

Removal of Equipment and Surplus Materials

Contracts usually refer to, or imply, this requirement under cleaning up, but the possible value of equipment and surplus materials justifies its separate mention. Also, their removal may prove costly and have legal implications. If a written notice of removal has no effect, the owner may have it done by

others. The items removed then become security for the costs of their removal. See Document A201-1987, Subpara. 3.15.[9]

Before selling property belonging to a contractor to pay for the costs of removal, it is best to obtain legal advice. However, the value of some materials and equipment left on a site may be virtually zero (e.g., gravel, sand, and gypsum wallboard), which is probably why they were not taken in the first place. The solution is retainage (see A201-1987, Subpara. 9.3.1).

Contract Document CCDC2-1982, GC 30, recognizes "final cleaning of the work" as distinct from periodic cleaning up on-site. "Final cleaning of the work" is the cleaning of the building itself (e.g., windows, fixtures, and floor coverings) by a subcontracted janitorial firm just before occupation. It is better to specify this cleaning as trade work in a separate section. The CCDC2 standard contract makes such final cleaning a prerequisite for "total performance of the work" (i.e., final completion).

Completion Documents

The collection from trade contractors at the completion of their work of special warranties, as-built drawings, maintenance, and operating instructions, and other **completion documents** is another area in which a super' may have difficulties. Because they take time and are classed as paperwork, such contractual requirements often are treated as mere formalities. Among completion documents this text includes those required by a contract's conditions including:

- A "comprehensive list of items to be completed or corrected" to be submitted at substantial completion (as in A201-1987, Subpara. 9.8.2, *Substantial Completion*): the so-called **punch list**

- *Warranties* for specific parts of the work (as in Subparas. 9.8.2 and 9.9.1)
- *Affidavits (statutory declaration)* that all wages and bills have been paid (as in Subpara. 9.10.2)
- A *certificate of insurance* as evidence that it is in effect and will remain so, as required by the contract (as in Subpara. 9.10.2)
- A written statement that the contractor knows of no reason the required insurance should not be renewed as required by the contract (as in Subpara. 9.10.2)
- Consent of surety (company), if any, to final payment (as in Subpara. 9.10.2)
- Any other evidence or information required by the owner establishing that a (sub)contractor's obligations have been met and his bills paid, and that there are no encumbrances on the owner's property arising out of the construction contract and work (as in Subpara. 9.10.2)
- Specific requirements of trades and suppliers with respect to their work or materials, as specified (e.g., as-built drawings, manuals, directions for operation, and so forth).

This is a considerable list of items to deal with before completion, to overlook any of which could cause trouble. Since all contractual requirements are a super's responsibility (on the contractor's behalf), a super' should search the contract documents. The most effective way to collect completion documents is to give notice of the requirements at a site meeting, stating the scheduled dates when the documents are due, and to record the notice and the required actions in the meeting's minutes. Site meetings are specially important in project completion and closeout, but like all management procedures, they should occur consistently throughout a project.

Deficiencies in Work and Performance

An owner's agent lists items of work requiring correction or completion at the time of substantial completion. Final completion requires the contractor to make good all the deficiencies, except accepted defective or nonconforming work. Punch lists are important in eliminating deficiencies, but they must be kept up to date and periodically reissued. As contractors make good deficiencies, the punch lists get shorter and that makes them a visual incentive to complete the outstanding deficiencies.

If a few deficiencies persist and seemingly cannot be made good for genuine reasons (e.g., the unavailability of materials), it may be better for a contractor to seek final payment with appropriate sums deducted to cover the costs of outstanding deficiencies. The owner–designer however may not agree and insist on total completion. Final completion and final payment go together and the issuance of a final certificate and the acceptance of a final payment have a certain contractual significance examined in Chapter 20. Also, total performance of a contract includes not only the work, but also fulfilling the contract in every other requirement, including:

- Submission of specified completion documents (previously mentioned)
- Submission of all notices and documents required by statute and regulation (e.g., to the building inspector, utilities, etc.)
- Payment and settlement of all assessments and fees required by statute and regulation (e.g., for sales taxes, unemployment and social insurance taxes, and workers' compensation assessments)
- Removal of all temporary work and facilities, equipment, and other things from the site

■ The fulfillment of any other obligation under the construction contract or the law.

11.5 COMPLETION OF CM PROJECTS

Up to this point everything about completion applies to both traditional and CM projects. Essentially, trade work is the same in both. Apart from contractual differences between a trade contractor in a CM project and a subcontractor in a traditional project, there is another important difference, and one of the main reasons for CM projects: phased construction. With phased construction, a construction manager's super' is constantly dealing with the completion and closeout of trade work, because trade contracts start and finish at different times. Consequently, a CM's super' needs the skills of a super' who specializes in completing and closing out projects.

Timely completion of contracts is, if anything, more critical in a CM project because phased construction makes timing, planning, scheduling, and coordination more critical. Each separate contract in a CM project has its own date for substantial completion, a punch list of items needing correction or completion, and its own final certificate and payment. Also, each contract requires the release of retainage, if progressive release is a provision. There are reports of lawsuits brought against owners and their construction managers for losses caused by delays, since the scheduling and management in CM projects is done by the owner's agent, the construction manager.[10]

As an agent of an owner in a CM project, a construction manager has much more to do with completion than a designer. The completion of contracts in a CM project requires more paperwork because each trade contractor has a prime contract with the owner. A superintendent can send some of his own workers to cleanup after a subtrade, and then back-charge the subcontractor by deducting the costs from monies due. A construction manager's super' should have the authority to do the same. However, a construction manager who does no part of the actual work has a practical disadvantage: there may be no workers onsite on whom he can call. Such a lack may be particularly noticeable during a project's closeout and completion.

On major CM projects, some construction managers engage the services of a company to do cleanup, back-framing, and similar jobs, and to provide certain minor facilities and services. Payment is by lump sum for certain items, and cost-plus-fee for others, such as cleanup. Other construction managers may employ their own workers for such items, but this is something many try to avoid, as it might identify them as contractors. According to its published precepts, the **GSA/PBS**, however, allows—indeed, requires—a construction manager to provide certain "general condition items" such as temporary facilities in its CM projects.[11]

Another reason many construction managers do not want to do construction work and employ construction workers is the assessment made for workers' compensation payments that vary according to the kinds of work undertaken, and which are higher for high-risk work. Finally, there is the question of responsibility for injury, damage, or death because of work and the need for indemnification and insurance, as discussed in Chapter 12.

Although the CM arrangement is commended for its fast-track construction, it has not been without its failures and lawsuits. Like some other innovations, CM once was hailed as a cure-all. In the 1970s, many general contractors became construction managers overnight with no change in staff and with no added expertise. They simply stopped pouring concrete and put on a tie.

It seems there is no refuting the fundamental criticisms of traditional and sequential designing and contracting: it takes too long. Subcontractors who do most of the work (sometimes, all) are too far removed from the owner–designer, and the superintendents who supervised and managed them are, too often, not knowledgeable enough about trade work and management. Unfortunately, often the construction manager's supervisor was last month a contractor's superintendent.

Compared to the alternatives, the CM arrangement has much to commend it. Its purpose, however, requires a high level of a wide range of skills and experience. There also remains the division between design and construction—as if one were all mind and creativity and the other all physical effort and the blind following of instructions. Until that is remedied, until there is one industry and an integrated education for it, probably no system or arrangement will fully succeed. In the early 1990s, the current movement is toward integrated information among **A/E/Cs**. Why not integrate the entire body?

SUMMARY OF MAIN POINTS

- Contract startup requires scheduling, budgeting, purchasing, hiring, and *mobilization*. Remote sites require more planning and expenditures. A contract's general requirements do not indicate everything needed.

- Entropy: typically, projects suffer from entropy, lose momentum, and slow down.

- Preconstruction preparation: a superintendent needs a good knowledge of a project's design and costs, a notice to proceed, and checklists.

- Substantial completion precedes and facilitates final completion; its achievement makes possible the use of a building (or other work) for the purpose for which it was designed; it is practical completion, not contractual or total completion.

- A punch list of deficiencies is needed at substantial completion, leading to final completion.

- To achieve completion: keep project on schedule, have effective (sub)contracts and good supervision, especially during the second half.

- Know the subtrades: a superintendent should know the (sub)trade contractors, the key persons, and the (sub)contracts.

- Liquidated damages (an amount per day for late completion) is stated in a contract as damages settled in advance. They can be effective.

- Changing superintendent during a project is not conducive to progress, unless it is to one specializing in the finishing of projects.

■ Equitable contracts and subcontracts and few changes in the work are conducive to proper and timely completion.

■ Project closeout and completion begins at startup; do not start closeout too late. Do all things like cleanup periodically and regularly, and not just in the latter stages.

■ Cleaning up shows the quality of a project's management, makes for a safer, more economic site, but requires a definition of "clean" for each trade.

■ Removal of equipment and materials by owner may need legal counsel, and proper contract provisions help.

■ Completion documents include the comprehensive punch lists of items to be completed: warranties, affidavits (statutory declarations), declarations and certificates of insurance (for continuance), consent of surety to final payment; and any other evidence or information as to

(sub)contractors' obligations met and bills paid.

■ Deficiencies in work are listed at substantial completion: correction is necessary for final completion, although if some items cannot be finished then final completion can occur and money withheld for outstanding items.

■ Final completion (total performance) includes not only the work, but all contractual obligations, including submission of specified completion documents (as previously discussed) and of all required notices and documents required by law; payment of all assessments and fees required by law; removal of all temporary work and facilities.

■ CM projects have same requirements for closeout and completion, but phased construction makes timely completion even more critical, and a multiplicity of contractors increases the administration required.

NOTES

[1]Specifications and subcontracts should require subtrades to inspect and approve the work of other trades that can affect their own work (e.g., painters should inspect and approve drywall before starting painting).

[2]The AIA contract documents refer to substantial and final completion: Canadian documents to substantial and total performance of work. Their definitions essentially are the same.

[3]See also, CCDC2-1982, GC 14, Para. 14.4, regarding payments and completion.

[4]CCDC2-1982 is similar in this matter. It also defines substantial performance of the work by

reference to "the lien legislation applicable to the Place of the Work." (*Definitions*, Para. 13).

[5]If planning to make a schedule a contract document, first consult a lawyer as to the implications in a specific contract or jurisdiction. There may be other reasons.

[6]Better supervision was called for by Aird (see Chapter 5).

[7]Designers should, however, use standard construction details wherever possible. Experience shows that university buildings designed only in outline and with requirements for many **design responses** (Chapter 18) by the contractors

proved much more economical than those fully designed and detailed by architects.

[8]See also, CCDC2-1982, GC 30, *Cleanup and Final Cleaning of the Work.*

[9]Also see, CCDC2, GC 30.

[10]See, Bruce M. Jervis and Paul Levin, *Construction Law: Principles and Practice.* (New York: McGraw-Hill, 1988) pp. 192–93.

[11]See General Services Administration, Public Buildings Service, *The GSA System for Construction Management*, Rev. ed. (Washington, D.C.: April 1975), Construction Management Contract, Article 25.

QUESTIONS AND TOPICS FOR DISCUSSION

1. Explain the concept and purpose of substantial completion in construction contracts.

2. What is the practical difference between substantial and final completion? Use several examples to illustrate your answer.

3. What significant contractual events can occur once substantial completion has been certified?

4. List and describe three common major obstacles to timely completion and describe ways of overcoming them.

5. Write a general condition to deal with periodic and final cleanup on a site by the contractors in a CM project. Also, write complementary specification clauses for cleaning up in the following trades: site works, including excavation and fill; cast-in-place concrete; and gypsum drywalling.

6. In the form of a letter to an owner's designer, present an argument by a contractor that work is substantially complete. (Make any assumptions required.)

7. Explain why the work of so many building construction contracts slows down in the later stages, and offer effective remedies.

8. Identify and briefly describe two specific contractual means that may be used by an owner–designer to achieving timely completion of contract work.

9. What incentives do most contractors have for completing work as rapidly as possible, and what conditions or circumstances may make it unattractive for them to do so?

10. Explain how the duties of a construction manager's supervisor vary from those of a prime contractor's superintendent in the completion and closeout of a construction project.

11. Explain the relationship of cash flow to project closeout and completion.

12. Explain why liquidated damages are not more widely included in building contracts?

13. Write an effective general condition to require a contractor not to change the superintendent during a project. Identify and explain any aspects of your general condition that remain difficult to enforce.

14. State and explain at least three effective axioms for efficient closeout and completion.

15. Write an effective general condition to control cleanup elsewhere, but related to, a construction site.

16. Define these terms and illustrate each with an example: punch list, deficiency, notice to proceed, completion document, and liquidated damages.

12

THE SITE AND GENERAL REQUIREMENTS

Location, location, location.
Anon. (Cited as the criterion of the value of real estate.)

Considering the significance of sites they deserve much attention, especially before making a design or a cost estimate. A main source of job overhead costs is general requirements, and many are directly related to a site. The topics of this chapter are the site and its effects on the costs of general requirements and site works and how these might be dealt with by designers and contractors.

12.1 SITES AND BIDDING DOCUMENTS

Bidding documents invariably exhort bidders to visit and examine the site of proposed work. As a warning, this provides the owner–designer with a response to fall back on if the contractor makes a claim because of unexpected conditions. He will be told:

The documents advised you to visit and inspect the site, and to do whatever was necessary to inform yourself of the conditions at the site. Therefore, we must assume your bid and the contract sum contain all the costs required to do the work according to the contract and the existing conditions.

Such a response may be only partly valid. However, if a contractor does not visit and thoroughly examine the site prior to bidding for a fixed-price contract, the situation is as if he had not examined the bidding documents. The law says, the contractor made a contract and now is obligated to do everything it requires.

Having advised bidders to visit and examine the site, some bidding documents also provide information about subsurface conditions. Often, this is obtained from test holes made at the site at the owner's expense. According to that information, the drawings then show footings at specific depths. The specifications should say that any necessary increases in the sizes of the footings will be priced at unit prices to be included with bids, and that the contract sum will be adjusted accordingly.

Other bidding documents may provide no information about subsurface conditions. There may be no mention of unit prices for variations in the foundations. The specifications for site works may put all the onus and risk on the contractor, who is obliged by the wording to allow for whatever proves to be necessary for the work. This is based on the fiction that as a bidder he had every opportunity to visit and examine the site, and if he thought it necessary, to have his own test holes drilled. (Can you imagine the situation on a site, and the costs involved, if 10 prospective bidders all hired drillers to make test holes?)

Worse, the specifications may say: "The Contractor shall have acquainted himself with all the conditions at the site prior to submitting a bid. Therefore, no adjustments to the contract sum for variations in the site works or the foundations will be entertained," or words to that effect. These are outlines of two radically different contract requirements touching on site conditions.

The site is the owner's, and it is he who decides to build on it. He contracts with a designer to design the work and then looks for a contractor to commit to a fixed price to perform the work on the site. If a contract says that whatever the conditions below the site's surface, it is the contractor's obligation to deal with them without extra payment, then that contract is unreasonable. An owner may buy a parcel of land at a low price because it has certain features

the changing of which are necessary before the site can be developed.

- A site may slope steeply, and retaining walls may be necessary to terrace and stabilize the ground
- A site may be marshy, and piles driven into solid ground 20 feet down may be necessary to support a building's foundations
- A site may appear normal at the surface, but on excavating for the foundations a ridge of bedrock might be uncovered several feet down. Possibly, test holes were drilled earlier and the results—which did not indicate rock—were included in the bidding documents

In the first case, the needed work is obvious, and providing the work is shown on the drawings, its costs can be estimated, and an equitable agreement can be made. In the second case, the piling work can be suitably contracted for at unit prices. The owner also should bear the costs of improving the site in the third case (i.e., the costs of removing some rock). If a contract's documents do not allow such costs to the contractor, the contract is not equitable, and the contractor should not have agreed to it. If he did, the contractor may have to bear the extra costs. The information of the test holes may have persuaded the contractor that no rock was present. The owner may feel that by ordering the test holes drilled he did all that could be expected. In some countries, an owner is considered liable for the costs of improving his own site so that it will allow building. That is not necessarily the case in the United States and Canada.

Subsurface conditions were discussed because they are the most unpredictable. (Chapter 13 includes more on this subject.) The principle is the same with all work affected by indeterminate site conditions. Bidding documents for fixed-price contracts should contain:

- All the design information available to the designer, which should be adequate to definitively design the substructure and superstructure
- Adequate contractual provisions for equitable adjustments to a contract sum (e.g., by unit prices) if changes in the work prove to be necessary

Bidders should examine documents to determine to what extent these exist, particularly for work below surface. If not there, a decision should be made whether to bid. If the decision is to bid, then other decisions should be made about the **contingency allowances** needed in the cost estimate to cover the risks. Many of the deficiencies in bidding documents are connected with sites and other subsurface conditions (dealt with in Chapter 13).

12.2 PHYSICAL CHARACTERISTICS OF SITES

On visiting a site, a bidder should make a site report on a standard form (the first part of which can be completed in the office with information from the bidding documents). A standard form makes a useful checklist and helps to prevent oversights. The information might include:

- Project title, as it appears on the documents
- Names of owner, designer, and construction manager
- Address of site and brief details of site location
- A key plan showing location, dimensions, roads, frontages, access, orientation, railways, etc.

- Brief description of site: aspect, topography, surface conditions, vegetation, etc.
- Existing improvements (buildings, etc.) on-site
- Existing services on and near site and their approximate locations
- Existing easements, rights of way, and roads and footpaths over the site
- Existing public utilities on site (e.g., power lines, pipelines
- Access points into the site (e.g., entrances)
- Distance from site to nearest communities and to any notable locations (e.g., railway, airport)
- Adjacent highways, roads, streets, sidewalks, streetlights, parking meters, car parks, bus stops, railways, airports, and other transportation and communication points
- Distances to communities, facilities, etc.

Some of this information can be obtained only at the site. Include details of rural locations, as addresses are not always helpful. Include a small key plan. Information not in the bidding documents about anything with significance to the work and its costs should be included; e.g., large trees, sloughs, water courses, ravines, and other features.

CASE

A vacant city lot was found to have a deep ravine that subsequently required special foundations. It was totally concealed from view by undergrowth. No mention of the ravine appeared in the bidding documents. Even the designer did not know it was there.

Do not assume that because bidding documents include a site-survey drawing, that someone walked over every part of it. Spot levels taken on a 25-foot grid can miss many features, even if all the levels are correct. When some individuals do a site survey, they avoid the difficult places; some may stand the levelling staff on rocks or other features, and others add details while sitting in a car. Take a copy of the site plan from the bidding documents and insert the additional information. Talk to local people who live nearby.

Useful information about sites often can be obtained from neighbors and local officials (e.g., the tax assessor, city engineer, and from staff of the city building department. Ask to look at any available drawings of any buildings built on the site. Details of foundations may suggest the nature of the subsurface conditions and the locations of existing services. A building inspector may know about the soil conditions. If possible, talk to a local builder or excavation contractor, and seek information about local places such as gravel pits, rental, repair, and welding shops.

Often, the worst sites are easier to deal with, because there is no question about what must be done; e.g., if a site is on an alluvial plain with ground water just below the surface, the remedy may be to preload the site with river sand. If that is what is required, there may be few problems with both the cost estimate and the work. Conversely, a normal-looking site may conceal an underground watercourse, which is why the grass is so green. Or the subsoil below a foot of loam may be clay of a type that shrinks and cracks after several hours of exposure to the air. If you are not familiar with the local soil and weather, talk to someone who is. Get geographical maps if available. Obtain statistical information about local weather.

The rapid removal of water is important. Try to visualize a site in the seasons during which the work will be done. A flowering park in June may become a wet bog in February. Besides looking at a site as it is, try to visualize it when weather is at its worst. Visualize it with the proposed work in progress, especially for

- Space to work, to set up sheds to store materials
- Space to store excavated material on the site
- Adjoining property to be supported or underpinned
- Exposed soil surfaces to be stabilized
- Existing services to be moved or removed
- Overhead wires that may obstruct cranes
- Access and egress for heavy equipment and trucks
- The effects of pile-driving or blasting or jackhammering on nearby buildings and occupants
- The need for dewatering systems, pumps, and drainage lines, etc.

The possibilities are many. A site must be related to the work and its performance if it is to be understood and the costs properly estimated. Local experience is the most valuable asset. Without it, you need to ask from those who have it. To be able to design the substructure, the designer should have asked the same questions. If he did, you cannot expect to do much better. But how can you be sure of what is in the bidding documents. If the designer did not ask the right questions, and did not get the correct answers, problems may remain hidden. The only solution in a fixed-price contract is equitable provisions for modifications to the contract.

12.3 SITES DURING CONSTRUCTION

Some designers try to retain as much as possible of a site's original features. Others prefer to strip a site down to the subsoil and put back the topsoil later as part of a landscaping contract. There are advantages and disadvantages to both approaches.

First, see which approach appears to have been used in the bidding documents, and then consider the consequences. Since an owner–designer is concerned mainly with the result, not all the requirements for the work's performance may be explicit in bidding documents.

- Retaining certain trees and original site features may delay the work and cause complaints and extra costs if displacement or damage is incurred
- Retaining existing natural features requires protection from damage and resulting expense
- Replacing a damaged mature tree may cost several thousand dollars
- Disposing of surplus excavated materials may require trucking costs, dumping fees, and costs of a burning permit with fire protection provided
- Stripping a site may expose the subsoil to weather that may create drainage difficulties and a morass
- Storing topsoil may be difficult, and extra handling is expensive
- Bases for new roads and parking areas may be laid early to provide better work traffic surfaces; gravel beds may sink into wet subsoil.

Try to economize by foresight and planning. Do not try to save by not providing the essential things. Some sites become littered with rubbish, and some contractors do not take the most rudimentary and common-sense precautions. As a result, when it rains surface-water runs over the site and collects in excavations. Temporary roadways turn into quagmires reminiscent of battlefields on which workers and equipment can only move at half-speed. Nowhere more than on a site does the old adage apply: A stitch in time saves nine.

Cleaning up a site has to be done in most contracts. To allow debris to accumulate causes delays, risks accidents, and makes a bad impression. Cleaning up is something to do when a crew has finished a job and there is time left before quitting. Leaving rubbish often creates extra expense, because at the end a big effort is necessary to get the cleanup done before a deadline.

Security often is a problem on sites. It is a question whether paying for guards or security personnel will cost more than the costs of things stolen. Neighbors can be helpful. At a remote site, it may be worthwhile to find a local person of influence who will support the project and provide some protection. People close to a site can be a valuable resource; or, they can be a hindrance and an obstruction. It pays to consider them.

12.4 GENERAL REQUIREMENTS

Many estimators believe job overhead costs are the hardest to estimate accurately because some are not related to tangible work, but to such things as project duration, size, cost, and location. **General requirements** sometimes are called **general condition items.** Some are referred to in contract documents and some are not. In an estimate, they should represent all the direct costs necessary that are not directly related to specific parts of the work. **Supervision** often is the most costly general requirement. Other more tangible job overhead items include temporary facilities and services, and the costs of statutory and contractual requirements (e.g., permits, bonds, and insurances). A checklist is included in the next section.

Often general requirements are underestimated because, like sites, they are variable. Too often, job costs are not fully itemized in estimates. Instead they may be shown as a percentage of the direct costs of the work. In CM projects, they are problematic for a different reason: there is no general contractor to provide them. Many construction managers prefer not to provide such things as temporary site facilities and services. Consequently, in CM projects general requirements usually are included in a contract for the structural work: a return to the tradition in which general condition items are provided by a general contractor. An alternative is a separate CM contract for their provision.

12.5 A CHECKLIST FOR GENERAL REQUIREMENTS

Construction companies and construction managers should develop comprehensive checklists (preferably in a computer system) of general requirements for the kinds of work they do, and for different kinds of sites. These lists are an aid in estimating costs to ensure that no general requirements are overlooked. The items that follow are from a checklist primarily for CM projects; other kinds of projects' requirements may differ. No code numbers are shown because all companies need to develop a cost code to suit their own requirements.[1]

CM Project Checklist

Field Supervision. Usually, supervision has the largest cost, and may represent as much as half of total job overhead. Normally, it includes all the site staff: superintendents, assistants, clerks, cost accountants, etc. However, certain projects have personnel on-site who normally work in a contractor's main office. Therefore, this category needs special attention.

General Labor. This is for minor, uncoded work, such as that not included in the work of separate contracts.[2]

Travel Expenses. Those directly related to a project, such as: truck rental and expenses; fares and minor travel expenses; board and lodgings for staff; travelling time for staff; costs of site visits by office staff.[3]

Computers. This category includes all on-site computer costs, as distinct from those in the head office.

Fees, Permits, and Licenses. All payments to authorities and public utilities, including

- Development permit
- Building and services permits
- Service connection fees
- Sewer connection fees
- Demolition permits
- Burning or rubbish permits
- City property rental fees
- Street and sidewalk rentals fees
- Temporary and permanent crossings

Insurances. All project-related premiums for different insurances, including

- Owner's property
- Employer's property

- General liability
- Completed operations
- Pressure vessels, boilers
- Business auto and aircraft[4]

As some contracting companies typically maintain continuous coverages not related to specific projects, insurance costs require care in allocation.

Bonds. All fees for project bonds, including:

Bid bonds
Supply bonds
Performance bonds
Labor and materials
Payment bonds
Special bonds

Testing. Costs of employing independent testing agencies for special testing (e.g., of windows)[5] and such materials and work as:

Concrete
Masonry
Metals
Wood and plastics
Moisture protection
Other special testing

Site Office Equipment. The rental costs of everything in a site's offices, including:

Furniture
Filing cabinets
Drawing files
Copying machines
Telephone sets
Calculators
Stationery
FAX equipment
Computers
CB and other radios

Survey Equipment. That rented to a project, such as

Transits
Levels
Staffs
Pegs
Measuring tapes
Chains
Rods
Field books

Safety Equipment.

Protective clothing
Hard hats
Boots
First-aid equipment
Fire extinguishers
Prefabricated barriers

Small Tools.

Axes
Hammers
Crowbars
Hand saws
Electric drills
Skill saws
Screwdrivers
Brushes and shovels
Wheelbarrows, etc.

Telephone and Communications. The costs arising from the use of all communication equipment and means, including:

Temporary telephones
Telephone rentals
Telephone calls
FAX costs
Courier costs
Radios
Car and CB telephones
Beepers
Postage costs
Telegrams, cables

Drawings and Prints. The costs of reproducing all project drawings for main office, site, approvals by authorities, owner, contractors, and mortgage and finance companies.

Textual Documentation. Costs of reproducing documents including specifications, correspondence, contract notices and modifications (e.g., change orders).

Progress Photographs. Those that show work progress and special conditions on site.

Temporary Buildings. Costs of providing, transporting, erecting, maintaining, dismantling, repairing, and removing from site such as the following:

> Site offices
> Storage sheds
> Workmen's shacks
> Temporary accommodations

Temporary Toilet Facilities. All charges for rental and maintenance of portable toilets are included in this category.

Temporary Power Services. Costs of the supply, installation, rental, operation, and removal from site of temporary power systems for tools and lighting; also the cost of rental of light fixtures and a supply of bulbs.

Temporary Water Services. Costs of installation and removal of temporary water supply systems to sites and the cost of the water supplied.

Temporary Heating. Costs of supply, installation, rental, and removal from site of heating units for drying and curing work, including fuel costs, are included here.

Temporary Roads and Ramps. Costs for the provision and removal of temporary roadways, ramps, and other means of access to the site and the work; including the supply of hog fuel, and gravel for these items.

Pumping. Costs of removing or diverting all unwanted water, including: wastewater pumps; dewatering systems; and labor for drainage work.

Barricades and Hoardings. Costs of materials, labor, and equipment for the supply, erection, maintenance, and removal from site of temporary fences, hoardings, barricades, screens, canopies, gates, railings, and similar temporary structures (to be identified and described as rented, or charged in full and salvaged).

Scaffolding and Staging. Costs of delivery, rental, and removal from site of temporary scaffoldings, staging, boards, and ladders; excluding scaffolding and supports for forms, masonry, and for other specific trades that should be charged to the work.

Security and Protection. Costs of security guards and all other security and protection of the work at the site are included here.

Climatic Conditions. All costs for snow removal, de-icing, and all temporary protection and enclosures against the weather are included in this category.

Heavy Plant and Equipment. Costs for the delivery, rental, erection, and dismantling and removal of general-use plant and equipment,[6] including operators, repairs, and communications for such items as

Mobile cranes
Climbing cranes
Tower cranes
Hoists
Lifting jacks
All general-use equipment.

Rubbish Removal. Includes all rentals of bins and their removal and related dumping costs, including costs of dumping hazardous materials.

Site Signs and Advertising. Costs of providing, painting, erecting, maintaining, and removing from site all project signs, site notice boards, and advertising (to be itemized) are included here.

Models and Mock-ups. Costs of such items provided for an entire project (and not for any particular trade work) are included in this category.

Final Cleaning. This category includes all costs of removing protective coatings, cleaning and polishing finished surfaces, such as floors, tiling, glass, and fixture surfaces, and vacuuming carpets. All as required to be ready for occupancy.[7]

Premiums and Bonuses. Included here are all costs of bonuses for staff and workers. (Experience shows that owners often will agree to an allowance for bonuses to be paid to key personnel on successful completion of a CM project.)

General Requirements. None of these headings or lists is complete or definitive. The test for inclusion in general requirements is: Can this item and its costs be attributed to a specific item or items of work? If an item can be so allocated, it should be. As a means to more precise estimating and costing, the allocation of general requirements should be exclusive, and not inclusive; i.e., items should be allocated to specific work whenever possible.

Some projects are managed and administered almost entirely from the site. On these, it is better to first allocate costs following a list of standard general requirements and to identify and separate those less common overhead items that normally would be part of **operating (office) overhead costs**.[8] Other aspects of sites and their requirements are mentioned in Chapter 11, concerning the startup of projects, and in Chapter 13, which deals with subsurface conditions.

Computer Applications for General Requirements

Because of the conditions and circumstances cited, special care and attention should be paid to all general requirement items, both before and after making a contract. More costing and analysis of general requirements are needed to get better cost information and estimates. This can be achieved more efficiently by maintaining checklists, requirements of specific projects, and cost records in a computer data base. For example, since supervision is a major job cost, it is worthwhile to analyze supervision costs in a spreadsheet program. Facts about individual field employees (supers, assistants, etc.) that may prove useful include

- Personal information
- Total employment costs to company
- History of productivity related to costs of projects, their success and profitability
- Productivity rating (on a scale of one to 100)

This information and data can be considered in calculating the markup in cost estimates. As a way of improving estimates and construction management economics, other major contributors to job costs might be similarly analyzed. It is not sensible to measure and price carefully so as to estimate the direct costs of work while paying no attention to much more significant costs, such as those of general requirements.

SUMMARY OF MAIN POINTS

- General requirements are those items which create job overhead costs; some are related to site conditions; often they are difficult to estimate.

- Bidding documents advise bidders to inspect the site of proposed work, in part because an owner–designer wants to ensure that a contractor has no grounds for a claim arising from the site.

- Shortcomings in bidding documents often are connected with a site, and bidders should investigate and calculate the related risks.

- Large risks on a contractor in a fixed-price contract may hurt the owner, as some bidders will increase bids in an attempt to cover the risks; others may not, but later a low bidder may become a disgruntled contractor trying to cut losses.

- A designer should have adequate information to design all work below ground; if he has not, he should not expect a contractor to complete such work for a fixed price, and should arrange for a more suitable contract.

- A site inspection should include completion of a site report. Owner–designers' site surveys and site plans may be deficient in information, but such may not excuse a bidder's mistake.

- Consider a site's conditions in bad weather, equipment's access, and space for work and storage. Get site information and local experience from as many sources as possible.

- Some surfaces of sites are preserved while others are remade; not all site works are specified, and therefore, site work requires care in estimating.

- Persons living near a site often are able to contribute to a project's security.

- Costs of general requirements are direct costs that cannot be allocated to specific work items; only to a job as a whole. They are among most difficult to estimate, and often are related to project's duration, size, or cost. Often costs are wrongly allocated to job overheads.

- Checklist of general requirements includes supervision, general labor, permits, insurances, bonds, site office and furniture, communications, temporary buildings, and services.

- Computer applications help with checklists of general requirements and their costs from past projects, and with work records of supers and other staff.

NOTES

[1] Bill G. Eppes and Daniel E. Whiteman, *Cost Accounting for the Construction Firm* (New York: John Wiley and Sons, 1984) provides a more detailed list of general requirements (but titled "general conditions") with *Masterformat* code numbers.

[2] In traditional contracts, "general labor" is provided by the primary contractor and certain subcontractors. In a CM project, special provision may be needed.

[3] Site visits from head office may become controversial if their costs are charged to the project.

[4] See Chapter 21 and its references for more on various insurance needs.

[5] Testing is more precisely classified as a direct cost of specific work. It is included in this list for construction management purposes, since testing in CM projects often is not included in the construction contracts, and instead is handled directly by the owner through the construction manager.

[6] Most equipment should be included as a direct cost of the items of work for which it is used. However, some equipment is of such widespread and general usage that sometimes it cannot be attributed to any particular work and so may be included here or under a separate heading in an estimate or cost account.

[7] Final cleaning often is specified as a separate section of trade work.

[8] This identification and separation of different overhead costs is important for several reasons: one of the most critical exists in a cost-plus-fee contract where the clear definition of "cost" and "fee" is essential.

QUESTIONS AND TOPICS FOR DISCUSSION

1. What obligations to bidders have an owner and designer concerning information about a site, and what should motivate an owner and designer in this matter?

2. Design a report format for use by a building company to record urban (suburban) (remote) (overseas) site information.

3. Use your report form (designed for Question 2) to make a detailed report on an actual construction site. Get a recorded critique of your report from a contractor on site.

4. Obtain bidding documents for a local building project and write a report criticizing the information provisions therein. In particular, point out any deficiencies in the information needed by bidders.

5. If bidding documents indicate existing buildings to be demolished at a site, and if, on visiting the site, a bidder finds the buildings are no longer there, what should he do? In your answer explain what is involved.

6. A scenario: A large site in a northern area is located on a remote plateau approximately 100 miles from the nearest town, and two miles from a small hamlet. There is a main highway approximately ten miles from the hamlet reached by a secondary road. There is no road to the site. The local industries are small farms, logging, and small handicrafts. Local labor is available, mostly unskilled. The nearest town has a railway station, a small airport, and four banks serving a population of approximately 50,000 persons. You have a bank draft for $50,000, two field engineers, a superintendent, two general foremen, and a small group of tradesmen. State any other require-

ments and any assumptions you need to make.

Make a sketch map and a detailed report telling how you intend to set up a project costing several million dollars on the site at which you have just arrived.

7. a. Define General Requirements for estimating purposes.

b. Define what General Requirements are not.

8. a. What costs are included under the heading "general labor"? Why are they necessary? Why are they classified as a job overhead? What limits should apply to them?

b. When should travelling expenses not be classified as a job overhead cost? What alternative allocations can be made, and what possible allocations can be made of truck rental costs?

9. a. Explain in detail why job overhead costs are so often underestimated.

b. What procedure should be followed to ensure that no general require-

ments are overlooked in cost estimating? Make the outline of a model to illustrate your answer.

10. What circumstances in a contract are likely to cause an increase in job overhead costs? What can be done to prevent it? What can be done by a contractor to improve the situation once it has occurred?

11. From the checklist in this chapter, select items that you believe might (not) be general requirements in almost every project. Explain your selections.

12. What facts will change the category of a cost from job overhead to operating overhead, or vice versa?

13. Offer arguments, pro and con, that a project owner should be responsible for all costs of work arising out of the site that are not specifically excluded from the scope of a fixed-price contract.

CHAPTER

13

SUBSURFACE
CONDITIONS

Dese are de conditions dat prevail.
Jimmy Durante, Comedian (1893–1980)

Since mutual understanding and agreement are essential to a good contract, physical below-surface conditions always are a potential source of trouble. Neither party knows for sure what is below the surface of a site, or below those of existing work. As a result their agreement may be flawed. This chapter considers the effects on contracts and management of subsurface conditions.

13.1 SUBSURFACE CONDITIONS

Usually the term subsurface conditions means conditions below the ground surface of a site. The term, however, has a broader meaning that includes the latent conditions of **existing work** that may affect new work. For example, subsurface conditions in an existing building might refer to

- Decaying structural timbers
- Corroding pipes of a mechanical system
- A concrete floor slab with no moisture barrier.

Examples abound, particularly in older buildings, and sometimes in new buildings. In North America, construction is considered as new buildings. However, much construction involves repairing, retrofitting, and renovating old buildings, and the proportion of that kind of construction work is increasing. This is good reason to consider the implications of subsurface conditions.

In construction there always is the possibility of discovering unexpected conditions. New work always requires contact with the existing, if only with the substrata of a site. So, we can say that most construction involves concealed, subsurface conditions. In a fixed-price contract, the economic and contractual implications of subsurface conditions usually are the same: they result in higher costs for one party or the other. Fixed-price contracts are the primary concern, because the risks are greatest in these.

13.2 RISK AND INFORMATION IN CONTRACTS

To the extent that a contract contains a fixed-price element (e.g., a unit price contract, or a cost-plus contract with a fixed fee) there is risk of a deficient estimate and bid, and an inadequate contract sum or fee. In the appropriate general condition of a standard fixed-price contract (AIA Document A201-1987, Subpara. 4.3.6, *Claims for Concealed or Unknown Conditions*), the wording is so general that, in the absence of more specific supplements, one might expect many claims by contractors for extra costs. The document uses the term "physical conditions of an unusual nature," and that seems wide open to interpretation. However, it is not possible to write a general condition in a standard document and expect that it can serve the purpose of every contract without amendment, or supplement, or specifications.

The relationship of risk to information in construction contracts is important.[1] Briefly, the smaller the amounts of **design information** and **experiential information** available, the greater a contractor's risk of financial loss. With absolute and superhuman prescience there would be no risk. With total ignorance of the facts, obviously the degree of risk is at its highest. How such risks are to be shared by contracting parties is this chapter's topic. In seeking more equitable contracts with fewer claims and disputes, some precepts to minimize the effects of risk follow:

- A risk in a contract is better taken by the party who has the greater control over the risk and its effects on the work and its costs.
- A risk over which neither party has any control should be minimized to whatever extent is possible, both contractually (e.g., by selecting an appropriate contract and conditions) and practically (e.g., by insurance); residual risk should be shared by both parties proportionately (e.g., most of the risk from bad weather is primarily a builder's; risk from a site is the owner's).
- A risk arising from subsurface conditions at a site is better borne by the owner because the owner owns the site, and because it is equitable that an owner should pay for what he receives as improvements (e.g., correction of unsuitable subsurface or other conditions); an owner, however, can contract to do otherwise, but should do so explicitly and without misunderstanding.
- All construction contracts should be specially designed and written for site conditions, the kind of work, the circumstances, and the foreseeable risks involved.

If a fixed-price contract clearly puts most risk of loss on the contractor, the owner should assume that he is going to pay the contractor a premium. Initially, the onus is on bidders to calculate perceived risks and to include the costs in their bids. If a bidder is in error and makes a serious mistake, the bidder should be allowed to withdraw.

If a fixed-price contract contains a contract sum that allows for foreseeable risks and then the expected risks do not appear, the contractor may expect to gain. If, however, a bidder ignores some risks, puts in a low bid and gets the contract, then, if the risks occur the contractor may suffer a loss. He might seek to recover either by reducing the quality of the work, or by making claims for additional costs.

If risks arising from concealed or unknown conditions and lack of information are large, it is better not to undertake the work with a fixed-price contract. Depending on the work and the design information available, another kind of contract (e.g., cost-plus-fee or unit-price) should be used.

If the risks from physical conditions are limited to one or two discrete parts of a project, and do not affect the whole then a fixed-price contract may be practical for the major part of the work. The minor parts (about which information is lacking and for which the risks are high) can be dealt with in several ways by using one or more of the following:

- **Unit prices** for specific items of work the quantities of which may vary, with provisions for pricing extra and omitted work
- A **cash allowance** within the contract for each discrete part of the work about which information is lacking, with contractual provisions for adjusting and expending the cash allowances as required
- A **separate contract** of a different kind (e.g., a unit-price or a cost-plus-fee) for each part of the work for which information is lacking

The most suitable kind of separate contract depends on the extent and nature of the work and on the available information, and a contract should be designed to suit. Unsuitable ways of dealing with or avoiding risks caused by lack of information in fixed-price contracts include

- Vagueness in and omissions from bidding documents (i.e., contract specifications and drawings)
- Catch-all weasel clauses in specifications, which seek to place risks with the contractor without providing information that enables him to calculate those risks.
- Requiring bidders to submit *alternative prices* for work of a different types or scope.

A designer should make clear in the bidding documents of a fixed-price contract all the assumptions (e.g., dimensions of foundations) affecting the quantities and quality of the work.

EXAMPLE:

The dimensions of concrete foundations have to vary according to subsoil conditions and load-bearing capacities. Assumed dimensions should be shown on the drawings according to the best information available. The contract should make proper provision for changes in the sizes of concrete foundations.

A fixed-price contract's bidding documents must provide a clear and measurable basis for the required quality and quantity of the work upon which estimates and bids can be made. Provisions in bidding documents for probable changes in the work also must be explicit. Bidders for fixed-price contracts should check bidding documents to ensure that such provisions exist. Where they do not, bidders should decide on a strategy that best suits their needs.

- Declining to bid, because the risks are not calculable or reasonable

- Bidding with the deliberate intention of increasing profits by taking advantage of any weaknesses in the contract
- Bidding with a contractor's contingency allowance made in the bid to cover indeterminate risks

It is important that each bidder decide on a policy for each project in which there are risks that cannot be properly calculated. Indecisiveness and imprecision increase potential risks. Decisions should be recorded in a cost-estimate file so that subsequently there will be no doubt why a particular bid was of a certain amount.

Under United States laws, collusion among bidders is illegal. Yet, that is not true of every country. In some places it is normal practice for bidders to hold pre-bid meetings about projects for which they are bidding.[2] It seems reasonable that there should be some means of communication among bidders that contravene no law or precept concerned with fair and honest bidding; a means by which bidders could arrive at a consensus as to the deficiencies and defects in bidding documents (if any) and, as a group, inform the bidding authority. If this were so, then improvements and corrections in design and documents could be made before there is a defective contract. The essential nature of a contract is, a bargain to both parties based on mutual agreement: a *consensus ad idem* (a meeting of the minds). Therefore, everything practical and necessary should be done to achieve this. Present methods of making contracts can fall short.

Experience shows that discussion often succeeds where mailed documents may not, and that through discussion better understanding of a contract's requirements results in lower prices. Such an exchange can be achieved by pre-bid meetings between own- ers, designers, and bidders and again, if necessary, just before submitting bids. Those who prepare contracts too often use a standard form of contract without amendments and special conditions, such as those needed to deal with subsurface conditions. Standard contracts are acceptable as far as they go, but they rarely go as far as needed. Virtually every project needs special provisions. Advice from a cost consultant can help an owner–designer. A cost consultant often understands best an estimator's needs, and what a contract should contain to minimize hazards with risks and their costs.

13.3 NATURE OF FIXED-PRICE CONTRACTS

One characteristic of a fixed-price contract is that the owner seeks assurance and freedom from risk. Within reason, and tempered by competition, the owner should be prepared to pay a contractor to carry those risks. Naturally, owners want to pay as little as possible. They hope that any premium will be small or nonexistent. Many owners also expect an agent, such as a designer or construction manager, to see that the contractor (who probably was the lowest bidder) does the work according to the contract. Standard contracts, however, do not (as published) provide for the kind of continuous and intensive supervision that may be necessary to enforce a contract that, because it does not equitably deal with risks, might cause the contractor financial loss. Bidders should first compare a contract with the nearest equivalent standard contract and carefully evaluate the risks and the contract being offered.[3] It also is important in the matter of unknown conditions to understand the fundamental nature of a fixed-price contract in common law. Without anything to the contrary stated, such a contract requires the contractor to provide and do everything necessary to complete the work for the general purpose for which it is designed and intended.

CASE

In one case, the absence of any reference to flooring in a fixed-price contract did not allow a contractor to claim an extra to the contract sum for the provision of flooring. On the contrary, when he refused to install the flooring unless he was paid extra, the owner seized the flooring material on-site and used it to complete the work. The court held that the contractor could not recover either the cost of the flooring material or the amount outstanding under the contract. This was because "it was clearly to be inferred from the language of the specification that the plaintiff was to do the flooring"; although the contract did not mention flooring.[4]

If not specifically mentioned, **work** that is indispensable to completion is included by implication in the stipulated sum of a contract.[5] Ultimately, however, a contractor's obligations always depend on the actual wording, meaning, and intent of the contract, subject to statute laws to the contrary. The AIA Document A201-1987, Subpara. 1.2.3, states:

> "The intent of the Contract Documents is to include all items necessary for the proper execution and completion of the Work by the Contractor."

The AIA Document's definition of "the Work" is "that required by the Contract Documents." (A201-1987, Subpara. 1.1.3).[6]

The Work is the same as that described in the Owner-Contractor Agreement (A101, Art. 2), where it says the contractor shall execute "the entire Work described in the Contract Documents."

If the work of a fixed-price contract is a residence, then with that definition of "intent," and drawings that show, for example, a residence, then it would seem the contract's work is a complete residence. Certainly, if the contract says the work is to be "completed and ready for occupation by April 1, 1984," or completion for occupancy were otherwise indicated, it seems reasonable that would go beyond an omission from the documents as to the specific type of flooring, for example, and that the contractor would be obligated to provide and install whatever flooring is reasonable and customary for that class of house. Several cases in American courts have upheld the principle of work that is reasonably inferable from the contract documents. One case[7] involved construction of a house. There was nothing in the contract about bathroom tiling, but the court said that "it was fair to assume that appropriate [tiled] walls and flooring are included [in a bathroom]."

An owner can remove practically all risk for himself in a fixed-price contract by prescribing that the contractor shall complete the work so that it will be ready for occupancy and use, as described and intended and evidenced by its design, by a certain date. That is the ultimate **performance specification**. However, an owner should consider the effect of such wording on bidders for the work. If they are prudent, the bidders will consider as many risks as they can foresee, calculate their probability and effect, and allow for them in their estimates and bids. For example, it may be more sensible for a contract's wording to limit, where possible, a contractor's risk by saying:

> "Allow in your estimate and bid for excavating in any material *except rock requiring blasting*. If blasting is necessary, it will be at an extra cost to be added to the contract sum." [Or,]

> "Allow for foundations to the depths shown on the drawings. If it is necessary to go deeper, *the extra work will be paid for by an addition to the contract sum* based on the unit prices in the schedule of quantities."

> "For the replacement of defective plasterwork, make a Cash Allowance of $5,000.00 (five thousand dollars), to be expended as provided for in the General Conditions. In the Schedule provided with the Bid Form, enter the percentage allowed for markup, and include your *unit price per square foot of wall-area for the replacement of defective plaster work*, as specified...."

The effect of such provisions in a fixed-price contract is to separate a minor portion of the work and to put it into a minor contract of a different kind: one that is a subset of the main contract.[8] In such ways, any specific risk can be isolated, described, and precluded. Provisions can be made to pay the extra costs should a contingency arise. Then it is unnecessary for bidders to assume the worst and to allow in their bids for contingencies and additional work that may not be required; or to take a chance, make no allowance, and perhaps to suffer a loss if a contingency does arise. To make such provisions it is necessary to make them quite clear. It is a matter for information, risk, and mutual agreement.

13.4 SUBSURFACE CONDITIONS AND CONTRACT CONDITIONS

If a fixed-price contract says that any necessary blasting of rock shall be paid for as an extra to the contract sum, the intent is clear. It is equally clear that if the contract says nothing about excavation work and blasting, *although both are obviously required by the work*, what is necessary for completion must be done as part of the contract and at no extra cost to the owner. The assumption will be that the contractor has assessed all the costs and the risks and allowed for them in the bid and the fixed-contract amount. If, however, the need for rock blasting is not obvious, and the documents say nothing about rock blasting, and it could not be foreseen by a reasonable builder, then it would seem reasonable that any blasting required should be paid for by the owner as an extra cost. But a court may not always see it that way.[9]

Precepts for Dealing with Subsurface Conditions

The following precepts are applicable in dealing with subsurface conditions that prove to be different from those previously assumed in a fixed-price contract:

1. The wording of a written contract expresses the entire agreement between the parties. It also supersedes any oral agreements between them (under the

parol-evidence rule). A court has no power to make a contract where none exists. Neither can it add to or subtract from the terms and conditions of a contract. It can only interpret a contract according to the law. Therefore, an owner–designer should ensure that a contract has a written instrument that includes everything needed, and both parties should ensure it includes everything agreed to; particularly wording concerning concealed conditions. Careful and precise interpretation of a contract's wording is necessary to understand the allocation of a risk.

2. In interpreting a contract, a court will apply the rule of reasonableness, which says that actions and intention shall be judged according to what a reasonable person would do under the circumstances of the particular case. Therefore, the word "reasonable" requires interpretation. However, actual use of the word "reasonable" is not essential to the rule of reasonableness.

3. In deciding whether subsurface conditions exposed during the work provide grounds for adjustments to the time and amount of a contract, the main question is: Were the discovered subsurface conditions foreseeable by the parties at the time of making the contract? If they were not, then a modification of the contract may be in order. The wording of a contract is definitive and paramount, but any ambiguity in a written contract will be construed against the party that made the document (under the rule of *contra proferentum*).

4. In deciding whether discovered subsurface conditions provide grounds for adjustments to a contract, there is another question: Are the discovered conditions materially different from the conditions as indicated or implied by the contract documents[10], or from those conditions usually encountered in work of the type in the contract?

5. The fundamental nature of a fixed-price contract is to provide a complete job for a stipulated sum, with all the inherent risks taken by the contractor, as previously explained. It is assumed a contractor understands this and the documents, their requirements, and the risks involved.

A contractor must assume in a fixed-price contract that if nothing is said about the type of soil, then he must excavate in whatever soil he uncovers. If it says nothing about blasting rock, and he uncovers rock that needs blasting, he still cannot assume that he categorically will be entitled to extra payment for blasting. It will depend on the likelihood of rock being there, the wording of the contract, and how a court might interpret it. If the situation looks potentially serious, a contractor should talk to a lawyer who knows construction practices in the district.

Common law is largely common sense, and the rule of reasonableness expresses it; as does also the question of foreseeability. The rule of reasonableness expects everyone to act reasonably, as would any reasonable person in like circumstances. However, in the same way that written law (statutes) can overrule common law, so written contracts can overrule common sense, custom, and whatever is reasonable; providing a contract is clear, explicit, legally valid, and enforceable. It is of no use for a contracting party to invoke the principle of reasonableness cry-ing, "that's not reasonable," if the wording of the contract that he has made clearly goes against what seems practical to a reasonable person.

Before considering a claim because of subsurface conditions, read again and fully understand the contract. The better way is to have bidding and contract documents reviewed and explained by a lawyer familiar with construction. This is especially important if there is any doubt or confusion, and particularly if there is anything unusual with the site, the work, or the contract. An axiom has it that the proper time for a contractor to read and understand a contract's documents is before making a cost estimate and an offer. Once an offer is made and accepted, a contract exists. It is then too late to find surprises under the surface or in the contract documents. Often with justification, contractors complain about the unfairness of contracts; particularly about requirements for work in fixed-price contracts involving subsurface conditions that may require the contractor to

- Excavate for the work in every kind of material
- Allow for pumping or otherwise removing all underground water
- Excavate to such depths as are required to provide a suitable bearing surface of not less than...
- Remove all rock, existing concrete and masonry, and other material exposed in excavations at the site
- Replace any piping that is defective
- Cut out and replace any defective plaster, and any plaster no longer fully keyed to the lathing

Such requirements are practically impossible to allow for in an estimate and a bid for a fixed-price contract with any de-

gree of accuracy. Test-hole results always are limited, and sometimes inadequate. (Owner–designers may proclaim such information as "not guaranteed," but this may not be admissible in a court.[11]) A bidding requirement that bidders visit a site to learn of all the site's conditions usually is impractical, both with respect to the time available and the costs of bidding for work. Designers may ask, "What are we supposed to do?" The reply may be

- Select, design, and prepare more precise, explicit, and equitable contract documents for a contract of a type suitable for the work and the conditions
- Use no unequitable and unreasonable wording in the documents: no weasel clauses, loose statements, or vague requirements
- Arrange pre-bid meetings to explain intentions, deal with questions, and issue and discuss addenda to bidding documents, and communicate information effectively.

Owners should be advised as to the different kinds of contracts and contracting methods: which contracts are more suitable, equitable, or economical, and about their implications. Many owners are not fully aware of the possible alternatives or of the need to consider them. If contracting companies made more protests and recommendations about documents containing unreasonable requirements, and if companies backed up their protests by refusing to bid for work unless unreasonable contractual requirements were changed, there would be improvements in bidding documents. Failing that, contractors and superintendents must learn how to deal with unreasonable requirements.

Procedures for Dealing with Subsurface Conditions

Assuming a fixed-price contract, here are some ways of dealing with unexpected subsurface conditions discovered on a project:

- Know the contract, the facts of the site and situation, the owner's situation and attitude, and the results of any similar cases.
- Work with the owner–designer in seeking a solution that is of mutual benefit. Avoid an adversarial attitude as long as possible.
- Try to find an alternative design for the affected parts of the work (e.g., foundations on rock[12]). Ideally, the alternative costs should be less than those of the work as originally designed, plus the costs of otherwise dealing with the discovered conditions.
- Try to propose a modification to the contract and changes in the work, supported by estimated costs, that will benefit both the owner and the contractor by avoiding a dispute and a delay.
- Simultaneously, prepare your case for a claim for extra costs and extra time. Consult legal counsel.

Making a Claim in a Contract

Although a contract's wording may preclude such a claim, if discovered conditions cause hardship, it may benefit a contractor to make a claim for adjustments to the contract sum, or time, or both. This is the principle of opportunism: You never know an outcome until you try. Not even lawyers always know what a court will decide. Consider the costs before making a claim. Emotionally, going into court may not be worthwhile. Sometimes the wording of a written claim and its impact on the owner–designer is sufficient to make a claim effective, although a contract condition may seem to preclude it. Also, sometimes it is possible to find other wording in a contract that gives one an advantage that can be traded off against a potential liability. (Chapter 17 deals further with claims.)

Changes and Interpretations in Contracts

Owners and contractors can mutually agree to make any changes in a contract they choose, providing the changes conform to the requirements for valid and enforceable contracts. A party to a standard-type contract can request a written **interpretation** of wording in the contract from the owner's agent named in the contract as the interpreter of the contract (e.g., the architect, in AIA and CCDC contract documents). Requesting a written interpretation often obliges an owner's agent to clarify his thoughts and understanding of a contract condition, since a written interpretation requires deliberation. A request for an interpretation by a contractor may be helpful and effective just before making a claim. Interpretations, however, should not necessarily be taken as final. In most contracts they are a first interpretation (i.e., not agreed to by the parties as final and binding). In any event, they always are subject to review, revision, or confirmation by an arbitrator or judge. AIA Document A201 makes an architect's decisions "relating to aesthetic effect" final and binding if consistent with the contract. However, the word "consistent" is open to interpretation. Sometimes, it may be worthwhile to seek an independent interpretation and to advise the owner–designer of a materially different interpretation, or to contest an interpretation by seeking arbitration.

Evidence of Discovered Conditions

Evidence of unusual or unexpected conditions should be recorded immediately on discovery. Take several photographs from different positions and show the dimensions. Include a measuring rule in the photographs to allow measurements to be compared in the prints. If a measuring rule is unsuitable or unavailable, standard-size products such as masonry units can be included as a scale in a photograph. The photographs should show the date they were taken. Photographs are cheap when compared with costs of the slightest delay. Other evidence includes entries in a job diary, dated and signed by a superintendent. Also, include measurements and descriptions of work recorded and signed by representatives of both parties. Where necessary, reference should be made to specific standard methods of measurement; or the method of measurement employed should be described and included. This is particularly important when measuring earth work, quantities of which always depend so much on the soil and the equipment used. Descriptions of soils should, whenever possible, be those as used in codes, ordinances, and manuals of practice.

EXAMPLE:

What is rock? Is it only solid and homogeneous bedrock; or does it include isolated boulders, and if so, in what sizes? How hard is rock?

It is better if such questions are answered by definitions before making a contract. If necessary, get independent inspec-tions and signed statements to establish the nature of soils and subsurface conditions. Do not delay in collecting evidence as conditions may change or disappear. This is especially true of conditions involving or affected by temperature, water, humidity, or the weather. In contracts for renovation that include several kinds of work, the definition of terms used in specifications is helpful in avoiding misunderstandings and disputes. Such terms might include

> *Replace*: means, remove the existing and put back in its place *work* of equal quality, appearance, and constitution, as the existing that was removed and the existing that may remain. Submit samples....
> *Work*: means, materials, products, and components, and the necessary skill and labor to install them in place in the building....

Subsurface Conditions with Other Kinds of Contracts

So far, subsurface conditions in fixed-price contracts have been considered because it is in that kind of contract that the associated risks are most critical. What of unknown subsurface conditions in other kinds of contracts? To the extent that other kinds of contracts contain an element of a fixed-price, the same applies. A cost-plus-fixed-fee contract might be made inequitable by the discovery of subsurface conditions that affect the contract's duration. In a unit-price contract, there may be no unit prices appropriate for the unexpected work needed; or the required quantities of work may be lesser or greater than expected. In such instances, the precise wording of the contract and the nature of the discovered conditions will affect the outcome. Unknown subsurface conditions conceivably might make a contract impossible to perform, or the intended work of a contract useless.

CASE

Excavations for a building uncovered, beneath a top crust of gravel and clay soil mixture, an indeterminate depth of black organic matter that made it necessary to design radically different foundations.

This discovery made it necessary to abandon the original fixed-price contract. If in the original contract the concrete foundations had been subject to remeasurement and repricing at agreed unit prices, a new contract could have been negotiated for only the foundations. If concealed and unknown conditions are part of the very nature of a contract, as in the restoration of an old building, it is likely that the only kind of contract fair to both parties is one based on the direct costs plus a percentage fee.

13.5 SUBSURFACE CONDITIONS IN CM PROJECTS

Because of their contractual makeup, **CM projects** often provide a greater degree of flexibility in the selection of a particular contract to suit a particular set of conditions affecting part of the project's work. In traditional contracting, a fixed-price prime contract is usual. Therefore, the work in a substructure—often more equitably done under a unit-price contract—usually is included within the scope of the prime fixed-price contract. Often, a fixed-price contract is without the necessary provisions (such as a schedule of unit prices and a specified method of measurement) to make simple and equitable modifications.[13]

In a CM project, it is simpler to have substructure work in a separate unit-price contract, as the other work of the project is in separate contracts. Also, a construction manager often is more at ease with other kinds of contracts and is more ready and able to use them.

REFERENCES

1. Robert F. Cushman, Esq. and John P. Bigda, Esq., Eds., *The McGraw-Hill Construction Business Handbook*, 2d ed. (New York: McGraw-Hill, 1985).

2. William Jabine, J.D., *Case Histories in Construction Law* (Boston, Mass.: Cahners Books, 1973).

3. Bruce M. Jervis and Paul Levin, *Construction Law; Principles and Practice* (New York: McGraw-Hill, 1988).

SUMMARY OF MAIN POINTS

- Site conditions and the conditions of existing work, either below ground or elsewhere, may affect the costs of work in a fixed-price contract, which should equitably provide for such contingencies.

- Concealed conditions may be below any surface; usually, they are those below ground, but may be part of any existing work. All construction potentially involves subsurface conditions.

- The level of contractual risk relates to the amount of information available; with little design or experiential information, there is a high level of risk.

- A risk is better taken by the party with more control over the effect of the risk. A risk over which neither party has any control should be minimized (e.g., by insurance) and any remaining risk shared proportionately according to each party's potential gain.

- Risk arising from a site's subsurface conditions usually is better taken by the owner, but an owner can contract to do otherwise, and should do so without any misunderstanding.

- All risks falling on a contractor must, in the first instance, be assumed to be allowed for in the contractor's bid and fixed-contract amount.

- A construction contract should be specially designed for the particular work and risks involved.

- In a fixed-price contract, if an owner seeks freedom from risk he probably pays for it.

- Another kind of contract should be used where there is a predictably high risk from concealed conditions (e.g., a cost-plus-fee or a unit-price contract) or, in a fixed-price

contract, cash allowances should be provided for specific contingencies.

- Unsuitable ways of dealing with or avoiding risks include: vagueness in and omissions from bidding documents; weasel clauses that unfairly seek to put unreasonable risk on a contractor; and alternative prices in bids.

- In a fixed-price contract's documents, the designer should make clear any design assumptions made affecting the cost of the work (e.g., depths of foundations), and the contract should provide for modifications (i.e., changes in the work).

- A fixed-price contract must provide a proper basis for valid bids, and bidders should find it in the bidding documents; otherwise, bidders should consider: (a) declining to bid, (b) bidding with a view to exploiting weaknesses in the documents, (c) making a bid that includes allowances to cover the indeterminate risks.

- Writing contracts: those who prepare bidding documents should consider and include what is necessary, equitable, and economic for both parties. In law, ambiguities go against the writer.

- The common-law requirement of a fixed-price contract is a completed project (e.g., building, railway, etc.) suitable for the intended purpose for which the work was designed. The wording, meaning, and intent of a contract is definitive, even if every detail is not specified.

- Specific risks often can and should be identified and provided for by a contract (e.g., by specifying work not included, such as the blasting of rock) so that a bidder need not have to assume the worst case and the highest probable costs.

■ Precepts for dealing with subsurface conditions: a written contract expresses the entire agreement (the parol-evidence rule) and courts will apply the rule of reasonableness (i.e., what was foreseeable at time of making a contract?).

■ If discovered subsurface conditions were not reasonably foreseeable at the time of making a contract, a modification to the contract may be in order, but a contract's specific wording is paramount. Courts will enforce harsh contract requirements.

■ Are discovered conditions materially different from those indicated or usually encountered? If so, a claim for extra costs or time may be valid.

■ A fixed-price contract is for a complete job for the contract sum: the contractor is assumed to know this and to have understood the documents and risks involved.

■ A contract can require anything legal and agreed to by the parties, providing it is valid and enforceable; therefore a contract should be made and used with care and understanding. If necessary, consult a lawyer.

■ The proper time to read and understand a contract is before making an offer. If necessary, have a lawyer explain a contract before bidding, particularly if confused or in doubt.

■ When writing bidding documents designers should make them equitable, use no weasel clauses, and arrange for pre-bid meetings to exchange information. Owners need to be aware of alternative contracting methods.

■ Making claims: if a contract and discovered conditions on-site cause hardship, even though the contract seems to preclude any claim, a claim should be made using well-chosen wording and with all the evidence.

■ Parties to a contract can agree to anything that is legal, even a new contract.

■ A party to a standard contract can request a written interpretation by the owner's agent named as interpreter of the contract. However, interpretations are not final; they can be subject to arbitration or taken to court. A lawyer's opinion and advice should be sought.

■ Evidence of discovered conditions: photographic and other recorded evidence (e.g., date, measurements) of discovered conditions that may lead to a claim should be collected.

■ Subsurface conditions in other kinds of contracts: To the extent that a contract has a fixed-price feature, so that contract may be affected by discovered conditions on site.

■ In a CM project (i.e., with separate contracts) it often is easier to deal with subsurface conditions by making the work the subject of a more suitable kind of contract.

NOTES

[1]For more on this topic, see Collier, *Construction Contracts*, 2d ed., (Englewood Cliffs, N.J.: Prentice-Hall, 1987).

[2]See Collier, *Construction Contracts* 2d ed., "The Method in The Netherlands," pp. 269–70.

[3]See Chapter 6 for more on reading documents.

[4]*Williams v. Fitzmaurice* 3 H & N. 844 (1858); quoted by Donald Keating in *Building Contracts* (London: Sweet & Maxwell Ltd., 1955), p. 48.

[5]A number of cases in courts in the United States have indicated that "strict compliance" by a contractor with a contract's specifications is required. However, other cases in certain courts indicate that the rule of strict compliance is not always applied. See, William Jabine, J.D., *Case Histories in Construction Law* (Boston, Mass.: Cahner Publishing Company, 1971) p. 27.

[6]Notice that the standard contract says "required by the Contract Documents," and not shown in them.

[7]*Granberry v. Perlmutter*, 147 Col. 474, 364P2d 211, 212 (1961); cited by Carl M. Sapers, Esq., "Harsh Contract Language Regularly Enforced," *The McGraw-Hill Construction Business Handbook*, 2d ed. (New York: McGraw-Hill, 1985) pp. 15-5, 15-6. This chapter is erudite and educational.

[8]Specifying some work in a fixed-price contract to be done for (say) unit prices, or (say) cost-plus-fee, is like pricing additional work in a change order by one of such methods, as described in Document A201.

[9]Carl M. Sapers, Esq., "Harsh Contract Language Regularly Enforced," *The McGraw-Hill Construction Business Handbook*, 2d ed., pp. 15-4, 15-5. The author cites the case of *Wunderlich v. State*, (65 Cal. 2d 777,56 Cal. Rptr. 473, 423 p. 2d 545, 548 (1967)) in which the court said "if one agrees to do a thing possible of performance, 'he will not be excused or become entitled to additional compensation because unforeseen difficulties are encountered.'"

[10]For an authoritative exposition, see: Marvin P. Sadur, Esq., "Interpretation of Working Conditions," *The McGraw-Hill Construction Business Handbook*, 2d ed. (New York: McGraw-Hill, 1985) pp. 16-7–16-11.

[11]The *Spearin Doctrine* says that an owner warrants the accuracy of such information provided in bidding documents. (*United States v. Spearin*, 248 U.S. 132, 39 S.Ct. 59, 63 L.

[12]The drawings may show standard concrete walls and spread footings. If substantial rock is encountered, much of the concrete foundations may be omitted, and little or no rock blasting may be necessary.

[13]Such a contract would be one that did not have the provisions of Document A201-1987, Subpara. 7.3.6, or something similar.

QUESTIONS AND TOPICS FOR DISCUSSION

1. Define the broad meaning of the term "subsurface conditions" and give several illustrative examples from construction.

2. Explain the relation between risk and information in construction.

3. Explain at least four of the five precepts given for dealing with risks in fixed-price contracts.

4. Describe one method by which unknown underground conditions at a building site might be equitably dealt with in a fixed-price building construction contract.

5. Describe the common-law nature of a fixed-price contract; also describe how the results of the omission of essential design information from a contract's documents

may affect the parties in this kind of contract.

6. Explain briefly (with examples from construction) the rule of reasonableness in law.

7. Examine several actual project specifications and find and cite examples of unreasonable and inequitable contract requirements. Explain why you consider them so.

8. Outline in tabular form the procedures to be followed by a contractor in dealing with subsurface conditions that he expects to be the cause of a claim for extra work.

9. Could unforeseen conditions under the ground at a building site be the cause for a claim and dispute in a cost-plus-fee contract? Explain your answer.

10. Within existing contracting procedures and law, outline a proposed procedure for the examination of bidding documents, the purpose of which is to discover potential inequities and causes of disputes, and to correct them before a construction contract is made.

11. Give an example of subsurface conditions that are not related to the ground of a site, but instead to the work in an existing building. Explain how such conditions might be equitably dealt with in a fixed-price contract.

12. Write definitions for the following construction-related terms to be used in contract documents:
   a. Rock
   b. Existing work
   c. Subsurface conditions
   d. Replace [work]
   e. Excavate [on-site].

13. With a written agreement for construction work at a fixed price that made no mention about changes in the work, what would be the position of each party should the owner wish to make a change?

14

INSPECTION OF WORK

A thing worth doing is worth doing well.
Anon.

This chapter discusses the general inspection of work. Specifically, as it applies to certain trades and their typical problems and deficiencies, you should refer to the many excellent publications of the manufacturers' and trade associations often found in the libraries of specification writers. Checklists are never complete, but they should be added to regularly through the experience gained from inspecting work.

14.1 WHO INSPECTS WORK, AND WHY

The purpose of inspection is to ensure that construction work is up to certain minimum standards of quality. The sources of these standards are:

1. Contract documents, particularly specifications

2. Laws, ordinances, and regulations of government and other authorities with jurisdiction over the work

Owners and designers write contracts stating the owner's requirements and specifying certain standards of work. The primary concerns of public law and regulation, however, are the standards of health and safety affecting persons and property. From the legal sources of these two kinds of standards also derived is the authority of different inspectors:

1. Those whose private authority originates in a construction contract

2. Those whose public authority originates in statute law

The second group is the larger, as there are many with the authority to enter a site and to inspect work. Yet public inspection does not ensure that work will be done according to the requirements of a contract. Through statutes and regulations, public authorities seek to ensure that buildings meet certain *minimum* standards for safety and health. Generally, comfort, style, appearance, and economy in buildings are not the concern of public authorities. A safe and healthy building is to that extent a well-built building, but most owners require more of their buildings and designers.

Inspection of Work Under Contractual Authority

Several people and their representatives may have contractual authority to inspect work in progress and completed:

- The owner
- The designer
- The construction manager
- The contractor
- Independent testing agencies hired by any of the above

To inspect, means to look over in critical appraisal, or to examine officially (Webster's) (i.e., not merely to examine). An inspection, therefore, implies a standard. It also implies approval or disapproval when remedial action may be needed. The standard depends on who is inspecting and with what authority.

Inspection by Owner and Representatives

Standard contracts make limited inspection a duty of the designer. Any other inspection on an owner's behalf requires particular mention and is paid for by the owner. Other contracts may contain other provisions. Legally, it can be assumed that an owner

has a right to enter his own site, unless he has agreed to be excluded. Whether an owner has a right to inspect the work depends on the contract. Even if an owner has no contractual right to inspect, usually there is nothing to prevent or inhibit him from examining the work, except certain safety regulations. Without contractual right, an owner may not, however, take any direct action because of his examination. That is the difference between inspection and examination.

If a contract says an owner has an agent to administer the contract and inspect the work, then the owner may only examine. Many contractors are thankful that usually construction contracts do not say the owner can inspect the work. However, the government, as an owner, usually does inspect the work of its contracts, which therefore should be read with care and understood by bidders and contractors.

Inspection by Designer and Representatives

Although we have seen that a designer usually has more authority on a site than the owner, usually a representative's authority is less than that of the principal. Sometimes, this causes confusion, and instructions without clearly established authority should be verified. At a project's outset, an owner and members of the **design team** should provide the names of their representatives and a description of their authority to the contractor. Most dealings are among individual representatives with limited authority; most of the time representation works, but sometimes there is abuse. The lines of privity of contract are few and clear, while those of authority and responsibility are many and sometimes confusing.[1]

A design team's inspections usually are limited. Depending on the work of a project, the members of a design team might include

- Structural engineers
- Soils engineers
- Mechanical engineers
- Electrical engineers
- Lighting consultants
- Acoustics consultants
- Interior design consultants
- Kitchen, hotel, restaurant, theater, stadium, and other special consultants for interior work
- Landscape architect, horticulturist, and other special consultants for landscaping, gardens, golf courses, and other exterior work
- Specialists in the design of particular and special construction (e.g., X-ray and nuclear protection, environmentalists, earthquake scientists, biologists, chemists, etc.)

The specialists employed are many and various. Their contracts often are with a designer and sometimes, an owner, and often include inspecting the work of their specialty. They are among those whose authority to inspect originates in a contract. In some contracts (e.g., those of government), the designer is not the owner's agent, but an employee (i.e., a public servant). Then the designer is not independent, and is unable to act as an impartial judge of performance or arbiter between the parties.

The purpose of a design team's inspections is to ensure that the quality of the work is consistent with the contract. It is a team effort with each of a designer's consultants dealing with his own specialty as a representative of the designer. As leader of the design team, the designer has the final word in design matters. Also, usually it is the designer who is designated by the contract as the interpreter of the contract and the judge of its performance, but only in the first instance. If you examine the AIA Document A201, Para. 4.1, *Architect*, and Para. 4.2, *Architect's Administration of the Contract*, you will note (in 4.1.3) that "in case of termination of employment of the Architect, the Owner shall appoint [another] architect"; since the contract requires an "Architect who will interpret and decide matters concerning performance" [of the Work] and that (4.2.2) "The Architect will visit the site at intervals…to become generally familiar with the progress and quality of the completed Work and to determine in general if the Work is being performed in a manner indicating that the Work, when completed, will be in accordance with the Contract Documents."

This means that the architect and his or her representatives will not inspect the work to the fullest extent. In fact, Subpara. 4.2.2 says the architect will not make "exhaustive or continuous on-site inspections." Other contracts, however, may require an architect or an engineer or other person to make exhaustive and continuous on-site inspections.

Inspections in a Construction Management Project

If a contract in a CM project is based on AIA Document A201/CM,[2] the situation does not change, and the architect still is the owner's prime agent, the interpreter of the contract, and the judge of its performance. A construction manager is then, in effect, a joint-administrator of the contract with the architect. Certain duties are allocated to each, but the primary duties are still the architect's. The construction manager is an advisor. In other CM projects, the roles may be reversed. Then a CM is the prime agent and the interpreter and judge of contracts, and the architect is the CM's advisor. In some other CM projects, an architect is solely the designer, and plays no part in contract administration at all. To avoid confusion, it is important that contractors in a CM project should know and understand the relative positions and the authority of the construction manager and the architect.

As we have seen, the significant difference between a traditional project and a CM project is the absence of a **general contractor.** Instead, there is a construction manager, represented on-site by a supervisor, and several specialist contractors, some of whom may have subcontractors. Their work is inspected by the construction manager's supervisor, by the designer, and in parts by the designers' consultants. Obviously, inspection in a CM project is easier if all the terms and general conditions are the same in all the separate contracts. It is better to have a standard subsection in all specifications that deals with inspection in general, with other subsections to deal with the particular inspection requirements of the work of each trade.

Inspections by a General Contractor

In a fixed-price contract the prime contractor is solely responsible to the owner for all of the contract work, including the work of subcontractors. (Refer to Document A201-1987, Para. 3.3, *Supervision and Construction Procedures.*) This means that the contractor, or his representative on-site, must inspect the work of the subcontractors. The inclination of some superintendents is to leave inspection of subcontractors' work to

public authorities and to the design team. There are several reasons for this:

- A designer's consultant (e.g., an electrical engineer) is more knowledgeable than a superintendent about the work of his specialty
- Public laws and ordinances require inspection and approval by a professional engineer or by a qualified public official or inspector of certain work
- If the designer (or a designer's consultant) and a public authority inspect and accept the work of a subcontractor, no one else is likely to find fault with the work
- A superintendent may believe he saves time, effort, and costs, if he leaves inspections to others more qualified
- If one of the design team rejects a subcontractor's work, a superintendent avoids conflict with the subcontractor

There is no question as to a contractor's primary responsibility for the proper performance of contract work even if the contract documents are not complete in every detail. Responsibility for and inspection of trade work requires an up-to-date and detailed knowledge of materials and methods. Specifications must be read, understood, and applied. For some contractors, however, approval and acceptance of the work by those with an official obligation to inspect is a practical criterion for saving their own time and effort. This, however, may cause carelessness, a reputation for ignorance of trade work, inadequacy as a manager, and work that is not consistent with the contract. The distancing of designers from exhaustive inspections, as indicated by the latest standard AIA documents, makes inadequate inspection by a contractor even more hazardous.

Inspection and Testing by Independent Agencies

Plumbing, drainage, water supply, electrical, elevators, conveyors, and other service systems usually are inspected and tested as required by law, by officials of public authorities with legal jurisdiction. Other work commonly tested by independent agencies includes

- Soils and other fill material (e.g., for moisture content and compacted density)
- Concrete (e.g., for compressive strength, entrained air, and other qualities)
- Structural masonry units and mortar (e.g., for compressive strength and absorptivity)
- Welding (e.g., for strength and integrity in structural steelwork and piping)
- Lumber (e.g., for moisture content and grades)
- Waterproofing, roofing systems, and sealants (e.g., for material content and integrity of applications)
- Metal-and-glass wall and window installations (e.g., for strength and watertightness)
- Coatings, such as paint (for product quality, thickness, and integrity of applications)
- X-ray protection work (for efficacy and integrity)
- Acoustical work (for efficacy)
- Lighting installations (for illumination)

Any other work may be specified by an owner-designer to be tested. The only constraint is the owner's willingness to pay. An increase in performance-type specifications has increased testing by independent agencies. Some inspection and testing agencies are private concerns, while others are organizations of trade associations. Instead of doing their own inspections and tests, some public authorities will accept tests by private companies and organizations.

In some jurisdictions, inspections by the professionals on a design team are accepted as fulfilling regulatory requirements. Incongruities exist in official testing requirements. For example, while most local authorities require public officials to inspect and test plumbing systems, they may leave it to the designers or independent agencies to inspect and test structural concrete. Both the structural and plumbing work, however, may be designed by professional engineers. If inspection by public authorities is necessary, why not make it consistent and apply to an entire building? Alternatively, why not rely entirely on professional designers (and independent testing) for the quality and conformance of the work they design?

Inspection and Testing by Authority of Law and Regulation

Federal or state laws empower public authorities to regulate and inspect and test certain work while retaining some powers for themselves. Federal authorities with jurisdiction include

- Department of Health and Human Services
- Department of Housing and Urban Development
- Department of Labor (including Occupational Safety, Health Administration, and Labor Management)
- Department of Energy
- Environmental Protection Agency
- Department of Transportation

State and other local authorities such as municipalities with jurisdiction may include those controlling

- Health (including pollution, litter, sanitation, environment)
- Land and natural resources
- Public utilities
- Environmental quality
- Labor and industrial relations
- Transportation (highways)
- Industrial safety
- Elevators and conveyors
- Buildings (including electrical, mechanical, plumbing)
- Water supply
- Planning
- Public works (including streets, sewers, sidewalks, engineering)
- Fire
- Housing
- Traffic
- Signs
- Noise, animals, pollution, and other nuisances and dangers

Delegation and distribution of governmental powers vary, and these lists are neither definitive nor complete. They show the more prominent and convey an idea of the extent of the jurisdiction of laws, ordinances, and regulations over construction. As populations increase, and as the public concern with pollution and the environment also increases, so will the numbers of regulations, and the number of officials to enforce them. Reasons for public inspection of work include

- Safety and health of workers and the public
- Safety of property (real and personal)
- Cleanliness of waterways, air, and sea
- Issuance of permits, occupancy permits, and certificates of completion
- Maintenance of public highways, streets, transportation, public works, and other public services

- Maintenance of public utilities
- Maintenance of environmental quality
- Suppression of pollution and other hazards
- General conformity with laws, ordinances, and regulations, etc.

The purposes and objectives of many inspections overlap. A solution might be to have one professional person responsible for each project for its conformity to all standards, both contractual and regulatory.[3]

14.2 INSPECTION AND TESTING REQUIREMENTS AND PROCEDURES

Inspection and Testing for Contract Requirements

Although standard contracts often combine inspection and testing in their references, we can understand them better if they are considered separately. Other than the cost of waiting for an inspection (a constant part of supervision) inspections generally require little expense, if any, for a contractor. There are three kinds of inspection mentioned in standard contracts

1. Inspection by an owner's agent(s) according to a contract condition and specifications
2. Inspections by independent testing agencies called for by contract specifications
3. Inspection by public authorities with jurisdiction over the work for legal compliance

Testing may be an extension of inspection, but because tests require active participation, so that a contractor incurs some cost, testing must be separately identified. If testing is specified, the contractor should have allowed for it in the contract. Contract wording decides who shall pay for tests. Most fixed-price contracts require a contractor initially to bear all costs of inspection and testing by public authorities required at the time of bidding. (See A201-1987, Subpara. 13.5.1.)

Additional Inspection and Testing

Some tests are not specified, but are called for when an owner–designer believes that part of the work is not according to the contract. AIA Document A201-1987 refers to additional testing and inspection, Para. 13.5 *Tests and Inspections*, Subpara. 13.5.2.[4] If the work in question is inspected and tested and found deficient, the contractor must pay all the costs of inspection and testing (including the costs of the designer's additional services and the remedial work). If the work is according to contract, the owner pays all the costs.

Whether such additional (ordered) inspection and testing could be required by an owner under a different contract with no such contractual provision is a question. If the work in question has been paid for by a progress payment, then the owner should be able to test it. Could a contractor resist ordered testing if the work is not yet paid for? It seems reasonable that a contractor might claim that such work is not yet complete, and therefore not yet ready for testing. Such a response, however, might be considered adversarial.

Payments for Inspections and Testing

Why might an owner in a fixed-price contract want to pay for testing directly, either through a cash allowance or out-of-pocket? One reason is a desire to ensure that the testing agency is truly independent. Another reason for using a cash allowance for payment is the possibility that the extent of certain testing may be indefinite (e.g., the number of samples of poured concrete to be tested). Another reason is that often an owner wants all a project's costs included in a contract sum, as that will be an important figure in obtaining a mortgage.

Inspection of work always adds to an owner's costs, directly or indirectly. Even the inspections that follow the issuance of a building permit are paid for indirectly by the owner. Some inspection on behalf of owners create additional expenses, right from the time of bidding:

CASE

Over decades the costs of certain kinds of work done at a university campus were higher than the costs of similar work done elsewhere in the community. The cause was the rigorous inspection procedures of the university's building department. Painting contractors spoke of adding 10 to 20 percent to their estimates to cover work that had to be redone because of excessively stringent inspection, and mechanical contractors said something similar.

One reason for the extra costs was the specifications that the designers were required to use: that and the inspectors' insistence on impractically high workmanship standards. Anecdotal information always is suspect, but this was checked and found true. Was the high standard of work really necessary, and if so was the resultant cost commensurate or excessive? A reasonable balance is needed between contract requirements, the costs of work, and the benefits received. Often it seems this is ignored when money is paid from the public purse. Specifications should be technically correct and appropriate for a particular class of work.

Some contracts say that "the contractor shall not be relieved of his obligations under the contract by any inspections or tests to completely perform the contract"; i.e., the contractor may have to do more than required for work to pass an official test, and inspections and tests that lead to approval of inspected and tested work do not relieve a contractor of his contractual obligations for the work.

Approval by a Public Authority

That a public authority has inspected and approved work does not imply that it is necessarily acceptable under the contract. A contract often calls for a higher standard of work than that required by an authority having jurisdiction over the work. Official standards for work are always minimum standards.

EXAMPLE:

A fixed-price contract says "provide and place 2500 psi[5] concrete." For his own reasons, the contractor provides concrete with a compressive strength of 3000 psi (e.g., the contractor believes it is better and may want to do a better job). In the long term, such a thing might be to the contractor's advantage, and he may have anticipated it and allowed for it when bidding.

There are however some situations in which stronger is not necessarily better.[6] So, a contractor should be careful when deviating from a contract, no matter his intentions.

Uncovering Concealed Work for Inspection and Testing

This can be a cause of trouble and dispute, consequently, it is mentioned in most contracts.[7] Contract specifications should mention any requirements for inspection and testing of work that ultimately is to be concealed. Specifications also should say how and when a contractor shall give notice that work is ready for inspection before covering the work. Dates for inspections should be in project schedules. If a contractor does not give notice when required, uncovering and recovering such work to the owner–designer's requirements will be done at the contractor's expense, even if the uncovered work is found to be correct.

For a member of a design team, it is sometimes difficult to judge the reason for a superintendent's objections to inspection. Is there something he wants to remain concealed; or is the superintendent really concerned over the disturbance of completed work needed to expose that which the inspector wishes to inspect?

CASE

The specifications required hollow concrete blocks to be filled solid with fine concrete at certain locations (e.g., jambs of openings, junctions of certain walls, etc.). The designer's inspector suspected the filling had not been done. Over vociferous objections from the super' some blocks were removed. There was no filling.

Had the uncovering showed that the blocks were properly filled, the designer would have issued a change order for the restitution of the work. As the blocks were not filled as specified, the owner and designer had to decide what to do. The designer proposed that the contractor should be required to redo the work according to contract. This would have meant extraordinary work and costs involving drilling and pumping fine cement grout into the block cavities. The owner decided to accept a credit. The assessment of the credit was difficult. The costs of the remedy proposed by the designer would be high. The contractor suggested it should be only the cost of the concrete fill omitted, which was a fraction of the estimated costs of remedying the omission. The designer proposed that the credit should be based on value, not cost.[8]

Precepts of Inspection and Testing

The purpose of inspection and testing within a contract is to ensure contract requirements are met, and particularly those of the specifications. Therefore, the precepts for writing specifications apply equally to inspection and testing: Be fair, realistic, current, correct, consistent, brief (not time-wasting), clear, and precise. Inspecting work requires deliberate and critical examination (sometimes, overseeing), knowledge, critical skill, fairness, and experience. An inspector is in a position of trust that can easily be abused. An incompetent inspector may do harm to both parties.

Inspection and Testing for Legal Requirements

A public authority's inspector is not directly concerned with the requirements of a contract. An official's concern is with the requirements of a code, an ordinance, or a regulation, which in turn is concerned with the health, welfare, and safety of persons and property. Consequently, an official's viewpoint is different from that of an inspector employed by an owner or an owner's agent. In parts, many codes are obsolescent: even obsolete. An official inspector has little choice but to enforce a code as it exists. Like the police, the official does not make the law but only enforces it.

If a public inspector seems unreasonable, and this becomes critical, a contractor may consider going over his head to get a ruling from a senior official. A building inspector may insist on a strict interpretation of a code because he believes that is the safer position to take. It does not necessarily follow that he will be offended if he is overruled. All codes contain some mistakes, deficiencies, and ambiguities. Sometimes, a code may require interpretation, and one person's interpretation may be different from another's. Some ordinances are scientifically questionable. For example, the fundamentals underlying the movement of moisture and its restriction within the fabric of buildings, are not all universally accepted.[9] Builders with experience are needed to contribute opinions when codes are drafted so that they are not made by scientists and bureaucrats alone.

14.3 INSPECTION OF PREFABRICATED WORK

Where appropriate, contract conditions should provide for the inspection of work at locations other than a site. **Prefabricated components** may then be inspected and approved before delivery. A building inspector cannot properly inspect glued-and-laminated or steel beams at a site, except to see that the beams have certificates to show that they meet required standards. Similarly, a testing agency may need to test window units in a wind tunnel. It has become increasingly necessary to certify components and products in factories and at testing laboratories as prefabrication has become more common. This also requires special provisions in subcontracts and purchase orders. The supplier of prefabricated components has become as important as a subcontractor, and the old contractual distinction between them may require modification.

Inspection of important prefabricated components frequently includes, when necessary for assurance of quality, destructive testing of samples selected at random by a testing agency. Such components might include glazed windows, glazed window-wall units, roof trusses, and mechanical and electrical system components.

The integrity of tested components must be protected until the completion of a project. Prefabricated components have to be delivered, and often this requires special packaging, temporary bracing, and other treatment to avoid damage in transit. This should be part of a contract's specifications, which also should provide for reinspection after delivery and unloading. Such testing may involve considerable time and expense. A contractor should, therefore, review contract specifications to ensure that their wording adequately describes such processes so that a proper cost estimate can be made. If, in the light of subsequent experience, contract wording is imprecise in the light of what had to be done, a claim for extra costs may be in order.

14.4 THE SUPERVISION OF TRADE WORK

The greater part of construction is the work done by specialist trade contractors. No matter what the contractual arrangement, in building construction it eventually comes down to **trade work**. Because of the fixed-price contract with a general contractor, it has become customary to think of building construction work as contractually divided into two parts:

1. The structural work done by the general contractor
2. All the rest of the work done by **subtrades**.

With the arrival of CM, building a structure has become another major part by another separate contractor, contractually equal to the other parts. Excavation and site work, formwork, reinforcing steel, concrete placing and finishing, all are specialist trades that must be coordinated and managed. The separation of construction management from contracting has occurred and construction can be better for it, providing the managers are qualified. Management is a specialist's work as much as building formwork, placing concrete, and installing mechanical systems. There are two primary measures of quality for all work:

1. The contract, specifically as expressed in the contract documents, and particularly in the specifications, referenced codes and standards (e.g., ASTM), and drawings, and
2. The customary trade practice, generally defined by practitioners and trade associations.

If you are new to supervision or inspection, you will learn not to be surprised at how often builders ignore drawings and specifications and follow their own ideas. Often they are technically correct.[10] Sometimes, they do not realize why something was drawn or specified in an unusual way. Inadequate details and specifications deserve to be disregarded. However, since they are part of a contract, a contractor does so at his own risk.

All contract specifications make references to published standard specifications. These include those of the American Society for Testing and Materials (ASTM), and the Canadian Specifications Association (CSA), and there are others by trade associations.[11] Be sure to have up-to-date copies available for reference; otherwise, it may be impossible to make much sense or use of project specifications. Some materials are more easily checked for conformity than others. Grades of lumber are not always easy to validate. Structural steel members are not usually a problem. Steel rebar may be a problem. Galvanized sheet steel might be questionable because it is not always easy to check its gauge, alloy, and the thickness of galvanized coatings. All trade work has its peculiar weaknesses and problems. Materials that are not easy to check usually are those that most need checking. An insufficient weight of asphaltic material in built-up roofing and waterproofing for example, may not be easily discovered without continuous supervision or by cut tests.[12]

A contracting company's reputation may be a general indication of work quality; it is not, however, an infallible guide. Even well-reputed companies sometimes inadvertently make a mistake or take on a second-class superintendent or worker. The better companies soon make corrections.

14.5 SUPERVISION OF TRADITIONAL PROJECTS

In traditional projects there is one prime contract, and the contractor is responsible to the owner for all of the work. Superintendents and their staff must therefore inspect the work of all subtrades to ensure that it conforms to the contract. In most contracts, the designer does not do full supervision, and a superintendent cannot rely on supervision by public authorities to ensure the specified quality of all work. Therefore, a superintendent must be capable of supervising all kinds of trade work. This is a demanding requirement. Deficiencies occur because trade work sometimes is not properly supervised, because the policy of some contractors is to leave it to the design team or a public inspector to criticize the trade work if necessary.

Mechanical and electrical (M & E) and conveying systems (e.g., elevators) usually are thoroughly tested by public inspectors in most jurisdictions. On larger projects M & E work is inspected by the designer's consultants. Most contractor's superintendents are not qualified to inspect M & E work. As new and complex materials, systems, and methods are used in construction, the matter of inspection and testing becomes increasingly important. "Smart buildings" wired for and operated by computer systems, and building components containing sections of built-in service systems (like those in aircraft), will demand even more sophisticated inspection.

14.6 SUPERVISION OF CM PROJECTS

In a CM project, the specialist trade contractors who would otherwise be subcontractors are full-fledged contractors with direct contracts with the owner. Supervision of all work is the responsibility of the owner's construction manager and his staff, particularly the supervisor on-site. Inspection of work in progress and its approval on completion are two of the primary responsibilities of a construction manager. Construction managers' supervisors must be capable of supervising most kinds of work.

Regarding supervision, there is no fundamental difference between a CM and a traditional project. However, dealing directly with a contractor (instead of with a subcontractor, indirectly through a contractor) should be more effective and efficient. Therefore, supervision in a CM project, by definition, should be superior supervision. If it is not, CM is diminished. Also, if a construction manager does no construction work, all of the work is inspected by a supervisor who represents a CM with no vested interest, and the relationship with trade contractors is an arm's length relationship less likely to be influenced by future work prospects.

14.7 COMPUTER APPLICATIONS TO INSPECTING AND TESTING

Think of computer systems with compact (CD-ROM) disks like those used for recording and playing music, but used instead for recording and reading massive amounts of information. Now envisage the many possible new computer applications to management. The development of computer systems will keep up with all the requirements for inspection and testing; especially given the time it takes for people to change attitudes and methods. Suppose a contractor/construction manager has on disk the following information:

■ The text of the local building code and related regulations with illustrative graphics
■ The contract documents of a current project (textual and graphic)
■ The diary of the project in progress

■ A data base of trade work derived from standard specifications and previous inspection and testing records of deficiencies and their frequencies

Now, with codes and project documents still in printed form, we file the records of completed projects—and they are hardly ever systematically compared. The only way such experience of a project can be used later is through individuals who can recall their experiences. If a specific need arises, they may search the paper files or their memories and say, "Yeah, that happened once before. Let me see, it was on such-and-such a project...." With the information on disk, the situation is radically different. A manager or supervisor can quickly look for key words such as "sealants, elastomeric, defects" (i.e., the key words of a topic, a code, or a contract). Not only is this faster and probably more fruitful than relying on the memories of one or two individuals, it also makes information available to all who can use the system.

Such computer applications, however, depend on the creation and maintenance of free-form text data bases of project records, including project diaries, and all the other documentation created by and for a project. If there is no input, there is no output. If standard management procedures, such as keeping a job diary, are modified to suit computers, an increase in efficiency should follow.

EXAMPLE:

Each on-site computer system in a site office has a comprehensive construction management program (such as that outlined in Chapter 3). Each day the program reminds the superintendent to do certain things (e.g., making diary entries, monitoring certain activities in the work schedule, and expediting a resource). By using a standard diary format (with headings that include, date, weather, inspections done, testing done, test results, etc.), the program automatically transfers diary information into a data base. From a data base, information and data about the results of inspections and tests can be retrieved for guidance in making cost estimates and decisions.

This simple example shows nothing more than the normal function of learning from and applying experience. Using a computer system makes this easier and enables everyone to contribute to and use a company's total work experience. This democratization of information and knowledge is unsettling for some, and so they oppose the use of computers.

SUMMARY OF MAIN POINTS

- The purpose of inspection is to ensure a certain minimum standard of work, according to: (1) the contract, and (2) public law and regulation, which is concerned with public health and safety. A contract's requirements usually go further.

- Contractual inspections may be by an owner–designer, a construction manager, a prime contractor, or an independent agency hired by one of the above.

- Standard contracts preclude inspection by an owner. Usually, an owner may visit his site and examine but cannot take unilateral action without contractual authority.

- Designers (or representatives) usually do limited inspections of the work they design. Members of a design team usually also inspect the work they design. The purpose is to ensure consistency with the contract, not to make exhaustive or continuous inspections.

- In CM projects, the relative authority of both designer and construction manager should be made clear. Usually, the latter does the more exhaustive inspections. In some projects, the designer does no site inspections.

- A general contractor is responsible for the work; however, some rely on public officials to inspect the work of some trades.

- Independent inspection and testing agencies may be hired to inspect work not usually inspected by public officials, including soils, structural concrete, welding, lumber, waterproofing and roofing systems, metal-and-glass assemblies, and coatings.

- Inspections and testing by authorities is widespread and increasing.

- Inspection and testing for contract requirements by owner's agents, independent agencies, and by public authorities, are all mentioned in standard contracts, which require the contractor to pay all fees for inspection and testing required at the time of bidding. Additional inspection and testing may be required (e.g., by Document A201), and if the work is found deficient the contractor pays all costs.

- Inspection required by some owners is excessive, and it increases the costs of work.

- Approval of work by a public authority does not necessarily mean it is consistent with the construction contract.

- Work to be inspected or tested before it is covered up should be specified and scheduled. Uncovering suspected work may be a subject of argument.

- Precepts for inspection require an inspector to be fair, realistic, current, clear, precise, and not to waste time.

- Inspection and testing for legal requirements requires a public official to enforce a code; if this appears unreasonable, it is possible to go to a higher authority. Some codes are obsolescent or flawed.

- Inspection and testing of prefabricated work off-site becomes increasingly necessary, and a contractor should monitor contract's requirements and the costs involved.

- The supervision of trade work follows both the contract's requirements and those of customary trade practice. Supervisors should have copies of standard specifications commonly cited (e.g., ASTM specifications), and a copy of the contract specifications.

NOTES

[1] A lawyer-engineer once said that when something goes wrong in construction usually it is a problem to know who to blame. In part, this is because of the separation of design from construction.

[2] AIA Document A201/CM, *General Conditions of the Contract for Construction—Construction Management Edition.*

[3] In some jurisdictions, architects, engineers, and other professionals can be certified by examination and qualification to approve drawings and specifications for proposed construction work for compliance with building code requirements.

[4] Additional testing is the testing of something already tested but not yet approved, and required by the owner, designer, or anyone with jurisdiction.

[5] psi = pounds per square inch (compressive strength).

[6] Two examples: (1) Masonry mortar that is excessively strong relative to the strength of the masonry units; and (2) certain adhesives that may be too strong for a particular base. This is discussed further.

[7] See AIA Document A201-1987, Article 12, *Uncovering and Correction of Work*, Subpara. 12.1.2; and CCDC2-1982, GC 32–*Inspection of Work.*

[8] Often, the value of work in place is much greater than its cost. But value may be more elusive.

[9] Popular theory in some quarters says houses should be highly insulated, virtually airtight, and with a mechanically controlled environment (e.g., the "R-2000" house). Some dis-

agree, and believe that wood structures should be built to breathe.

[10]Detail drawings of such work as framing, for example, are often ignored by skilled workers, who may know better.

[11]Some trade associations publish excellent technical material that is among the best guides and references for specifiers and inspectors.

[12]Sample pieces of the installed roofing are cut out for examination, weighing, and testing, and the roof system is repaired. This test borders on the destructive and should be a last resort.

QUESTIONS AND TOPICS FOR DISCUSSION

1. Identify the two main sources of quality standards in construction and explain their basic purposes.

2. Does a designer usually inspect construction work, and if so, on what terms?

3. If it is a primary duty of a construction manager to inspect construction work, what need is there for the designer of the work also to inspect it?

4. Discuss an owner's right to uncover and to inspect construction work on his own site when the construction contract contains no specific provisions for inspection by the owner or his agents.

5. Find out and report on the technical equipment and methods used by testing agencies to test
   a. Concrete
   b. Built-up roofing
   c. Structural lumber
   d. Painting

6. Which public authorities have powers to inspect construction work, other than those listed in the text?

7. Investigate the possibility of a civil lawsuit for damages against a local authority with a statutory obligation to inspect construction work, by an owner who finds his work is not according to the building code.

8. Argue for (or against) the proposition that the conformance of construction work with law and regulation should be the responsibility of professional designers; i.e., argue for or against dispensing with all inspections by public authorities.

9. Identify and describe three different kinds of inspection mentioned in construction contracts, and explain the differences among them.

10. If, according to most standard forms of construction contract, a designer (architect or engineer) will only inspect work periodically to see that the work is generally done according to the design, who assures the owner that the work is done according to the contract in all other respects? Is this adequate? Explain your answer.

11. Define: (a) trade work, (b) trade contractor, (c) customary trade practice, (d) defective work, (e) work consistent with the contract.

12. While inspecting work at a construction site, what things should the inspector have? Explain why.

13. On inspecting work you see a serious deficiency. You check the specifications, but find that particular point is not included. What other contractual authority might you be able to turn to support your rejection of the defective work? Use a specific example and give a detailed answer.

14. On inspecting work, you find that certain specified work has not been done. Instead, you find that the contractor has substituted other work of equal quality. What should you do? Give a detailed answer, first stating any assumptions.

15. Define the following terms: (a) level, (b) straight, (c) even, (d) smooth, (e) plumb.

16. Why is an architect's inspection of work under a lump-sum contract governed by AIA Document A201 not necessarily sufficient for an owner?

15

REJECTED WORK
AND DEFICIENCIES

Labor disgraces no man, but occasionally men disgrace labor.
Ulysses S. Grant (1822–1885)

Following inspection, construction work may be found defective or otherwise not according to the contract, and so may require remedial action. This chapter examines the nature of defective and other nonconforming work, and the procedures for rejecting, correcting, or accepting it. Warranties and tolerances in work also are discussed.

15.1 CONTRACT QUALITY REQUIREMENTS

Reviewing the four major elements in construction contracts:

1. Contract quantity: quantities of work indicated in a contract's documents
2. Contract quality: qualities specified for the parts of the work
3. Contract time: time agreed to for completion of the work

4. Contract sum: that agreed to for the work, that is, the contract amount

This chapter deals primarily with the quality of work; however, the other three elements are affected. Quality of work is dealt with generally in the conditions of a contract, and specifically in the specifications and drawings. It also is a subject of common and public law. Contract sum and contract time are stated in a contract agreement (e.g., AIA Document A101). Contract quantity is either implicit in the drawings or explicit in **schedules of quantities.**

Contract Conditions of Quality

Most **general conditions** contain some expressed liability of the contractor for the quality of work for a period (usually one year) after substantial completion. See the index of AIA Document A201-1987, under

Warranty. The references are many, and we look at some aspects of warranties below. Even in the absence of an expressed warranty in a contract, the law says there is an implied warranty that work will be of a standard that is normal in the industry and its trades. If an owner requires more than that, there should be an expressed warranty and pertinent specifications in the contract.

Contract Specifications

The specifications of a contract state specific requirements for the quality of work. To avoid conflicts, drawings should be limited to showing and noting only the different kinds of materials and work, their scope, and extent. Specifications alone should indicate quality. In practice there is some overlap, and as a result often conflict. For small projects, it may be sufficient to write the specifications on the drawings. Whether notes on drawings supersede separate specifications is questionable. It depends in part what a contract says. Contracts like CCDC2 say specifications supersede drawings. The AIA documents say only that they are complementary (A201-1987, Subpara. 1.2.3.)[1]

Because so much is related to the quality of work, including both contract sum and contract time, contract specifications must be carefully written and fully understood. However, a survey of the memberships of the two North American specification institutes probably would reveal few superintendents. Similarly, a survey of courses for foremen and superintendents probably would show that the reading and writing of specifications form only a small part of the syllabus; if the subject is there at all. This is one cause of the problems with construction quality and specifications: there is a lack of education in reading and writing specifications and other contract documents.

Whereas most individuals in designers' offices prefer working on drawings, quality of work can be defined only by words or samples. Training in the writing and understanding of specifications is one of the best ways to learn about materials and methods; it also encourages clear thinking and more effective communication. Also, experience shows that a specification writer is more likely to discover errors and discrepancies in drawings.

Published Standard/Master Specifications

Some information and working examples of specifications come from the standard specifications published by several manufacturers' organizations. There is an axiom for their use: Know the contents of standard documents to which you refer, and supplement them as needed for a particular project. Specifications of the American Society for Testing and Materials (ASTM) and of the Canadian Standards Association (CSA) are well known. Trade association standards also are widely cited. Yet, sometimes these are misrepresented by inappropriate references made by persons who have never read their contents. Remember that most published specifications set minimum standards to be met or surpassed. Like building codes, they do not always state the higher standards sometimes required. The purpose of referring to published standard specifications is the improvement of project specifications through

- Conciseness, and greater readability
- Uniformity, and consistency of standards and practices

- Agreement, as to the minimum standards of materials and workmanship
- Efficiency, in specification writing and production

Better specifications are easier to read and they make it easier to understand a contract's requirements and when work is defective. (It is easier to define what is wrong when you are quite clear about what is right.) Construction managers should not only be competent in reading, writing, and understanding specifications; they should be familiar with all the standard specifications referred to in the codes of the localities in which they work. This means that they must have current copies. How can a contracting or construction management company explain that they have no technical library when so many specifications and building codes refer to standard specifications and trade association standards?

As owner–designers write more performance specifications and as design–build contracts become more popular, so contractors and construction managers will find it necessary to write specifications for trade contracts. Specification writers were among the first to use computers. Word-processing programs and master specifications now make specification writing more efficient, while other programs make it easier to refer to and search specifications.

Despite the great improvements in specifications over the last few decades, conflicts between drawings and specifications still exist. In the 1960s, a specification writer found that two-thirds of his working time was spent checking and correcting the architectural and structural drawings. Some drafters in design offices still cling to obsolete terms and practices (e.g., galv. iron instead of galv. steel). When pencils are replaced by CAD, the same standard terms can be used in both drawings and specifications, and a common language and integrated design and construction information can be used. In the meantime, for a contractor, searching out conflicts among contract documents can be time profitably spent.

The Quality of Work Under the Law

Chapter 14, examined inspections and testing by public authorities and also referred to customary trade practices. Apart from codes and regulations, which are creatures of statute, there are standards recognized by common law: the current and customary trade practices that most specifications cite in order to cover everything not otherwise included. Even without specifications, a contractor owes a certain minimum standard of quality in the work he performs. There is an implied warranty recognized by the law.

15.2 WARRANTY IN CONTRACTS

The AIA Document A201-1987 does not limit a contractor's warranty to any specified period, and making a final payment does not constitute a waiver (by an owner using that form of contract) of any claims against his contractor for defective work, or for work that does not conform to the requirements of the contract documents (as in Subpara. 4.3.5). Other contracts may differ from the standard documents.

A **warranty period** stated in a contract makes its start date critical; i.e., contingent on certification of substantial completion, which is the preferred starting date for warranties.[2] For example, Document CCDC2-1982, GC 24, *Warranty*, requires a contractor to make good "defects and deficiencies in the Work which appear prior to and during the period of one year from the date of Substantial Performance of the Work... or such longer periods as may be specified for certain products or work." Some legal experts hold that work done under warranty during a warranty period does not extend the warranty period.

A prime contractor has the obligations of an **implied warranty** if no warranty is mentioned by a contract. The implication is that work shall be done according to a normal and reasonable standard, given the class of work, its location, and other circumstances. Since a prime contractor always has the obligations that flow from a warranty, it is important that such a contractor ensure that all his subcontractors have similar obligations. The AIA Document A201-1987 also refers to "special warranties" (4.3.5.3) that include warranties expressly required by a contract for such work as roofing and waterproofing. Usually, these are for a specified period.

A construction contract is still in force for the period of its stipulated warranty, but usually there is a statutory limitation. A contract's warranty is not without value, but since it depends on many things, in an owner's mind its value may be overrated. Some things that may detract from a warranty's effectiveness include

- The disappearance of the corporate contractor (some are incorporated for only a single contract)
- The owner's inability to prove that defects and deficiencies appearing in the work are the contractor's responsibility (a common response is that they are design deficiencies)
- Counterclaims that the owner–designer or an occupant have caused or contributed to defects that have appeared.

Perhaps the main value of a contract's expressed warranty is the continued existence of the contract itself, within which legal action may be taken more effectively than otherwise. (See Chapter 5 for subcontractors' and suppliers' warranties.)

In the AIA Document A201-1987, Para. 3.5 (*Warranty*) for the "warranty period" you have to look to Subpara. 12.2.1, *Correction of Work,* to find out that, not the warranty, but the contractor's obligation to correct work "not in accordance with the Contract Documents" is limited to a period of one year (or by the terms of a **special warranty**). As usual, the AIA documents are among the most comprehensive (but sometimes, the most complex) and the most instructive for the student.

An **expressed warranty** is desirable, especially if the intent of a contract is for work of a higher-than-average standard. (An implied warranty requires interpretation.) Some may wonder if an expressed warranty is more an attempt to limit a contractor's contractual liability than to create a benefit for an owner. Therefore, it is advisable for owners to seek legal advice regarding warranties, and particularly about those in contracts for large projects or for construction work of high-quality. A contractor's warranty however covers only the materials and workmanship; it does not imply the adequacy of the completed work as a structure. That is the subject of warranty by the designer, and there is an implied warranty as to the efficacy of the design as shown and specified in the contract documents.

Clearly there are potential conflicts between a contractor's warranty and a contract's specifications. Generally, the primary duty of a contractor is to properly perform the work according to the contract—including the specifications. If specifications or drawings show details or methods that prove ineffectual, it is not the fault of the contractor, providing the contractor has followed the contract documents. However, that is not always easily shown and many contracts shift responsibility onto a contractor, as in the AIA Document A201-1987, Subpara. 3.2.2, which requires the contractor to study the documents and report any errors or inconsistencies. If the contractor finds any and does not report them, he may be liable for their results. That does not seem reasonable or equitable. A design team may spend several years working on a design and producing dozens of drawings and hundreds of pages of specifications: yet a contractor is expected to "carefully study and compare the Contract Documents" and "assume appropriate responsibility" if he does any work "knowing it involves a recognized error."[3]

15.3 REJECTION OF WORK

Rejection of Work by an Owner's Agent

Standard contract conditions provide for defective work to be rejected by the **owner's agent** named in the contract agreement.[4] The rejection of work is not left to an owner because of the presumed absence of technical knowledge and the presence of an understandable bias. In standard contracts, the designer is the interpreter of the contract documents and the judge of contractual performance by both owner and contractor. Obviously, this duty of interpretation and judgment sometimes includes the rejection of defective work. If no architect, engineer, or construction manager is present and is given the responsibility of rejecting work,

then the contractor and the owner are the only people who can decide if work is according to the contract; although, the opinion of either is likely to be biased and to cause dispute. However, many contracts that do not follow a national standard give the owner full powers to reject work. A builder should know this before bidding and consider its probable effect.

Work may be rejected if it does not conform to the contract. That includes work that may be sound but nonconforming. Also, a contractor may be required to show evidence that materials and products used in the work were according to the contract (as in Document A201, Subpara. 3.5.1, under *Warranty*). Most contracts require a contractor to remove nonconforming and defective work and materials from the site unless subsequently accepted by the owner. Such acceptance should be in writing or immediately followed by a change order, and a credit to the owner should be assessed where appropriate.

When an owner decides to accept nonconforming or defective work, usually he will expect a reduction in the contract sum. The critical question is, how much? Standard contracts say different things about how this shall be settled, but it always comes down to negotiation.[5] The rejection of work and the subsequent settlement always should be in writing. The assumption should be that this is an action that eventually may go to arbitration or a court of law. Evidence, therefore, should be established from the outset to prepare against the worst situation. If the worst does not happen, nothing is lost. (There is more on this topic in Chapters 16 and 17.)

When work is not done according to the contract, a consideration for an owner's agent is the effect on his authority in the future should he not reject the work. There also is the effect and result of a possible, subsequent failure of the defective work. To what extent is an owner's agent responsible for the performance of work during and after a contract? There is no simple answer: it depends on the facts and on the interpretation of a contract. The standard contracts clearly say the contractor is completely responsibile for the work. This does not, however, free a designer from responsibility for a bad design, a bad decision, or a wrong interpretation.

The entire question of responsibility in construction is exceedingly complex. Conditions in standard forms of contract often seek to remove the architect–engineer from responsibility on the grounds stated: "The contractor shall be solely responsible for and have control over construction means, methods, techniques, sequences and procedures, and for coordinating all portions of the Work under the Contract, unless Contract Documents give other specific instructions concerning these matters."[6] Also, a contractor in a standard contract must indemnify and hold harmless the owner and the architect (or engineer) and their agents and employees against all claims; except those arising from documents and instructions issued by the owner's agent. However, upon discovering a serious defect or a failure, often it is difficult to decide whether it was the design or the execution of the work that was at fault; or if both are to blame, and how the blame and damages should be apportioned. Presumably, if a designer approves nonconforming work, this would amount to giving an instruction to the contractor, and thereby the designer would take on a responsibility and risk. Some consider this as an argument in favor of a master builder who is responsible for

both design and production of construction work.

Disputed Rejections of Work

Rejection of work frequently will be disputed by a contractor, and some advocate contesting any rejection on principle. Designers and their representatives cannot always judge the correctness of certain trade work. Therefore, their rejection (or approval) cannot always be accepted as final. The judgment of a designer's consultant normally will be accepted; e.g., that of a mechanical-engineering designer-consultant of a mechanical installation. If work is inspected and approved by a public authority, that is a first step toward contractual acceptance. However, it may not go far enough to meet the specific requirements of a contract (e.g., a plumbing code may say nothing about the orderly installation to building lines or the concealment of piping).

A general contractor is responsible for all the work, but most of it is done by specialist subcontractors, and a contractor's superintendent is not always competent to judge the quality of specialists' work (e.g., mechanical systems). A primary requirement is that a super' should know and understand the prime contract's requirements. With mechanical or electrical work, even that may not always be possible. This often puts a prime contractor in an awkward position; with a responsibility for work that the prime contractor does not fully comprehend. Therefore, the prime contractor has to rely on others, the designer's consultant and a public official, to say that certain work is acceptable. This shows up the critical nature of certain (sub)contracts (e.g., for mechanical work) and the content of their documents.

Notices of rejection of work should always be in writing. The procedure followed should be similar to that in making changes in work, described in the next chapter. A written notice of rejection that precedes actual rejection and an order to replace unaccepted work is an intermediate step during which disagreements can be aired. If the rejected work was by a subcontractor, the superintendent should pass on a copy of the notice of rejection. If a notice of rejection is not acceptable and the intention is to contest it, a written disputation should be given to the designer or construction manager. The procedure continues in the same manner as the suggested procedure for change orders. Grounds for disputing a notice of rejection of work and for justifying the work as done might include

- The work was done according to the contract
- The work was done according to a valid modification of the contract
- The work cannot be done according to the contract

There are no other valid grounds for contesting a notice of rejection of work. Let us examine each one.

The work was done according to the contract

This requires an interpretation of the contract documents and a demonstration that the work in question conforms. According to the standard contracts, the owner's agent (designer) is the designated interpreter of the contract's requirements, in the first instance. One cannot say that a contractor can have no opinion as to the meaning of the contract to which he or she is a party. It can be said that in a dispute between a contractor and an owner the de-

cision of the owner's agent governs, subject to interpretation by an arbitrator or a court of law. This is in accord with the dual position of an architect or engineer as both owner's agent and a quasi-arbitrator or referee in a construction contract.

In a dispute over rejected work, a superintendent can request from the owner's agent a written interpretation of the appropriate part of the contract. There is nothing better than writing things down to clarify thinking. Therefore, it is possible that having to write an interpretation may cause an owner's agent to see the contract's requirements more clearly. Meanwhile, the superintendent should write his own interpretation to compare it with that of the owner's agent. If in a fixed-price contract a specification does not specify certain work, the contractor has some latitude.

The work was done according to a valid modification of the contract

This first requires that a valid modification exist. A valid **modification** becomes part of the contract, and the argument then is as above; that the work is according to the contract. Of course, production of a valid change order is the best evidence. If one exists, however, it is unlikely that a notice of rejection of that particular work would be issued. Nevertheless, confusion and mistakes do happen.

By definition, in a standard contract a modification (e.g., a change order) must be in writing. If no modification or other document touching on the subject of the work in question is issued before the notice of rejection, the contractor's position is weak. Substantial evidence, such as a recorded conversation or a diary record relating an oral instruction or direction, might be of some value. So might the evidence of actions taken by the owner's agent before the issuance of the notice of rejection. For example, actions showing that the work in question was done with the knowledge and approval of the owner's agent; particularly if the work in question is nonconforming, but not defective technically. Nonconforming work can sometimes be made acceptable through negotiations; e.g., by an offer to offset the nonconforming with other work (a *quid pro quo*). Another defense by a contractor might be that the work was done according to an inference of the contract.

The work cannot be done according to the contract

This requires the contractor to bring proof. The work shown and described in the contract may be contrary to law, ordinance, or regulation governing the work; or it may be impractical, technically wrong, or physically impossible. Or, the work may be a hazard if it is done in the manner set out in the contract; or it might cause deterioration or damage to other work because it is poorly or wrongly designed. In such cases, the obvious response is that the contractor should first seek an interpretation of the contract; or ask for alternative instructions before performing work that does not conform. Under some circumstances, there may be a justification for not first seeking an interpretation; e.g., an owner's agent may not be available when instructions are needed, and the work may have to proceed nevertheless.

Impossibility of performance of work puts an onerous requirement for proof on a contractor. Why did not the contractor raise this matter at the time of bidding, or at the outset of the work? In such cases, a lawyer's advice may be needed. In court cases, so much depends on local law, the facts of the case, and on the court itself. Therefore, it is not easy to predict an outcome, even if similar cases have been decided. Some general guidelines follow.

The Supreme Court of Colorado has said that impossibility (of performance) is a defense against breach of contract. The Court defined impossibility as having a practical rather than an absolute meaning. It said that "impracticability because of extreme and unreasonable difficulty, expense, injury or loss involved..."[7] was a suitable defense. The Supreme Court of Colorado also said the important question was not the distinction between impracticability and impossibility, but "whether any unanticipated circumstance has made performance of the promise vitally different from what should have been within the contemplation of both parties when they entered the contract. If so, the risk should not fairly be thrown upon the promisor": the contractor, in the case in question.[8] These words are confirmation of the precept in this text that a contracting party is not obligated by anything that was not foreseeable at the time of making the contract.

In construction terms, a contractor is not obligated to do anything that he could not have foreseen while making his estimate, and until the time of submitting a bid. If during the performance of work, something appears that was not foreseeable that causes the contractor unreasonable difficulty, expense, or loss, the contractor may claim that it is impossible under the law, even if it is not absolutely impossible, but only highly impractical. Clearly, such a claim must involve a degree of impracticability assessed in the light of the circumstances and facts of a particular case. It appears it is a valid defense if a contractor can show that the something was not reasonably foreseeable before the contract was made.

Impossibility of performance may be a valid defense for not doing work. There is less likelihood that it can be a defense for doing nonconforming work in place of work deemed impossible without first getting approval. On finding that part of a project's work is practically impossible to perform, the contractor should give the owner and his agent notice and request instructions. The only reason or justification for performing nonconforming work without instructions is that it is essential work done in an emergency. (Emergencies are discussed in Chapter 21.)

It should be noted that law courts have not always insisted on absolute compliance with the drawings and specifications in construction contracts. There are circumstances under which only substantial compliance (not full compliance) may be acceptable. If a contractor believes he has acted in good faith in the performance of the work, part of which was rejected, the contractor might consider contesting the rejection. If he does, he should proceed with care and properly document everything in preparation for a court action should that become a reality. Evidence might include photographs, written reports, diary records, written expert opinions, and other substantive evidence.

Remember that preparation for legal action does not imply an intention or even a desire to take a dispute into court. Rather, it reflects an intention to ensure that all possible evidence is obtained and documented. Also, it helps in a way to ensure that a dispute will not go to court. A dispute may go instead to arbitration; or it may be settled between the parties through discussion and negotiation. Whatever the recourse, proper evidence is vital. That is why an attitude that anticipates going into court is recommended.

Substantial performance is an important idea in construction contracts. Everyone should be familiar with it as set out in the standard contracts (see Chapter 11). Strictly speaking, the law requires total and exact performance of a fixed-price contract before the contractor receives payment, but practical considerations and contracts usually have made substantial performance sufficient. This does not mean, however, that an owner, acting on the advice of his agent, cannot hold back some payment; i.e., to the extent that certain minor parts of the work were not done; or to the extent that certain deficiencies in the work have not been made good. Usually it does mean that an owner cannot withhold substantial payment because the contract has not been totally and exactly performed. Here we see the doctrine of reasonableness applied.

No decision by an owner's agent is absolutely final, even when a contract says it is final. Many contracts follow the national standard contracts and provide for arbitration of disputes to avoid, if possible, a court action. Even if a contract makes no such provision for arbitration, disputing parties may mutually agree to seek it. Sometimes, written notice of an intent to seek arbitration or a judgment is enough of itself to bring about a settlement. If arbitration cannot be reached by mutual agreement, it cannot be enforced. Everyone is entitled to due process, and therefore nothing can legally prevent a plaintiff from going to court. The pertinent question is, can a plaintiff afford it? (Arbitration is discussed in Chapter 17.)

In dealing with situations that may lead to a court action, a limited knowledge of legal principles is useful in recognizing that such a situation exists.

Specific legal problems, however, cannot be solved by reading a book. As with all contractual and legal matters, the advice of a lawyer should be obtained.

Everyone involved in construction should know of at least one lawyer who regularly deals with construction cases. To seek counsel from a lawyer who is not familiar with construction and construction cases may prove expensive.

Rejection of Work by Official Inspectors

Successful appeals against rejection of work not conforming to law, ordinance, or regulation are uncommon, but they do happen. That fact should encourage a builder to believe that there really are times when his opinion is more creditable and valid than that of a public official. For most practical purposes, however, assume there is no recourse for a contractor whose work is rejected on statutory grounds. Provisions for appeal and due process may exist, but usually the time and effort required may make anything other than the correction of rejected work impractical. However, in some situations, an official may be conservative simply because he does not want to take a chance on being wrong. If a superior overrules the official, he may not mind, since the responsibility has shifted.

If work is rejected and the work is sound, but correction of the work is impractical or impossible, the contractor should negotiate a tradeoff or find a way to get the rejection set aside. The advice of an expert consultant as to a code's interpretation may

be helpful. Often, regulations are like nets: they catch fish, but they are full of holes. Sometimes, regulations can be turned against themselves. For example, when forbidden by a code to use a particular exterior facing, the builder threatened to apply paint in garish colors—which was not proscribed by the code.

Permits for construction usually are issued after building officials check the documents for compliance. Providing the work is according to the approved documents, a builder does not expect work to be rejected for not conforming. However, sometimes it happens. A plan-checker may make an oversight. Or, on the grounds of public safety, a fire chief may require work to be changed even though it is according to the approved drawings and specifications. The justification is that life and safety supersede all else, which is difficult to dispute despite the problems and costs it may cause. Normally, such changes justify a change order and adjustments to the contract. A contractor cannot be expected to carry such costs, although some contracts may unfairly say otherwise.

Contracts require work to be according to current laws. Once documents are approved for the issuance of permits the work must be done accordingly. In the case of an onerous decision by a building inspector, however, the possibility of an appeal to higher authority need not be ruled out.

15.4 CORRECTION OF DEFECTS IN WORK

Correction by Contractors

Most standard contracts require a contractor to "promptly correct the work rejected." But what does "promptly" mean? Usually it means what an owner's agent says it means. Words such as "promptly" and "immediately" in contracts should either be defined or replaced by more definitive terms. The word "immediately" was found by courts to mean within a reasonable time, and the meaning of "reasonable" depends on the circumstances. Some may consider several days reasonable. One day may be too long for others. If contract time is critical, specific time limits for action on all notices given in the contract should be made part of the contract's conditions. In one contract, the following general condition was used:

> On receipt of a written Notice of Rejection of Work, the Contractor shall respond within 48 hours to the Construction Manager with a plan and schedule for the correction of defects for the Construction Manager's approval, and shall start to correct the defects within 5 days of receipt of the Notice of Rejection of Work, and shall complete the correction of the defects within the time indicated in the approved schedule. If correction of defects is not started or completed within the time limits indicated in the approved schedule, the Owner may, subject to the Construction Manager's approval, implement the provisions of the Condition— *Owner's Right to Carry Out the Work.*

Such a condition does not avoid or solve all the problems of making good defects and contract time; it does give an owner's agent more power than the word "promptly." Time limits for starting and completing work need to be reasonable according to circumstances. On completion,

corrective work should be inspected by the owner's agent. To ensure that the record is complete, written approval should be issued if the correction is acceptable. Frequently it is not possible to remove and replace defective work, and additional remedial work must be done while part or all of the defective work remains.

EXAMPLE:

It may not be practical, for example, to remove a reinforced concrete column in which the embedded reinforcement is inadequate. The only solution may be to jackhammer away the part of the concrete, and to place extra reinforcing steel and concrete around the column's perimeter.

Where all or part of defective work remains, consideration of the loss in value and appropriate recompense may be necessary and equitable. In this case, because of the additional work to the column, it is made larger in diameter; consequently, floor space is lost and possibly, therefore, rental income.

Acceptance by an Owner of Defective or Nonconforming Work

An owner may decide that it is more expedient to accept rejected work and to obtain some adjustment of the contract sum. Parties to a contract always can mutually agree to make changes in their contract. Common sense and legal precedent show that more than just the actual costs of remedial work may be involved. A screw may be worth only a few cents, but like the proverbial nail its absence may be critical and cause a disproportionate loss.

EXAMPLE:

Without incurring great expense, it may not be possible to install omitted insulation on concealed pipes after the piping work is covered. However, the total cost of the heat loss caused by the absence of insulation might be much more than the costs of the missing insulation.

Common sense and legal precedent say that the loss in value of a building, or the economic loss, may be considered when a contract sum is adjusted for the acceptance of defective or nonconforming work; e.g., in the case of enlarged columns, the owner might claim a credit calculated from the lost floor area at a going rental rate for a number of years. A contractor's responsibility lies in the intent of a fixed-price contract (e.g., the construction of a commercial building for rental) and not simply for the installation of several products. This illustrates that often the value of a project is greater than the sum of its parts. The value of insulation should be greater than its costs, otherwise it was foolish to require it in the first place.

Correction of Work by Owners

If a contractor fails to correct defects, or to replace nonconforming work, the owner can have the necessary corrective work done by others. This right usually is in a condition entitled "Owner's Right to Carry Out the Work,"[9] or something similar. Under such a condition, if a contractor defaults, the owner may undertake the entire work or any part of it. The standard contracts spell out the details of the relevant rights and duties. Practically, however, it is not always easy for an owner to find another contractor to complete the work of another without paying a premium. Such a condition may, therefore, be a last resort. The nature of the work in question and the scarcity of work are the main factors affecting the use of this contractual right.

If by default an owner undertakes to perform work in a contract, subsequent disputes over costs are probable. Therefore, the work should be done with care and probity, and meticulous records kept. The operating assumption should be that a court action will follow. Detailed diary entries should be made, and records of all work and all costs should be complete. Additional services required of the owner's agents and their consultants and staff also should be recorded. Make detailed records and take photographs of any extra work needed because of the interruption, any changes in the work, and any exposed subsurface conditions.

Termination of Contract by Owner

The ultimate reaction of an owner to a contractor who has breached the contract is for the owner to terminate the contract. Standard contracts state specific causes for termination and the need for written certification by the owner's agent that sufficient cause exists. This must include a breach or repudiation of contract by the contractor that shows no intention to be further bound by it, nor to any longer accept its obligations. Obviously, only a serious default on a contractor's part constitutes a breach or repudiation. The AIA Document A201-1987, Para. 14.2 *Termination by the Owner for Cause*, lists four causes for an owner's termination:

1. Not supplying enough proper workers or materials

2. Not paying subcontractors
3. Not obeying laws and regulations
4. Substantial breach of contract

If an owner's agent certifies in writing that such cause exists, the owner may (following certain contractual requirements) accept the contractor's repudiation and seek certain legal rights, and may

- Terminate the contract
- Take possession of the site
- Take over all the work, materials, equipment, etc.
- Withhold further payment to the contractor until completion of work

Failure to correct defective work may not constitute a breach of contract; it depends on the nature of the defects, the wording of the contract, and on its interpretation by the owner's agent. The AIA Document A201 does not mention failure to correct work as a cause for termination by the owner. An owner should seek legal advice before taking such drastic action.

15.5 REJECTION OF WORK IN COST-PLUS-FEE CONTRACTS

It is a common question as to who pays for defective work that has to be redone in a cost-plus-fee contract? No matter what happens, some believe that the owner always pays for everything in a contract of this kind. That is not reasonable. An owner should only be expected to pay for work properly performed.

EXAMPLE:

In a cost-plus-fee contract, if because of faults a wall is built, demolished, and rebuilt, the owner gets only one wall.

Why should the owner have to pay for more? That is not within the essential nature and intent of a cost-plus-fee contract unless the contract or owner-designer indicates otherwise.

There is no reason a contractor should apply less construction expertise in a cost-plus-fee contract: a type of contract that implicitly relies on a greater degree of trust in a contractor's skill, experience, and honesty. A cost-plus-fee contract should not protect a contractor from his own mistakes.

The common misunderstanding apparently stems in part from the practical difficulty of separating the costs of work from the costs of correcting mistakes. It is a situation that requires careful supervision and honesty. In a maximum cost-plus-fee contract, there is a limit to the cost that an owner pays, and that limit mitigates the effect on the owner's expenditure for correcting defects. However, the same precepts about costs apply in all kinds of cost-plus-fee contracts. To avoid misunderstandings, cost-plus-fee contracts should explicitly deal with this topic.

15.6 REJECTION OF WORK IN CM PROJECTS

The subject of this chapter is applicable to all trades, their work, and all contracts. Everything concerned with rejected work applies equally to a contract with a general contractor and a contract with a specialist contractor in a **CM project**. Connections and interfaces among the work of the different contractors in a CM project always require special attention; especially from the construction manager responsible for coordinating all the work. A CM project inevitably involves an owner's agents in those aspects of work that exist near the boundaries of separate trade contracts; including the physical connections, interfaces, and tolerances between the work of two or more trades. Although in a traditional project the division of work among trades is the prime contractor's responsibility, in a CM project it is decided by the owner's agents who write the documents the of several separate contracts. Whereas a general contractor has some room to shift the boundaries and scope before subcontracts are let (and given the nature of subcontracting, possibly even later), an owner–designer must commit to the division of work among separate contracts by describing them precisely in the documents of the separate contracts. Otherwise, problems with defective work in a CM project are no different. An owner of a CM project should receive better supervision and coordination because these are primary duties of a construction manager.

15.7 TOLERANCES IN CONSTRUCTION WORK

This is not a common subject, yet it is an essential part of design, construction work, and quality control. Physical tolerances are essential in all work, but frequently none are specified. This can make the approval or rejection of work argumentative. When one discusses tolerances, accuracy and quality are implied, as are the degrees to which deviations from a specific standard will be tolerated. The word tolerance means the allowable (tolerable) deviation from a standard. Usually the term is associated only with weight or dimension, but it applies to any standard and to acceptable deviations.

EXAMPLE:

A metal window, 4 feet by 5 feet in size, cannot be installed in an opening in a masonry wall that is also 4 feet by 5 feet. The window opening must be larger than the window itself, within certain tolerances that should be indicated.

Masonry and concrete walls cannot be built to specific dimensions except to within certain tolerances. Also, the tolerances for masonry and concrete work are much larger than those for metal windows. Different work requires different tolerances.

EXAMPLE:

An architect may specify exposed concrete to be finished to a smooth and solid surface. Without actual examples, it may be difficult for a bidder to know exactly what will be acceptable. In such cases, approval first of a sample is a prerequisite. Also, the specification should state acceptable tolerances in trueness, smoothness, and solidity of surface.

Absolute accuracy is impossible, and high precision is sometimes impractical or unnecessary. The acceptable tolerances in one field are very different from those in another. Therefore, it follows that:

All dimensions and all qualities in construction must be subject to specific tolerances. Unless tolerances are specified, it is not reasonable to reject work based on deviation from a loosely specified standard.

Similarly, such terms and phrases as: level, plumb, straight, true to line, and true to plane are all meaningless unless the specifications also state acceptable tolerances.

EXAMPLE:

What is accepted as level for a concrete slab in a house may not be level for a concrete slab in a laboratory. In the house, tiling or carpet may be laid on the slab. On a laboratory floor sensitive machinery may require levelling to very fine tolerances.

What is acceptable as level in a house may be quite unacceptable in a laboratory. Not only are tolerances in dimensions necessary to fit things together, they also are necessary to permit joints to be made, sealed, and controlled, and for machinery and equipment to be properly installed.

EXAMPLE:

A space of approximately $\frac{1}{8}$ inch between a metal window frame and the surrounding masonry may just suffice to install the window frame; it may not be enough however to enable the perimeter joint to be properly sealed.

A space of ½ inch may be too wide, and ¼ too narrow, depending on the type of sealant to be used. Paradoxically, a wider space between wall and window sometimes may result in a better-sealed joint.

It is a mark of good specifications that they contain specific tolerances for both dimensions and specific characteristics of all kinds of work. Without specific tolerances one must resort to arbitrary opinions. Without specific tolerances in a contract, a court of law probably would seek to establish reasonable and customary tolerances for the trade work in question. Far better to avoid a dispute in the first place and to state the tolerances for work in the documents.

Even if contract documents omit tolerances, they are nevertheless necessary and are implicit in the nature of work. Upon the rejection of work, an effective defense by a contractor may be that the dimensions and characteristics in question are within the customary tolerances for the particular class of work and that anything more onerous should be specified. Evidence of customary tolerances may be obtained by requesting expert opinions from established practitioners in a particular trade.

Some standard specifications and manuals of practice give tolerances in work. Establishing tolerances later may and be an expensive procedure resulting in a modification. If a designer decides not to specify tolerances, they are by default left up to the contractor, and probably there will be no ground for complaint by the owner–designer. For some parts of the work, a designer may specify shop drawings to be prepared and submitted for approval. Shop drawings normally show required tolerances. It is the prime contractor's responsibility to check and approve shop drawings for acceptable tolerances and for the accuracy of dimensions. Providing the work conforms to the general design, the designer may not be concerned with the tolerances shown in shop drawings.

15.8 COMPUTERS AND DEFICIENCIES

If contractors and designers recorded in free-form data bases[10] all the documentation of projects, from contract documents and their modifications to the superintendent's project diary; if we had the history of every project on computer disk; if we then examined these and discovered why deficiencies occur in the performance of construction work, we would find that often the cause is defective communications.

SCENARIO I:

The contractor's estimate, which made his bid the lowest, was produced manually and in too short a time; it contains errors of omission and several errors in arithmetic. Even with no errors, the bid still would have been the lowest. The contractor doubts he will make any profit. On site, the contractor's superintendent has no copy of the estimate. He has had no training in specifications, dreads paperwork, has read only parts of the specifications, and has only an incomplete comprehension of the project's details. Meanwhile, the project manual remains largely unread, because it is practically unreadable and the superintendent is daunted and does not know how to read it effectively.

SCENARIO II:

In a project's specifications, 15 percent of the selected products will eventually prove to be bad choices.[11] The result is several deficiencies in the work, the responsibility for which can never be categorically determined. The designer blames the contractor, and the contractor blames the specifications.

These scenarios illustrate all-too-common situations. The industry is divided by a chasm across which the designers attempt to communicate with the contractors. Frequently, however, the gap is too wide, and their dialects differ. They could communicate with a newfangled electronic system, but the problem of dialect will still remain. They need a common language.

REFERENCES

1. *A/E/C SYSTEMS Computer Solutions* (published quarterly), P.O. Box, 310318, Newington, CT, 06131-0318.

2. Robert F. Cushman, Esq., and John P. Bigda, eds., *The McGraw-Hill Construction Business Handbook*, 2d ed. (New York: McGraw-Hill, 1985).

SUMMARY OF MAIN POINTS

- Quality of work is dealt with generally in a contract's conditions and specifically in its specifications. More knowledge of specifications is needed.

- Standard specifications issued by trade and manufacturers' associations establish minimum standards; they should be used properly and appropriately.

- Writing specifications is a skill needed by prime contractors and construction managers.

- Discrepancies and inconsistencies between drawings and specifications remain a major source of disputes and claims.

- Quality of work and design generally is covered by implied warranties recognized by law.

- Warranties expressed in AIA standard contracts are not limited by a stipulated period. An obligation to correct defects usually is limited to one year from substantial completion.

- A contractor's contractual obligation to study the contract documents and report any errors and inconsistencies is onerous and possibly unreasonable.

- Rejection of work as defective in AIA contracts is the designer's duty, as judge of performance. If work is sound but not consistent with contract, a designer must consider his duty and the possible failure of that work. If an owner agrees to accept sound but inconsistent work, usually the contract sum is reduced.

- A contractor is responsible for work's performance and for means, procedures, and coordination, unless specific instruc-

- tions say otherwise (A201). Many claims and wasteful disputes are caused by the separation of design from construction.

- Disputed rejections of work may be countered by a claim that the work was done according to the contract, or the work was done according to a valid modification, or the work cannot be done according to the contract.

- Impossibility of performance has been held by a court as a defense against breach of contract. Also, a court may not insist on absolute compliance with a contract, and may instead accept substantial compliance.

- Specific legal questions and problems should be taken to a lawyer.

- Work rejected by an official inspector, if nonconforming but sound, might be the subject of an appeal or a tradeoff.

- Correction of defective work is required to be done promptly, a term which requires clear definition.

- Defective work may not be removable, in which case other contiguous work at the contractor's expense may be needed. Any resultant loss in building's value should be compensated (e.g., for loss of rental space, for heat loss).

- An owner may correct defective work and charge the contractor if he or she will not comply.

- Termination of contract work by owner may be valid if the contractor does not supply enough resources, pay subcontractors, obey laws and regulations, do what is required, and so breaches the contract. Termination should only be undertaken following legal counselling.

- Work rejected in a cost-plus-fee contract should be made good at contractor's expense.

- In CM projects, rejected work may cause more contractual problems because there are several separate contractors.

- Tolerances in construction work are necessary, but often neglected in contracts; if not specified, they are by default left up to the contractor. Tolerances are required for both dimensions and workmanship.

- Deficiencies in documentation and communication contribute to conditions that lead to deficiencies in construction work.

- Computer systems can help to solve communication problems in the construction industry, but there is need of a common vocabulary.

NOTES

[1]Some owner–designers amend Document A201 to make specifications govern drawings in the event of conflict.

[2]Substantial completion is best declared and certified by the designer or construction manager. Final completion is less suitable as a starting date for warranties because it may be too long after substantial completion and occupation by the owner, and post-completion damage could occur.

[3]Read A201-1987, Subpara. 3.2.1, and ask yourself: How much time and cost is involved in doing what is required? Also, Marvin P. Sadur, Esq., "Interpretation of Working Conditions," *The McGraw-Hill Construction Business Handbook*, 2d ed. (New York: McGraw-Hill, 1985) pp. 16-2–16-20.

[4]See A201-1987, subparas. 3.5.1 and 4.2.6.

[5]The Document A201-1987, para. 12.3, "Acceptance of Nonconforming Work," says the reduction in a contract sum will be "appropriate and equitable." An owner should consider both reduction in value and in cost.

[6]AIA Document A201-1987, Subpara. 3.3.1.

[7]William Jabine, J.D., "Case Histories in Construction Law" (Boston, Mass.: Cahners Publishing Co., 1973), p. 58.

[8]Ibid., p. 59.

[9]As in A201-1987, Para. 2.4.

[10]Such as, *askSam* by askSam Systems.

[11]See Mark J. Kalin, "Trends and Tips in Specifications Management," *A/E/C Systems Computer Solutions*, Winter-Spring, 1992, p. 18. In his article, Mark J. Kalin cites a "major building product manufacturer" who claims this proportion of mistakes. He also cites *Engineering News-Record's* cover (dated 17 June 1991) saying, "84% of Contractors say specs have major omissions."

QUESTIONS AND TOPICS FOR DISCUSSION

1. Describe the four main elements of work and its performance stipulated in fixed-price construction contracts.

2. In which construction documents is "quality" mainly described, and what should the relations be among contract documents concerning the quality of work required? What of quality of work not mentioned in a contract? What may an owner expect?

3. Describe in detail the procedures for a contractor contesting the rejection of construction work in a contract.

4. On what several specific statutory grounds can public officials reject construction work in your locality? Report on appeal procedures.

5. Discuss and compare the significance of defective work in fixed-price and cost-plus-fee contracts, and the effect of its correction on contract time and contract sum.

6. For the following items of work, write a suitable specification clause for each and select and include practical tolerances:

    a.   Level concrete floor slabs to receive resilient flooring
    b.   Concealed surfaces of concrete foundation walls
    c.   Exposed exterior surfaces of concrete walls above-ground and in an institutional building

7. Explain and compare the different kinds of warranties in construction.

8. Obtain the drawings and specifications for a building project and look for discrepancies and inconsistencies between them. Describe those discrepancies discovered.

9. Looking at AIA Document A201, on what contractual grounds may construction work be rejected?

10. Explain the difference between "cost" and "value" of building work using illustrative examples, and explain the significance of this to an owner who has deficiencies in the work of a construction contract.

11. When might it be expedient for an owner to accept work that is sound but inconsistent with the contract? On what grounds and to what practical extent may such an owner seek recompense from the contractor? State your answer in terms of precepts and principles.

12. Write an argument for (against) the proposition: That deficiencies in documentation and in communications between designers and contractors contribute to deficiencies in construction work.

C H A P T E R

16

CHANGES IN WORK AND OTHER MODIFICATIONS

A change is usually for the worse.
Anon.

This chapter examines modifications to contracts, especially changes in work, which are common and significant in fixed-price contracts. For that reason the published standard contracts deal with them in some detail; particularly the AIA Document A201.

16.1 THE NATURE OF MODIFICATIONS

Modifications to Contracts, Generally

The definitive term **modification** is useful in referring to changes of all kinds made in contracts.[1] Not all contract modifications are changes in work; e.g., a modification might change the calendar date for progress payments. **Change orders** for changes in the

quality or quantity of work, and resultant changes in contract time or contract sum, also are examples of modifications. Modifications to a written contract must be in writing and may include drawings and other documents.

Change Orders

Changes formalized by change orders are one kind of modification to a contract that comes in several forms and arises from several sources:

- **Changes in the work** (its quantity or quality) within the general scope of a contract required by the owner.
- **Minor changes** consistent with the contract issued by an owner's agent (architect/engineer) that do not cause a change

in the contract sum or in the contract time.

- An increase in contract sum or contract time, or both, because of changed contractual conditions or other causes claimed by the contractor.
- A decrease in contract sum or contract time, or both, because of changed contractual conditions or other causes claimed by the owner.
- An adjustment to contract sum or contract time, or both, initiated by either party because of the discovery and effects of previously unknown physical conditions at the site.

We shall examine each of these in more detail. Our primary concern is with changes in fixed-price contracts, and in other contracts with a fixed-price element; i.e., unit-price contracts and contracts in which there is a stipulated maximum cost or a target figure. Even cost-plus-fee contracts may have changes of certain kinds, especially if the fee is fixed.

Changes in Work Required by an Owner

Changes generally are possible only in a fixed-price contract if the contract says the owner can make changes; i.e., the possibility of changes was agreed to in principle and in advance of any change by the owner and contractor, as in a contract with conditions such as those of the AIA Document A201. Otherwise, changes cannot be made in a fixed-price contract except by subsequent mutual agreement, and except in the case of a contract based on Document A201 that employs a **Construction Change Directive**, (*sic*) discussed later.

Changes may be simple changes; i.e., an addition to or a deletion from the work; or they may be complex changes involving both addition(s) and deletion(s) resulting in a net addition or a net deduction; or there may be changes resulting in a balance and no adjustment to the contract sum, which, nevertheless, should still be formally made.

As a matter of principle, although changes are allowed, there is a limit to the kind and extent of changes that an owner can make in a fixed-price contract without the contractor's consent. An owner cannot change or go beyond the essential nature and general scope of the contract. Where that limit lies is, like most things in contracts, a matter of fact to be determined from the contract documents and other evidence.

Standard contracts require all change orders to be issued with the authority and signatures of the owner and the owner's agent. Except that, in contracts based on Document A201, minor changes (as defined) can be issued by the architect acting alone. Another contract may, however, authorize changes to be made by the owner's agent without reference to the owner; although, now, designers are less inclined to act unilaterally.

In many contracts made by government and certain private corporations in which a designer is a regular employee, the owner and the designer are essentially one and the same. This may have implications for a contractor, as such a designer will not be able to act independently or impartially as arbiter or referee between the contracting parties.

If a fixed-price contract says changes can be made, the contractor already has agreed to changes in principle. The owner–designer then asks the contractor to agree to a specific change order and its effects on time and costs. If the contractor signs the change order, he indicates his agreement and the change order becomes a contract document.[2] Considerable negotiation between the parties, with the owner's agent acting on the owner's behalf, may be necessary to arrive at this state.

To avoid issuing a change order to which a contractor will not agree, some owner–designers first issue a **notice of change**. A notice of change is not a modification of a contract; it is merely an administrative means to a change order. The alternative procedure is to issue a change order that later may have to be modified or cancelled.

In AIA Document A201-1987 (Para. 7.3) a "construction change directive" is directed to be used "*in the absence of total agreement on the terms of a Change Order*" (Subpara. 7.3.2.) [emphasis added]. In other words, if a contractor cannot agree to an owner–designer's change order, the owner–designer can issue a written construction change directive, which is a contract document, and to which the contractor has already in principle agreed. However, there is the key question: How will it affect the contract and the contractor's profit? That has to be answered. In part, it already is answered by the contract condition in Subpara. 7.3.6, of Document A201, which prescribes how the designer will assess the costs. The Document A201, Para. 7.3, deserves study. Notice, however that even with a construction change directive, a change cannot be ordered unless it is within the "general scope" of the contract: a term that remains open to interpretation.

On receiving a notice of change, a change order, or a change directive, a contractor should examine it with care and consider its implications. The superintendent may be the first to receive a notice of change and an immediate response may not be helpful. Assume that there is a notice of change[3] for a complex and major change in the work. Also, assume that after consider-

ing the notice of change, the contractor does not want to implement the proposed change. What courses of action may he take, and on what contractual grounds may he reject the change?

The first ground for rejecting a change is that the contract does not make provision for changes in the work. All standard fixed-price contracts and most others, however, do make provision for changes. Another ground for rejecting a change is that a particular change is beyond the general nature and scope of the contract. If the contract is in a standard form, first a written interpretation of the contract regarding this question by the owner's agent may be requested. As the designer probably is circumspect, and has already considered this question, any interpretation probably will support the proposed change. (If the owner's agent believed the change to be beyond the contract's scope, probably she would never have issued it.) Nevertheless, it is better for the contractor to request an interpretation. Requesting an interpretation emphasizes a contractor's concern about a proposed change. Also, it may cause the owner's agent to pause and possibly reconsider. If the contractor does not agree with the interpretation offered, the contractor may then seek arbitration. Or, finally, following legal advice, and if he thinks it worthwhile, the contractor can seek support from a court of law in contesting a change.

If the contractor accepts the architect's written interpretation of the contract and the notice of change, what is the next step? Probably, to calculate the effect of the change on the contract sum and the contract time. Sum and time are related, since an increase in one probably will mean an increase in the other; it depends on the nature of the change. An increase in contract time normally will lead to an increase in the contract sum because of an increase in job overhead costs, and particularly of supervision. There is more information about pricing changes in Section 16.3.

Minor Changes in Work Required by an Owner's Agent

The fixed-price contract conditions of Document A201 provide for an architect unilaterally to make minor changes that, by definition, will not require changes in the contract sum or contract time. The intent of the provision for **minor changes** is to allow a designer to make changes which are necessary for improved performance of the contract, but that will not affect the contract, its time, or amount. Minor changes are binding on both the contractor and the owner, but they must be consistent with the contract documents. In CCDC2-1982, such minor changes are better described as "additional instructions" (GC 2).

Whether a change is a minor change may be debatable. What a designer considers minor may not be by a contractor who has to make the change. The general idea of minor changes is valid; it is practically impossible to design and perform complex work without some minor changes. Although not primarily intended to correct errors in the documents, this may be a valid reason for making a minor change; providing the contract sum and the contract time remain unaffected. If it appears they are, the contractor should seek a change order and an appropriate modification.

Often there is a certain amount of compromise between a contractor and an owner's agent over minor contractual discrepancies and minor changes. This is acceptable if it is in the best interests of the owner and the project; it also requires a professional attitude by both the owner's agent and the contractor. Here the difference between the strict and sometimes inadequate letter and the spirit of a contract should be acknowledged. Both letter and spirit should have the same purpose, but sometimes the spirit can reach where the written letter cannot.

Claims for Additional Costs by a Contractor

There are specific provisions for claims in the AIA standard contract conditions. This is not true of all contracts. Nevertheless, a contractor always can make claims for additional costs even if a contract says nothing about them. However, if a contract says that no claims for extra costs will be considered (and some have stated that), then the contractor who agreed to it will have to live with it.

The existence of specific provisions for claims provides a head start. They show that, in principle, the owner and his agent will consider claims and modifications to the contract. Primarily, claims are a matter of changes to the **elements of a contract**, or changed conditions under which the work of a contract has to be done. Changes in time and timing, season and weather, are among the main causes. Additional overheads are among the possible increases in costs and may include increased operating overhead costs and increased job overhead costs at the site. (Chapter 17 deals with claims in more detail.)

Claims by an Owner for a Reduction

Possible causes for reduction claims by an owner and the resultant modifications to a contract might include

1. A reduction effected in the costs of the work in a project started not at the

originally agreed time, but at a time more propitious for the contractor.

2. A reduction in the costs of work because of other unforeseen causes that materially affect a contract's time or cost, or both.

Such claims by owners are not common. However their possibility must be recognized, at least as the counterpart of claims by a contractor. A contractor might make a claim for additional costs because a project starts in the winter instead of the summer as previously agreed. Conversely, an owner might seek a change for a later start in the spring instead of earlier in the winter, thereby eliminating the need for temporary enclosures and heating. The AIA Document A201-1987, Para. 4.3, *Claims and Disputes*, defines a claim as "a demand or assertion by one of the parties ... " as might be expected. Later, in the same paragraph, claims for additional costs or additional time refer only to a contractor as a claimant. It would appear more equitable if claims by a contractor in a standard contract were balanced by reference to similar claims by an owner. Perhaps the reason is that owners have no hand in drafting standard contracts.

Claims Because of Exposure of Unknown Physical Conditions

Standard contracts provide for a modification should physical conditions prove to be different from those assumed and upon which the contract was based:

EXAMPLE:

It is not unusual to find that excavation on a site exposes subsurface conditions significantly different from what were expected. A similar situation may occur when altering or renovating an existing structure and concealed work is uncovered.

As before, the same principle applies: Could the exposed conditions have been foreseen at the time the contract was made? If not, grounds for a claim may exist. To avoid misunderstandings and disputes, it is important to state in contracts the assumptions made about subsurface and other concealed conditions. This is necessary to provide a clear and firm basis upon which the costs of the work can be estimated. If the assumptions are mistaken, the contract should be adjusted by change orders. (Subsurface conditions are discussed in Chapter 13.)

An important fact should be remembered. An owner makes a fixed-price contract and pays to limit risk by passing it to the contractor. Also, an owner usually retains the right to make changes in the work through provisions in the contract. Without such provisions, changes in a fixed-price contract would not be allowable. Also, the site, which so often causes changes in work, belongs to the owner. Because of this, it appears reasonable that if there is any doubt about a change and its effect on a contract, the decision should be made in favor of the contractor. An owner should pay a fair price for all the work received.[4]

Disputed Changes

As with all contractual disputes, disputes over changes in a contract based on a standard contract are initially referred to the owner's agent for settlement. Usually it is a requirement for an owner's agent (architect or engineer) to be impartial, as stipulated in some contracts (e.g., AIA Document A201-1987, Subpara. 4.2.12). That, however, is not the case with all contracts, and a contractor should ascertain at the time of bidding the authority of the owner's agent to judge performance and to make interpretations. If either party is not satisfied with a decision or an interpretation, they may agree to seek arbitration, as explained in Chapter 17. A contractor can contest or resist a change order in two ways:

1. By claiming the change is beyond the nature and scope of the contract
2. By requiring a cost or credit for the change that is prohibitively large and in his favor (a high cost or a low credit).

If a contractor's disagreement with a change order is ineffectual, and if the owner insists on the change, under the wording of AIA Document A201-1987, the designer (architect) can issue a construction change directive, and the contractor must proceed and implement the change. The costs of such a change must then be determined by the architect (owner's agent) in the manner specified.[5] For a contractor in some contracts such wording would be considered unreasonable. The precise wording of a contract in all such matters, however, is decisive.

A contractor receives a notice of change and makes an offer. He may negotiate the content with the owner's agent, who should have his own estimate of the costs of the change. If they cannot agree, the owner's agent may withdraw the notice of change or replace it by another. Under Document A201 he may issue a construction change directive. In considering a change and before negotiating the costs of a change, a contractor is advised to consider such questions as

- Can a proposed change be carried out by another contractor, either during or at the completion of the contract?
- Can the work of the contract proceed without the change?
- Is the reason for the change a mistake in the design, or is it a requirement of the owner?

Changes in fixed-price contracts rarely are simply a matter of adding or deducting dollars and days. Besides the reasons for a proposed change, there are other considerations such as

- Disruption of work, and apparent, but not always assessable, extra costs (i.e., due to temporary disorganization, loss of productivity).
- Extra time and effort required of the superintendent, the contractor, and his staff (i.e., extra operating overhead costs).
- Risk of loss due to the inherent inaccuracy in estimating the costs of small amounts of work involved in a change; also, the practical difficulties or virtual impossibility of accurately defining or estimating the costs of deleted work.

The proper calculation of costs related to a change needs an experienced estimator or cost consultant. It is not a matter of simple accounting; it requires a good knowledge of construction and costs. Often there is little or no saving for a contractor in the deletion of small quantities of work. Quantity surveyors and other cost consultants are often better equipped than designers to deal with construction costs. Also, designers often lean toward their client, the owner, in trying to keep down costs, and in this matter it may be difficult for a designer to be objective.

16.2 DOCUMENTATION OF MODIFICATIONS

The importance of proper documentation cannot be overemphasized; especially when we hear of disputes in which a settlement is made more difficult because certain things are stated or imputed without supporting evidence. The importance of putting everything in writing goes far beyond changes and other modifications to contracts, and affects all aspects of contract administration. Always, those involved in contract administration and management should act on the assumption that they are recording evidence in preparation for a judicial hearing—even when there is no such intention. Such an assumption is a preventive measure. The intention is not to cause disputes, but to discourage them. Fundamental to this attitude is the consistent maintenance of project records. For example, among the diary entries should be references to current conditions, including

- Natural conditions (e.g., weather, soil conditions)
- Work conditions (e.g., work done, work completed and started, materials delivered)
- Personnel conditions (e.g., workers, visitors)
- Contractual conditions (e.g., modifications to contract, references to all correspondence and documentation issued and received on matters of contract administration)

Particular attention should be paid to change orders and the notices of change that precede them, and to all other possibly contentious matters and documents. Diary references may be but brief annotations.

EXAMPLE:

April 1, 1992
- Weather: Cloudy, light showers and sunny intervals. Temp. 58–62 degrees
- Received Notice of Change No. 69, d. March 30, 1991, re: substitution of vinyl sheet flooring for carpet in all Type 4 units. Passed to H.O. for estimate of costs. To respond by April 4
- Windows installed up to 11th floor
- Wallboard completed up to 10th
- All plumbing 1st rough-in up to 21st
- All electric 1st rough-in up to 20th

Such entries can be made more easily by providing a standard diary page with printed headings. What a journal is to an accountant, a diary should be to a superintendent: a daily record of events from which stem other events, actions, and other records. A diary is a factual outline of a project's history. A signed diary may be admissible evidence in a court.

Special files for notices of change, change orders, and construction change directives should be set up. All documents should be numbered sequentially and entered on a control form with all the essential information, including dates of replies and other actions. As a cross-check, only the number and date of the notice or change order then need appear in the job diary. All documents, notices, directives, instructions, correspondence, and other material should at least bear the following information:

- A standard project title and number
- Date of preparation and address of place of origin
- Name and title of writer and addressee, and the signature and name of the writer

- A document title consistent with the contract, where appropriate (e.g., Change Order)
- Distribution of copies with names of recipients
- Appropriate cross-references (e.g., in a change order, to an earlier notice of change).

Printed standard forms should be used for all documents used in large numbers. These should be in the concise format of a memorandum (to be completed by hand), with noncarbon copies as required. Documentation and its organization and handling can be efficient. Contract administrators and managers should use the best systems and techniques available. The onus is on management to provide them, and on each individual involved to use the systems provided and to write clearly, concisely, comprehensively, and contractually.

Contractors who are not prepared or able to deal properly with claims, changes, modifications, and disputes in contracts, will lose money. Their lack of preparedness often is in part due to a lack of their own documentation. Meanwhile, other contractors will continue to make money with such contractual matters as are to their advantage. It is healthy for the industry that they should do so. If contract documents were better, fewer claims would succeed.

16.3 PRICING CHANGES IN WORK

Provisions for determining adjustments to a contract sum for changes in the work are set out in detail in the standard contracts.[6] A change in work can be understood as an ancillary contract specially made for the change. It need not be of the same kind as the original contract. Any change can be made and priced by any of the following three methods:

1. Stipulated sum mutually agreed to at the time of making the change.
2. Unit prices mutually agreed to either at the time of making the contract (better), or at the time of making the change.
3. Costs to be determined in a way mutually agreed to, plus a fee to be mutually agreed upon, either when making the contract (better), or later.

There are other requirements, details, and refinements, but these are the three main ways of pricing changes, and they reflect the three fundamental kinds of construction contracts:

1. Stipulated (fixed) price
2. Unit price
3. Cost, plus a fee

Some practical aspects of each method of pricing changes in construction contracts should be examined.

Changes Priced by a Stipulated Sum

Both parties make estimates of the costs of a change and then compare them. If they are close, agreement may be quickly reached. If there is a big difference, both should review the notice of change or the change order. Initially, misunderstandings and different assumptions may cause wide variations. If, after a review there still is a big difference between the amounts, it may be better to try to reach agreement by another method. (There are fewer ways to price omissions than additions.)

Standard contracts require supporting information from a contractor for the stipulated-sum and cost-plus-fee approaches to pricing changes. The AIA documents state the detailed requirements. Presumably, AIA Document A201, requires "sufficient supporting substantiating data to permit evaluation" (7.3.3.1) from both parties, but it does not say so. Additional work may require additional information about the site or the design from the owner-designer.

Some contractors are not willing to take the time to carefully estimate the costs of proposed changes. Instead, they may jump at a price, add an amount as a margin for error, and submit the total cost for approval. Such stipulated prices usually are high, and a contractor may be prepared to negotiate. Often the outcome depends in part on how much the owner and his agent know about costs. The stipulated-sum approach is therefore generally accepted by most contractors, but by fewer construction owners. It is difficult for a buyer (the owner) to negotiate a price when the buyer has no choice but to deal with one seller: the contractor. That is part of the price to be paid for the privilege of making a change in a fixed-price contract. Also, for that reason, a contractor should consider including in the cost estimate of a change an allowance for any expected disruption and increased risk. Changes in the work of fixed-price contracts are really inconsistent with the fundamental nature of the contract, which is why an owner is at a disadvantage.[7] The owner-designer's alternatives are

- Not to make a change, or
- To make a change and agree on costs with the contractor according to the contract, or
- To wait until the work is complete and then hire another contractor to do the work required by the change

Depending on the nature of work and the change, the last alternative may some-times be impractical, but at least it should be considered.

Changes Priced by Unit Prices

If an owner–designer anticipates changes in quantity of work, it is in the owner's interest to have bidders submit an appropriate schedule of unit prices. It is easier to negotiate changes in unit prices with a contractor before accepting his bid. This is the best way for an owner to price changes: before the change is needed. However, it is necessary to be able to anticipate the kinds of changes needed. (In some unit-price contracts and in contracts with quantities, there are unit prices for most work already in the contract documents. Therefore, pricing changes of quantity in such contracts often is straightforward.) For a contractor, unit prices agreed to at the time of a change sometimes are advantageous because of an owner–designer's lack of familiarity with unit prices.

To wait until they are needed to agree over unit prices leaves an owner in much the same position as negotiating the costs of a change by stipulated sum. For an owner, unit prices included in a contract are better. Unfortunately, it is not customary to use unit-price contracts in building projects as fixed-price contracts based only on a stipulated sum are normal. That may change when more designers and contractors become more familiar with the uses of unit prices.

Changes Priced by Cost-Plus-Fee

Most owners are reluctant to proceed with a change in work based on cost plus an agreed fee. Sometimes, it may be the only way; sometimes it may be the fairest way. If the contractual definition of "cost" is clear, and if work will be properly supervised, there should be no problem with a change order priced at cost plus a fee. That is the way set down in Document A201, under Subpara. 7.3.6, following the issuance of a construction change directive. However, the amount allowed for profit and overhead is to be determined by the architect.[8] Also, there may be some difficulties in keeping separate certain costs. There is no reason a major change cannot be priced by cost-plus-fee with a stipulated maximum cost, as with a contract of that kind. Any of the terms and conditions normally found in that kind of contract, such as a cost-savings clause, can be incorporated. The standard fixed-price contracts do not mention this, probably because a change in work sufficiently large to justify use of this method is not anticipated. Nevertheless, as we have seen, any changes in contracts can be made using any other kind of ancillary contract. In judging the ways of pricing changes, consider the pros and cons of the features of other kinds of contracts.

16.4 CHANGES IN OTHER KINDS OF CONTRACTS

Changes in unit-price contracts warrant the following considerations:

- Changes in quality: negotiate new unit prices as needed, based on any appropriate unit prices in the contract (this should be stated as a contract condition)
- Changes in quantity: negotiate new unit prices if a change in quantity is greater in amount than a specified percentage of the contract quantity—often 10 to 20 percent (this should be stated as a contract condition)
- Change in contract time: negotiate new unit prices if overhead costs generally are

included in unit prices; or negotiate a lump-sum adjustment for affected job overhead costs (this should be stated as a contract condition)
- Changes in contract sum: as for contract time
- Changes in contract conditions: as above

View each unit price and its extension (unit price × quantity = cost) as a separate contract sum, and deal with it accordingly. Similarly, for changes in contract time and contract sum, view the entire contract as if it were a fixed-price contract, as time and sum affect the overhead costs and profit.

Changes in the work of cost-plus-fee contracts may affect the fee. If it is a lump-sum, fixed fee, and the changes are significant, then changes should be dealt with as if the contract was a fixed-price contract. The significance of changes depends on their costs, and on the extent to which they affect contract scope, contract time, and fee. Changes in a cost-plus-percentage-fee contract may justify a change in the fee percentage for the same reasons. Changes in maximum cost-plus-fee contracts also may justify modifications to the contract, as if it were a fixed-price contract. No matter the kind of contract, if significant changes are made in its elements, then the whole contract justifiably may be subject to review.

16.5 CHANGES IN WORK IN CM PROJECTS

CM projects consist of several contracts between specialist contractors and an owner. Therefore, all that has been said previously about changes in work applies equally to the separate contracts in CM projects. One difference with a CM project is that the owner's construction manager deals directly with specialist contractors for changes in their work. In traditional projects an owner-designer deals with a general contractor. Dealing directly with the company doing the work, instead of through another, may simplify negotiations. Also, there is no markup for a general contractor in a CM project, although this probably is offset, at least in part, by the management fee (the subject of a separate contract). (A CM fee may be fixed, and unaffected by normal changes in the work, or it may be a percentage fee.) The benefits to an owner of a construction manager's knowledge of costs should be apparent when it comes to negotiating with contractors for changes in work. Because of the construction manager's function, it is imperative that a CM have a wider knowledge of costs than a prime contractor, who often relies on subcontractors to estimate costs.

16.6 COMPUTER APPLICATIONS AND CHANGES IN WORK

We have yet to examine the nature and use of a schedule of values in a fixed-price contract as the basis for applications for progress payments (see Chapter 20). Since they have relevance here, this text will briefly define a **schedule of values** (SV) as a breakdown or analysis of a contract sum according to the various parts of the work, so made as to enable an owner–designer to check and confirm subsequent applications for payment.

Already the standard fixed-price contracts give designers considerable authority in requiring supporting evidence to confirm the accuracy of an SV. With this authority, with the cooperation of the contractor, and with a sufficiently detailed SV in a computer system, it would appear possible for the

valuation of many changes to be arrived at systematically. The idea can be better illustrated by referring to current practices in other countries that employ bills of quantities made by professional quantity surveyors as part of the documentation for fixed-price contracts.

A contract's bills of quantities constitute the ultimate schedule of values. They contain unit prices and are a detailed breakdown of the contract sum. Stored in a computer system available to both parties, bills of quantities can facilitate the pricing of changes, which can be done almost automatically. Programs in the system would have provisions for the input of additional information regarding a particular change in work (e.g., an adjustment to certain unit prices for an increase or decrease in the total quantity of a work item beyond stipulated percentage limits).

Present practices of fixed-price contracting are hampered and made more time-consuming and liable to dispute by a lack of communication and a restriction of the information about a contract and its work. On the one hand, full and complete design information does not always get to the bidder–contractor. Conversely, cost information does not flow easily from contractor to owner–designer. As a result, often there are nonproductive actions and reactions between the parties and their representatives, to the loss of all concerned. A free flow of all information is needed while simultaneously protecting a contractor's right to privacy regarding the division of a contract sum between direct and indirect costs. The knowledge and techniques exist. They need only to be brought together and used to mutual benefit. A computer system is the means.

SUMMARY OF MAIN POINTS

- Modifications in Document A201 refer to all kinds of changes in a contract including change orders, minor changes, written interpretations, and construction change directives.

- Changes in the work of a fixed-price contract are only possible by mutual agreement; they are limited by the nature and scope of a fixed-price contract, even under a construction change directive.

- A notice of change issued by an owner–designer seeks to make a change with the contractor's agreement, and if agreement is reached a change order is issued. (Not used in A201.)

- A minor change in an AIA contract is one that does not affect contract time or contract sum; its purpose is improved performance of the contract. That a change is a minor change may not be accepted by the contractor, who may request an interpretation.

- A claim for additional costs in performing a contract can always be made, even if the contract makes no specific provision. A201 does make such provision. Changed contractual conditions are the usual grounds.

- A claim by an owner may be valid on certain grounds (e.g., omission of temporary heating costs due to a shift in season).

- Fixed-price contracts generally favor the owner.

- A change order can be disputed in two ways: (1) by showing the proposed change is beyond the contract's nature and scope, and (2) by requiring a prohibitively expensive cost or credit (which in Document A201 can be overcome by a construction change directive.) The wording of a contract is decisive.

- A contractor should consider whether a proposed change can be carried out by another contractor, whether the contract work can proceed without the change, whether the change is to correct a mistake, or whether it is a requirement of the owner. The answer may affect a negotiated cost.

- Changes may cause disruption of the work, need for extra supervision, or risk of loss due to inaccuracy in estimating its costs. Often, it is practically impossible to accurately estimate the costs of some changes.

- Documentation of modifications is required in written contracts. As a general rule, view all documentation as preparation of evidence for possible adjudication.

- Methods for pricing changes reflect the main kinds of contracts: fixed price, unit price, and cost-plus-fee. Unit prices are better agreed upon when a bid is made, or when a contract is awarded.

- Changes in unit-price contracts may warrant revised unit prices for changes in quality, quantity, and in contract time and contract sum (if unit prices include overhead costs). Each unit-price item, like the entire contract, is for a fixed price.

- Changes in cost-plus contracts may justify a change of fee, even a percentage fee in some cases.

- Changes in contracts in a CM project are no different but may be easier, since an owner–agent in a CM project deals directly with the contractors. A construction manager should be valuable to an owner in dealing with pricing changes and costs in general.

- Computer applications can make dealing with contract changes easier (e.g., with a detailed schedule of values and a contract bill of quantities in a computer system).

NOTES

[1] The term, "modification", is defined in AIA Document A201-1987, Subpara. 1.1.1, *The Contract Documents*, as: (1) a written amendment to the contract signed by both parties, (2) a change order, (3) a construction change directive, or (4) a written order for a minor change issued by the architect.

[2] A change order is better viewed as a separated but ancillary contract; especially since it can be of a different nature from that of the parent contract.

[3] Some believe that an initial "notice of change" is more reasonable than direct a change order, or a construction change directive. As a contract document, the AIA document's construction change directive reinforces the idea that changes are normal to fixed-price contract. This may not be to the advantage of construction owners. The remarks that follow concerning a notice of change, however, generally are applicable to a change order and a construction change directive, both of which may be challenged by a contractor.

[4] In Canada, at least one lawyer who specializes in construction cases has observed that the courts are generally more inclined to support an owner than a contractor. It can be argued that the same inclination prevails in England. This may not be so in the United States.

[5] AIA Document A201-1987, Para. 7.3, *Construction Change Directives*, Subpara. 7.3.3 requires: (1) mutual acceptance of a lump sum, or (2) unit prices stated or agreed to, or (3) cost plus a fee. The architect decides on a "reasonable" markup.

[6] For example, see AIA Document A201-1987, Article 7, *Changes in the Work*.

[7] The existence of *Construction Change Directives* in Document A201-1987 appears to put an owner–designer in a strong position when it comes to negotiating the costs of a change. Provisions in other contracts may vary.

[8] Percentage markup amounts for overhead and profit, like unit prices, are better agreed to at the time a contract is made.

QUESTIONS AND TOPICS FOR DISCUSSION

1. Explain the contractual difference between a "change order" and a "construction change directive" in a contract based on AIA Document A201.

2. Explain the purpose of a notice of change. Why not issue a change order directly?

3. a. Why should an owner be required to approve of and sign all changes made in a contract? Is it absolutely necessary?

b. How is a minor change defined in A1A Document A201, and how does it differ from a regular change?

4. How can a contractor dispute a change in the work ordered by an owner in a fixed-price contract? Explain in detail.

5. In a standard AIA contract, what specific part does the architect play in making changes in work, and why?

6. Explain the most important prerequisites for a valid change in the work of a fixed-price contract.

7. Discuss the proposition that most problems with changes in work are the result of contractual requirements for pricing changes, or the lack of them.

8. As an owner in a contract, which method would you prefer to use to arrive at an agreement with the contractor as to the costs of extra work? Explain your answer in detail.

9. If an owner expects to make many changes in the work of a proposed project, are there advantages in using a construction manager's services and making it a CM project? Explain your answer.

10. What are the implications of changes in the work of a unit-price contract?

11. What are the implications of changes in the work of a cost-plus-fixed-fee contract, and in a cost-plus-percentage-fee contract?

12. Discuss the purpose and implications of a minor change, as defined in Document A201.

13. Suggest other contractual means for dealing with changes in the work of contracts, other than those found in AIA standard contracts.

14. Outline a proposal to use computer systems for the administration of construction contracts for large and complex projects in which the criteria are economic advantage and the avoidance of litigation.

17

CLAIMS, DISPUTES, AND ARBITRATION

Extra labor and materials costs...$36.35
Mental effort and stress...$ 1000.00
A Contractor

Chapter 16 examined changes in work, and introduced the subject of claims. This chapter further discusses claims. Claims frequently give rise to disputes and arbitration, which also are discussed. Specific legal problems, however, cannot be solved by a book; an experienced lawyer should be consulted. Since claims often indicate problems in contracts, experience with claims should help to produce better contracts.

17.1 CLAIMS IN FIXED-PRICE CONTRACTS

Most claims occur in fixed-price contracts, not only because they are the most common contract, but also because they are the least flexible and, for a contractor, the most onerous. We are mostly concerned with claims that may initiate contract changes. We may classify changes in contracts as follows:

- Changes initiated by an owner–designer that begin with a notice of change, a change order, or a construction change directive
- Changes initiated by a claim made by either party
- Changes classified (in A201) as minor changes and ordered unilaterally by the designer

Out of ignorance or reluctance, a contractor may neglect to make a claim. Some look for claims as a way to make money, and the owners who contract with them complain that it was not long after the work started that the claims began. However, that should not be surprising if, when examining contract documents, deficiencies or inconsistencies are discovered, some of the documents are inappropriate, and possibly a different kind of contract should have been used. For purposes of discussion, two main types of claims can be identified that might lead to changes in a contract:

1. Claims arising from changed physical conditions (of site or work)
2. Claims arising from changed contractual conditions

Expect some overlap with these classifications; nevertheless, they are useful providing one does not confuse classifications with the reality they attempt to reflect.

Claims from Changed Physical Conditions

Claims arising from changed physical conditions often are easier to support and prove because frequently the conditions are self-evident, and may include:

- Different subsurface conditions from those presented in the contract documents, or from those expected
- Physical obstructions or other hindrances on the site that could not have been foreseen
- A reduction in facility or access that could not have been foreseen
- Premature and unexpected occupancy of the work or of part of the work by the owner or others
- Unusual weather or other working conditions that could not have been foreseen

There are other causes, but these suffice to illustrate the related principles and proce-

dures. Because subsurface conditions are critical and are commonly identified with sites, they were dealt with separately in Chapter 13. The fundamentals of claims discussed in this chapter, however, can be applied also to subsurface conditions generally.

Physical Obstructions or Other Hindrances

The first question to ask is, "Could an obstruction have been foreseen by the contractor prior to bidding?"

EXAMPLE:

Standard contracts refer to "separate contractors" employed by an owner on the same site. Should there be no mention of separate contractors in a contract, and should they later appear, the contractor might have cause for a claim, as other contractors possibly could cause obstruction.[1]

The amount of such a claim may be difficult to establish. That is one test for the validity of a contractor's claim: Can the contractor show reasonable grounds and a calculated result (e.g., the loss of a specific sum over a specific period because of certain unforeseen conditions)? Other various physical obstructions may occur.

EXAMPLE I:

In renovation work, the expected departure of occupants may not occur on time, thus making it necessary for the contractor to delay work or to work around them.

EXAMPLE II:

Prior to the start of new work, there may be a delay in demolitions to be done under a separate contract. Or, later, the debris from demolitions is not cleared away by the scheduled date.

Both might be reasons for claims for extra costs or extra time, or both. Extra time relates to actual delays; extra costs, to extra time and the resultant increase in overhead costs, and possibly to reduced productivity caused by hindrance or obstruction. As evidence of loss, a contractor might point to appropriate parts of his cost estimate and compare the estimated costs (demonstrated to be reasonable) with the actual costs incurred.

Reduction in Facilities or Access

If a site, its access, or its facilities are different from that expected at the time of bidding, this may be a reason for a valid claim; it is similar to the one before, and also relates to reduced productivity. Also, the absence of an expected facility on-site may make it necessary for a contractor to provide and pay for alternative facilities, such as

- Temporary water supply brought from elsewhere
- The absence of previously existing facilities, such as a ditch or other means of drainage
- The loss of a site access, requiring the use of less convenient access, or the making of another
- The loss of the use of existing buildings for temporary offices and storage

Claimed costs may include the costs of providing something originally not required (and therefore not included in the estimate and bid), and of increases in overhead costs related to loss in time and production. However, all claims are governed by the contract's wording and intent.

Premature Occupancy of the Work

Bidding and contract documents should clearly state an owner's requirements for any occupancy required prior to substantial completion of the work.[2] Some standard contracts may be imprecise about an owner's right to partial occupancy, and this should be clarified, if necessary, in supplementary conditions. Otherwise, a contractor may assume that he will have a clear run of the site and the work until substantial completion.

Premature occupancy may cause obstruction and related losses. If for example, a tenant's fixtures are moved in prematurely, it might constitute partial occupancy and cause an obstruction. A contract's wording is critical.

Unusual Weather and Other Unexpected Conditions

Unexpected weather conditions can be cause for a contractor's claim for extra time under A201-1987, Subpara. 4.3.8, but not all contracts are the same. A related claim for extra costs may be in order under "reasonable grounds" cited in Subpara. 4.3.7. A contractor might first make a successful claim for time and then, on that basis, claim an extension of time and extra overheads. Also, inclement weather may be cause for claim for time and costs if a connection can be traced to some action, or inaction, by the owner or his agents that caused a delay; or if it can be shown that the weather is unusual and not expected.

Delays by an owner may put a contract's duration between different dates from those first agreed. Then a contractor might argue that a certain condition detrimental to the work and its progress (such as bad weather) would not have arisen if the owner had not caused a change of date. Other "reasonable grounds" might include:

- A *force majeure* (an extraordinary force or event, such as an act of terrorism, or revolution)
- An act of God (an unusual natural phenomenon)
- Any extraordinary condition or occurrence that reasonably could not be foreseen

The success of such claims depends largely on a contract's wording and the disposition of the owner–agent involved. Notice also, in A201-1987, Subpara. 4.3.8, the reference to "data substantiating weather conditions"; an indication of the kind of information and data commonly expected to be used in cost estimating and contract management.

Having considered examples of changed physical conditions, we shall now turn to examples of changed contractual conditions. However, there is some overlapping, and one kind of claim often affects another.

Claims from Changed Contractual Conditions

Changed contractual conditions that may cause claims by contractors include

- A change in a contract's starting date caused by other persons or circumstances beyond the contractor's control

- An extension of contract time for causes originating with the owner, his agents, or his representatives, or other causes beyond the contractor's control
- Interpretations of the contract, instructions, or minor changes made by the owner's agent that the contractor believes are not consistent with the contract
- Delayed payments by the owner to the contractor resulting in additional costs for the contractor
- Anything required by the owner from the contractor that was not part of the original bidding documents; or that the contractor can reasonably contend is outside the intent or scope of the contract as it was made

Undoubtedly, there are other conditions that may justify contractors' claims, but those listed are sufficient to illustrate the principles involved. Notice that A201-1987, Subpara. 4.3.7, acknowledges the possibility of claims by a contractor for additional costs arising from, among other things: interpretations of the contract, and minor changes ordered by the architect. This is an important acknowledgment that an architect's interpretation may not always be valid.

Changed Starting Date

Contractors should always seek a specific starting date for the work as part of a contract agreement, and the owner–designer should issue a **notice to proceed**.[3] A stated contract time without specific dates ignores the possibly critical impact of timing and therefore of season and weather on a fixed-price contract. Other things that may cause additional costs because of a delayed starting date include: possible wage and price increases, and increased costs of materials that might have been avoided had the work started earlier.[4]

Extended Contract Time

If a contractor is able to obtain an extension of contract time, then a related claim for extra overhead costs also may be valid. Some do not understand that a day's delay may cost a contractor several thousand dollars in lost time and wasted expense. Short-term financing costs for a project costing millions of dollars can amount to several thousand dollars a day.

Interpretations of a Contract and Minor Changes

If an **interpretation** of a contract is given, the contractor may have grounds for a claim if the designer's interpretation causes unexpected costs. Normally, a bidder makes whatever assumptions are necessary and reasonable. If a designer's subsequent interpretation differs from what was assumed, there may be grounds for a claim. As evidence, the contractor might produce the original estimate. The legal rule of *contra proferentum* construes an ambiguity in a document against the drafter; therefore a designer's interpretation possibly may be contested on that ground.

A **minor change** may go beyond a contract's intent or scope and require instead a modification of the contract (e.g., a change order). A contractor, however, should not immediately dismiss a designer's point of view just because it is different. A designer may live with a design, its drawings, and its other documents for months or even years before construction begins. To the designer and staff, the documents are so familiar it may never occur to them that the contract's content and intent are not obvious. They may not be able to see certain omissions and discrepancies. However, for a contractor, it might be obvious that something is missing. Initially, therefore, patience and tact are the better way.

Delayed Payments

Delayed payments probably will result in extra financing costs for a contractor. A contractor may suffer other losses, such as noncollectable cash discounts on materials, because of delayed payments. Prolonged delays in payment cause the even more serious effects of a restricted cash flow, such as

- Inability to pay bills
- Lowering of credit rating
- Discontented staff and workers
- Liens on the work
- Financial failure

Many contracting companies operate almost entirely on short-term credit. The harm caused by a drying up of cash flow can be more serious than the extra cost of interest. As mentioned, the standard contracts are quite liberal when it comes to allowing a contractor extra time to complete work; too liberal for some owners.

If a fixed-price contract contains a condition that requires the contractor to pay liquidated damages the question of extra time then becomes critical. In such a contract, however, it is probable that the conditions governing extensions of time will not be as liberal as they would be otherwise. In a more common contract with no liquidated damages, contractors may be less than vigorous in seeking extensions of contract time. But they should seek them vigorously, because extra time causes extra expense, and a granted extension may be a first step in a claim for extra overhead costs. In the early stages a contractor does not know how valuable accrued extra time may prove later when the contract is close to completion.

17.2 CLAIMS IN COST-PLUS-FEE CONTRACTS

In simple cost-plus-percentage-fee contracts, usually no contract time or sum are stipulated: only "costs" (direct costs) and "fee" (indirect costs) are defined. Although it is possible to state a contract time in a cost-plus-fee contract, it is not always necessary, and in a contract with a percentage fee it is not likely, or if a contract time is stated, it may not be significant. In a cost-plus-fixed-fee contract time is significant because of the makeup of the fee.[5]

In **maximum cost-plus-fee contracts,** the stipulated maximum cost is similar to a fixed price, and the maximum cost is adjusted for extras and omissions; therefore, maximum-cost contracts usually stipulate a contract time. So, for the purpose of claims, we can view a maximum cost-plus-fee contract as one for a fixed price.

In simple cost-plus-fee contracts (with no maximum cost), the possibility of claims for extra costs still exists, despite the absence of a contract sum. Mention of a fixed fee should provide the clue—it resembles a fixed price. Usually a fixed fee includes the contractor's **indirect costs** (operating overhead costs and profit). The **direct costs** in a cost-plus-fee contract usually are in the "cost"; sometimes called the **reimbursable costs.** AIA Document A111, perhaps misleadingly, calls indirect costs "nonreimbursable costs." Of course they are reimbursed, as part of the fee.

A careful contractor will only enter a cost-plus-fee contract for a fixed fee if the amount of design information provided is sufficient to allow a reasonable estimate of the fee. A fixed fee is largely dependent on the duration of the contract. If the duration of a fixed-fee contract is extended, the fee may not be enough to cover the overhead costs and the expected profit. Therefore, contract time should always be stated in a cost-plus-fixed fee agreement. If the contract time is extended, the contractor should have a valid claim for additional fees for the increased overhead costs.

In cost-plus-percentage-fee contracts, contract time is usually indeterminate; otherwise, it would be better for the owner to reduce his risk and make a contract with a fixed fee. Does this mean that in a cost-plus-percentage-fee contract a contractor can never make a valid claim for an extra fee (i.e., at a higher percentage of cost)? There are times when such a claim may be valid.

Consider that even in a cost-plus-percentage-fee contract some estimating of costs is needed to establish the fee. A fee covers the profit and the indirect costs. To arrive at a suitable fee, a bidder (or negotiator) has to consider the contractual conditions, the work involved, the probable duration and scope of the contract, the probable total direct costs of the work, the site, and the amount of supervision required.

On some projects, a 10 percent fee is inadequate; on others a 1 percent fee may do. To help the bidder decide, it is probable that some information about the work and the site will be needed. (It also is probable that some is available, as few construction contracts are made without any idea of the work.[6]) Having made the best judgments possible with the information available, a bidder/negotiator then decides on a percentage fee.

Assuming one has a contract with a percentage fee and as it progresses the contractor finds that the contract work is significantly different from what he expected from given information, it is possible the contractor may have a reason for a valid claim for an increase in the fee. Simply put, all contracts require mutual understanding between the parties: some measure of a *consensus ad idem*, (a meeting of the minds). If it is necessary to make an estimate of time and costs before bidding for a contract (and invariably it is, even if it is not done, or done properly), the estimate has to be made with some information and assumptions about the work and the site. If any of these can be shown as erroneous, it is possible that one party may have cause for a claim. The more specific the contract, the greater the possibility of a difference between it and the actuality, and the greater the possible validity of a claim for an adjustment.

A contractor supposedly is an expert, should know the risks in construction, and should be prepared to deal with them. However, it is not always a matter of risk, or of a contractor's knowledge and experience; it is also a question of design information and what is agreed in the contract.

17.3 CLAIMS IN UNIT-PRICE CONTRACTS

Often, unit-price contracts are fixed-price contracts because, although the **quantities of work** are subject to change, and the parties jointly measure the completed work, a total fixed price for the work is stipulated.[7] Conversely, a unit-price contract may be quite different from a fixed-price contract; e.g.,

when a contract's quantities are described as approximate, or patently exist primarily for the competitive selection of a contractor. If a unit-price contract is for a fixed price, then there should be a stipulated contract time; therefore claims for extra costs and extra time may be valid. Once again, the wording of a contract must be examined.

Changes ordered in unit-price contracts are priced by applying to measured quantities appropriate unit prices in the contract. Where there are no appropriate unit prices in the contract, prices should be negotiated. Unit-price contracts often say that any negotiated unit prices must be based on any relevant unit prices in the contract. If a contractor can point to changed conditions, different unit prices may be justified. Often, unit-price contracts say that if actual quantities of work vary from those in the contract by more than a certain percentage (typically between ±10 and ±30 percent), new unit prices must be negotiated to reflect the changes in quantity. Due to the fixed nature of certain costs, it is reasonable to have different percentages for an increase or a decrease in quantities. We already have examined changes and claims related to contract quantity, quality, time, and amount. Next, this text examines some other things that may go to the root of a contract and give rise to claims.

17.4 ILLEGAL WORK IN CONTRACTS

An essential ingredient of a valid and enforceable contract (i.e., one that a court will support and enforce) is a legal object. In the eyes of the law, without a legal object a valid contract cannot exist. The legality and validity of an entire construction contract is not often in question, but it is possible.

EXAMPLE:

If the work of a contract infringes on a development or zoning bylaw, the contract may be considered wholly or partially invalid.

Issuance of a change order for nonconforming work is more likely than a project that is entirely illegal; e.g., a change order for the enlargement of a building space to increase capacity beyond that allowed by law. But some contracts may be wholly illegal.[8] Other illegal change orders have included those for

- The conversion of a designated attic space into living space beyond that allowed by regulation
- The extension of a basement beyond that allowed[9]
- Reduction in exits required for public safety
- The omission of fire barriers and fire stops in roof, floor, or wall spaces
- The use of hazardous materials that support combustion or cause sickness
- The installation of doors unsuitable to prevent the spread of fire
- The installation of wrong hardware on exit doors
- The omission of necessary exit signs, fire alarms, and firefighting equipment

As a whole the contracts were valid; the work subsequently ordered was not, as it contravened certain regulations. The end results of such orders could be disastrous. A contractor therefore is justified in refusing to undertake such work. No contract can overrule the law, and any such change order would be invalid. A contractor who is mis-led and who enters a contract subsequently invalidated by a court (e.g., one that contravenes a zoning code) probably could collect damages from the owner or the designer, or both, depending on the facts. However, it also is possible that a contractor might be found negligent through ignorance of the relevant laws and regulations.

Although AIA Document A201-1987, Article 2, *Owner*, requires an owner to provide specific information about a site and project (legal title, survey, and financial arrangements), there is no specific mention of information regarding the project's legality. However, at law there is an implied warranty that project drawings and specifications are legal and suitable for the purpose intended. If there is any doubt, the advice of a lawyer should be obtained.

17.5 IMPOSSIBILITY OF PERFORMANCE OF A CONTRACT

Unexpected conditions may make it impossible to carry out the work of a contract; or the work may be possible only if done by different means from those originally anticipated. In other words, performance of a contract, or a part of a contract, may be frustrated by conditions beyond the expectations and control of the parties. In such cases, a court may grant relief to a contractor faced with an impossible situation. That does not mean that a contractor can obtain relief from a contract that he merely finds extremely difficult, inconvenient, or too expensive to perform. The fact that the contractor will lose money by performing the work is not of itself a frustration of the contract; although it may be frustrating for the contractor. The wording of the contract will have great significance in making a decision.

Should such conditions arise that a contractor believes they entitle him to relief from a contract, he should first seek legal counsel. If the contractor is unable to achieve satisfaction through the contract itself, he may then consider arbitration, or a court action. However, the costs involved should be weighed carefully against any relief that might be gained.

17.6 LACK OF MUTUAL AGREEMENT

Mutual agreement is essential for a valid and enforceable contract, and a party can seek relief from a contract because there was a lack of mutual agreement because of the following:

- Mistake, as to existence of someone or something
- Misrepresentation, as to the truth of facts
- Nondisclosure, of materially significant facts
- Fraud, deliberate or careless assertion of untrue facts
- Duress, by using threats or intimidation
- Undue influence, coercion through power or other influence

As grounds for obtaining relief from a contract, none of these **torts** may be easy to prove, but all should be understood. Some examples follow.

Mistake

A mistake may be made about something, or of some person. The company with which a person believes he is contracting may not exist. Or, the site conditions may

not be as they were believed to be. How far can a mistake be allowed as a reason for relief? Suppose a contractor believes he has to excavate in sand below the topsoil on a site and can prove that he so believed, and later finds he has to excavate in solid rock. Is that a mistake and is he then entitled to receive extra payment? An answer can be found only in all the facts, but relief is not readily granted.

Errors in an estimate could cause a mistake by a bidder (i.e., an erroneously low bid) and invalidate the bid. To be significant a mistake must be factual and material (e.g., a major arithmetical error). However, if gross negligence can be shown, a mistake may not be allowed. Courts will consider such aspects as the effect on both parties of allowing or not allowing relief. If a wrong estimate and bid would lead to a contract that could financially ruin the contractor, withdrawal of the bid might be allowed. As to whether a contract already exists, and the mistake was not discovered until later, the situation would be different. As to whether a mistake is material and factual and can be proven, a contractor should seek legal advice. An owner–designer has some responsibility to verify a bid's accuracy. The deliberate withholding of important information by one party also could cause a mistake by the other.

Misrepresentation

Misinterpretation may be innocent, negligent, or fraudulent. Information about a site included in bidding documents in good faith, but later shown to be untrue, is misrepresentation; it may make a contract invalid. Should a contractor discover important information provided to be untrue, he should consult a lawyer about having the contract modified or set aside. It is important to note that misrepresentation, although innocent, may be enough to invalidate a contract in whole or part. A contractor may not desire such a drastic remedy as complete invalidation, and might seek only changes in contract conditions and adjustments in the contract time and amount. A contractor should not delay over misrepresentation, since a delay may be construed as acceptance of the existing conditions.

Nondisclosure

If material facts about a site or its work are deliberately not revealed by the owner, a contractor may have grounds for the invalidation of the parts of the contract affected. However, as always, the wording of a contract has the greatest bearing on such matters. An owner must provide all relevant and available information about a site and the work. Withholding information in testhole reports made before bidding may be grounds for a claim for extra costs and extra time if a contractor discovers unexpected subsurface conditions. Such a claim might be based on nondisclosure. Again, the advice of an experienced lawyer is essential.

Fraud

Unlike some misrepresentation, fraud is the deliberate and wilful statement of untruths; or the making of statements without caring whether they are true. If fraud leads a party into a contract the contract may be invalid. Again, immediate action is necessary to avoid the appearance of acceptance of the situation. Delay might mean loss of the right to have the contract invalidated. Therefore, when the possibility of fraud becomes apparent, seek a lawyer's advice.

Undue Influence

Undue influence is the domination of one person by another by a variety of means, and so it is more extensive than duress. It might be duress for an owner to threaten a **low bidder** with a ruinous lawsuit if he will not agree to enter a contract, because the owner realizes there is a mistake in the estimate that led to the low bid. In some instances, a question might be raised about undue influence of an owner over his agent who has the authority to interpret the contract and judge its performance by both parties. This might not touch on the validity of the contract, but it could be grounds for relief.

Duress, or Undue Influence

If a contract is made by coercion, threats, or the improper use of power or influence, the contract may be invalid. Duress is less common, in that it involves direct threats. This is not a practical problem in the making of most construction contracts, although many bidders do make offers that owners believe cannot be refused. However, given the alleged involvement of certain syndicates in construction, duress does appear possible.

17.7 INCONSISTENCIES IN A CONTRACT

Some contracts say that certain contract documents shall govern others if discrepancies are found among them; usually in a declining order as follows:

Agreement
Supplementary or special conditions
General conditions
Specifications
Drawings[10]

In this way, some inconsistencies may be removed in advance, but others in the same document may remain to confound and cause difficulties. If a dispute over a contractual matter arises, it may be worth looking for contractual inconsistencies that touch on the matter in question. Inconsistencies often are the cause of disputes since each party will favor the interpretation that better suits his or her position. The first recourse is to ask the designer for an interpretation of the contract (if the contract provides for this procedure). What if the designer's interpretation is unacceptable to one or both parties? Or, suppose that an inconsistency is the designer's fault, and his interpretation appears less than totally objective, and perhaps is intended to eliminate a conflict in the documents? A court case probably would be protracted and expensive. The answer may be to go to arbitration. First, seek advice from an arbitration body such as the American Arbitration Association.

Some contract documents state that, should discrepancies and inconsistencies exist among them, the interpretation that results in the lesser cost to the owner shall be taken as the correct reading. This is an example of a so-called weasel clause; however, if a contractor signs a contract containing such a clause, he may be stuck with it. Again, consult a lawyer who knows construction.

17.8 CHANGE IN A CONTRACT'S NATURE

As mentioned before, there is a limit to the extent of changes an owner can make in a fixed-price contract. The limitation is that they must be consistent with the intent and scope of the contract and the nature of the work. Exactly what that means is a matter of fact in each contract. However, if many changes are proposed, at some point a contractor can say no more changes unless both parties can come to an agreement over new contractual terms and conditions (in effect, to make a new contract). Again, in such a case consult a lawyer.

A contractor does not have to go to court before using a legal argument in negotiations. After consulting a lawyer, a contractor might also seek an interpretation from the owner's agent. If, however, the contractor does nothing and accepts the change orders without protest, his behavior might be construed as tacit agreement to a new contract that includes the new work. If the project is large, and even if the contractor is not immediately concerned with ordered changes, it would be prudent to obtain early legal counselling.

17.9 CLAIMS FOR LIQUIDATED DAMAGES

A contract may contain provisions for liquidated damages. In essence, it says that if the work is not completed by the date named in the agreement, the contractor shall pay to the owner a certain sum of money as liquidated damages for every day the work remains substantially incomplete after the date for substantial completion. In this context, "liquidated" means settled; in other words, damages settled in advance by mutual agreement.

If late completion will cause financial loss for the owner, and if assessing future actual damages will be difficult, and if a contract's intent is to avoid that difficulty and to provide for and settle on possible damages in advance, then a contract's provisions for liquidated damages likely will be upheld by a court.

Some contracts go further and say that if in the opinion of the designer liquidated damages are due, the owner may deduct them from any money owed to the contractor. If the contractor disagrees with the damages withheld, he is then in the position of having to sue to collect. There are several defenses against payment of liquidated damages by a contractor.

- Actual damages were not incurred by the owner, although the completion of work was delayed
- Actual damages were less than the liquidated damages
- The scope of the contract was extended
- Delay was caused by the owner, his agents, or his employees
- Delay was beyond the contractor's control
- No delay in the work occurred.

Because the precise wording of a contract always is critical, these can only be discussed in general. In contracts with no provision for liquidated damages, a contractor is still liable for actual and proven damages due to late completion of work, and can be sued for such damages by an owner.[11] Similarly, a contractor delayed by the owner also can seek damages. See references to "Damages for delay" in the Index of AIA Document A201.

Actual Damages Were Not Incurred

In writing liquidated damages into a contract, an owner–designer should relate the amount of liquidated damages to the actual damages that probably could be incurred if there is a delay. An owner should make and record realistic calculations of anticipated damages and be ready to produce them if required to prove the amount of liquidated damages stipulated in the contract. If a contractor can show, or lead the court to find out, that no actual damages were incurred, or that actual damages were less than the stipulated liquidated damages, the contractor may obtain relief.

Courts apparently do not look favorably at contractual penalties for delayed completion, especially if the contract contains no provisions for a bonus for early completion. Such symmetry, however, is not always realistic. Time lost may cause a financial loss, but time saved does not always create a financial gain. Also, no matter whether called a penalty or damages, it is how construed by a court that counts, and that depends more on the facts and the figures than on the words in the contract.

Actual Damages Were Less Than the Liquidated Damages

If a contractor can show that the actual damages incurred were less than the liquidated damages claimed, and that the difference would be a penalty if paid, then the contractor may be given some relief. It is often likely that in assessing liquidated damages an owner will err on the high side and make the amount of liquidated damages stated in a contract, in part, a penalty. A contractor's difficulty may be in proving it.

Scope of the Contract Was Extended

If the scope of a contract is altered, it is possible that any provisions for liquidated damages will become ineffectual unless new terms for damages are agreed. Although a contract allows an owner to collect liquidated damages, it is reasonable that the owner should be able to agree with the contractor to add to the scope of the work and still collect damages for late completion after the new completion date, since in effect they create a new contract. Obviously, clear wording is necessary, so that there is no doubt about what the parties have agreed. To that end, a lawyer should be consulted.

Delay Was Caused by the Owner

If an owner causes a delay, the contract period is not extended, and if the date for substantial completion is not changed, it is reasonable that any provisions for liquidated damages should no longer apply. If a contract's time is extended, it seems reasonable that the contract's provision for liquidated damages should remain effective for delays beyond the new completion date, as in the previous case, but this will require mutual agreement. Again, a contract's wording is critical. Also, we must recognize timing when it is significant.

EXAMPLE:

A contract to build a hotel includes provision for the payment of liquidated damages based on loss of income. An acknowledged delay caused by the owner puts back completion until after the high season. A completion after the later date will not cause a loss to the extent originally expected because the season is over.

Every case must be judged by the facts. The parties should be sure to record them all from the outset.

No Delay in the Work Has Occurred

If due to changed conditions there is a dispute as to a contract's completion date, and if the contractor contends that he is entitled to an extension of the contract time, the settlement of such a question may also result in the conclusion that no delay has occurred and that there is, therefore, no liability for damages.

17.10 CLAIMS FOR ORDINARY DAMAGES

Following the discussion of liquidated damages, a word about ordinary damages is relevant, because the awarding of ordinary money damages is a common judgment in a contractual dispute. (Alternatively, in some cases, a court may issue an order for specific performance; or, if appropriate, an injunction prohibiting some action. Damages, however, are the most common remedy and are easier to enforce.)

Monetary damages are payment to an injured party who has suffered a loss by the person who caused the loss. The principle of damages is to put injured parties into the position they would have been in (as far as money can) had the damage not been incurred. If there is no contractual provision, this will require judicial action. With liquidated damages, the object is to achieve a settlement without recourse to legal action. There is, nevertheless, a strong similarity between liquidated damages and ordinary damages, since one is a substitute for the other.

In dealing with damages and other legal matters, and particularly the topics of this chapter, a person should get legal counselling. In addition, certain important procedures and an attitude of preparedness should be adopted by

- Carefully reading and understanding a contract, and governing oneself accordingly
- Acting promptly when a potentially contentious event occurs, and preparing as if expecting an arbitration hearing or a court case
- Establishing and collecting evidence (e.g., records, written statements, interpretations, and confirmations)
- Not waiting to see what develops; since by then it may be too late
- Getting legal counselling at the first sign of a potential problem, dispute, or inequity

Do the necessary minimum of preparation of evidence as a matter of routine (i.e., keep a job diary, put everything in writing, get written confirmations, make records, and maintain files). A computer system and information-management software are most useful. Most problems do not develop into an arbitration hearing or a court case. The recommended preparatory efforts will help to make either less likely. In any event, the result will be of value in better administration and management, and possibly in reaching a settlement.

17.11 AREAS OF CONTENTION IN CONTRACTS

Any dispute may go to arbitration or court; its subject might include

- **Modifications** to contracts (as defined in AIA Document A201), particularly changes (minor and regular), and (in A201 standard contracts) construction change directives

- **Designer's Instructions** and **Interpretations**,
- Disapprovals of samples, shop drawings, test results, and other items submitted according to contractual conditions and instructions
- Notices given or required by contract conditions
- Discovered subsurface conditions (of site and work)
- Claims for adjustments to a contract sum, contract time, or contract requirements for changed conditions and other causes
- Alleged inconsistencies, faults, and deficiencies in the contract documents or other information provided by the owner–designer
- Alleged inconsistencies, defects, and deficiencies in work
- Substitutions for subcontractors and suppliers named and listed in a contract
- Allegedly wrong information given to subcontractors[12]
- Alleged improper performance of the work

The list is incomplete, but the point is made: many contractual topics are potentially contentious and should be carefully handled when they arise, as if a dispute were imminent or already existed, and as if it were already the intention to take the dispute to a tribunal. Lest there is a protest that such a strategy is precipitous and liable to give rise to disputes, we might compare it to strategies among nations. Some say that armed preparedness will lead to war, but history shows that unpreparedness is more likely to do so. Similarly, efficiency and awareness may persuade a party that reason and care are needed if adjudication is to be avoided.

17.12 THE NATURE OF ARBITRATION

Arbitration may be defined as an arrangement or procedure for settling disputes by obtaining the judgment of selected impartial experts. Arbitration is an alternative to judgments in courts of law; its origins are as old as civilization. Its purposes are

- To obtain an early settlement of a dispute by avoiding the delay and costs of going to court
- To obtain the judgment of a person or persons selected because of his(their) objectivity, knowledge, and experience in the field of the dispute
- To keep the hearings and evidence private
- To reach a settlement as economically as possible

Early Settlement of Disputes

Courts of civil law are overburdened by cases. In some courts the backlog is so large that some cases wait for years to be heard. Even after a court hearing and a decision, usually it is possible for one or both parties to make an appeal.

Judgment by Impartial Experts

Usually, arbitrators are selected by disputing parties for their expert knowledge and experience. The parties may agree to ask an impartial person of knowledge and experience, or a body such as the American Arbitration Association (AAA), to appoint one or more qualified arbitrators. Anyone who can make a contract can be an arbitrator, but usually expert knowledge also is required. Judgments by judges or juries are not always the most equitable or effective for disputes involving technical and other

esoteric systems, conditions, and information. A judge listens to opinions of expert witnesses brought by both sides. Frequently these are in conflict because the opinions are of selected expert witnesses. Also, decisions handed down by courts sometimes appear arbitrary, or based mainly on points of law instead of on practical considerations. In arbitration, the rules of evidence are less strict. Therefore, an arbitrator may be able to get a better insight into a construction case than a judge bound by strict rules of evidence and procedure.

Private Hearings

Arbitration hearings are a private matter arising from an agreement between disputing parties, and there is no right of public knowledge. For businesses, the question of privacy is important.

Reduced Costs

There is no guarantee that an arbitration hearing will be less expensive than a court case; however, because an arbitration award cannot be appealed unless there was flagrant misbehavior, the total time spent in arbitration usually will be less than that spent in court. Also, in arbitration there is no pretrial discovery of evidence as there is in a court case and the involvement of lawyers is not obligatory in an arbitration hearing.

Other Factors Concerning Arbitration

Many contracts contain provisions for arbitration. Even if they do not, arbitration always is an open door for disputing parties, but they have to agree to enter either before a dispute arises, or later. Disputes still reach the courts for several reasons.

- Arbitration is a matter for agreement. If the parties to a dispute have not or cannot agree to arbitration, neither can force the other to go.
- Parties may mutually waive their agreed right to go to arbitration and agree to go to court instead.
- One or more of the disputing parties may find parts or the whole of an arbitration award unacceptable. The next step may be to go to court.

Everybody is entitled to due process. It is not legally possible to prevent somebody from going to court, except refusal by a court to hear a case. Neither is it possible to make a valid contract that says the parties shall not take a dispute to court.

Legal precedent suggests that a court will not overturn an arbitration award unless there has been misconduct, corruption, or a refusal to hear evidence in the arbitration. In which case, under the Uniform Arbitration Act for Commercial Disputes, a court is required to confirm an arbitration award and to enter a judgment according to the award. A party dissatisfied with an award may seek the opinion of a higher court, but if the award is proper, it will be upheld.

17.13 ARBITRATION IN CONSTRUCTION CONTRACTS

All standard contracts in the English language appear to contain provisions for arbitration, or at least refer to it. You are therefore urged to examine the wording of more than one standard form on this subject. The wording in AIA Document A201 is comprehensive and instructive. Also, you are advised to obtain and examine a copy of the local arbitration statute in your state or province. There are variations in statutes and in standard contracts.

Standard contracts in some countries provide that all disputes arising from the contract shall go to arbitration, and that the "award of such Arbitrator shall be final and binding on the parties." The AIA forms, however, preclude certain matters from arbitration.[13]

The exact wording and meaning of arbitration provisions in contracts are important, but not all jurisdictions will enforce such arbitration provisions. Before drafting a contract, and before making a decision whether to include arbitration provisions, or whether to seek arbitration, it is advisable to find out the laws applicable in the locality of the proposed work and obtain advice from a lawyer.

17.14 ARBITRATION PROCEDURES

Frustration of Arbitration

If a contract contains arbitration requirements, and if a dispute arises over a matter not precluded by the contract's arbitration provisions, a contractual agreement to settle the dispute by arbitration already exists. However, as has been illustrated, some jurisdictions will not enforce arbitration provisions. Although previously agreed, if one party does not wish to seek arbitration, that party may be able to frustrate arbitration, since the other party cannot proceed unilaterally. Both parties have to agree, and both have to participate. Arbitration thus differs from a legal action, which one party can begin unilaterally, and the other party must then appear in court as a defendant.

Location of Arbitration Hearings

The location of an arbitration hearing may be significant. Locale may be fixed by mutual agreement. If no agreement can be reached, and if the contract contains no provision for deciding on a locale, there may be a problem. For a party to attend an arbitration hearing far from home may create a burden of cost and inconvenience. This may influence a decision whether to proceed or to give in to the other party. The AAA appears to favor as a locale the place where the demand for arbitration was first filed. The fairest and surest way is to make a previous agreement as to locale and to make it part of a contract's provisions for arbitration.

Multiparty Disputes

The AIA standard contract documents limit multiparty disputes and say an architect cannot be called to arbitration as a party without his written consent.[14] There are other limitations in the AIA documents to involving persons other than the owner and contractor in arbitrations. The preclusion of the architect from disputes between an owner and a contractor in arbitration is new. It first appeared in the 1976 edition of AIA Document A201 and probably originated because of earlier multiparty disputes. Should an architect seek arbitration of a dispute between himself and his client, the owner might try to make it a multiparty dispute. The owner might introduce another topic about which he finds himself also in dispute with the architect. To combine two disputes into a multiparty dispute might be advantageous to one or another party; for an architect, it might be a disadvantage. In a dispute over fees, for example, an architect might have a good case. If that dispute is combined with another over the quality of work in which the owner seeks redress from both architect and contractor, the architect's case for fees might be overshadowed or tainted.

Parties should be careful in choosing strategies for the arbitration of disputes: in deciding whether to seek arbitration; in deciding the locale; and in consolidating disputes for arbitration.

Strategies in Arbitration

Not all in construction prefer contracts that make the arbitration of disputes obligatory. Some prefer to have the option to seek arbitration by agreement at the time of a dispute. In that way, they can first consider their chances of winning at arbitration, and go to arbitration only if the chances of winning are good. One contractor who has consistently followed this strategy claims he has never lost an arbitration. He will not go to arbitration unless he has a strong case and believes he can win.

One cannot, however, always judge one's own case or know in advance the development of a dispute: whether one will be a mover or a resister; whether it will be advantageous to have multiparty arbitration, or whether it is better to seek separate arbitrations for different disputes. Consequently, it may be impossible to prescribe or negotiate contractual provisions that will be favorable to oneself in future disputes should any occur. Also, keep in mind that standard contracts are prepared by committees of designers and contractors and that owners are not directly represented. Owners, therefore, are advised to obtain legal counsel when it comes to arbitration provisions in contracts, and they may find modifications to standard contracts advisable.

In contracts with obligatory arbitration provisions, a move toward arbitration by one party may be sufficient to create a change in the attitude of the other who may not want arbitration on a particular topic. Initiative usually is superior to inertia, and sometimes the person who takes the initiative wins by default.

Multiparty disputes can be advantageous to all persons in a situation in which there is derivative liability along a chain of responsibility. An owner has a contract with an architect. The architect has a contract with the mechanical-engineering consultant. If a mechanical design fault is proven, the owner should get damages from the architect who, in turn, should recover from the consultant. In such a dispute, a multiparty arbitration will save time and money. The same is true of disputes involving an owner's complaint about the work of subcontractor. However, with a system in which there are both design and installation faults, there may be nothing to be gained by the owner by joining designer and contractor in a multiparty hearing. Also, an owner should remember that the designer is his agent and representative. He may need his services and goodwill in later disputes with the contractor.

Arbitration Panels

Parties may agree in advance to leave the selection of an arbitrator or arbitrators (usually three) up to an impartial body such as the AAA, or the AIA, or to an impartial person named in the contract. Parties also may delay selection by mutual agreement until such time a dispute arises. It may be difficult, however, to make a mutually agreeable selection in the atmosphere of an acrimonious dispute.

Another procedure requires each party to appoint one arbitrator who then appoints a third as chairman. The wisdom of this procedure is questionable, because the selected persons may simply become champions for their respective designators. The third individual then must act as a referee in a two-sided match. It might be more economical and effective to have just one arbitrator appointed by an impartial person, or persons. If someone other than the disputing parties appoints an arbitration panel, it is not uncommon for one member to be a lawyer and the others, technicians. Another reason for provision for appointment by another, and not by the parties, is to avoid "stonewalling" by a party who may have something to gain by delaying an arbitration hearing.

Proceedings in Arbitration Hearings

Because arbitrations are private they may be as informal as desired, as long as there is no misconduct or corruption. However, it seems that most arbitrations follow the main procedures of a court of law. Guidelines for arbitrations can be obtained from associations such as the AAA. The presence of a lawyer on a panel may be an advantage, providing the lawyer allows for the differences between a court of law and an arbitration hearing. If it follows proper guidelines, an arbitration hearing will be more effective, and there is less chance of misconduct. An arbitrator is not normally legally liable for misconduct on his part (he is liable only for fraud), but he may be removed for misconduct. Duties of an arbitrator may include the following:

- To accept the appointment in writing
- To study the submission to arbitration

(which sets out the substance of the dispute), including

a. The legal rights of the parties to arbitration
b. Verification that the dispute is within the scope of those rights and of the submission made

- To act in concert with the other arbitrators if more than one is appointed
- To give proper notice of meetings
- To hear all parties and witnesses in the presence of both parties
- To take evidence under oath
- To avoid communicating in private with any party or any of their witnesses

There usually is no discovery of evidence prior to an arbitration as there is prior to a court case. Therefore, evidence may be called for during a hearing.

The First Arbitration Meeting

At the first arbitration meeting, the following might occur:

1. Appointment of arbitrator(s)
2. Reading of the submission to arbitration
3. Preliminary statement by the moving party
4. Arrangements for production and examination of evidence, times and dates of future meetings, and arrangements for visits to the site.

Subsequent Arbitration Meetings

At subsequent meetings, the following procedure may be followed (in sequence):

1. Examination, cross-examination, and reexamination of each witness of the moving (initiating) party

2. Examination, cross-examination, and reexamination of each witness of the other party or parties
3. Reply, if required
4. Final argument on each party's behalf

The procedure is similar to that in a court hearing. Parties may mutually elect to be or not to be represented by legal counsel in an arbitration.

Arbitration Awards

An award in arbitration is a written decision of the arbitrator, or arbitrators, appointed to adjudicate a dispute. A good award should be

1. Within the scope of the submission to arbitration, which limits the powers of the arbitrator(s) to the substance therein
2. Made within the prescribed time
3. Unambiguous, unconditional, complete, and final
4. The judgment and decision of the arbitrator(s) and of no one else

Awards may be set aside by a court on the grounds of legal misconduct (e.g., mistake in legal procedure such as would cause an injustice), collusion, or fraud. Otherwise, arbitration awards generally are not set aside by courts. A court may correct or otherwise modify an award if it contains a mistake or miscalculation, but a court will not act as an appeal court and set aside a valid award. In that respect, an award is not unlike a contract, which a court will interpret, rule on, and enforce when necessary. A court will not nullify it or set it aside if it is valid.

REFERENCES

1. Robert F. Cushman, Esq. and John P. Bigda, Esq., eds., *The McGraw-Hill Construction Business Handbook*, 2d ed. (New York: McGraw-Hill, 1985).

2. Bruce M. Jervis and Paul Levin, *Construction Law, Principles and Practice* (New York: McGraw-Hill, 1988).

SUMMARY OF MAIN POINTS

- Most claims in contracts are made in fixed-price contracts, and may give rise to, or arise from, contract changes.

- Changes in contracts include those initiated by a notice of change, a change order, or (as in Document A201) a construction change directive; those arising from a claim; and those called minor changes in A201.

- Many claims may indicate a defective contract, or a contractor with a liking for making claims.

- Claims may arise from changed conditions, either physical or contractual; or from defective documents.

- Changed physical conditions include different subsurface conditions from those shown or expected, unexpected physical obstructions, reduced facility or access on site, premature or unexpected occupancy, unusual weather or other unexpected conditions.

- Changed contractual conditions include a change in starting date beyond the contractor's control; an extension of contract time for a cause of the owner; those arising from an interpretation of the contract, a minor change, or an instruction by the designer; a delayed payment; or anything required of the contractor allegedly outside the contract.

- In cost-plus-fee contracts, to the extent there is a fixed-price element the same causes for claims may exist as in a fixed-price contract.

- In unit-price contracts, to the extent there is a fixed-price element, the same causes for claims also may exist.

- There is an implied warranty that drawings and specifications are legal and suitable, but work may be ordered that is not legal, and the order therefore is neither valid or enforceable.

- Contract work may be impossible of performance, and the contractor may get relief from a court, but impossible does not mean only difficult or excessively expensive.

- Lack of mutual agreement may make a contract defective, and may arise from a mistake or misrepresentation (not deliberate), nondisclosure of facts, fraud, duress, or undue influence (deliberate).

- Inconsistencies in contract documents are common, and may cause disputes and claims. Some contracts say there is a hierarchy of documents (e.g., first an agreement, then supplementary or special conditions, general conditions, specifications, and drawings).

- Changes ordered in a fixed-price contract are limited by the scope and intent of the contract.

- Claims for liquidated damages for late completion can be made if a contract contains the provision; otherwise, an owner can sue for ordinary damages. A contractor's defense against damages: damage was not incurred, actual damages were less than the liquidated damages, the contract's scope was extended, delay was caused by owner or his representative, delay was beyond contractor's control, or no delay occurred.

- In dealing with damages and other legal matters certain procedures and an attitude of preparedness should be adopted. Know the contract, and act accordingly; prepare as if for a judicial hearing; establish and collect evidence; get legal counselling.

- Common areas of contention in contracts include modifications of all kinds; a designer's instructions and interpretations; disapprovals of samples, shop drawings, tests, and submissions; notices given or needed; discovered subsurface conditions; claims for adjustments to contract terms and conditions; alleged inconsistencies, defects, deficiencies in contract documents and work performed; allegedly wrong information; and allegedly improper performance.

- Arbitration is a judicial alternative to a court case to get an early settlement from knowledgeable experts, through a private hearing, and economically.

- Standard contracts recognize arbitration differently; some make it obligatory, while others only propose it.

- Arbitration always requires an agreement between disputing parties to use it; either when contract is made, or later when arbitration is needed.

- Multiparty disputes at arbitration are sometimes an advantage, and sometimes not. Under Document A201, an architect is precluded from certain multiparty arbitrations if he gives no consent.

- Arbitration awards should be: within a submission's scope, in time, unambiguous, unconditional, complete, and final, and made only by the arbitrator(s). Awards are not usually set aside by a court, unless there is: misconduct, a mistake in law causing an injustice, collusion, or fraud. A court may modify an award if it contains a mistake or a miscalculation.

NOTES

[1] See the Index of AIA Document A201 for references to "Separate Contracts and Contractors."

[2] The AIA Document A201-1987, Para. *9.9 Partial Occupancy or Use*, says "Consent of the Contractor to partial occupancy or use shall not be unreasonably withheld."

[3] The AIA Owner–Contractor Agreement, A101-1987, Art. 3, refers to a "notice to proceed." This is important to establishing a completion date when a contract's duration, but not a calendar date for completion, is stated. It also may bear on the payment of liquidated damages, and the commencement of warrenty periods.

[4]Inflation is more usual than deflation, but the latter too should be kept in mind.

[5]Fixed-fee contracts are practically the same as fixed-price contracts when it comes to overhead costs.

[6]While negotiating a cost-plus contract, a contractor should try to find out why an owner is willing to enter such a contract, and why a fixed-price contract is not considered. Sometimes, it is because an owner feels the need to go ahead before the design or other things (e.g., leases) are determined. Sometimes, it is because an owner wants to keep his design options open. Knowing why should help in negotiating the fee.

[7]In building contracts with bills of quantities, the quantities provided usually are accurate quantities. In engineering contracts, (especially those for such as earthworks), quantities provided in the schedules usually are approximate. On this, the contract wording is important.

[8]A classic case in nineteenth century England involved a notorious lady who ordered a custom-made carriage for business purposes. She took delivery of the carriage and then declined to pay. A legal action to collect was thrown out because the contract with the carriage-maker was deemed invalid, since its object, the carriage, was for an immoral and illegal purpose.

[9]In one case, such a change order was carried out. After its discovery, an order was issued by the municipality to fill the extra space with sand.

[10]Supplementary and special conditions are commonly added to the general conditions found in standard contracts, and are therefore deemed more pertinent. Drawings of larger scale may supersede those of smaller scale, and those of later date supersede those of earlier date, if the contract says so: as in CCDC2, and as common sense dictates.

[11]See Jervis and Levin, *Construction Law* (New York: McGraw-Hill, 1988) Chap. 7, "Liquidated Damages," for one lawyer's view of this topic. For another, and several cited cases, see W. Robert Ward, Esq., "Liability for Liquidated Damages," *The McGraw-Hill Construction Business Handbook,* 2d ed. (New York: McGraw-Hill, 1985), pp. 32-2–32-8.

[12]For example, see Document A201, Subpara. 9.6.3 Or, information not so authorized might be given to subcontractors, thereby causing a complaint from the contractor.

[13]See AIA Document A201-1987, Subpara. 4.5.1, which excludes "controversies or Claims relating to aesthetic effect and except those waived [by the owner] as provided for in Subparagraph 4.3.5"; referring to a waiver of claims by the owner in connection with final payment.

[14]See A201-1987, Para. 4.5, *Arbitration,* and Subpara. 4.5.5, *Limitation on Consolidation or Joinder.*

QUESTIONS AND TOPICS FOR DISCUSSION

1. a.   Briefly describe four different physical conditions that might be valid causes for a claim by a contractor, and explain why.

   b.   Briefly describe four different contractual conditions that might be valid causes for a claim by a contractor, and explain why.

2. In a unit-price contract that stipulates a fixed price for all of the work and also permits changes in the work, on what ground could either party request an adjustment to certain unit prices?

3. Assuming you are a contractor in a fixed-price contract, write a formal claim

for increased job overhead costs. State the grounds and a valid argument.

4. Explain the differences between mistake, misrepresentation, and fraud.

5. Explain the contractual limits to changes in the work of a fixed-price contract that can be ordered by the owner.

6. Define ordinary damages and liquidated damages, and point out the essential differences between them. Explain how they may be awarded and how claims for them may be settled.

7. State in the most fundamental terms the basis for most valid claims by parties to valid construction contracts.

8. In what kind of situation might a multiparty arbitration be helpful to both parties?

9. Describe at least five duties of an arbitrator.

10. Obtain a copy of your local arbitration statute and make a synopsis of the main points under appropriate headings.

11. Describe in general terms the relationship between claims and the changes in work made in a fixed-price construction contract.

12. Define the following terms used in this chapter on claims:
   a. Reduced access
   b. Partial occupancy
   c. *Contra proferentum*
   d. liquidated damages
   e. ordinary damages

13. In a cost-plus-fee contract, what are primary criteria for a claim by a contractor for extra overhead costs?

CHAPTER

18

DESIGN RESPONSES BY CONTRACTORS

God is in the details.
Mies Van der Rohe, architect, (1886-1969)

In earlier times, the designers of buildings were master builders, many of whom started out as mason's apprentices. Today, at least in the English-speaking countries, and since the nineteenth century when architects decided to specialize in design, most builders are technicians and managers and have little opportunity to design. It is hard to determine what this has done for architecture and building. This chapter deals with what contractors may have to do with a design and its details.

18.1 DESIGN RESPONSES DEFINED

Most contracts require a contractor to provide certain information about the work to the owner–designer, including

- Samples of materials
- Shop drawings, or fabrication details
- Product information
- Mix designs

The information is required because of deliberate omissions of **design information** from the contract documents, and the transfer from the designer to the contractor of some minor parts of the design initiative and responsibility. There are several reasons for this, including those that are

- Economic: to increase competition among bidders through a wider choice of materials and methods
- Technical: to enable components, mix designs, and tests to be made according to site conditions

- Contractual: to place responsibility for work with the contractor

This chapter discusses how best to deal with these bits of information. To identify them, they generally are called design responses. They all are subject to approval by the owner–designer, as consistent with the general design and the contract.

18.2 SAMPLES OF MATERIALS AND WORKMANSHIP

Samples are either physical examples of materials to be installed, or specific and completed parts of the work (e.g., a masonry wall). A designer selects and approves certain materials from the samples provided; or the designer approves a sample of workmanship before the work represented by the sample can be started. As the designated work is done, it is compared with an approved sample.

As in the standard AIA and CCDC contracts, the general requirement for samples and their handling usually is stated as a contract condition.[1] The AIA Document A201-1987, *General Conditions of the Contract for Construction*, states that the contractor shall submit samples, shop drawings, and product data "required by the contract documents," (Subpara. 3.12.5). Specific requirements are found in appropriate sections of specifications: which samples are required, the number, scope, type, and other requirements. Some contract conditions allow an owner's agent to ask for samples not specified in the contract documents. In such a case, the contractor should be paid any additional costs. Some contracts are vague on this point.[2]

At the outset, the superintendent should go through the contract documents and note all requirements for samples and other design responses in the project schedule and diary, and later communicate them to the appropriate subcontractors and suppliers. Samples not specified and asked for during the work generally should be treated as modifications possibly involving extensions of time and additional payments to the contractor. Document A201-1987, Subpara. 3.12.5, refers to samples, etc., "required by the Contract Documents." Subparagraph 3.12.4, says: "Shop drawings, Product Data, Samples and similar submittals are not Contract Documents."

Costs of Samples

Do not assume that because samples often are supplied free by suppliers and manufacturers, that there are no costs for a contractor in providing them; or that the scope and quantity of samples required never makes a difference to the costs involved. Most architects are particular about choosing the proper sample, and a contractor may have to return to a supplier several times before finding a suitable sample.

Sometimes, a designer is late in making a selection, and as a result scheduled work may be delayed. If this happens, a contractor should consider making a claim for an extension of time. It is better, however, to avoid this problem by conferring with the designer beforehand about dates for submission and approval of samples required and including them in the project schedule.

Samples of workmanship can be even more expensive; especially if the first samples are not approved. A designer is in a strong position when the contract says that no part of the work for which samples are required shall begin until the samples are approved:

CASE

According to a project's specifications for decorative precast-concrete structural units, the units were to be made and cured by an approved precast manufacturer. Alternatively, with certain provisions, the units could be made on-site by the prime contractor. Samples had to be approved by the designer before general production started. One reason the contractor's bid was the lowest was because he intended to make the precast units on-site. First, they used plywood forms, which buckled during steam curing. The architect rejected the first sample. Next, they lined the forms with steel sheet. It also buckled. The architect rejected the second samples. Before the contractor found a successful method and samples finally were approved they had cost the contractor several thousand dollars more than he had estimated.

It is difficult—sometimes, practically impossible—to specify workmanship; especially if the work contains a natural material, such as stone. Photographs and references to actual examples of work in existing buildings may be the only effective way of specifying such workmanship:

CASE

A performance specification required exposed exterior concrete with a fine, smooth, even, and solid surface. The specifications cited tolerances for straightness and trueness; they did not specify the method of achieving the finish. The contractor insisted that poured concrete could not have a polished mar-

ble finish, which he said was what the architect apparently required.

Was the architect at fault in writing the specification, or did the contractor's estimator misunderstand? In such a case, a sample of the work is necessary. The contractor should have questioned the specification at the time of bidding. Perhaps he decided to take a chance—and so got the contract.

Designers and specification writers must not expect inspection and approval of samples to be a substitute for an adequate description of work in specifications. Contractors must not expect that ordinary standards of work will be accepted if a specification says otherwise. However, if work cannot be properly described, it cannot be accurately priced in estimates. Clearly, requirements for samples cannot be taken lightly since they may involve considerable costs of handling, delays, repeated requests for samples, and much valuable time.

18.3 SHOP DRAWINGS AND PRODUCT DATA

With shop drawings, usually diagrams, schedules, and other information (product data) about construction work are included. Document A201-1987, Para. 3.12, defines both shop drawings and product data.[3] For purposes herein, they may be defined as information about work required by a contract, to be submitted by a contractor to the designer, or construction manager, for approval before the work is started.

Shop drawings usually represent parts of the work custom-designed by a contractor, or (probably) by a subcontractor. Some shop drawings are not much more than published diagrams of standard products.

Others are specially drafted detail drawings for fabrication work in a shop, or factory, showing tolerances for installation with the work of other trades.

Custom-designed work not detailed by the designer requires its details to be designed by a contractor, or (more often), by a subcontractor and shown in detail in shop drawings. Shop drawings often have an effect on the quality of the work of a project, as often they represent a significant proportion of the total work.[4] Contract procedures for both shop drawings and samples generally are similar. Shop drawings however require more time and attention and are checked by

- The general contractor, or construction manager, for consistency and accuracy of dimensions and tolerances in relation to other work
- The designer (architect or engineer, or a designer's consultant) for consistency and conformance with the general design as shown in the contract documents.

A designer's responsibility for shop drawings is limited to seeing that they conform to the general design and the contract. The contractor is concerned with fitting the work together and its performance. Although shop drawings usually are made by subcontractors, the prime contractor is responsible for shop drawings and for the work they show. A superintendent, therefore, should review all shop drawings carefully to verify that they

- Show the correct field dimensions and tolerances for fitting with the work
- Conform to the contract's requirements for the general design and other specific requirements.

According to standard contracts, deviations from the contract made in shop drawings must be pointed out to the designer at the time of submission for approval. This is an important obligation.

CASE

Contract specifications for aluminum windows stated they were to be glazed with the glazing beads on the outside, and shop drawings were to be submitted and approved. No deviation from the contract was indicated by the contractor when the shop drawings were submitted for approval by the architect, as required by the contract; they showed only a section-detail of the windows, and did not show which were the inside and outside surfaces. Apparently believing the windows as shown met the specification's requirements, the architect approved and stamped the shop drawings: "Approved for general design purposes only."

The first batch of windows was made and installed with glazing beads on the inside. After a site inspection, the architect's representative gave the contractor written instruction to remove the installed windows and to modify and reinstall them according to the contract, with glazing beads outside. The contractor protested that the approved shop drawings showed glazing beads on the inside. The shop drawing was ambiguous. Since the contractor had not given the written notice of the deviation in the shop drawings as required by the contract, the contract's requirement for outside glazing was upheld.

The primary purpose of shop drawings is not to reduce the number of drawing details made by the designer, although that is the result. The primary purpose is to increase competition and thereby lower the costs. By showing only the general design requirements and by leaving the details to others (subject to approval) more sub-bids and greater competition should result.

Product data includes just about every other kind of published information that might be required, and the difference from shop drawings often is unclear. Shop drawings better describe custom-made drawings, and product data is everything else.

18.4 MIX DESIGNS

Mix designs are particular kinds of product information that are different because they may vary. (They are not specifically mentioned by the AIA Document A201.) Mix designs are common for

- Asphaltic concrete (commonly called blacktop)
- Soil-cement mixtures (used in road bases)
- Gravels and soils used as aggregate or fill
- Portland cement concrete
- Cement grouts and toppings
- Masonry mortars
- Roofing compounds
- Wet plaster coatings

Mix designs are used for compounds for which there is a performance specification. As a safeguard against failure and resultant trouble, and against imperfect performance specifications (which are difficult to write), some designers require the submission and approval of mix designs before work starts. The minimum proportions of major ingredients (e.g., portland cement)

and maximum proportions of others (e.g., water) also may be specified.[5]

EXAMPLE:

A project specification requires cast-in-place concrete with a compressive strength of 3000 psi at an age of 28 days (20–21 MPa, in metric). Nothing more may be specified, except that before mixing and placing the concrete, the contractor shall submit the proposed mix design for the structural designer's approval. However, with such a performance specification, some prescriptive requirements also may be specified, such as

- Minimum cement content
- Maximum water content
- Maximum aggregate size
- Maximum slump of a sample

The minimum cement content specified may exceed the amount needed for the required compressive strength, but may be necessary for greater durability or finish. Similarly, excessive water content reduces durability, and aggregate size may affect appearance. Slump tests will show plasticity, flow, and water content.

It is not unusual to allow a masonry contractor to design mortar mixes within certain limits according to variable conditions and requirements. Formal approval by the designer is not always required.

18.5 TESTS OF MATERIALS AND WORK

Inspection and testing were introduced in Chapter 14. There are two classes of tests in construction:

1. Tests required by **authorities with juris-diction over the work** through laws, ordinances, and regulations
2. Tests required only by **owner–designers**, as specified in contracts

Tests by public authorities may be mentioned in specifications, but not always. Frequently, it is a general condition that work shall be done according to all laws, ordinances, and regulations. (See A201-1987, Article 13.) These may require working tests for performance made on completed systems, such as those for plumbing and drainage. Tests required by owner–designers are mostly tests of certain materials, products, and components specified in a contract.

If products or components are to be tested in ways that will damage or destroy a sample, a specific number of tests and samples must be specified; especially with tests of expensive custom-designed components such as metal-and-glass units, fire doors, and similar items. Keep in mind that tests are not always successful. Some may have to be repeated, and adequate time should be allowed; especially for any tested materials and systems on a project's critical path. It is in an owner's interests to have certain testing done by an independent agency. Samples to be tested should always be selected at random from the general supply.

The costs of tests are significant, and some are very expensive. The extent and number of tests sometimes is difficult to foresee. If a project's costs of tests exceed what was allowed in a cost estimate and bid, the contractor should review the circumstances to determine if there are grounds for a claim for extra costs. The wording of a contract about tests is significant, but there also is a rule of reasonable-ness. These precepts apply also to the other design responses made by contractors.

18.6 REQUIREMENTS IN OTHER CONTRACTS

In Unit-Price and Cost-Plus-Fee Contracts

The requirements for design responses in such contracts are similar to those in a fixed-price contract. In cost-plus-fee contracts, the only related concern for a contractor may be the effect of any delays in approval upon a contract's duration and a fixed fee. In unit-price contracts, the costs of some requirements for design responses may be included in the unit prices for work items. This may create a problem if the quantity of a major item (e.g., concrete) changes. Others may be the subject of a separate **lump-sum item,** which is the better way.

In Construction Management Contracts and Projects

The owner's agent responsible for approving a particular design response may be either the designer or the construction manager, and this should be made clear. Selections of samples involving aesthetics probably will be made by the designer. Where fast-track construction is employed, the times and timing of submissions and tests are more critical, and this should be reflected in the specified and scheduled periods allowed.

In Design-Build Contracts and Projects

In **design-build projects**, there is no division of responsibility between designer and builder. Therefore, the need for defined design responses apparently does not exist. Nevertheless, certain samples and tests may still be required by an owner; or of a trade contractor. However, there is an even more important consideration: the warranty of an entire project, its design, and its subsequent performance. On the one hand, an owner of a design–build project has only to look to the one corporation for satisfaction. On the other hand, an owner probably has no technical ability to check such things as shop drawings and mix designs. Is it reasonable for an owner in a design–build contract to have to wait for delayed tests before use of an entire building? Simple utilitarian structures (e.g., storage tanks) can be tested in a short time by independent agencies. Defects in the design and construction of a commercial or institutional building might not appear for a long time. In part, a solution may exist in skillfully written performance specifications and related tests, together with some of the traditional design responses already discussed. An owner intending to enter a design–build contract for a large or complex structure should therefore employ an independent construction consultant, and possibly a project manager.

18.7 COMPUTER APPLICATIONS TO DESIGN RESPONSES

Although the use of computer systems in this part of contract administration and construction management is similar to other uses that require data bases for the storage and manipulation of information and data, there are places for special applications.

- **CAD** (**D**) for shop drawings will make for faster design, transmission, and approval
- Free-form information managers for product data will make for faster creation, transmission, checking, and approval
- Engineering–design applications employing mathematic models and graphic solutions will speed up the testing of materials, especially of complex components and structures
- The life histories of hundreds of buildings and other structures collected and distributed by professional associations of property managers would be of great assistance in the selection of construction materials and methods
- Cost estimating and other programs for design and management will enable more objective and faster decisions to be made about design–build proposals. (Criteria would include the economics of development; i.e., land-use economics; *capitalized budget estimating*; **feasibility studies**; **cost-benefit analyses**; **cost engineering**; and **value engineering**.)

All of these are made more feasible and effective by a computer system. Perhaps the greatest savings will come from the use of libraries of proven, standard graphic construction details and product information[6] stored and distributed on *CD-ROM* disks so that the proverbial wheel (i.e., construction details) need not be reinvented in design offices.

REFERENCES

1. The AIA Document A201, *General Conditions of the Contract for Construction.*

SUMMARY OF MAIN POINTS

- Design responses are samples, shop drawings, product information (i.e., mix designs) so-named because all are in contracts to deal with design information deliberately omitted and left to a contractor.

- Samples usually are specified; if not, their costs should be extra, but some contracts do not allow extra costs.

- All samples entail costs because of the contractor's time involved, and samples of workmanship are the most expensive to produce.

- Specifying workmanship is difficult, and samples of suitable existing work are most effective.

- Shop drawings and product data include diagrams, schedules, brochures (catalogs): all represent information about work required by the contract to be submitted (after checking by the contractor for accuracy and tolerances) by the designer for conformity with the general design. Standard contracts require a statement with shop drawings indicating any deviation from the contract.

- Mix designs are called for several compounds; (e.g., cast-in-place concrete and masonry mortar); typically they allow adjustment of a mix to suit current conditions.

- Tests of materials and work should be scheduled; some may have to be repeated. Their costs are not insignificant and may justify a claim.

- A general precept for design responses: If costs appear excessive, review cost estimate and circumstances with a view to making a claim.

- Design responses in other kinds of contracts and projects are similar:
  - In a cost-plus-fee contract, delays in approval may affect the sufficiency of a fixed fee
  - In a unit-price contract, costs may be included in unit prices, or lump-sum items
  - In CM projects with fast-tracking, scheduled times may be critical
  - In design–build projects, design responses are not needed, but without them it is difficult to ensure quality

- Computer applications to design responses might include: CAD for shop drawings; free-form information managers; engineering–design applications; the use of recorded building histories; and cost estimating and other programs to evaluate design–build proposals by the techniques of land-use economics.

- Computer libraries of graphic design details and product information should reduce design and construction costs.

NOTES

[1]The AIA Document A201 refers to shop drawings, product data, and samples. CCDC2 1982 refers only to shop drawings. Presumably, the intention in CCDC2 is that the others should be dealt with either in special conditions, or in trade sections of specifications, or both.

[2]The 1974 edition of the Canadian standard document CCDC-12 was a case in point. It said: "The Contractor shall submit for the Architect's approval such standard manufacturers' samples as the Architect may reasonably require." Since most samples come from subcontractors, a contractor might not object; but some might. The word "reasonable" always is a signal of possible contention.

[3]Product data is better called product information. There is a useful distinction to be made.

[4]In the 1970s, at the University of Reading, England, a study of comparative costs of construction in the United Kingdom and the United States was made. The study showed that, unlike construction in the United Kingdom and some other countries, the American construction industry used shop drawings for the design of a larger proportion of its construction details.

[5]Pure performance specifications are not common. They are difficult to write, and their testing is of necessity delayed. Therefore, designers oftern play safe by prescribing some critical characteristics.

[6]Such as a more developed and updated version of *Sweet's* catalogs on a CD-ROM disk.

QUESTIONS AND TOPICS FOR DISCUSSION

1. Explain the contractual purposes of shop drawings and the advantages and disadvantages of using them.

2. What precepts should be observed when including requirements for different kinds of samples in fixed-price contracts?

3. Is it necessary that a contract require the submission of mix designs to the designer for approval? Why not simply rely on a performance specification for the work?

4. Write two paragraphs dealing with samples for a contract: one as a general condition and the other as a specification for a particular trade. Include relevant precepts mentioned in the text.

5. Write an effective specification for materials and workmanship for a natural-stone, random-rubble walling as a decorative veneer.

6. Explain the respective obligations of an architect and a contractor in dealing with shop drawings in a building contract based on AIA Document A201.

7. Write a specification clause for the testing of the performance of large, glass-and-metal window units to be installed in a high-rise building.

8. What information do shop drawings normally show that is not normally shown in the contract drawings? What is the reason for this difference?

9. Define "product data" as used in Document A201, and distinguish it from shop drawings. Give examples of both.

10. Define and explain the use of mix designs, using typical examples. Explain how mix designs differ from other classes of product information.

11. What would you advise a contractor to do if he found that the costs of a series of particular tests by an independent agency (and required by the contract) were much more than originally allowed in the cost estimate and bid? Explain in detail.

12. Discuss the implications of a design–build contract to an owner's need for design responses, as defined.

13. Offer suggestions as to other ways that computer systems could improve the implementation and approval of design responses.

14. Discuss the pros and cons of a lesser (greater) use of shop drawings in fixed-price building contracts.

CHAPTER

19

ACCELERATING AND DELAYING CONSTRUCTION

*The wind and waves are always
on the side of the ablest navigators.
Edward Gibbon (1737–1794)*

It is said that time is money, and in the cost-of-borrowing equation, time is one of the factors. To reduce design and construction time and the costs of financing, developers originated CM projects with phased construction. To save project time, developers plan and schedule work, and sometimes write contracts requiring liquidated damages. However, these steps often are not taken soon enough. Projects need planning and organizing as part of design. They need controlling as part of their execution. Sometimes, other contracting methods are needed to get an earlier start or finish. This chapter examines several such methods. There are times when it is desirable for an owner to delay a project already under way because, although extra costs will be

incurred, they are considered acceptable in the light of other considerations. Therefore, after a decision to delay work is made, it is important to minimize losses. This chapter also examines ways to do this.

19.1 ACCELERATING TRADITIONAL PROJECTS

Decisions as to contracting methods, types of contracts, and contractual arrangements should be among the earliest, especially by an owner who wants to complete a project quickly. Therefore, contracting decisions should be made even before the decisions concerned with design. Yet, frequently it is done the other way around.

Owners not familiar with the contractual alternatives and their respective advantages and disadvantages need expertise and unbiased advice. When offering their services, contractors, construction managers, and designers may be biased. Most of the criteria in selecting a contracting method are economic; therefore, at the outset of a project, a construction cost consultant may be the most unbiased and most useful adviser to an owner.[1]

An owner–developer should seek the guidance of a qualified and experienced cost consultant before talking to anyone else. Contrary to some opinion, for many kinds of construction it is not necessary to have even preliminary drawings to obtain useful, early advice on probable construction costs and contracts. If an owner who wants to build an ordinary type of building knows the size and the **outline specifications,** and already has a site, a cost consultant can make a preliminary estimate of the probable costs. Probably, too, he can offer advice on contracting methods. Some designers also are knowledgeable and proficient in making cost estimates and know the criteria for selecting a method of contracting. If an owner insists on a traditional, fixed-price contract with a prime contractor, the possible phases for separate contracts might be

1. Building's substructure
2. Building's superstructure
3. Machinery installations
4. Fixture and fitting installations
5. Landscaping and outside parking, etc.

Each of these could be the work of a separate contract; however, many separate contracts require a construction manager. In a traditional project, even if there are to be separate contractors, the project design must first be substantially complete, so as to prepare the bidding documents needed for competitive bidding.[2] (If a contractor could be competitively selected by another way, then it would not be necessary to wait until a design is completed.) Often it takes as long to complete a design and the bidding documents as it does to build the building. Saving design time therefore reduces the total time of a project. Contractual means of accelerating a fixed-price project include

- Extensive use of **design–build drawings** for construction designed by a contractor
- Extensive use of **cash allowances**
- Several contracts with **separate contractors**
- A **unit-price contract** for some or all of the work, to be measured as completed.

Any one or all of these might be used in a project to gain time by reducing design time. A description of each procedure follows.

Extensive Use of Design–Build Drawings

Shop drawings are commonplace in construction, and the idea of design-build drawings is similar. Often there are differences among contractors and designers about construction details, especially those in architectural drawings. Because time is short, estimates and bids frequently are made without paying much attention to detail drawings (e.g., the connection details for structural steel framing usually are designed by a contractor after a contract is made). A similar but more widespread and contractually formalized procedure can be used when time is critical and an early start to construction is needed, as follows.

The designer makes a design illustrated by small-scale drawings and with few larger-scale details. The design drawings are accompanied by specifications as detailed as the owner–designer wants to make them. Some are performance specifications; others describe in outline acceptable alternative systems (e.g., for heating). Bids are called and one or more fixed-price contracts are awarded.[3] While the site works and construction of the substructure are under way, the building contractor submits design–build drawings of all required details for designer approval. Details must be according to the contract's and contract documents' intent. Time is saved in the design phase when fewer design drawings are needed. Practical design solutions are applied and disputes over details are minimized. This technique is similar to that already established for shop drawings, but is larger in scope. In other respects, it is similar to design–build, but with the general design made by the owner's designer. In a project of several contracts, this technique can be used in some or all parts.

Extensive Use of Cash Allowances

This technique also is tried and proven, and is described in detail in Chapter 3. Standard contracts describe the principle and procedures. The effect of this arrangement, in which almost all work in a project is covered by **cash allowances**, is similar to that of a CM project with several separate contractors. It requires a prime contractor as manager, or a management contractor, or a construction manager. Its traditional format— with a fixed-price contract—may be more reassuring for some owners. This approach requires a surefooted agent-administrator to deal with project finances.

Contracting with Several Separate Contractors

This practice too is commonplace in traditional projects, but usually limited in application. As indicated, at its largest extent this method becomes the equivalent of a CM project. How many **separate contractors** need management by a construction manager or a management contractor depends on the owner, the designer, and the nature and size of a project. (The use of separate contracts and contractors is referred to in several places in the Index of AIA Document A201.)

Unit-price Contracts and Cost Consultants

Any part, or an entire project can be handled by using unit prices; however, in order to gain time by starting work before a design is finished, the following things are needed.

- **Schedules of quantities of work** yet to be designed, in which bidders insert unit prices to arrive at a total of the direct costs (quantities are approximate)
- **A standard method of measurement of construction work** (described in the documents)
- **Contractual general conditions** dealing with the measurement of work, adjustments to the contract sum, and adjustments to unit prices for variations in the quantity or type of work

This contracting procedure is common in some countries,[4] and is not foreign to North America where it is used almost exclusively in engineering projects, since earthworks and such are difficult to premeasure. (As explained in Chapter 2, engineering work often is relatively simple in variety of work relative to project size.)

North American builders, however, do not use this method in building construction except for pricing changes in work.[5] However, there is no reason why unit-price contracting should not be used more widely, except for the lack of a generally accepted standard method of measurement and the skill and the experience that comes with its use. Another temporary obstacle to using unit-price contracts for building work might be the preparation of proper bidding documents, particularly the bills or schedules of quantities. A demonstrated need, however, would soon attract the necessary skill.

At the outset of a project, a quantity surveyor often is able to agree with the designer about a major portion of the specifications for the work before the working drawings are produced. A quantity surveyor can then produce approximate quantities of work and complete the specifications. This is simple when the proposed construction is of a common type, such as housing and many kinds of commercial construction. It is less simple with uncommon buildings, for which more information and time are needed. Meanwhile, the costs of the proposed work can be estimated and monitored by the quantity surveyor. Unit-price contracts should contain a requirement that if there any items of work for which there are no unit prices stipulated, unit prices for those items shall be negotiated and agreed to on the basis of any similar unit prices in the contract.

This method requires skill and experience in the analysis and negotiation of unit prices. Such a contracting method can get a project started before completing the design and the working drawings, and an owner using it does not take all the risks inherent in a cost-plus-fee contract.

19.2 ACCELERATING DEVELOPMENT PROJECTS

Nobody is more inclined to say that time is money than a developer who has borrowed for a major development. Some developers, seeking advice on contracting and costs, get involved with a contracting company too early. Often they have no assurance that the company they are dealing with is either suitable or that its participation will be economically advantageous. Because a developer wants to start work, he may think that he should find a contractor and get advice immediately. By doing so incautiously, a developer runs the risks of getting biased information, getting into an unsuitable contract with an unsuitable contractor, and losing some control of the project.

There is, however, a way by which a developer can competitively obtain a construction company's services while remaining independent.[6] The method is similar to that just described and involves the use of unit prices. Since it brings forward the selection of a contractor to a time prior to design and does not use traditional bidding, there are certain requirements:

- *Schedules of general requirement items* (as distinct from, but similar to schedules of quantities and unit prices)
- *Contract conditions* dealing with the management of trade contractors and subcontractors and prices for the prime contractor's operating overhead costs for managing them.[7]
- *Schedules of approximate quantities* for basic items of work, the need for which can be readily anticipated (e.g., concrete in foundations).

This information in the bidding documents excludes that design information traditionally included (i.e., complete working drawings, construction details, and specifications). If more information is available, it should be given to bidders (e.g., a site plan and preliminary drawings to show the general nature of the proposed work). Otherwise, the bidding documents include only the general requirements and the measured quantities of certain basic items of work the need for which is anticipated. These form the basis for competitive bidding by selected companies.

This procedure enables the earliest possible selection of a prime contractor, and many variations are possible, depending on

- The specific needs of an owner for construction, speed, risk handling, and protection
- The amount of design information available
- The availability of innovative professionals as owner's agent-consultants, and of innovative companies as contractors and subcontractors

As already observed, there is a connection between an owner's control over work and the extent of the risks the owner carries. Also, there is a connection between the design information available and the risks in doing construction work in a contract with a fixed price or fee. Different contracting methods cannot succeed unless the participants are knowledgeable and flexible.

Providing an owner–developer is ready to pay, there is no need to go far with a development without the advice and skill of a cost consultant and a construction manager. With some owners, there has long been a reluctance to pay for anything as intangible as information. With the increasing realization that information is the new coin of commerce that attitude is changing.

Another alternative for an owner–developer who wants a builder's expertise and advice from the outset of a project is employment of a construction manager during both design and construction in a CM project.

19.3 ACCELERATING CM PROJECTS

As previously discussed, a primary purpose of a CM project is to accelerate it by phased construction, as described in Chapter 2. Another means of acceleration (or avoiding delays) is advanced purchasing. Also, in a CM project it is possible to use any of the time-saving techniques described for use in traditional projects within the separate contracts.

Generally, in a CM project for a standard-type building an owner may be better off with a fixed-price contract with each contractor. It is possible, however, that in certain contracts, such as those usually awarded earlier, that time can be gained by using other kinds of contracts; particularly since the earlier work usually is site work, which by its very nature often does not fit as well into a fixed-price contract.

There is a great variety of contracts and contractual arrangements. In a CM project it is possible to use several, each selected and designed to suit the work and circumstances. Unfortunately, too often alternatives are overlooked or deliberately ignored; and traditional contracting with a fixed-price contract is undertaken either because of ignorance or because there is no incentive to suggest alternatives. Also, with a contract other than for a fixed-price and with a general contractor, there usually is more work and risk for an owner's agent. Today's propensity for litigation also may discourage innovative contracting. For certain works, expeditious completion might be aided by any of the following:

- Machine excavation: by a unit-price contract; or if quantities of work cannot be easily measured, for cost-plus-fee
- Work in a substructure (i.e., up to ground floor level): by a unit-price contract if the design is not yet complete and the subsurface conditions are not yet fully known
- Structural work in superstructure: by a maximum cost-plus-fee contract, or by a fixed-price contract if the design is sufficiently advanced
- Protection trades and finishing trades generally: either by fixed-price contracts or by unit-price contracts, depending on the available design information and the nature of the work
- Underground services outside the building: by a fixed-price contract if quantities are readily ascertainable; otherwise by a unit-price contract
- Underground services inside the building: by a fixed-price or unit-price contract
- Plumbing and air-conditioning: possibly by a maximum cost-plus-fee contract (established by cost-per-unit); the system layout to be designed by the contractor with design-build drawings; the fixture specifications and locations to be shown on plan by the owner and the designer–consultant
- Electrical: the same as for plumbing, or by a unit-price contract

If necessary, all such contracts, can be arranged and let by a construction manager in a matter of a few weeks following the completion of preliminary design sketches; for some contracts, design sketches may not be necessary. Yet, in none of these contracts

need an owner be exposed to the risks inherent in a simple cost-plus-fee contract. The examples given are illustrative and other arrangements are possible.

To manage a CM project effectively, it is essential to have an effective budget estimate as the primary guide for budgeting costs and choosing a contract type. Development and contracting are done for profit, and usually within a limited budget; therefore, that good design, good contracting and good economics go together.

19.4 DELAYING CONSTRUCTION IN TRADITIONAL PROJECTS

The terms an owner is able to negotiate for a delay in construction will depend on several conditions and circumstances, including

- The type of contract to be delayed
- The stage at which a delay commences
- The length of the delay.

The Type of Contract to Be Delayed

Special circumstances aside, the most significant consideration in a decision to delay a project is the type of contract. For comparison, two fundamental kinds of contracts are considered.

1. Fixed-price contracts
2. Cost-plus-fee contracts.

Delay of a Fixed-Price Contract

The AIA Document A201-1987 provides for the owner in a fixed-price contract without cause to "suspend, delay, or interrupt the Work in whole or in part for such period of time as the Owner may determine" (Subpara. 14.3). The standard contract's condition also provides for "an adjustment [to be] made in the cost of performance" for such suspension or delay by the owner. Without contractual provisions like those, no delay is possible without a contractor's agreement. The contracting parties have to agree mutually to an interruption and in effect create a new contract for later continuation. Alternatively, at a price, contractors might agree to abandon entirely a contract and its subcontracts. Delay or abandonment undoubtedly will create a cost for the owner; therefore, for an owner, it is a question of how much of a cost, and will it be worthwhile?

Delay of a Cost-Plus-Fee Contract

Depending on its wording and intent, in a cost-plus-fee contract with a percentage fee and no stipulated completion date, delay or even abandonment may cause little or no extra expense for the owner. Anything that indicates a particular scope of work, however, may create an obligation of the owner that may require recompense for the contractor's loss of expected profit. In a contract with a lump-sum fee and a stipulated completion date (the fee and date are related), the costs of delay or abandonment probably would be higher.

The Stage at Which a Contract Is Delayed

The point at which an owner wishes to delay work in a contract's progress is significant to the costs, and may include

- Costs of returning materials ordered but returned for restocking
- Costs of handling, storing, and securing delivered materials at the site, and possible losses while stored
- Extra payments to discharged workers and staff

- Demobilization and transportation costs for equipment, or idle time for equipment kept on-site during a delay
- Subsequent remobilization costs
- Payment of wages and expenses to a superintendent or any other staff required by the owner during a work stoppage
- Continued payments on short-term financing

Besides extra direct costs, there are the extra indirect costs. These are more difficult to assess because they occur at a contractor's office (as distinct from a site). Possibly, there could be extra costs resulting from a change in timing caused by the postponement of completion, such as increased costs from

- Higher interest rates, inflated prices, or new wage agreements
- Performance of work under less desirable weather or other conditions
- Extending a contract into the period of a labor shortage
- Shortages of other resources (although, as with labor, a shift to a more favorable period also is possible)
- Disruption in work flow, and loss of expected cash flow and profit

All issues such as these may be subjects for negotiation. The time in a project at which work is stopped should be the first item for agreement. Factors to be considered include

- The degree of completion of a building (whether the work is close to completion of an important stage; e.g., "closing in" to make weathertight)
- The season and the weather, and their effect on uncompleted work left standing during a stoppage (e.g., exposed subsoil, exposed or unfinished surfaces)

■ The effect of delay on existing permits, and other arrangements with public authorities and public utilities

The deliberate delay of work is a subject for mutual agreement and carefully considered action by both parties; otherwise, an owner may be in breach of contract. Even in a contract based on AIA Document A201, and with the provisions for "suspension by an owner for convenience" (Subpara., 14.3), there remains much to be settled by negotiation. All the AIA document does is show previous agreement in principle to the idea.

19.5 DELAYING CONSTRUCTION IN CM PROJECTS

In CM projects, the situation for an owner who wishes to delay work in progress is much the same as in a traditional project, although possibly less onerous. It may be easier for an owner to interrupt and delay a project's work simply by awarding no more contracts; e.g., for specific finishing trades, on completion and closing in of the structure. If a CM project has advanced to the stage where all contracts are let, the owner who wishes to delay may be in no better position than one in a traditional project.

19.6 COMPUTER APPLICATIONS FOR ACCELERATION AND DELAY

Among the factors affecting decisions about accelerating and delaying projects the first is the prime contract. Next, what can the parties agree to beyond the existing agreement?

Finally, there are the economic aspects to be considered by both parties. One can imagine:

A SCENARIO:

The owner has good reason to delay work, and he raises the subject of delay with the contractor. Each tries to foresee and calculate the several possibilities and their economic effects. The contractor studies the cost estimate and work schedule and calculates the effects of stopping and starting work for different periods at different times. He also considers what may be gained, and how. Meanwhile, the owner proceeds similarly, but the owner has economic considerations that suggested the delay in the first place. The parties need to make proposals that are feasible and equitable. The possible permutations may be many. Without computers, they might never come to an ideal conclusion. Using a computer spreadsheet in the "what if" mode, each one can input criteria and select the best solution for himself. They then have a basis for negotiations. There may be other advantages in using a computer, since when dealing with many alternatives serendipity sometimes happens and unexpected information and insights appear.

SUMMARY OF MAIN POINTS

- Decisions about costs, contracts, and contracting methods need to be among the earliest decisions made by an owner; therefore a construction cost consultant may be the first needed.

- Save construction time by planning both the designing and the contracting before designing, and by using separate contracts and phased construction.

- In a traditional fixed-price project phased construction is limited to a few separate contractors; more contractors require a manager.

- To reduce the time in the design phase before construction can start, use one or more of the following: design–build, a large number of cash allowances, several separate contractors, or a unit-price contract for some or all of the work.

- Design–build drawings are like shop drawings applied to any or all construction and its details; with the general design and scope of the work shown by the designer in small-scale design drawings and outline specifications.

- Extensive use of cash allowances effectively divides up a project's contract into several smaller contracts with separate contractors managed by a prime contractor, a construction manager, or by a management contractor. The result may be similar to a CM project.

- Traditional contracting with several separate contractors, like the previous method, also creates something similar to a CM project.

- Unit-price contracts can be used for a whole project or any part. They enable work to be started before a design is completed.

- A contractor can be selected competitively by using as bidding documents schedules of unit prices for approximate quantities of basic work items and of certain general requirement items.

- A CM project with phased construction is a notable way of accelerating construction, and the contractors may have different types of contracts.

- Delaying a project already under way will cost an amount dependent on the type of contract to be delayed, the stage at which a delay begins, and the length of the delay.

- The type of contract delayed—fixed-price or cost-plus-fee—is important; usually it is easier and cheaper to delay one of the latter.

- Delaying a fixed-price contract is dealt with only generally in Document A201, which gives an owner the right to delay without cause. Terms, however, must be negotiated with the contractor.

- The stage at which a contract is delayed will affect the owner's additional costs, possibly including costs of returned materials, severance payments, demobilization, any subsequent remobilization, wages for staff retained during shutdown, and costs of any extended financing.

- The point at which project work is stopped is important because of the season and weather, and the effect on permits and arrangements made with authorities and public utilities.

- Suspension of work in a CM project may be easier, since it consists of several separate contracts.
- Computer systems offer the opportunity to consider the economic effects of many

alternative methods and procedures in accelerating and delaying projects.

NOTES

[1]Cost consulting and a construction management service often may be obtained from the same company. Some are cost engineers; some are quantity surveyors.

[2]"The design...substantially complete" means: except for those parts of a design not yet decided and made the subjects of cash allowances, or shop drawings, or of separate contracts.

[3]Depending on the size, scope, and complexity of a project, there may be one or more prime contractors from the outset, or later in the project.

[4]Mostly, in those countries where the profession of quantity surveying is established.

[5]As in A201-1987, Article 7, *Changes in the Work*: "[by] unit prices stated in the Contract Documents or subsequently agreed upon."

[6]If an owner–developer hired a cost consultant, probably there would be no need to deal with a contracting company prematurely.

[7]Usually, operating overhead costs would be expressed as a percentage of the prime costs of subcontractors' work, which in turn is paid for out of cash allowances; all subject to adjustment according to actual amounts and paid costs of work performed.

QUESTIONS AND TOPICS FOR DISCUSSION

1. Explain what advice the owner of a proposed construction project needs right at the outset, and from whom this advice is best obtained.

2. Define precisely the following terms, and give an illustrative example of each:
   a. Separate contractor
   b. Phased construction
   c. Cash allowance
   d. Design–build drawings
   e. Quantity surveyor

3. List and briefly describe the separate phases of a building project for a major commercial or institutional building that can be performed under separate fixed-price contracts.

4. Other than fast-tracking in a CM project, list and outline three different kinds of contract provisions that might be used to accelerate a project.

5. Take one of the contract provisions described in Question 4 and describe it in detail; its contractual features, their purposes, and applications.

6. Of what value to contracting would be a national standard method of measuring construction work? Explain your response, making references to different kinds of contracts and construction.

7. Explain an effective method for selecting competitively a contractor prior to the preparation of design drawings.

8. What are the three main considerations for an owner in arranging a delay in a contract?

9. As an owner–developer proposing to develop a shopping mall and expecting that because of tenants' leases it might be necessary to have a delay at some point in the development, what contractual preparations would you make in order to be able to call for and get a delay with a minimum of difficulty and expense?

10. Explain the concept and the pros and cons of using design–build drawings (as defined) in a fixed–price contract.

11. Explain briefly the effect of the stage at which a project is delayed on a prime contractor and his contract.

12. Make an outline specification for a computer system (hardware and software) to deal efficiently with the economic considerations of accelerating and delaying projects. Outline the economic considerations and describe appropriate software programs to aid in decision-making.

13. As bidding documents, of what use are schedules of approximate quantities of work, and what do they achieve?

20

FINANCING AND CONTRACT PAYMENTS

The borrower is servant to the lender.
(Proverbs, 22:7)

Most of this chapter deals with financing construction and the progress payments in contracts. First, there is a brief review of the persons who borrow and pay for construction work.

20.1 LIMITED AND PERSONAL LIABILITY

Construction produces an expensive and durable asset that requires a large investment. Therefore, almost every project requires capital in amounts larger than most owners can provide, and so most *owner–developers* and governments borrow.[1]

It is significant that in business schools, although finance and accounting are common subjects there is little time spent with financing and accounting for capital projects, and even less on how to make a

realistic project budget based on cost estimate. Not all projects are for construction. Software engineering, for example, requires designs, budgets, estimates, and cost controls.[2] It also is significant that many of the problems with capital projects are spawned at the very beginning when budgets are established.

In construction, lenders become the financial partners of those who borrow, while surety companies become the guarantors of contractors' performance. The strengths and weaknesses of the companies that borrow are therefore of vital concern to a lender and surety company. Should a contractor fail, a lender or a surety company might be obliged to take over a construction contract or development project. That is not their preference, however, as lenders prefer to be regularly paid.

Limited Liability

Its charter describes the purposes of a corporation. It is prepared and filed by those who incorporate a company, and states the name of the corporation, followed by the word "Incorporated," or the abbreviation "Inc.," to show it is a corporation with a limited liability. Incorporation ensures that the owners of a corporation are liable for the liabilities of the corporation only to the extent of their investment in it. However, that does not mean that lenders and sureties cannot demand more security than a corporation itself will provide.

EXAMPLE:

In providing performance bonds, surety companies commonly require principals or directors of contracting companies to take on a personal liability for nonperformance of a construction contract. Similarly, financial institutions may look to personal liabilities as a condition for financing construction work.

Simply put, given the nature and risks of construction, those who deal with construction companies seek to protect themselves against losses that they might otherwise incur because of limited liability.

20.2 CREDIT FINANCING FOR CONSTRUCTION

Credit is an old term whose origin goes back centuries (i.e., Latin, *creditum* means loan), which suggests long-established practices. Credit implies three fundamental things:

1. Capital: used for making wealth
2. Time: or the duration of a loan
3. Return: the interest or profit on a loan

Often the time that a builder needs credit is short; perhaps, less than a year. For a developer, it may be short-term in the initial stages, but long-term credit usually is needed for a real-property development; e.g., a mortgage for a term of years. These variations in duration and risk create different kinds of credit financing.

Qualifications for Credit

Besides stability, credit requires certain things of the borrower, called the three Cs: character, capacity, and collateral. Character refers to a borrower's predisposition to repay a debt, and for this a person's credit rating is examined. Capacity refers to a borrower's subsequent ability to repay a loan, as well as current financial status. If a developer needs a loan, a lender may be more experienced and in a better position to judge the probable outcome of the development than the borrower and, therefore, in a better position to judge the borrower's capacity to repay. Collateral refers to something of value required by a lender to protect the lender against loss should the borrower not make repayments as agreed: something by way of security that is of more than adequate value, and which can be converted or used by the lender. For a real-property development, the land may be the collateral. For a short-term loan to a contractor, it may be the company's assets.

What is satisfactory for a lender depends on the amount and duration of a loan, the condition of the borrower, the attitude of the lender toward the borrower, and the purpose of the loan. If a lender is more than satisfied by all the requirements, the lender may make the loan at a lower rate of interest. If one or more of the three Cs appears deficient, the lender may still be prepared to make the loan, but at a higher rate, since it is at a greater risk. The return required is commensurate with the risk.

The three Cs cited here are essentially the same as those for bonding (in Chapter 22), except that instead of the usual collateral, cash or other such assets are the third C (collateral) required to get a bond. If you need specific advice about credit, financing, and any related matters, consult a reputable financial consultant.

Financing Construction by Credit

Credit always has been part of civilization, and reportedly even preceded the coining of money.[3] Contractors need loans to bridge the gap between doing work and getting paid for it. The cost of short-term financing usually is a job overhead cost. A late payment or late completion means extra interest and less profit. For a developer who borrows, an inadequate cash flow may be disastrous:

EXAMPLE:

Two entrepreneurs found a site ripe for development and borrowed heavily to purchase it. They went to an architect, paid a lump-sum for design sketches, and got short-term financing. They entered a construction contract, but could not make the final payment to the contractor. As a result, the lender took over the substantially completed project and the two entrepreneurs lost their entire investment.

Here is what one banker[4] said about construction lending:

> Construction lending is a highly profitable but risky form of real estate lending. Banks engaging in it must, by and large, take the development process as they find it and refrain from treating it as they wish or hope it would be.

In the same article, a successful developer described his life's work:

> It is...a cacophony of activity in which zoning commissions cry for fees they never had, undercapitalized contractors rail for payment for work they will do tomorrow if they get paid for it today, and architects, engineers, accountants, lawyers, and bankers attack your plans with a dizzying array of conflicting (and only sometimes relevant) requirements, only to retreat until the time they can say, "We knew that wouldn't work."

Term Loans and Standby Credit

Books on credit describe several kinds of loans. We referred to several, including one written by several financial experts.[5]

Revolving Credit. A line of credit for more than a year (usually for several years), during which time the borrower pays a fee (interest) on the daily average of the unused portion of the credit. Revolving credit is typically used for financing construction. A busy season followed by a slack season affects a construction company's cash flow. Revolving credit allows a borrower to terminate the credit by giving notice and to reduce the amount of credit available (and thereby the fee paid) when the original amount of credit is no longer required.

Standby Credit. Similar to revolving credit, but it differs in that the borrower cannot repay and borrow again as with revolving credit. On completion of a construction project, the borrower with standby credit either sells the development or obtains permanent financing (a mortgage). Sometimes, a lender-bank will seek a take-out letter (a commitment for a mortgage) from an investor (e.g., a mortgage company) providing the interim standby credit for construction; therefore the term, take-out loan.

Serial Term Loans. Obtained by a borrower with revolving or standby credit, the terms of which allow a conversion to a serial term loan to be repaid over several years. This provides credit for construction and then a shift to a term loan for such as operating capital to be repaid by income from the new building.

Equipment Leasing. Through a bank and often via a leasing company is another means of construction financing. Cash flow in construction and its variability is the primary cause of the need for most construction financing.[6]

Financial Institutions (Financiers) and Loans

This is only a concise survey of credit financing, but anybody in the construction business must be familiar with the subject. Some financiers[7] publish useful literature. They are in business to lend money as partners of their borrowers. When you look for a loan, start by thinking of the lender as your financial partner, and expect to provide all the information that you would

expect. As your financial partner, a financier is not only interested in why you need a loan of a certain amount, he is even more interested in exactly how the loan can and will be repaid. Therefore, a loan officer wants to see from a construction company at least the following:

- Balance sheet
- Income (profit and loss) statement
- Retained earnings account reconciliation
- Source and application of funds statement
- A detailed estimate of costs for a project.

The terminology of finance and accounting can be confusing. So many things have different names, and financial documents come in so many different formats.[8]

Accounting Standards

Anyone in business should be aware that because of the limitations of business accounting, financial statements do not always reveal all that they should reveal. For evidence of this fact about financial statements two of many critics will be cited.

> A proposed change in the accounting rules will make financial institutions' reported earnings much more realistic—which is to say, much more volatile. [Forbes][9]

Why does the article in this long-established business magazine have this header? Because, as the author explains, for years financial institutions have reported their "huge portfolios of fixed-income securities" at higher than actual values by calling them long-term investments and reporting the historical values. Meanwhile, all the time they are trading in securities, selling off those of high value to increase institution earnings, and sitting on those securities that have depreciated; but with their original, higher values still on the books. The author quotes a member of the Financial Accounting Standards Board: "It is not appropriate for us to encourage people to buy long-term debt by setting up accounting standards that mislead them."

Another, different source of information about financial statements is the book, *The Truth About Corporate Accounting*,[10] that should be read (especially the last chapter) by all in business. Among other things, in that chapter the writer calls for the need

- "To make the independent auditor responsible..."
- "for a joint congressional committee on corporate accountability"

Therefore, realize that there often is more or less to a financial statement than may appear, and that some preparation is necessary for reading them. If as a contractor and potential borrower, you need to take your company's financial statement to a loan officer, be sure that you understand it well enough to explain it. Do not be shy about asking the most simple questions of your accountant.

Key Business Ratios

For a concise overview of a company's financial condition, a lender may look at the four basic financial statements cited; or, for an even more concise view, the financial ratios derived from them, some of which follow.

Net profit on net sales, or the profit margin, is:

$$\text{Formula: } \frac{\text{Net profit after taxes}}{\text{Net value (sales) done}} \times 100 = x\ \%$$

This ratio commonly is a measure of business efficiency, but it should be looked at with the next ratio (N.B. all ratios should be viewed together and compared with the typical ratios for a particular line of business or an industry; e.g., residential construction as distinct from commercial construction.)

Gross profit on net sales:

$$\text{Formula: } \frac{\text{Gross profit}}{\text{Net value (sales) done}} \times 100 = x\ \%$$

This ratio is one to read with the first ratio: Net profit on net sales.

Net profit on tangible net worth:

$$\text{Formula: } \frac{\text{Net profit after taxes}}{\substack{\text{Net worth less intangible} \\ \text{assets}}} \times 100 = x\ \%$$

Intangible assets in a construction company are mostly goodwill—a thing not easily measured. This derives from a good reputation and may be of considerable value. Since it is not readily accountable (and is always changeable), it is not considered in these calculations.

Net profit on tangible net worth, also called return on investment (ROI), is among the most important ratios. The amount should be more than that currently available from short-term government securities; otherwise, why bother to invest in a construction company? For some the answer might be: Because I like construction and I like being my own boss.

Net sales to tangible net worth:

$$\text{Formula: } \frac{\substack{\text{Net sales} \\ \text{(value) done}}}{\text{Tangible net worth}} = \text{Rate of IT}$$

Tangible net worth excludes intangible assets (e.g., goodwill). Another name is the rate of a company's investment turnover (IT); i.e., the number of times the investment turns over during a fiscal year. In some businesses, a high turnover may not be a good thing as it means greater debt to finance the necessary inventory and accounts receivable. They call this high turnover "overtrading." Therefore, the upper and lower quartiles of this ratio often are reversed, as with the next rate to be described. This does not apply to construction, which usually does not require inventory.

Net sales to net working capital:

$$\text{Formula: } \frac{\text{Net sales (value) done}}{\text{Net working capital}} = \text{Rate of WCT}$$

Often called, the rate of working capital turnover (WCT). As with the previous rate of IT, a high rate here may suggest overtrading and a heavy resultant debt, and as noted before the quartiles may be reversed. (Consider how misleading such rates could be if not reversed, or if misunderstood!) The next rate also should be reviewed with this one.

Current assets to current debt:

$$\text{Formula: } \frac{\text{Current assets}}{\text{Current debt}}$$

Here the kinds of current assets are important, since too much of the wrong kind (nonliquid assets) could mean an inability to pay current liabilities; e.g., too much money tied up in construction equipment. Another similarly current rate also is significant.

Liquidity ratio:

$$\text{Formula: } \frac{\text{Cash and equivalents} + \text{net receivables}}{\text{Current liabilities}}$$

This rate is a measure of a business' liquidity. A ratio of 1 to 1 would suggest good liquidity, but less than 1 to 1 might not suggest nonliquidity; it depends on the type of business. As stated earlier, comparisons should be made among similar businesses and industries. It is a matter of enough cash on hand to pay bills when due. (The equivalent of cash would be, for example, government securities and other assets readily convertible to cash.)

Fixed assets to tangible net worth:

$$\text{Formula: } \frac{\text{Fixed assets (net value)}}{\text{Tangible net worth}} \times 100 = x\ \%$$

Fixed assets might be equity in a building and equipment; i.e., the value less any related liability. This however may not be very significant for a contracting or construction management company whose assets are primarily people and an organization.

Current debt to tangible net worth:

$$\text{Formula: } \frac{\text{Current liabilities}}{\text{Tangible net worth}} \times 100 = x\ \%$$

This too may not tell much about a contracting or construction management company that operates almost entirely with borrowed money. There are other ratios used to assess a company's financial condition:

- Inventory turnover
- Total debt to tangible net worth
- Inventory to net working capital
- Accounts payable turnover
- Long-term debt payback.

Not all of these ratios are useful for examining the condition of a construction company. As always, the type of business is critical, and not all classes of construction are comparable (e.g., framing with excavation, or residential construction with heavy commercial).

Construction Loans

Construction is project-oriented, and so are its loans. (An exception is revolving credit, for a company doing such work as renovations and insurance restitution work.) Therefore, since a lender becomes a business partner of the borrower for the purpose of a particular project, before a lender's finance officer approves a loan she will want to know about the project, its design and its prospects, the cost estimate and bid, and about the capacity of the contractor who seeks financing. If the project is a builder's speculative development, the finance officer also will want to know about projected sales or rentals, and everything else related to the development.

Given the complex technical and financial nature of construction development, a lender may employ a construction cost consultant, or a project monitor,[11] to verify the validity of a contractor's bid, the terms of the construction contract (especially those affecting payment), and the contractor's ability to perform. The cost consultant's service to the lender also may include monitoring the project from start to completion to assure the lender that

- The contract sum and contract time are realistic
- The contractor's personnel and capacity are adequate
- The construction contract contains all the necessary provisions for bonds, insur-

ances, indemnity, and protection for all concerned

This may require a consultant to make an independent cost estimate, cash-flow projection, and schedule for the project; or the consultant may only examine and check those of the developer–builder and major subcontractors. In other words, a lender seeks assurance from an independent construction expert that a project is on a sound contractual and financial basis and that it is safe for the lender to have an interest in the development to the extent of the loan. Besides these assurances, a lender also will require an independent appraisal (valuation) of the completed project. A lender is not only concerned with the viability of the construction project, he also is concerned with its later viability as an income-producing real property, so that if there is a default on the loan the lender will have sufficient equity in the project to cover the loan by a safe margin.

All the costs of this reassurance and monitoring required by a lender are part of the fixed costs of a loan to a borrower. On an intermediate-size project, the costs amount to several thousand dollars. Typically, a cost consultant's fees are part of a project's costs and are included in the amount of the progress payments to the contractor. Despite the precautions by lenders to ensure the security of loans, other things may influence the attitudes and actions of loan officers:

CASE

A financial institution is in the business of lending money for a profit. So, although an institution needs to protect its interests, and despite a statement by the cost consultant that the amount of work done to date on the project did not warrant a draw in the amount requested, one lending officer approved the amount of an excessive progress payment to a contractor.

This occurred apparently because the lender knew of another larger project already planned by the borrower. The lender indulged the borrower and approved the draw in the hope of making a larger loan. In other words, the lender took a risk on a smaller loan to get the chance of making a larger loan in future.

Latent Credit

Besides financing by direct credit (i.e., by short-term or intermediate-term loan), there also is a form of internal, short-term, latent credit that regularly helps to finance construction projects. It is provided by everyone employed on a project: designer, designer's consultants, construction manager, cost consultants, contractors, subcontractors, suppliers and, not in the least, the workers. All are paid in arrears, and all therefore have an equity and interest in the project on which they are working that gives rise to their right of protection by lien rights.[12]

Also, in a buyer's market, when demand for construction is low, to encourage construction work and to create a demand for their goods, manufacturers and suppliers may extend credit far beyond the normal periods. In leaner times, there is yet another kind of credit in the construction industry. This credit (if it can be called that) comes from the contracting companies who do work for only a bare markup, and trade contractors whose only resources are knowledge and labor. They accept lower prices because their workers will accept lower wages in order to work. By temporarily lowering costs, they effectively create credit. It is called credit because those who provide it expect a return in higher wages and prices when the demand for work returns. Others' investments in projects may be the fees for consulting services. Others may take bonds or stock for payment, or an equity interest in a project.

Cost of Credit

The use of money has a price. The cost of credit for construction is a job overhead cost, the amount of which depends on the interest rate and the loan period. Another cost of credit (and overhead cost) are the costs to process a loan, or to arrange a line of credit. Such administrative costs increase proportionately as the amount of a loan and its term decrease; i.e, the processing costs of small, short-term loans is proportionately higher.

Theoretically, lenders set interest rates according to their assessments of the three Cs of each borrower, and according to the prime rate in the money market at the time of making the loan. Lenders also use other guidelines in establishing interest rates, including the economy and the current construction market. Interest rates reflect, in part, the changing nature of a cyclical economy. Unfortunately, economic cycles usually do not coincide with the seasons or the cycles of construction demand. Like farmers, contractors need credit to tide them over their winters of discontent; credit is an essential part of both construction and agriculture.

Time of Credit

In development and credit financing, for both borrower and lender, timing may be critical. Time is fundamental in the cost of credit. Good timing shortens the period, minimizes the cost of credit, and helps in selling. Also, a primary duty of an owner's agent is the timely certification of correct payments to be made by the owner to the contractor. An owner's primary duty is to pay the contractor the amount certified on time, according to the contract.

Many contracts now contain provisions for the payment of interest on an owner's overdue payments, as any delay creates an extra cost for a payee. (Also, a delay in payment becomes even longer for the subcontractors and suppliers.) A standard construction agreement, (AIA Document A101), now provides for insertions to make it mandatory to pay interest on unpaid payments due. Such interest should be compounded daily at the prime rate plus an agreed premium. The premium can be either stipulated in bids or a subject for negotiation, and included in a contract's agreement. Further, AIA Document A201-1987, Article 2, *Owner,* Para. 2.2.1, requires an owner to provide the contractor at his request "prior to execution of the Agreement and promptly from time to time thereafter,...reasonable evidence that financial arrangements have been made to fulfil the Owner's obligations under the Contract."

Cash Flow in Construction

Every contract is a promise to perform, and every construction contract is a promise to pay for work completed. On the strength of a promise, hundreds of other promises to pay are made: by prime contractor to subcontractors; by subcontractors to sub-subcontractors; and by all of them to suppliers and workers for materials supplied and for work done. A supplier gives credit for a period of days. Subcontractors usually are paid each month. On the strength of payments to come, workers also obtain credit for themselves.

The flow of cash through the contractual system of a project is like the flow of water through an irrigation system. It flows from lender to owner, who periodically pays the contractor who, holding the payment in trust (as in a holding tank), then pays the subcontractors, suppliers, and workers. Cash-flow requirements are an essential part of project scheduling, and often a lender or his cost consultant wants to examine a cash-flow schedule before approving a loan.

20.3 CONTRACT PAYMENTS

Most owners contract to make periodic progress payments to the contractor during the work. For smaller projects, payments are made at specified stages: for larger projects, usually every month. (See AIA Document A101-1987, Article 5, *Progress Payments,* and A201-1987, Article 9, *Payments and Completion.*[13] Usually, only minor contracts require the entire completion of the work to precede payment, and this kind of entire contract should be so described in its documents.

The effect of periodic payments is to share the financing of a project between the two contracting parties, and to create incentives for the contractors and subcontractors. Because payments are fundamental, their main terms and the procedures for payment are in the contract agreement (as in AIA Document A101-1987, Owner–Contractor Agreement, Article 5).

In addition, with the site as collateral, often an owner can obtain financing more cheaply than a contractor.

Terms and Conditions for Progress Payments

As in Document A101, Article 5, the latest day in each payment period by which progress payments will be made should be stipulated. The most suitable date is not always the last day of the month, as it may not be convenient to the owner, the owner's bank, or to the mortgagee. The latest day for the receipt of an application for payment and for the certification of payment should be established by counting backward from the day stipulated for making the payments. An agreement also should state the percentage of the contract sum that will be paid for work completed and for materials delivered to and stored at the site. Also, the percentage held back as retainage, if any, must be stated together with any later reduction or limitation of retainage, as will be described. Notice that standard forms of agreement in a fixed-price contract, usually refer to

> that proportion of the Contract Sum properly allocable to completed Work as determined by multiplying *the percentage completion of each portion of the Work by the share of the total Contract Sum allocated to that portion of the Work* in the Schedule of Values...." (A101-1987, Article 5) [Author's emphasis]

Words of similar meaning should show that what is payable is not the actual value of labor, materials, and equipment expended by the contractor, but that portion of the contract sum that can be allocated to the completed work as a proportion of the entire work.

EXAMPLE:

Consider a contractor with a fixed-price contract obtained by making the lowest bid. Assume the bid was erroneous and the contract sum too low: that partway through the job the contractor finds he is losing money, and that by the date of completion the contractor has spent approximately 10 percent more than the contract sum. Obviously, from the time the contractor started to lose money the amounts of the progress payments should have been less than the amount he had spent on the work up to the date of each payment (ignoring any retainage).

A contractor's applications for payment must be based on the proportion of total work completed, and not on actual costs expended, based on the contractor's schedule of values submitted earlier for approval.

Retainage, or Holdback

In standard contracts, and many others, a provision is usual for the retention, by an owner, of a percentage (often, 5 or 10 percent) of the amount of payments due, often up to a stipulated limit. The purpose of such retainage is to ensure the contractor has a continuing financial interest in a project; it also gives the owner some security against deficiencies or default by the contractor. Retainage, however, has its costs in the form of interest paid by the contractor on the amount withheld, which cost a contractor should have allowed for in his bid and in the contract sum. It is therefore in an owner's interest to balance his need for security against the related cost he pays. To this end, a common practice is to stop deducting retainage from progress payments when a project reaches 50 percent completion.[14]

Schedule of Values

These schedules are so important and fundamental to proper contract payment procedures and to the administration of a contract's finances that some believe they should be identified as a contract document in all but the most minor contracts.[15] A **schedule of values** (SV) is a creature of a construction contract; it is an analysis of the contract sum made by the contractor to show the owner–designer the amounts of several parts of the work. An SV can and should be an important source of information and therefore merits careful attention and use.

If you examine a standard form of contract conditions (e.g., AIA Document A201, Article 9) you will observe from the condition dealing with the SV that its stated purpose is to be "a basis for reviewing the Contractor's [subsequent] Applications for Payment" (A201, Subpara. 9.2.1). A contractor must initiate payments by applying for them to the owner's agent who is responsible for checking them. This is done by comparing the applications with the approved SV and with the work completed on-site.

Checking and approving an SV is an important first step. The best way for an owner's agent to check an SV for accuracy and approval is to have an accurate estimate of the costs of the work and to make comparisons. No owner should seek bids for a fixed-price contract without an accurate estimate of costs of the work made by an expert. How else can anyone judge the worth of the bids received? How else can anyone properly check the accuracy of an SV? Additionally, without a valid and proven SV, how can anyone check an application for payment and with confidence issue a certificate of payment?

Supporting Evidence for SVs

Some standard contracts, such as A201, require a contractor to submit supporting evidence for the accuracy of his submitted SV, and this should be the normal procedure. How much evidence does an owner's agent need to check an SV? How much can be requested? It depends on the nature and location of the work, but it is reasonable to require an SV to show at least the actual costs of all major parts of the work—not only the amounts of subcontracts, but also analyses of the costs of major subtrade work and the contractor's work, if any. To illustrate, a partial list follows of possible parts of a project, for which separate costs are readily available from trade contractors and from a general contractor, that might be required in an SV:

Division One—General Requirements

1. Mobilization costs, including: bonds, permits, and all other initial, nonrepetitive mobilization costs, setup costs, and costs of layout.
2. Continuous general expenses, including rental (or charge-out) costs and all other repetitive costs of all temporary facil-

ities and services; plant and equipment not allocable to specific parts of the work; small tools, site supervision and staff, and all other job overhead costs and operating overhead costs and profit not included in (1) mobilization costs, and (2) demobilization costs.

3. Demobilization costs, including all nonrepetitive demobilization costs and closeout costs.

4. Cash allowances, if not included by the bidding documents in the several trade sections of the specifications.

Division Two—Site Work

1. Demolitions
2. Moving structures
3. Clearing and grubbing
4. Site grading
5. Excavating
6. Backfilling
7. Filling (imported)
8. Dewatering
9. Piling
10. Site utilities, etc.

It is not necessary to list more because anyone can go to the same source: *The Masterformat* and its narrowscope headings. The specific main headings in an SV are those of the sections in the contract's specifications. So that an SV will contain adequate supporting evidence as to its accuracy and correctness, the supporting information provided by a contractor must be in sufficient detail to enable it to be checked and subsequently used to check the accuracy of all **applications for payment**. This means that certain sections of work will need breaking down.[16] An owner–designer, therefore, should create the outline of an SV, include its pro forma with the bidding

documents, and identify it as a contract document. Some believe, however, that there are hazards in making an SV part of a contract.[17] An illustrative example is shown in **Figure 20.1**.

Some contractors may balk at the detail for SVs proposed because instinctively they do not like to release such information. An owner's agent (designer or construction manager), however, can and should insist on whatever information is reasonable and necessary. It is essential to be able to check completely the accuracy of applications for payment, and only such detail makes that possible. Also, by requiring an analysis of Division One—General Requirements, as shown here, in the first progress payment a contractor can be properly paid the necessary mobilization costs and an accurate proportion of the job and operating overhead costs and profit (all lumped together and not shown separately). This should make the *front-end loading* of SVs and payment applications no longer necessary. Further installments of overheads and profit are included in the subsequent payments.

From the viewpoint of a general contractor, making an SV from an estimate summary need not be time-consuming; especially if using a computer program. The markup for profit and operating overhead can be concealed by including it with those costs that cannot be analyzed or compared (i.e., the costs of the work done by a prime contractor's own forces and the job overhead costs). If a bidder comes across an SV pro forma that appears to require the exposure of markup, then a protest before submitting a bid should be made.

Front-end loading in an SV is justified, some say, because owner–designers, not knowledgeable in construction costs and economics, often do not pay a contractor enough in the early progress payments to cover the costs of mobilization. If successful, front-end-loading gives a temporary increase in cash flow, but there always is an equal decrease and a related risk from a reduction in cash flow later.

Applications for Payment

The designer, construction manager, or other agent or employee of an owner checks the applications for payment (APs) for accuracy with the approved SV. Reasons for inaccuracies in APs include

- An overvaluation of the work completed
- An unintentional error in its preparation
- An intentional error, in hope that an overpayment will be made

Overvaluation of earlier work (i.e., front-end loading) is a common reason for wrong APs. Seemingly intentional errors in APs may include wrong percentages of work completed, and claims for work not yet done. Confusion over the deduction of all previous payments from the "total value of work completed to date" is not uncommon. Causes for the approval of a wrong AP include

- Lack of a detailed cost estimate
- A reluctance to spend time checking or disputing
- An incorrect SV wrongly approved in the first instance

The most reprehensible causes for approval of a wrong AP are the lack of an independent cost estimate, and a wrong or inadequate SV, since proper certification and payment are primary duties of an owner and his agent. Other things that may bear on APs and distort their contents include:

- An approved, front-end-loaded SV
- Errors in an SV that are adjusted in an AP
- Calculations of the values of completed work by estimated percentages that are inaccurate
- If payments by an owner often are late, so that there is more work completed by the time a payment is made, at some time in the future APs may be inflated in anticipation of a recurrence
- A contractor or subcontractor may be working at a loss and may apply for payments based on actual expenditures for work, instead of on the proportion of the contract sum according to the proportion of the work completed, as stipulated in the contract.

Estimates of the proportions of completed work should be accurate at the time of submission. Overassessment in order to include work expected to be completed before payment is common and may lead to overpayment.

When an owner's agent tries to protect the owner against overpayments and the contractor tries to get as large a payment as possible, tensions may arise.

When it was reported (by Aird) that contractors generally lacked cost information, no mention was made of owners and designers who generally have even less cost information. This should not be, and need not be, if the owner employs the cost consultant's skills needed.

Measurement of Work Done

Among the information in an application for payment, the most critical, and probably the most difficult to ascertain, is the proportion of work completed as of a specific date.

SCHEDULE OF VALUES

THIS SCHEDULE IS REQUIRED BY THE OWNER AND ARCHITECT UNDER THE GENERAL CONDITIONS OF THE CONTRACT FOR CONSTRUCTION TO BE COMPLETED AND SUBMITTED IN DUPLICATE PRIOR TO THE FIRST PAYMENT. WHERE BIDS HAVE BEEN DEPOSITED IN A BID DEPOSITORY, THE ACTUAL AMOUNTS OF DEPOSITED BIDS SHALL BE INSERTED BELOW. ALL CASH ALLOWANCES REQUIRED BY THE CONSTRUCTION CONTRACT SHALL BE DEDUCTED FROM SUBBIDS AND INCLUDED SEPARATELY AS INDICATED.

JOB TITLE *Sandown High School* CONTRACT SUM *$1,160,000.00*

OWNER *Island School Board* ARCHITECT *A. Bolton King*

CONTRACTOR *W. Brice Ltd.* CONTRACT DATE *29 Jan. '74*

Sections of Work	Name	Value of Work ($)
1. General Expenses	General	
(a) Initial Expenses	Contractor	18,000
(b) Continuing Expenses	ditto	84,000
2. Site Works	ditto	36,000
3. Reinforced Concrete		
(a) Formwork	ditto	110,000
(b) Steel Rebar	ditto	65,000
(c) Concrete	ditto	95,000
4. Blockwork Massonry	Acme Ltd.	33,000
5. Metals		
(a) Miscellaneous	Ferrous Ltd.	28,000
(b) Structural	Cansteel	5,500
6. Woodwork		
(a) Rough Carpentry	General	5,000
(b) Finish Carpentry	ditto	12,000
(c) Millwork	Foursquare Ltd.	28,000
7. Protection		
(a) Roofing	Blackspot Ltd.	21,000
(b) Waterproofing	ditto	7,000
8. Openings		
(a) Aluminum & Glass	Alspec Ltd.	40,000
(b) Interior Doors	Portico Ltd	12,500
9. Finishes		
(a) Lath & Plaster	Stucco Inc.	51,000
(b) Acoustic tiling	Denman Co.	20,000
(c) Resilient Flooring	Vyner Ltd.	10,000
15. Mechanical		
(a) Plumbing	Cobre Inc.	52,000
(b) Heating & Venting	Cobre Inc.	214,000
16. Electrical	Sparks Co. Inc.	104,000
Total Value of Work		$1,051,000

Add: Cash Allowances:

    Contingency Allowance $10,000
    Finish Hardware (supply) $63,000
    Testing and Inspection $5,000
    Electrical Fixtures (supply) $21,000
    Landscaping $10,000

	=	+109,000
TOTAL: CONTRACT SUM		$1,160,000

Figure 20.1 A schedule of values

Application for Payment

APPLICATION FOR PAYMENT NO. 4. This application is required by the Owner and the Architect under the General Conditions of the Contract for Construction and is to be completed and submitted in duplicate to the Architect at least 5 days before payment becomes due and is to be based on the previously approved Schedule of Values

JOB TITLE *Sandown High School*   CONTRACT SUM *$1,160,000.00*

OWNER *Island School Board*   ARCHITECT *A. Bolton King*

CONTRACTOR *W. Brice Ltd.*   APPLICATION DATE *25 May '74*

Sections of Work	Values	Amount Completed	Value Completed	Remarks
1. (a) Initial				
G. Expenses	$18,000	100%	$18,000	
(b) Contin.				
G. Expense	84,000	25%	21,000	(4/16 months)
2. Site Works	36,000	20%	7,200	(bldg. excav.)
3. Reinforced Concrete				
(a) Formwork	110,000	85%	93,5000	(some to be removed)
(b) Rebar	65,000	100%	65,000	
(c) Concrete	95,000	100%	95,000	
4. Massonry	33,000	33%	11,000	(see attachment)
5. Metals	28,000	50%	14,000	
(a) Miscellaneous				
(b) Struct. Steel	5,500	100%	5,5000	
15. Mechanical	266,000	(allow)	2,000	(sleeves, etc.)
16. Electrical	104,000	(allow)	1,500	(concealed conduit)
		Sub-total	$333,700	

Add: Amounts of Cash Allowances Expended:

    Contingency Allowance:

Extra work in foundations			+5,300	(Change #3)
			(nil)	(Change #2)
			(nil)	(Change #1)

Total Value of Work

Completed to Date $339,000

                                          −33,900

Less: Retainage (10% of above total) $305,100

Less: Previous Payments

Payments Nos. 1 and 2   = $100,000

Last Payment No. 3   =   86,000

                                =   − 186,000

Amount Now Due: Payment No. 4   = $119,100

Figure 20.2 An application for payment.

Often an owner's agent has accepted an AP with the percentages of completion intuitively assessed, or eyeballed by the superintendent, and nothing more. **Figure 20.2,** shows an example of a completed application for payment, with its supporting schedule of values.

AIA Document A101, Owner-Contractor Agreement, Article 5, *Progress Payments,* para. 5.5 says, "Applications for Payment shall indicate the percentage of completion of each portion of the Work...." Frequently, a percentage gives a false impression of accuracy (e.g., 66-2/3 percent), and usually percentages are better derived from actual measured quantities of completed work. Percentages that are multiples of five or 10 may be suspect. (Ten percent is the percentage of choice, 90 percent of the time.)

Only a person with a good knowledge of construction and its costs can properly check SVs and APs. Also, one has only to consider the detail and complexity of work and estimates of costs to realize how difficult it often is (sometimes impossible) to eyeball accurately the proportions of uncompleted work. For some trades the amount of work completed is easy to assess (i.e., to count the number of windows installed or of doors hung). Some trade work, however, needs much more effort to assess the proportion completed.

The primary means to accurate and efficient measurement of the quantities of completed work is a detailed cost estimate. Measurement, however, does not always take tremendous effort. On site, the estimate's quantities can be compared with the completed work. If the estimate is well organized, the quantities of completed work often can be extracted easily. When work is approaching completion, it is easier to mea-

sure the work not yet done as a deduction from the total quantity in the estimate.

The ease or difficulty with which such measurement can be done depends largely upon an estimate's accuracy and layout. In addition to trade sections and subsections, estimates should show quantities according to floors, or bays, or other modules of a building. This makes for easier and more accurate measurement in the estimate, and it makes the estimate more useful later.

In Figure 20.2, the Application for Payment shows "Concrete" as "100 percent complete," and "Forms" as "85 percent complete." The reason for these apparently contradictory figures is that some forms have yet to be stripped. Note on the same application a statement: *"Total value of work completed to date."* Such totals must appear on every application.

Every application must contain an accurate evaluation of each part of the work done to date, and the total value to date. From this, deduct the total of all previous payments made to the contractor. In this way, errors are not carried forward to subsequent applications and to progress payments. If a contractor does not make accurate measurements of completed work in a month, or if he simply increases the amount by the amount done in the previous month, an incorrect AP will be made.

Although accurate APs and progress payments are required, accuracy always is relative, and striving for total accuracy is a waste. It is foolish to spend $100 worth of effort to save $5 of financing costs. On the one hand, carry out one's obligations properly; on the other, we should use common sense and be economic. Descriptions of the procedures for dealing with APs are found in the AIA Document A101, Article 5,

Progress Payments. Note the provisions of subparagraphs 5.7.1, 5.7.2, and 5.8 for the modification of certain progress payments at the time of substantial completion and final completion of work.

Value of Delivered and Undelivered Materials in APs

A construction contract may, or may not, provide for progress payments to include the value of materials delivered to the site, but not yet incorporated into the work at the time of an application for payment (see A101-1987, Article 5, subpara. 5.6.2). If an owner pays for unincorporated materials, they then become the owner's property and may not be removed from the site. Some contracts stipulate that certain materials shall be paid for by the owner before delivery to the site, in which case the owner's title should be protected and the need for insurance considered. This aspect of progress payments becomes increasingly important as prefabricated components are increasingly used.

20.4 CERTIFICATES FOR PAYMENT

In all national standard forms of contract, payment of the contractor by the owner always is dependent on and initiated by a certificate for payment (CP) issued by the owner's agent named in the contract (usually, an architect, engineer, or sometimes a construction manager or quantity surveyor). In many contracts, including those based on the standard forms, the issuance of certificates for payment is the most important single function of an owner's agent, because under the standard contracts an owner can pay the contractor only on issuance of a CP.

Yet, the obligation to pay for the work is an owner's primary contractual obligation.[18]

The issuance of CPs demonstrates a prime example of the owner's agent (designer, or other) acting as arbiter and interpreter of a contract's requirements and the judge of its performance. Issuance of a CP also is an indication to an owner, and the contractor, that the owner's agent represents, to the best of his knowledge, that the contractor is entitled to the payment certified because the work it relates to is according to the contract, except for any noted exceptions. See the AIA Document A201-1987, Article 9, *Payments and Completion*, Subpara. 9.4, *Certificates for Payment*, for the subject-clause[19] and other details.

Further exposition of the architect's powers as arbiter and judge of performance is found in AIA A201-1987 under Subpara. 9.5, *Decisions to Withhold Certification*, where seven reasons are given for such withholding. In other words, as a developer once said: "He who controls the money has the clout." Document A201 provides an architect with clout—and responsibility.

Carefully read the wording of a construction contract to find the precise contractual significance of a certificate for payment. Although standard contracts are commonly used, there is nothing to stop an owner from changing any part, providing the changes result in a legal contract. Changes and differences in matters of payment are commonplace, especially when an owner is government or a corporation.

At law, the responsibility for full and proper performance of the work of a contract lies with the contractor. In practice, therefore, it is unlikely that a contractor can claim the issuance of a CP as a categorical approval of the work, the value of which is in the CP, so as to contest a disapproval of specific parts of the work by the owner's agent. However, a final certificate of payment and the final payment by an owner to a contractor does have considerable contractual significance.

Even though, under Document A201, a CP may be taken as an indication of limited approval of the work by the owner's agent, a contractor should not think that he is in any way relieved of any responsibility for the work because of the issuance of a CP. On its face, a CP in effect says: So much work is complete according to the contract, therefore the contractor is entitled to so much money. It usually does not say that categorically the work is approved and accepted.

AIA Document A201-1987, Section 9.4, on the subject of the progress and approval of work, although quite long, does not commit the architect to very much. It says: "However, the issuance of a Certificate for Payment will not be a representation that the Architect has...", followed by four preclusions intended to keep the obligation for proper performance squarely where it belongs: with the contractor.[20]

In many contracts, an owner's agent is not obliged to issue a CP in the amount claimed by the contractor in his application for payment if the owner's agent has reasonable cause. There are several reasons stated why an owner's agent may withhold part or even all of the amount applied for in an application for payment. Some reasons are

- Work not performed according to the contract
- Failure of the contractor to pay bills and subcontractors
- Lien claims made against the work by third parties

- Evidence that the work specified in the contract cannot be completed within the contract time
- Evidence that the work specified in the contract cannot be completed for the unpaid balance of the contract sum

The primary reason for withholding payment is to protect the owner against a probable loss arising from the conditions just cited. Probably, none of these (except the first) would be valid if they were not specifically set down in a contract's documents. As always, a contract's wording is paramount.

If an owner's agent and a contractor cannot agree as to the correct amount due in a progress payment, the owner's agent may, if the contract so provides, exercise his contractual power as judge of the contract's performance and interpreter of its requirements and issue a CP in the amount that he, the owner's agent, believes is due the contractor. In that event, a contractor's only recourse is to seek arbitration, or an action in court.

If no CP or payment is forthcoming within the times prescribed in the contract, usually a contractor can stop the work. However, he cannot stop work because he disagrees with the amount of a CP, unless the contract so provides. Again, the actual wording of the contract is paramount. Decisions in legal cases dealing with construction contracts vary among jurisdictions. Consult a construction lawyer for cases and precedents in your area.

20.5 PAYMENTS IN CONTRACTS

Many supply goods or services to a construction project, and all deserve and expect proper payment. Under the typical terms and conditions of construction contracts, an owner pays only the contractor (not the subcontractors and suppliers). Money paid by an owner to a contractor is considered to be held in trust by the contractor for payment to those who have supplied goods or services to the work. Some lien statutes (and some construction contracts) state as much and identify a contractor as a trustee with a legal obligation to pay first all those who have a legal right to payment.[21]

The existence of statutory provisions, and the existence of contractual provisions for sworn statements made before payment, are evidence of an area of construction contracts that requires special vigilance—that of payments. Whenever it is necessary to pay money to one person for distribution to others, expect some delays at best or, at worst, misappropriation. It happens in all walks of life and with all kinds of people.

Final Certificate and Final Payment

It is important to read and understand exactly what a construction contract says about these last things, because they bear on a contract's performance. Not all contracts, standard or otherwise, are identical. Usually, a final certificate and a final payment are distinctly different from all preceding certificates and payments. It is as if all preceding certificates were only a means to paying advances on the contract sum; as if the final certificate and final payment only are contractually significant; and as if all preceding certificates and payments were washed away and replaced by the wording and figures of the final certificate. Particularly in a final certificate, where the total amounts of all preceding payments are deducted from the total value of work done, leaving "the amount now due" to the contractor to be paid in this the final payment. As stated in A201-1987: "The making of final payment shall constitute a waiver of claims as provided in Subparagraph 4.3.5" (Subpara. 9.10.3) [and] "Acceptance of final payment by the Contractor, a Subcontractor or material supplier shall constitute a waiver of claims by that payee..." (A201, Subpara. 9.10.4).

By making a final payment, an owner also waives all claims against the contractor, with certain important exceptions stated in the contract[22] and other exceptions that simply may be called unsettled claims; excepting any further claims that may subsequently arise during the period of the warranty for the work, often set at one year after substantial completion. Obviously, it is good practice for a contractor to reaffirm in writing any outstanding claims at the time of making an application for final payment; thereby emphasizing their exclusion from the final payment and their exception from the contractual waiver.

Similarly, at the same time, it is a good practice for an owner's agent to restate any outstanding claims by the owner against the contractor.

Before final payment, it is common practice to require contractors to provide an affidavit, a statutory declaration, or a sworn statement, to the owner, to declare under oath that the contractor has paid all the contractor's bills for the work, all payrolls, and all other debts arising from the work. The purpose is to assure an owner that there will be no claims against the owner or his property arising from work by third parties. Experience has shown, however, that some sworn statements are not reliable. Therefore, it is good practice for an owner's agent to have a title search made of the property (the work site) to ensure that no one has registered a lien against the property for work done at or for materials supplied to the job site. A main point is whether a final payment to a subcontractor can or should be made before the contractor's final payment; this a matter for mutual agreement explicitly expressed in a subcontract.

20.6 FINANCING AND PAYMENTS IN CM PROJECTS

The fundamental differences between CM projects and traditional projects affect financing and payments. Instead of making payments to one contractor, an owner in a CM project makes payments to several prime contractors each of whom must submit a schedule of values and subsequent applications for payment. Therefore, there are many more checks for an owner to sign. There is much more administrative work for the owner's agent in making payments in a CM project. The extra work is not without a return, since as a result an owner has more immediate control over the CM project's finances. Does an owner really want more control? What, if any, are the advantages to an owner in a CM project with respect to payments? Are there disadvantages?

One disadvantage already mentioned is the increase in administrative work paid for by the owner in the fee for the construction manager. If, however, the claims made for CM projects are realistic, and particularly the claim of a shorter construction time because of phased construction, an owner's financing costs in a CM project should be less. Because each specialist contractor in a CM project has to submit a schedule of values before submitting his first application for payment, the owner's agent will get more information about the CM project's actual costs. Similarly, more information

and more accurate estimates of the quantities of completed work may be obtained in applications for payment from specialist contractors, than from a general contractor in a traditional project. This should help to ensure against overpayments and assist in contract management.

The increase in information and control gained by an owner pertains throughout a CM project. In a CM project, there are fewer subcontractors but as many suppliers as in a traditional project. However, almost all the suppliers in a CM project are suppliers to a contractor. This means that all payments to these suppliers can be the objects of sworn statements (affidavits) made by contractors. Similarly, a large part of the work in CM projects is the subject of warranties by contractors, and not subcontractors.

20.7 COMPUTER APPLICATIONS TO FINANCES AND PAYMENTS

A good example of the need for integrated construction information occurs in the administration of contract finances; particularly, with schedules of values (SVs), applications for payment (APs), and certificates for payment. In a fixed-price contract, the contract time and contract sum are part of the agreement. Progress payments are fundamental. Much time and effort could be saved if SVs were required to be computerized extracts from computerized cost estimates. It is possible to devise ways (through software) to protect the confidentiality of a contractor's overhead and profit. All else should be open to scrutiny.

Expect to see a reduction in paperwork with the increased use of digital transmission of information. Eventually, the paperless office will become a reality. Already information can be stored and transferred by means of FAX, modems, laser disks, and other paperless means. As financial markets are now electronic, so will be project administration. There are no real obstacles, except the costs of the systems and their acceptance. As with other electronic technology, the costs of information interchange are falling. Acceptance may take a little longer.

REFERENCES

1. H. V. Prochnow, ed., "Commercial Bank Real Estate Lending," *Bank* *Credit* (New York: Harper and Row, 1981).

SUMMARY OF MAIN POINTS

- Property developments usually require borrowed capital; lenders become partners of developers, and therefore need to know about them and their developments.

- Limited liability of a corporation does not mean the owners have no personal liability when they borrow or obtain a performance bond.

- Credit financing is common in construction. For a builder, credit often is short term (i.e., less than a year), or medium term (i.e., a few years); for a developer it often is longer (e.g., a mortgage for a term of years).

- Three Cs of the borrower are: (1) character, (2) capacity to repay, and (3) collateral to secure a loan (like the Three Cs of bonding).

- The many kinds of credit available include: revolving credit, to deal with seasonal rise and fall of work volume; standby credit, or a take-out loan, as interim financing for development; and serial-term loans.

- As a borrower's partner in a development, the lender needs to know the reason for a loan and how it will be repaid; therefore, a loan officer also needs certain information about the borrower and the project.

- The four primary financial documents and sources of information about a company are: (1) balance sheet (2) profit and loss statement (3) retained earnings reconciliation, and (4) source and application of funds statement. Also, a loan officer will want to see the cost estimate for a project.

- Accounting standards do not always require financial statements to make the facts as clear as many think they should be. Understand your own company's financial statement when you take it to a lender.

- Key business ratios are simple indications of a company's financial condition; some mean more than others, depending on the kind of business and how the ratios compare with the norms. All relevant ratios should be examined together and compared to reported norms for a particular class of business.

■ Construction is project-oriented, complex, and often lenders hire a construction consultant to verify a bid and contract, to monitor a project and its finances, all to protect the lender's investment.

■ Latent credit comes from many sources, including all those in construction who have a financial interest in a project and a lien right of claim.

■ Cost of credit for a builder is an overhead cost; it depends on an interest rate and loan duration.

■ For a borrower, time affects the cost of credit, but timing also is important.

■ Timely certification and payment in a construction contract is a primary obligation of the designer and owner.

■ Late payments to a contractor create a burden for him and for all who depend on his payments.

■ An owner's finances and ability to pay are of concern to the contractor. Document A201-1987 allows a contractor to ask for "reasonable evidence."

■ Cash flow is critical. Like irrigation water, cash flows through a project to all who do work and provide materials and services.

■ Contract progress payments generally are made monthly; only "entire contracts" require total completion of work before payment.

■ Progress payments are like advances, they do not signify acceptance of work; they should be commensurate with the proportion of total work completed, not with the actual costs expended.

■ A schedule of values (SV) is a breakdown of a contract sum into the costs of discrete parts of the work; it is required to establish the basis for checking applications for payment. The format should be prescribed.

■ An application for payment (AP) is based on the costs in the SV and on the proportion of work completed (and of materials delivered, or accepted elsewhere, if allowed) to date; it is to determine total value of work done to date, from which are deducted all previous interim payments.

■ Assessment of amount and proportion of work completed often is problematic. The solution is an accurate cost estimate by an owner's agent, an accurate SV with adequate supporting evidence from the contractor, and measured quantities of work done.

■ Values of materials and of products accepted may be included in an interim payment, if provided for by the contract; this becomes more important as the amount of prefabricated work increases.

■ Certificates for payment (CPs) are a primary duty of an owner's agent, since the fulfillment of the owner's obligation to make payments depends on them. A CP for a progress payment does not indicate acceptance of work done.

■ A final certificate of payment and a final payment are different from earlier certificates and payments. In most contracts they both represent waivers by each party of undisclosed claims.

■ Affidavits and statutory declarations as to the fulfillment of financial obligations

- cannot always be accepted at face value, and a title search for liens is advisable.

- CM project payments are essentially the same, except there are several prime contractors, which makes for more administration, but gives an owner more information and security.

- Computer applications to SVs, APs, and progress payments, should be part of integrated information open to all (but with markups concealed). Project finances can emulate financial markets in the use of electronic systems.

NOTES

[1]Real property development generally consists of a site, a concept, and borrowing to make it materialize. Problems include ideas that do not endure, slow startups, economic cycles, and poor timing. As a result, development bubbles burst, sometimes leaving owners with properties that do not appreciate quickly enough; or worse, depreciate quickly.

[2]See, Brooks, *The Mythical Man-month*, in Chapter 7.

[3]Sidney Homer, *A History of Interest Rates* (New Brunswick, N.J.: Rutgers University Press, 1963) p. 17.

[4]Herbert G. Summerfield, Jr., Vice President, Pittsburgh National Bank, in "Commercial Bank Real Estate Lending," an article in *Bank Credit*, Herber V. Prochnow, ed. (New York: Harper and Row, 1981) p. 181.

[5]Herbert V. Prochnow, *Bank Credit*. A collection of short writings by experts on numerous aspects of bank credit.

[6]*Ibid*. Chapter 19, "Equipment Leasing."

[7]Financier is used here as a convenient term for a bank, a mortgage finance company, or any such financial institution that lends money for property development.

[8]A profit and loss (income) statement shows the bottom line by accounting for gross value of work done, net value done, gross profit or loss, net profit or loss, and net profit after taxes. A retained earnings statement (net worth reconciliation) shows retained earnings at year's start, net income for the year, cash dividends paid out in the year, and retained earnings at the end of the year. A source and application (use) of funds statement shows changes in available working capital: that part of current assets (after deducting current liabilities) available for the business; noncurrent assets might be an office building and construction equipment; noncurrent liabilities, a mortgage on the building.

[9]Dana Wechsler, "The Bankers' New Headache," *Forbes*, Vol. 145, No. 1, January 8, 1990, pp. 76. Events in this decade, such as the Savings and Loan debacle and the failure of real estate to go on appreciating in many major cities of the world, have drawn more attention to the need for better accounting methods.

[10]Abraham J. Briloff, *The Truth About Corporate Accounting* (New York: Harper and Row, 1981). This author has written at least two other books in this field.

[11]In Canada, often a project monitor is a quantity surveyor. Some financial officers are not knowledgeable enough about construction and its costs and contracts and still neglect to obtain expert advice.

[12]Lien rights of different persons vary in different jurisdictions. See, p.374 Chapter 23, "Laws and Liens in Construction."

[13]See also, CCDC2-1982, GC 13, "Applications for Payment," and GC 14, "Certificates and Payments."

[14]In some jurisdictions, retainage is required by a lien statute. Should a lien be filed, the retainage is then paid into court for dispersement to valid creditors.

[15]Document A201 is not specific about the nature of a schedule of values. Subpara. 1.1.1, *The Contract Documents*, does not name it; but neither does it exclude it, and it refers to the "other documents listed in the Agreement."

[16]There is a close relationship between the breakdown of work needed for a schedule of values and that for a work-breakdown structure as used in planning and scheduling. Both are derived from the cost estimate.

[17]Jervis and Levin, *Construction Law, Principles and Practice* (New York: McGraw-Hill, 1988) p. 91. The expert opinion, however, is without explanation. Therefore, each owner–designer and contractor should obtain appropriate legal advice.

[18]Often standard contracts are changed by amendments. Here we refer to standard documents as published.

[19]That is, "subject to an evaluation of the Work for conformance with the Contract Documents upon Substantial Completion..." (A201-1987, Subpara. 9.4.2.).

[20]Document CCDC2-1982 flatly says: "No payment made by the Owner under this Contract or partial or entire use or occupancy of the Work by the Owner shall constitute an acceptance of work or products which are not in accordance with the Contract Documents." (GC 14, *Certificates and Payments*, Para. 14.10); and "By issuing any certificate the Consultant [architect, engineer, construction manager] does not guarantee the correctness or completeness or the Work." (*Ibid.*, Para. 14.11).

[21]As in, for example, the *Builders Lien Act* of British Columbia, in which the provision whereby the "Contract price constituted [*sic*] a trust fund" is a thing separate and apart from the statutory lien rights, although set down in the same statute.

[22]As in AIA Document A201-1987, Subpara. 4.3.5 *Waiver of Claims: Final Payment.*

QUESTIONS AND TOPICS FOR DISCUSSION

1. Explain the meaning of the following terms:
   a. A contractor's equity in a project
   b. A corporate person's limited liability
   c. A revolving-credit loan
   d. A serial-term loan
   e. Retainage

2. Describe the main kinds of credit financing available to builders.

3. Identify and explain the Three Cs of financing.

4. Explain why a contractor usually needs credit to perform a construction contract, and how and why this affects the costs of construction work.

5. Explain in detail why a financial institution that has made a substantial loan to a property developer should employ its own construction consultant.

6. Why do owners usually make progress payments to contractors? Discuss the alternatives.

7. What are the most common major deficiencies in schedules of values submitted by contractors, and how can these be guarded against?

8. What are the most likely major deficiencies in applications for payment?

9. Discuss the contractual significance of an interim certificate of payment and a final certificate of payment.

10. What are the five financial documents a developer–contractor seeking finance needs to show a loan officer? Explain the main content of each.

11. Explain why cash flow during a project often is more critical to a contractor than the profit at the end.

12. What do a worker's wages and the site of a construction project have in common?

13. Discover and explain four financial ratios that are most appropriate to an understanding of the financial condition of a construction company.

14. Explain in detail the meaning of front-end loading with respect to progress payments.

15. Regarding contract payments, explain why
a.   A certificate of payment is required
b.   An owner needs technical advice as to the amounts of progress payments
c.   Accountants typically are not equipped to deal with progress payments
d.   Progress payments are different from a final payment
e.   In an interim certificate, the total amount of all payments made to date is deducted

16. Explain the purpose and limitations of retainage.

CHAPTER

21

PROTECTION AND INDEMNIFICATION

A thing done between two persons
ought not to injure another.
(Legal maxim)

Protection of persons and property, and (should injury or damage occur) the question of liability, always is a matter of concern in construction. Construction work is complex and hazardous, and with many possibilities for injury or damage. Buildings are designed for the safety of the occupants. However, most of the time during construction, protective features are not yet installed. Construction sites are dangerous. The responsibility is onerous. So, it is not surprising that contracts speak at length of protection, liability, indemnification, and insurance. This chapter examines all of these, except insurance which is examined in Chapter 22.

21.1 OBLIGATIONS IN CONTRACTS

Indemnification of an Owner by the Contractor

Standard contracts are specific about a contractor's obligations, some of which are

- To supervise and direct the work
- To be solely responsible for all construction means, methods, techniques, and procedures
- To indemnify and hold harmless[1] the owner and his agent(s) and their agents and employees against all claims, damages, losses, and expenses arising out of or resulting from the work

The contractor is responsible for the execution of the work and generally may do it in whatever way he chooses, provided he performs it according to the contract. Therefore, the contractor is primarily responsible for any injuries and damages to persons and property that occur as a result. Not only is a contractor responsible, he also specifically agrees and contracts (when the contract contains the wording) not to allow the owner and his agents to suffer any damages, loss, or expense resulting from claims (i.e., by third parties) arising out of performance of work.

Owners and their agents, knowing what sites are, and often using standard contracts as a guide, write contracts as best they can to protect themselves from liability for all that goes on at a site. However, they cannot rid themselves of every obligation simply by seeking to place them all on a contractor. An owner and his agents will be responsible for certain damage (e.g., that resulting from misinformation or from a defective design). Such responsibility often is described in a contract.

An owner and a contractor are mutually obligated and affected by their contract. If an owner requires a contractor to take more risk or to provide more protection, the extra costs should be passed to the owner in the contract sum. Standard contracts, and particularly the AIA Document A201, *General Conditions of the Contract for Construction*, describes at some length indemnification of the owner and architect by the contractor. Study copies of this and other standard contract documents. If they appear difficult, try underlining or highlighting the key wording, and ignoring at first the wording between parenthetic commas.

The gist of Document A201-1987, Article 3, Paragraph 3.18, *Indemnification*, is that the contractor shall indemnify the own-

er and the architect against all claims arising out of the work caused by any negligent act or omission of the contractor or anyone under his control. This article begins:

> To the fullest extent permitted by law, the Contractor shall indemnify and hold harmless the Owner, Architect, Architect's consultants, and agents and employees of any of them....

You cannot be more to the point than that; it really is a matter of common sense. If the contractor did not have control over the work, and could not decide how and when the work would be done, or could not direct the work, then he could not be responsible for the work and its effects. A contractor, however, usually does have control of the work: as stated in Paragraph 3.3, *Supervision and Construction Procedures*:

> The Contractor shall supervise and direct the Work,...[and] shall be solely responsible for and have control over construction means, methods, techniques, sequences, and procedures...unless Contract Documents give other specific instructions concerning these matters.

The contractor decides the means and methods of doing the work. If the contractor is negligent and something goes wrong, then he is responsible for any resultant injury, damage, or destruction of persons or property. Similarly, under Article 10, *Protection of Persons and Property*, which begins: "The Contractor shall be responsible for initiating, maintaining and supervising all safety precautions and programs...." The contractor is in charge and carries the main responsibility because the work is the contractor's to perform, and the responsibility is his to take. Other contracts, however, may say other things; therefore, every contract must be read and understood.

Each project is unique, so each contract requires particular attention by both parties, their agents, and employees. Nothing can be taken for granted because, although the wording of certain conditions in many contracts may be similar, differences among contracting parties, sites, and the work of projects are many.

Owner's and Designer's Obligations

Both owner and designer have obligations in contracts for which they are liable if they are negligent. Specific indemnification of a contractor by an owner is, however, not usual. That is not to say that a contractor has no legal recourse against an owner (or others) should he suffer loss because of their negligence; only that he may not be able to take action under the contract.[2] Nevertheless, a contractor who believes he has suffered damage through the owner's (or anyone else's) action or inaction can sue for damages; as can any person who has, or believes he has, suffered damage because of another's fault or default.[3]

EXAMPLE:

Some contracts stipulate that the owner shall indemnify the contractor against all claims and losses arising from a defect in the owner's title to the real property known as the site. If this is not a contract provision, and the contractor suffers a loss because of a defect in title, the contractor can take action and seek damages through the courts.

A typical general condition in the earlier AIA Document A201-1976 (Article 7), said that should either party suffer damage because of the acts or omissions of the other party, or of anyone for whom the other party is legally liable, including employees and agents, a claim shall be made in writing by the injured party.

In AIA Document A201-1987, there is no longer a heading "Claims for Damages" as before. Instead the document's index shows such claims as a general topic and refers to several paragraphs and subparagraphs of the standard document. See Article 4, Para. 4.3, *Claims and Disputes*, and specifically, 4.3.9, *Injury or Damage to Persons or Property*, which begins:

> "If either party to the Contract suffers injury or damage to person or property because of an act or omission of the other party,...written notice shall be given..."

Article 4 provides for the definition and settlement of a claim for additional cost, or time, or both, initially through the architect. Also, in A201-1987, the owner does indemnify the contractor and the architect (and others) from and against claims and damages arising out of work in areas affected (contaminated) by asbestos or polychlorinated biphenyl (PCB) on site.[4]

In these matters, not all contracts are the same. Read copies of different contracts on the subject of protection and indemnification. Try rewriting in your own words to arrive at an understanding of pertinent parts; especially of a contract for which you propose to bid. In specific instances, a lawyer's advice should be sought.

Construction Manager's Obligations

If a construction manager is an agent of an owner, then the construction manager's obligations[5] in such matters as legal liability are generally similar to those of an architect, as outlined in a construction contract, although specific obligations depend on the contract between them. Generally, a contractor also indemnifies a construction manager as an owner and an architect are indemnified. Other contractual positions of a construction manager are examined at the end of this chapter.

Obligations of Others to Protect and Indemnify

A designer normally has the protection of professional liability insurance, better known as **errors and omissions insurance**. Should an owner require indemnification from a designer? Although a designer generally is not responsible for the means and methods of construction (and most standard contracts stipulate that a designer is not, and that the contractor is responsible), is that protection enough? It would appear not always to be so.

For instance, a specification written by a designer may prescribe the means and methods of work. Also, there is the design of the work itself for which the designer obviously is responsible, from which effects and causes of damages may arise that might produce third-party claims. These are enough of a potential risk for an owner to seek indemnification from a designer. And, if an owner, why not a contractor? Also, what of a designer employed in a design–build contracting company? Similarly, there are other consultants of an owner who might not be protected and indemnified by a contractor in a contract who, therefore, should seek such protection and indemnification through their contract for services to the owner or the owner's agents.

A professional designer (and his independent consultants) owe a client (an owner) a normal and reasonable standard of performance in the work he undertakes and the advice he provides. Apart from the contract for consulting services between them, if a designer is negligent in his service, a client-owner (and a contractor who works for him under the designer's supervision) have recourse at law for damages. It is a matter of **tort,** or breach of duty. However, acting as an arbiter between an owner and a contractor puts a designer in a quasijudicial position in which he is not liable for his decisions to either, except for bad faith or fraud.[6] (There is more on the topic of tort in Chapter 23.)

The entire question of liability and protection is complex, particularly in construction management arrangements, and all involved should seek competent professional advice from insurance consultants and brokers and legal counsel. Perhaps one solution to the need for protection and indemnification is a standard contract condition for comprehensive protection and indemnification similar in idea to that of wrap-up insurance (see Chapter 22).[7]

21.2 PROTECTION: PRACTICAL CONSIDERATIONS

Temporary Works

Temporary works are dismantled and removed and do not become a permanent part of the work. They may include

- Batterboards and shorings for trench excavations
- Formwork for cast-in-place concrete
- Scaffolding of all kinds (for formwork, masonry, plastering, etc.)
- Temporary supports for lintels, arches, and other masonry work
- Temporary supports, braces, struts, and other supporting members for structural

precast concrete, steelwork, and heavy timbers
- Temporary enclosures for protecting, heating, and curing concrete and other wet work
- Temporary enclosures to prevent damage to persons and property

Depending on the kind of permanent work, there are other kinds of temporary work. Contract drawings and specifications do not show temporary works because they are only a contractor's concern: not that of the owner or designer. AIA Document A210-1987 says nothing about them. In contrast, Canadian standard document CCDC2-1982 specifically refers to temporary works. The general condition GC 25 states that the contractor is solely and totally responsible for temporary works from design and erection, operation, maintenance, and removal, and requires the contractor to "engage and pay for registered professional engineering personnel...to perform these functions where required by law or by the Contract Documents and in all cases where such temporary facilities and their method of construction are of a nature that professional engineering skill is required to produce safe and satisfactory results." (Para. 25.3)

This requirement in one national standard document and the complete absence of any mention in another draws attention to temporary works and to a contractor's responsibility for them. The CCDC2-1982 document, in Paragraph 25.4, states:

> *where such Contract Documents include designs for temporary structural and other temporary facilities or specify a method of construction in whole or in part*, such facilities and methods shall be considered to be part of the design of

the Work and *the Contractor shall not be held responsible for that part of the design or the specified method of construction.* (Emphasis added.)

Formwork for cast-in-place concrete is temporary work that usually is not shown in contract drawings, and usually is designed by a contractor. However, there are examples of cast-in-place concrete work that, because of a unique design, may require special formwork that may be designed by the designer and shown in the contract documents. Also, some formwork might have to be left in place because removal is practically impossible. Is formwork left permanently in place part of the work? Following the wording of CCDC2 such formwork could be "considered to be part of the design...or specified method of construction," if the design of the concrete work made the formwork's removal impossible (e.g., beneath stairs).

It is a fact that temporary works are a common cause of accidents. Understandably, sometimes there is a desire to minimize the costs of temporary works and to build them as cheaply as possible. The responsibility for designing and carrying out temporary works efficiently and safely is one of the greatest responsibilities placed on a contractor. Temporary works have to be dismantled and removed soon after erection, which means although they must be strong enough they also must be easy to remove. Since movability and impermanence normally are not consistent with strength and stability, often it is easier to design and erect a permanent component than a temporary one that can be dismantled and moved.

For less common kinds of temporary works, special design expertise may be necessary. On site, the contractor's superintendent has the immediate responsibility for temporary works, and for the protection of persons and property. His experience must be equal to his duties. A superintendent, however, is not always a professional engineer. When designing certain temporary work is beyond his knowledge and experience, he should be the first to recognize it. He should then insist that such temporary work be designed and supervised by a qualified person, even if the contract does not require it. Ultimately, the responsibility for temporary works and for any claims for damages arising from them is the contractor's. But a superintendent also might be sued for damages incurred. In the event, nobody wants injury or damage to persons or property. Safety is every person's responsibility, but a superintendent has a particular responsibility.

The costs of temporary works are easily underestimated. We have said that a superintendent should be able to make an estimate of costs, and that on a project he should check the estimated costs of all major items of work. If he believes that the estimated costs of temporary work are low, he should make this opinion known. A superintendent should think of the risks involved before trying to keep below what may be an unrealistic cost estimate by making savings in temporary works.

Temporary Works and Computer Applications

A computer system can store and retrieve verbal, quantitative, and graphic data of typical designs for such temporary work as

- Shoring for excavations in different soils
- Formwork for all kinds of concrete structures

- Falsework for masonry arches, openings, etc.
- Temporary support work for various kinds of permanent construction.

The advantages of using a computer system for the design of temporary works include

- The capacity for storing CAD drawings and design information and data, and the ease of analyzing, revising, and updating them
- The speed, ease, and reliability of adapting standard designs to specific site conditions to produce working drawings by computer, on site if necessary
- The ability of a software program to calculate quickly and accurately the sizes of members and components and to compare and check design results, and thereby reduce risk of error
- The ability to transmit information electronically
- The ability to produce printed (hard) copies of information

21.3 EMERGENCIES ON A CONSTRUCTION SITE

Under Article 12 of AIA Document A201-1987, emergencies are in the contractor's realm of responsibility and allows for claims for additional compensation or time as a result. In an emergency, the probability is that the contractor and designer will not be on site, and in the event it is not likely that either can deal with an on-site emergency any better than a superintendent. In an emergency, first-line responsibility lies with superintendents, and they must be prepared.

- Have a list of top-priority emergency telephone numbers prominently posted by all site telephones, including those of the police, ambulances (at least two), fire protection, hospitals, clinics, doctors, and a paramedic service. This list should be permanent and clearly printed.

- Have a list of second-priority telephone numbers that includes those of the emergency departments of all public utilities (transportation, electricity, gas, water, and telephone), and all similar companies whose plant and equipment may be involved in an emergency, of the contractor's permanent office, and those of the owner's agents.
- Have an effective safety program, and make the necessary provisions for project safety, as mentioned later.

In an emergency, the first consideration is protection of persons against injury or death. The second is the protection of property, including the uncompleted work. Procedures to be followed should be published and practiced on site. Procedures to set in motion all the required precautionary and protective services needed when an emergency happens on site might include

- In an emergency, render such first-aid as is appropriate and do whatever is proper to minimize the hazard[8]; (e.g., enable breathing, stop bleeding, protect against shock)
- Inform the first-aid officer on site about the type of emergency, any injuries, its location
- Inform the superintendent on site as to the location of the emergency and the type of injury sustained
- Inform appropriate authorities (e.g., city engineering, police, utilities, police, fire service, etc.) as required
- Inform the designer (architect, engineer, or other) who should decide whether to inform the owner and others (e.g., engineering consultants)

Procedures will vary according to the nature of the emergency, the work, and the site. The important thing is that the procedures must be established following expert advice and publicized at the start of a job. Local authorities and utilities (e.g., electric, gas, earthquake) may have their own procedures that should be known, incorporated into those at a site, and followed in an emergency. Possible conflicting procedures should be recognized and reconciled before an emergency arises.

When an emergency has subsided and things are under control, the superintendent should write an accident report. It is important to record the facts as soon as possible, and before they become distorted by conjecture, gossip, and imagination. Witnesses should be interviewed and statements recorded. As much evidence as possible should be photographed. If in doubt as to the seriousness of an accident, one should assume that the worst may yet develop from hidden injuries or damage.

Contractual procedures similar to those applicable to the discovery of subsurface conditions (Chapter 13) and to changes in work (Chapter 16) should be followed in an emergency involving the work and the performance of the contract; including possible changes in the contract sum and the contract time. Actions required by law, ordinance, and regulation, and by insurance companies must be taken without delay. If this is not done, certain protections and coverages may become ineffectual or void, and responsibility for effects of the emergency may fall on the contractor.

An emergency resulting in injury, damage, death, or destruction of persons or property, may create extra work and costs that possibly cannot be recovered. The economic impact alone is enough to justify the costs of preventing or minimizing the number and effects of accidents and other such emergencies. In these matters, a contractor's and superintendent's posture should be as in contractual matters, following the maxim: This may yet become a court case; therefore we must immediately mitigate any deleterious result, and begin to prepare by gathering evidence.

In an emergency, there is a responsibility to prevent the situation from becoming worse (i.e., further damage or injury); to take those actions required by a safety program, insurance carriers, regulation, and law); and a need to prepare evidence for possible legal action. Other statutory requirements touching on accidents and emergencies exist (e.g., workers' compensation and OSHA standards and regulations). For government work, there are additional requirements.

21.4 SAFETY OF PERSONS AND PROPERTY

Importance of Contractor's Obligations for Safety

As has been shown, apart from not being responsible for faults and defaults of the owner and his agents, a contractor usually bears first responsibility for any injury, damage, or death, or destruction of persons and property because of performance of the work on site. The primary reason for this is the contractor's right and responsibility to direct how and when the work shall be done. An owner cannot direct construction work, so he hires a contractor. On site, a contractor has control of the work, so safety

is a contractor's responsibility. AIA Document A201-1987 states this responsibility of the contractor in Subpara. 10.2, *Safety of Persons and Property*.

Lawyers and others have observed that in construction it often is difficult to allocate responsibility for failure or damage. Injured persons and their lawyers usually look to all who possibly can be implicated. Also, contracts and their results always are subject to interpretation by courts, and actions for damages can never be precluded by contract agreements.

Safety in Construction Contracts

Safety is not an explicit subject in all contracts, but it is in AIA Document A201-1987, under Article 10, *Protection of Persons and Property*. In that article, safety is a responsibility of the contractor. There have been court cases in which plaintiffs have sought damages from designers because, it was argued, they were responsible, in whole or in part, for the safety of persons and property. Generally, as common sense would suggest, this is not so. AIA Document A201 makes it clear that it generally should not be so.

CASE

The supreme court of Arkansas at least has found "that the supervisory duties of the architect or designing engineer on a job does not [sic], unless specifically provided for in the contract, include the inspection or control of measures taken for the safety of the men employed on the job."[9]

A designer or other supervising agent of an owner generally is not responsible for the safety of persons and property on a project. Responsibility usually is with the contractor. A contractor's responsibility for safety on a job does not, however, remove from the designer and his agents and consultants responsibility for the design of the work and for the safety of persons and property as it relates to the design of the work. If damage or injury is caused by the failure of a beam of faulty design, possibly the designer is responsible.

Safety has become a popular concern and an important responsibility for contractors, and many publications are available to provide a safety officer on any job with all the information he or she requires. According to AIA Document A201-1987, Article 10, the contractor's superintendent is to have the responsibility and duty for the prevention of accidents unless the contractor designates another employee. On many large jobs, some person other than the superintendent is the safety officer. AIA Document A201 is a good information source about a contractor's duties with regard to the protection of persons and property.

Besides the contractual responsibility, a contractor has inherent responsibilities for the protection of persons and property through both statutory and common law. Therefore, the absence of anything about safety from a contract's documents does not remove from a contractor the responsibility for safety. Safety provisions also are a requirement of the insurers who provide the insurance protection required by construction contracts. (Insurance is a topic in Chapter 22).

The AIA Document A201-1987, Article 10, *Protection of Persons and Property*, makes specific mention of asbestos and PCB, a volatile liquid accused of being cancer-causing. We may expect to see more of such requirements in future construction contracts. The related costs of safety often are considerable.[10]

Safety in Practice

The Four Es are the most important aspects of safety:

1. Engineering for safety
2. Education for safety
3. Enforcement of safety measures
4. Economics of safety measures.

Engineering for safety. Engineering for safety is necessary in all aspects of construction work, including its design (particularly the design of falsework, temporary supports, formwork), and in the planning and execution of work on-site. Falsework is important because of the increasing use of large prefabricated components. Accidents may occur because of the failure of falsework. It is customary for contractors to design their own falsework, but it is better if building codes, regulations, and contracts require falsework to be designed by qualified engineers.

Engineering for safety also is necessary in the planning and execution of the work and in planning a safety program. This can be achieved through an accident prevention plan, such as is required by the terms of contracts for work to be paid for by federal government funds. In such a plan, the contractor is required to submit to the contracting officer (the owner's representative), or to one of his representatives (such as a designated safety engineer), a report on his general safety policy, the safety measures that will be taken, and the responsibilities for safety that will be assigned according to the phases of the work and the major work activities. The measures include such things as

- Safety instruction and training of employees
- Reporting of accidents on-site
- Medical facilities and arrangements for emergencies
- Identities and qualifications of safety personnel
- Provisions for the prevention of fire and other hazards

Before starting any major work activity (e.g., excavating trenches or placing concrete), a contractor in a government contract must submit a written report[11] analyzing the potential hazards of the work to be undertaken and listing specific provisions to prevent accidents.

The nature of construction gives the industry a high frequency of accidents and a high severity rate for the injuries that occur. Frequency of accidents in the construction industry is related to the unique and complex nature of the work, which makes it difficult to maintain safety standards and consistent safety measures because the needs of each site, project, and trade are different. Also, the heights and depths at which work is done above and below ground mean that people often are in danger of falling and suffering injuries from falling objects. Also, a mobile work force and a lack of personal familiarity among journeymen and foremen may add to the hazards.

Sites often appear as a confusion of workers, materials, and equipment with an ever-changing medley of sound and action. Small companies are less likely to have employees with specialized expertise in safety measures and accident prevention. That smaller companies do most of the work on most projects also contributes to accident frequency. The severity of accidents in construction relates in part to those same things that cause their high frequency, including

- Handling large quantities of heavy and volatile materials
- Handling large and heavy components, machinery, etc.
- Using heavy equipment in restricted locations
- Using and restraining large loads and forces
- Using power tools for cutting, drilling, inserting, driving, and compacting

The speed and urgency of much work and the unique combinations of different work forces, materials, and equipment on a unique site make it difficult to use defensively all the safety experience gained from previous projects. A factory ensures a flow of work under constant conditions, and enables the possibility of well-established safety measures suited to those conditions. The situation on a construction site is quite different.

Education for Safety. A superintendent should see that foremen of all trades are educated in safety and that they, in turn, educate the workers they direct. In this way, attention can be drawn to the hazards peculiar to particular trades and the measures to be taken to avoid them. Current statistics about accidents and their causes in construction are instructive if clearly and simply presented.

Safety education should make clear the primary goal: That your safety is everybody's concern—including your own. The purpose of safety is to keep individuals from injury and accidental death. That safety measures are a matter of law and a contract requirement is not enough. Education requires both stick and carrot. Supplies of literature and posters on safety are obtainable from official sources. In addition, the following might be noted and applied

- Safety signs and posters are more effective if replaced when damaged or dirty; since neglected safety signs and posters evoke a negative attitude to safety in general.
- Regular reminders and meetings about safety are necessary, and their need and frequency should be monitored; some call weekly site meetings.
- Safety policies and accident prevention measures should be identified with a company, rather than a national body; therefore, all new employees should be informed in writing of the company's policy and regulations and the consequences of ignoring them.
- Specific notices, equipment, and installations on-site to prevent accidents should be pointed out to all workers who are then asked to help in maintaining them.
- Even if they only consist of a first-aid kit in the site office, first-aid facilities should be made conspicuous. A large red cross on the office wall is an effective sign and reminder of "safety first."
- Workers should be employed on periodic clean-ups of a site, and all subcontracts should require such clean-ups.
- All temporary installations (e.g., guardrails) and all equipment (e.g., ladders) should be well-made, prominent, and regularly inspected.

Enforcement of Safety Measures and Accident Prevention.

In construction where the frequency and severity rate of accidents are high, enforcement is essential. On-site it is primarily a superintendent's responsibility; although of necessity he may delegate enforcement to a safety officer and foremen. Enforcement is easier if a safety policy and safety rules are in writing as part of a published accident prevention plan. As with all preventive measures, routine enforcement is necessary to combat the apathy with which most of us meet such things as fire drills and medical checkups. Enforcement, however, is practically impossible if individual workers are not educated in safety.

Economics of Safety Measures and Accident Prevention Programs.

The economics of safety sometimes are hard to determine, but there is no doubt that accidents are expensive, and that, apart from being a legal and moral obligation, accident prevention is good business. The annual cost of industrial accidents in the United States is in the billions of dollars. Some estimates place losses as high as 1 percent of the national income. The cost of lost time alone is significant to a contractor when an accident happens on one of his jobs, and even a minor accident can be expensive. Cuts and bruises may cost an employer tens of dollars. With a major accident or, infinitely worse, an accidental death, the costs of disruption and loss of time may run into hundreds or thousands of dollars, to which must be added the costs of making reports and carrying out other related duties, and that is not all.

It has been estimated that the direct loss of time caused by industrial accidents results in at least an approximately equivalent loss in time by other workers rendering aid and discussing the accident. Anyone who has witnessed a serious accident can attest to the shock to those nearby that invariably causes a breakdown of normal activity. In any accident, there always is a loss in time and expenses to be paid by a company; also, a seriously injured worker will suffer financially. Other economic aspects of industrial accidents include

- Increases in the costs of insurance
- The possibility of loss of business and key employees due to a reputation for frequent accidents
- The possibility of an injured worker not receiving adequate compensation, and considerable family hardship as a result[12]

It is estimated that generally an injured worker usually receives only a small part of his income loss in compensation payments and damages received.

21.5 PROTECTION AND INDEMNIFICATION IN CM PROJECTS

In CM projects, indemnification by contractors should include the construction manager. Unless he does work on a site as a contractor, it should not be necessary for a construction manager to provide indemnification to the owner and his other agents and their consultants. As explained in Chapter 2, in certain other respects also it is better for an owner and his construction manager if the contract between them for CM services precludes performance of any part of the actual work of the CM project by the construction manager. Even if a construction manager does only so-called general condition items (i.e., job overhead items such as temporary services and facilities, and possibly general labor for clean-up and such) then the construction manager, like a contractor, should be required to provide indemnification under the CM contract to the owner, designer, and others.

In federal government CM projects, each contractor has to take responsibility for safety in the performance of work. In addition, a construction manager must review and supervise each contractor's safety program and provide an overall and comprehensive safety program for the project. This procedure is equally suitable for private projects. Most contracts in CM projects can use published standard contracts, and the standard conditions about safety indemnification and insurance are as applicable to CM projects as they are to traditional projects. Questions of insurance, particularly wrap-up insurance, which is well-suited to CM projects, are introduced in the next chapter.

21.6 COST CONTAINMENT IN DISASTER LITIGATION

Cost containment, or cost limitation, in disaster litigation[13] appears as an important aspect of disasters in construction about which all should be aware and know where to obtain expert advice and help. To quote from an authority:

> Disastrous fires, building collapses, and other construction-related catastrophes are not recent phenomenon. Nevertheless, major lawsuits arising from these disasters are increasing with future-shock rapidity. There is little reason to believe that this trend will reverse.
>
> Construction disaster litigation is unique. It combines the most difficult aspects of at least three other complex areas of litigation—construction claims litigation, product liability, and multidistrict litigation. Moreover, at a minimum it

involves complex and technical facts, large claims, multiple parties, and, usually, wide geographic dispersion.[14]

The article discusses the management of litigation to economize and increase the probability of success. It also discusses mass document control by using computers.

21.7 COMPUTER APPLICATIONS TO LEGAL AND OTHER ASPECTS

Lawyers have spoken and written of the advantages gained from using a computer system in research and in the preparation of evidence presented in numeric and graphic form.

CASE

In a case involving breach of trust, the lawyer compiled financial evidence using a well-known spreadsheet program. In part, he credits his ability to convey the complex financial information to the court and winning the case for his client to the graphic capabilities of the software.

Lawyers may be next only to accountants in using computers to store, search, and retrieve verbal information. There is no reason any other profession or trade should not use the same technology. As for specific applications to matters of protection and indemnification, it appears useful to have all available information about the subjects in a relational data base for textual materials so that answers are quickly available

when a question arises. Such a data base might contain information about protection and indemnification from many sources, including

- Safety regulations
- Standard contracts
- Standard insurance policies
- Contracts commonly used for owners
- Standard documents of the user company
- Reported cases on indemnification, safety, etc.
- Safety programs and reports generated by the user

In the article referred to (in the last section) there are five pages devoted to this topic as it relates to disaster litigation: the recommendations therein are positively in favor of using computers for storing, handling, and searching large numbers of documents. In such an area as protection and indemnification, with its abundance of related information and documentation, a practical and efficient way of correlating all the information and data is essential in order to avoid confusion or ignorance of the many requirements.

If a company uses or plans to use a computer system for any other construction-related application (as proposed here), it is economic to use such a system for as many purposes as possible. If a company uses a computer for general accounting, then it makes sense to use it also for job costing; if for job costing, then for cost estimating, and so forth—for work planning and scheduling, resource management, purchasing, work and cost control. The overhead costs diminish as the scope of use increases.

REFERENCES

1. Robert F. Cushman, Esq. and John P. Bigda, Esq., eds., *The McGraw-Hill Construction Business Handbook*, 2d ed., (New York: McGraw-Hill, 1985).
2. Bruce M. Jervis and Paul Levin, *Construction Law: Principles and Practice* (New York: McGraw-Hill, 1988).
3. *Handbook of Professional Practice* (Washington, D.C.: The American Institute of Architects).

SUMMARY OF MAIN POINTS

- A contractor has control of the work, its methods and procedures; so owner–designers require a contractor to contractually indemnify them (and theirs) against claims, damages, losses, and expenses.

- Owners and designers do not usually indemnify a contractor, but either owner or contractor may make a claim against the other in a contract (and also outside a contract) for damages, losses, and expenses.

- Indemnification of an owner and others by a designer, and the designer's responsibility, is a complex subject. A designer owes a responsibility for reasonable performance of duties to both an owner and a contractor. A breach of duty is a tort. (Review commentaries elsewhere by construction law experts.)

- A contractor is responsible for temporary works, their design, and construction, which by their nature often are potentially dangerous and underpriced in cost estimates. Use of CAD and engineering-design programs can improve design and reduce risk of error.

- Site emergencies require preparedness with priority telephone numbers and a safety program. Emergency procedures include immediate action (as required by first-aid, common sense, insurance terms, regulation, and law), stabilizing an emergent situation (to prevent further damage or injury), and collecting evidence.

- The Four Es for safety include: (1) engineering (e.g., good falsework design and a safety program), (2) enforcement (by super, or safety officer), (3) education (through signs, posters, meetings), and (4) economics (loss of time and money through accidents and injuries).

- Cost containment in disaster litigation can be expensive, and construction managers should have some knowledge and training in this area. (Consult cited authority.)

- Computer system applications to information handling and retrieval as practiced by the law profession might be emulated in design and construction, especially in dealing with large amounts of information and documentation.

NOTES

[1]Hold harmless means to protect against harm or loss.

[2]AIA Document A201, Subpara. 10.1.4 requires an owner to hold harmless the contractor for a specific cause, as stated. There is no contract between a contractor and a designer, or any other agent of the owner, but the law of tort (breach of duty) applies, the usual remedy for which is money damages.

[3]The Canadian CCDC-12 (1979) referred to "a negligent act or omission of the Owner, the Architect, Other Contractors, their agents and employees." CCDC2-1982, which replaced CCDC-12, refers to "claims [that] are: caused by negligent acts or omission of the Contractor or anyone for whose acts he may be liable, and made in writing within a period of six years from the date of Substantial Performance of the Work..."(GC 19, *Indemnification*). Also, under GC 22, *Damages and Mutual Responsibility*, "If either party to this Contract should suffer damage in any manner because of any wrongful act or neglect of the other party...then he shall be reimbursed by the other party for such damage."

[4]This book's first edition (Reston, 1982) said: "Responsibility for protection has become increasingly onerous in recent years, and it is possible that legal responsibility may extend to the specification and use of hazardous materials such as asbestos and volatile compounds." (p. 248).

[5]The term, obligation, embraces both rights and duties.

[6]The subject of indemnification by a designer and his or her responsibility is complex. See, Bruce M. Jervis and Paul Levin, *Construction Law: Principles and Practice* (New York: McGraw-Hill, 1988), Chap. 4. pp. 59–80; also, Theodore W. Geiser, Esq., "Liability of the Architect–Engineer," *The McGraw-Hill Construction Business Handbook*, 2d ed. (New York: McGraw-Hill, 1985) for authoritative explanations.

[7]See the appropriate AIA publications regarding particular legal concerns, including the *Architect's Handbook of Professional Practice* and various documents and instruction sheets.

[8]This requires at least some minimal first-aid training. There are risks in moving an injured person, for example. Consult publications by appropriate authorities.

[9]William Jabine, J.D., *The Engineer's Responsibilities: Case Histories in Construction Law* (Boston, Mass.: Cahners Books, Division of Cahners Publishing Company, Inc., 1971), p. 174. The case being referred to is *Walker* v. *Wittenberg, Delony & Davidson, Inc.*, 412 S. W. 2d 621.

[10]The cost-effectiveness of regulations is sometimes surprising. It was reported that car seatbelt standards (issued 1984) cost $100,000 for every premature death averted, while the ban on asbestos (issued 1978) cost over $110 million per averted death. Reported from United States government sources in *The Economist*, Vol. 325, No. 7780, p. 22, Oct. 10, 1992.

[11]This may sound onerous, but actually the contract requires only a memorandum, properly designated and prepared. This is more easily done by using a standard pro forma suitably modified and completed. Its issuance may prove to be useful evidence of concern and attention to safety.

[12]When dealing with a bureaucracy, an injured worker often seems to become a victim, and so suffers doubly.

[13]Information was obtained from an article by John A. Baughman, Esq., Robert F. Cushman, Esq., and Irvine E. Richter, "Cost Containment in Disaster Litigation," *The McGraw-Hill Construction Business Handbook*, 2d ed., Chapter 59, and other sources.

[14]*Ibid.*, p. 3-59.

QUESTIONS AND TOPICS FOR DISCUSSION

1. Discuss the difference in meaning as between protection and indemnification.

2. Why should a contractor be required to indemnify the owner and his agents in a construction contract?

3. From a standard contract, in your own words, make a synopsis of all the conditions dealing with indemnification and protection. Use plain English and explain uncommon words.

4. What contractual means does an owner employ to protect himself against risk and loss resulting from damage, injury, or death from any cause? Tabulate and briefly describe them.

5. Describe an owner's and a designer's positions regarding temporary work done by a contractor in the event of damage resulting from the work.

6. Identify and briefly discuss the Four Es of safety in construction practice.

7. Identify, list, and describe the measures usually required in a local program for safety in construction.

8. Why is construction particularly hazardous? List and describe 10 major specific reasons.

9. Make an economic study of the impact of an actual industrial accident on a construction project. Describe how the employee and the contractor–employer are affected economically.

10. List and describe five means to safety education on construction sites and discuss their probable impact and effectiveness.

11. Define a tort, and explain how it might apply as between a designer and a contractor.

12. (a) Report on the statistics of accidents in construction in your area, their frequency and severity. (b) Compare the assessment rate for workers' compensation insurance for three trades in your area with the highest and the lowest rates in the United States.

13. Explain how a computer system could help to ensure the efficacy of the design of forms for poured concrete walls.

14. Discover what regulations in your area require as safety equipment on construction projects for buildings of different sizes, costs, and types.

15. Obtain authoritative literature on the subject of safety on construction sites, and write a short report on each of the following topics:

   a. The main cause of accidents to workers

   b. Recommended ways to avoid such accidents.

22

BONDS AND INSURANCE

*He that is surety for a stranger
shall smart for it.
(Proverbs, 11:15)*

Construction bonds and construction insurance are different. Bonds provide guarantees and offer protection to owners against loss due to the default of contractors who do not perform. Insurance provides protection against losses due to damage or injury. Perhaps the reason bonds and insurance are so often confused is that often the same companies provide them.

22.1 BONDS IN CONSTRUCTION

Bonding requirements and costs vary according to location and whether a project is public or private. Usually, bonding requirements for public works are more onerous.[1] All bonds involve three persons,[2] and in construction usually they are

1. The owner, who requires bonds as guarantees that
2. The bidder or contractor[3] will do the things he should do, and

3. The surety company that provides at a price bonds that guarantee bidders or contractors will do certain things. Otherwise the surety company will pay certain specified damages to the owner.

The most common types of bonds in construction are

- Bid bonds
- Performance bonds
- Payment bonds

Let us examine each of these types of construction bonds and the reasons for their use.

Bid Bonds

If an owner requires a **bid bond**, then a bidder must provide one. If a bidder cannot, it is unlikely that without a bond his bid will be accepted. Bid bonds guarantee that a bidder who provides a bid bond will enter a construction contract if his bid is accepted. Otherwise, the bid says, in effect, that the surety will recompense the owner for the loss (by having to accept the next higher bid) by way of money damages up to the face amount of the bond.

If a bid is successful, why should the bidder who submitted it not make a contract? Perhaps, because after he has submitted the lowest bid he finds out the amounts of all the other bids and realizes that his bid is too low, immediately followed by a conviction that an error was made, and simultaneously a reluctance to do the work for such an amount. Or, perhaps, after bidding, a bidder may find that circumstances have changed, and that a new contract is not the good idea that it seemed a short time before. Whatever the reason, if a low bidder is convinced that he no longer wants the contract, the owner's immediate alternative is to accept the next lowest bid:

A SCENARIO:

A surety company provides a bid bond for a bidder that in effect says in the bond that if the bidder does not enter a construction contract when his bid is accepted, the surety company will pay the owner a sum of money to make up the difference between the contract sum in the contract the owner finally makes (by accepting the next lowest bid) and the contract sum he would have had if the bidder had entered a contract. But, as it says in the wording on the bid bond, the surety company will not pay more than the face amount of the bid bond: usually, 5 or 10 percent of the amount of the bid.

Since the relative amounts of bids may vary significantly, the outcome for an owner, too, may vary.

EXAMPLE:

Assume that an owner receives six bids, and the lowest two bids and the accompanying 10 percent bid bonds are as follows:

Lowest bid $900,000
  Amount of bid bond is $90,000
Next bid $1,000,000
  Amount of bid bond is $100,000

If the owner accepts the lowest bid of $900,000, but the bidder wants to withdraw and will not enter a contract, the owner has to go to the next bidder of $1,000,000 for a contract and, on the face of it, the work will cost the owner $100,000 more. The owner then seeks forfeiture of the lowest bidder's bid bond, because he would not make a contract at $900,000. The surety company pays only up to the face amount of the bid bond to the owner; i.e., $90,000. Theoretically, the owner is still $10,000 short. He may consider suing the lowest bidder for that amount, but such an action may be neither successful nor worthwhile.

As we can see, if the face amount of a bid bond is 10 percent of the bid it guarantees, and if the difference between the lowest bid and the second lowest bid is more than 10 percent of the lowest bid, then, if the lowest bidder will not enter a contract, the owner will not be fully compensated by the face amount of the lowest bidder's bid bond. Also, in the preceding example, the owner's apparent loss was $10,000. Such a loss, however, can only be described as theoretical, since it cannot be stated for sure that any particular contract sum is correct. The reason for the difference between the two bids in the example might have been an error in the lowest bid, and the more correct price for the work might be $1,000,000. Except for amounts of the bids submitted, everything else is conjecture.[4]

The fee for a bid bond is nominal, and the reason is that a surety company who provides a bid bond expects also to provide a performance bond if a client's bid leads to a contract. It is with performance bonds that a surety company makes money. There is, however, no guarantee that because a surety company has issued a bid bond to a construction company, it will also issue a performance bond to that same company. Although it is a surety company's intention at the time of issuing a bid bond to issue a performance bond later, it is possible that a contractor's ability and capacity to perform a construction contract may change in the short time between issuance of a bid bond and the need for a performance bond. Nevertheless, bid bonds generally are more acceptable than a certified check issued by a bidder as guarantee of a bid, because the issuance of a bid bond suggests the strong possibility that a performance bond will follow. A certified check is not insignificant, but it does not guarantee that a low bidder will enter into a contract, neither does it imply that a performance bond is forthcoming. The difference between the two lowest bids may be so great—due to an error in the lowest bid—that the low bidder prefers to give up a deposited check and cut his losses!

Withdrawal of Bids

A bidder generally can withdraw his bid any time before its acceptance, even if he has submitted a bid bond; except that in public works a bidder may be required to withdraw a bid before the opening of bids, according to regulations set out in the instruction to bidders; or withdrawal may not be allowed at all. For protection of the public purse, they regulate bidding for public works, and there are several court cases dealing with the withdrawal of bids for public works.[5] Conversely, the withdrawal of bids for private work, is much more open as a private owner can accept any bid or none, while a public authority generally is bound to accept the lowest proper bid.

CASE

Instructions to bidders were part of the contract documents for a school's construction and said that bids could be withdrawn before the time set for the opening of bids by written request and personal appearance of bidder. One bidder sent a telegram requesting withdrawal of his bid. This bid was the lowest bid. Later the low bidder claimed that there was a mistake in his bid. Nevertheless, the lowest bid was accepted, and so the low bidder sought in court to enjoin the school authority from acting on his bid and to have the bid declared void. The bidder was neither successful in a lower court nor through an appeal in a higher court.[6]

A court has held that "a competitive bid is an option based upon a valuable consideration, namely a privilege [for] bidding and the legal assurance to the successful bidder of an award as against all competitors [Citations]."[7] As such, a bid is then both a purchased right (of the owner), a unilateral contract, and an offer that when accepted is mutually binding. This legal interpretation is significant.

Assessment of a Contracting Company's Bonding Capacity

Bonding companies (sureties) assess a contracting company's ability and capacity to perform before they issue a bid bond by considering the Three Cs of bonding:

1. Capacity: resources and ability to perform
2. Cash: liquid assets of the company
3. Character: that of the company's principals, and the company's reputation

By considering these, a bonding company assesses the limit up to which it will go in issuing bonds on behalf of a client for the performance of construction work. If a construction company is doing more work than it can handle, this increases the risks of improper performance. Bonding companies therefore assess their clients' capacity to do work and issue performance bonds accordingly. However, bonding companies also may make mistakes:

CASE

Construction Company X is in business for a few years and then in the middle of a contract the company goes bankrupt. Later Construction Company Y appears with a president who previously was the president of Company X. Yet Company Y is able to provide a bid bond when bidding on public work. Were all Three Cs sufficiently considered?

Facts to keep in mind: (1) surety companies are in the business of selling bonds, and (2) despite their solid appearance, similar to other companies, surety companies also may fail and go out of business.

CASE

A developer was winding up a construction management project. Before releasing the final payments he asked a consultant to review all the contracts and other documents to ensure there were no loose ends. The consultant discovered the surety company that had issued the project's largest performance bond—supposedly still valid, and to be so throughout the warranty period—had gone out of business. The developer insisted on getting another bond from another surety before releasing funds to the contractor.

Nothing is absolute, nobody is infallible, and sooner or later every company and institution fails, dies, or is dissolved. Therefore, at critical times (e.g., at project completion) the validity of everything should be checked.

Performance Bonds

If an owner has required a bid bond, it is likely that a performance bond also will be required. If a bidder is unable to get a surety company to issue a performance bond, it is unlikely he or she will get the contract. Performance bonds guarantee the full and proper performance of a contract by a construction company. Usually they issue performance bonds in face amounts of 50 or 100 percent of the contract sum, depending on the amount required by an owner. The face amount of a bond sets the limit of the bonding company's liability under the bond. The cost of a 100 percent performance bond is considerably higher than the cost of a 50 percent performance bond, but not usually double.

The cost of a performance bond is a job overhead cost to be included by a bidder in an estimate and bid. Therefore, the owner pays for it, directly or indirectly. Some owners, apparently on the advice of a consultant or agent, call for a 50 percent performance bond on the supposition that if a contractor is not going to perform, work stoppage probably will occur before the work is more than 50 percent complete. That is not always true, and therefore some owners require and pay for a 100 percent bond. The Small Business Administration, for example, requires all bonds for performance and payment to be for 100 percent.

If a contractor who has provided a performance bond does default, and if consequently the surety company has to make good its bond, it will hire another construction company to come onto the site to complete the contract. Because a new company has to mobilize for a partially completed job and pick up the loose ends before proceeding, usually it will cost more than the unpaid balance remaining to complete the work. Also, the surety's liability is limited to the face amount of the bond. Later, the surety company will seek to collect from the client-contractor who has defaulted the full amount it has had to pay out. It is on this point that many confuse bonds with insurance.

A bond is not like insurance, and a surety agrees to and expects reimbursement from a defaulting contractor for the costs it incurs by making good on a performance bond. Although some think otherwise, the small cost of a performance bond is not

enough to buy a contractor freedom from a construction contract's obligations. The purpose of a performance bond is security for an owner. Also, limited liability is no refuge for the principals of a bonded construction company in default of a contract, since before issuing a performance bond surety companies usually require them to accept personal liabilities.

On the face of a performance bond, the wording says (in effect) that if the contractor does what he has contracted to do then the obligation of the surety issuing the performance bond is nullified. Otherwise, the obligation (to the owner) shall remain in effect.

Labor and Material Payment Bonds

Payment bonds are common in public works contracts where the construction site belongs to government; therefore a lien cannot be registered against it. This removes from workers and subcontractors the right of claim against the property upon which they have done work, or to which they have delivered materials, should payment not be forthcoming. The purpose of a payment bond is to provide a practical alternative to the right to lien; a means by which those not paid may obtain the payment due. Payment bonds are used in some private contracts for essentially the same purpose. The wording on the face of a payment bond says (in effect) that if the contractor makes payments for labor and materials, the obligation of the surety is nullified. If a bonded contractor defaults on payments, the surety is obligated to pay amounts totalling up to the face amount of the bond. Later, the surety company will collect from the defaulter.

Under the Miller Act,[8] certain United States federal government projects must be bonded for performance and payment. In addition, state statutes require similar bonding on state public works, but the requirements vary from place to place.[9] The forms for construction surety bonds published by the AIA are recommended by experts.

Other Kinds of Bonds

Other kinds of bonds are less important in construction projects and include

- Maintenance bonds that guarantee the maintenance of specific plant over an extended period. (Note: This is not the usual maintenance required of a contractor in most construction contracts during a one-year warranty period following substantial completion of the work.)
- Supply bonds, to guarantee the proper and timely delivery
- Fidelity bonds, that guarantee the honesty of sales agents, bookkeepers, and others in positions of trust
- Bonds to guarantee public safety from physical harm, such as might be caused by the work of gas-fitters, and from financial harm arising from the illicit actions of persons such as real-estate agents, brokers, and auctioneers
- Bonds to guarantee payment of taxes collected for the government
- Bonds to guarantee the performance of duties by trustees and executors arising from court orders

These and all other kinds of surety bonds involve the same three persons and the same principles found with all bonds: (1) A party with an obligation to perform properly, (2) a surety company that guarantees that proper performance, and (3) the person or persons protected by the bond. The earliest surety companies were bankers, and it is in the origins of bonds and insurance that most clearly demonstrates the fundamental differences between bonds and insurance. When a surety pays out on a surety bond, the bonded party eventually has to pay. When an insurer pays out on an insurance policy, the insured party does not have to pay anything (other than any deductible amount) because the insured has already paid the premiums, as have all the others similarly insured.

22.2 INSURANCE IN CONSTRUCTION

The insured person who suffers a loss benefits from the mutual support of the other insurers similarly insured by the same company. (Therefore, "mutual" is a common word in insurance company names.) By definition, surety companies are not insurance companies, and bonds are quite different from insurance. Insurance and bonding have different origins and principles. Bonding, as we have seen, involves just three persons: contractor, surety, and owner. Insurance involves any number of persons who, as a group with similar insurable interests, mutually seek to protect and insure themselves against specific risks.

The Principles of Insurance

Insurance involves the principles of an insurable interest and indemnification—of payment as compensation to any member of a mutually insuring group who incurs a specified loss. It also requires the payment of cash premiums during the period of insurance. The following example of marine insurance best illustrates the principles of insurance.

EXAMPLE:

A group of sixteenth century merchants each owned a ship loaded with spices returning from the East Indies. From experience, each knew there was a 10 percent chance of losing a ship at sea. So each merchant paid 10 percent of the value of his ship and cargo into a mutual fund. With the objective of returning them to the position they would have been in had a loss not occurred, each owner of a lost ship would be paid a sum proportionate to his loss.

That is an oversimplified description of mutual insurance. Today, an insurance company, or insurer handles such a fund. As a result, there are additional costs for management and profit. Also, there may be various options and additional premiums; e.g., for ships whose captains are under 25 years of age, and for those who previously have lost ships.

Two General Classes of Risk and Insurance in Construction

They say that one can insure against anything, and although film actors can insure against the loss of physical attributes, there are limits to insurance coverage. Generally, an insurable interest and the related risk must be measurable, and it must be a physical risk, not a moral one. Physical risks can be divided into two main classes:

1. Risks to persons
2. Risks to property

Insurance against a risk arising from an obligation to pay damages to a third party[10] usually is provided by the same insurance companies that also insure property. Life insurance is a separate branch of insurance. Some companies insure the lives of their key personnel.

In construction there are many risks that can be covered by insurance, and standard contract documents refer to only the most common. Builders and contractors should remember that owners and designers usually prepare the contract documents, and they assume that a construction company knows its own business, the risks involved, and the insurance it needs. Therefore, contract documents mention only the least requirements, and many risks taken by contractors are not mentioned by owner–designers in their documents. However, since a contract mutually obligates an owner and a contractor, anything that affects one may affect the other. Therefore, in many respects, their requirements for insurance protection are the same.

Although the AIA Document A201-1987, Para. 11.1, is entitled *Contractor's Liability Insurance*, and is described as to protect the contractor against third-party claims arising out of the work, the owner also requires it, and will pay for it through the contract because the owner does not want the contractor to be impaired by a legal action and not perform the contract. Also, the owner does not want to be sued by a third party because the contractor is not covered and cannot pay a claim. The same document also refers to an owner's liability insurance (Para. 11.2).

For a specific contract and project, no matter what the contract's conditions say,[11] a contracting company should obtain independent advice on the insurance coverages it needs from its own insurance broker–consultants.[12] One major difference between the risks of a contractor and those of an owner is that an owner in a fixed-price contract pays the contractor to take most of the risks (according to the kind of work and the contract's wording); therefore, the conditions for insurance in a contract presumably reflect the owner's wishes, or his agent's advice. A contractor, however, requires more comprehensive and varied coverage than an owner because a contractor's exposure to risk is greater.

It is a common practice, required by many contract conditions, for a contractor to purchase comprehensive general liability insurance to provide protection for all the persons involved in the work, and for the owner to purchase property insurance to provide protection against loss resulting from damage to the work. The reasons for this are that a contractor has the greater exposure to risk arising from third-party claims, and a contract usually requires the contractor to indemnify the owner and others against such claims. As for property insurance, the owner of the property and the work done on it needs to maintain the property insurance when the work is complete and the building is occupied. There is no rule about this, however, and different construction contracts provide for different insurance arrangements. Also, different contracts deal with insurance in different ways, and careful consideration is essential in every contract. We can identify two main groups of insurance that an owner and a contractor require in a construction project:

1. General liability insurance, to protect against the general risks of loss arising from claims of third parties affected by the work
2. Property insurance, to protect against the risk of loss resulting from damage to the work

These two kinds will now be examined. Consult with insurance experts regarding specific needs.

General Liability Insurance

Liability insurance has many names, but generally it is for protection against risks such as the following:

- Claims by employees of the contractor for personal injury, or by their dependents for death of an employee occurring during his or her employment, beyond and distinct from any claims covered by workers' compensation law
- Claims for injury, death, or property damage made by others not employed by the contractor
- Claims arising from acts or omissions of the contractor and his subcontractors
- Claims arising from the use of vehicles owned by the contractor and vehicles not owned by the contractor, but used by a person during his or her employment by the contractor
- Claims arising from the construction contract and its work against one of the parties who has assumed certain obligations of the other party under the terms of the contract; for example, indemnification by the owner and his agents by the contractor against all claims and damages (called contractual liability insurance)
- Claims arising from cross liability between the parties to a construction contract
- Claims arising from the subsequent use of the completed work
- Claims arising from the use of elevators and hoists
- Claims arising from work done below ground (e.g., excavating, blasting, demo-

lition, pile driving, shoring, underpinning, and other work often not covered by ordinary liability insurance).

Insurance brokers have pointed out that many contractors do not have adequate liability insurance and that some insurance agents are not knowledgeable about the insurances they sell and the coverages provided.

CASE

One excavation contractor worked for many years with only an ordinary liability insurance policy that specifically excluded coverage for most of the work that he normally did (i.e., excavation work).

Other forms of liability insurance often are required, including those providing protection against claims arising from automobiles, aircraft, and equipment, and from certain operations. Contractors must read and understand construction insurance policies, or have them explained by an expert. Generally, they are better off dealing with an insurance broker who deals with more than one company and who places insurance in order to get the best value for its client-customers, the contractor.

Liability insurance should be comprehensive to cover risks of loss arising from claims by others for injury, damage, and destruction of persons and property; therefore the most widely used name: comprehensive general liability insurance. Comprehensive, however, usually does not mean what it says.[13] Post-construction liability insurance also may be needed.

Liability insurance usually is in the name of the contractor and called "contrac-

tor's comprehensive general liability insurance." An owner may get his own liability insurance, or a contractor may have to take out an owner's protective liability policy. Liability insurance also may be in the joint names of the owner, contractor, designer, and construction manager, and may cover as "unnamed insureds" their consultants, employees, and subcontractors. The combinations are many and variable.

Property Insurance

Property insurance (often called fire insurance, builders' risk insurance, all-risks insurance, or named-perils insurance) is for protection against

- Loss resulting from damage to the work and materials on site, caused by fire and other hazards (if included by an extended coverage endorsement) such as windstorm, hail, explosion, riot, civil commotion, aircraft and other vehicles, and smoke and water damage
- Loss resulting from damage caused by earthquake (requires special endorsement and coverage)
- Loss resulting from the explosion of boilers or other pressure or vacuum vessels and equipment
- Loss resulting from vandalism, malicious damage, and the like
- Loss resulting from theft

Property insurance usually is for all who have an insurable interest in the work of a project, including: (1) the owner, (2) the contractor, and (3) all subcontractors and sub-subcontractors, who may, or may not, be named individually.

For complete and detailed information on all kinds of insurance coverages for different risks you should consult a professional insurance consultant and broker. Different owners and different contracts and contractors each have their different insurance requirements. This brief introduction to the subject is not sufficient to decide particular insurance requirements.

Post-Construction Insurance

Post-construction insurance (or, completed-operations insurance) extends insurance protection beyond the duration of a construction contract and its warranty period. Legal cases have shown that liability for damages to persons and property arising from a project may continue long after the project's completion, and long after a contractor, subcontractor, or designer may have assumed that he is no longer liable for the work of a completed project.[14]

Contractors and owners should consult an insurance broker before purchasing any construction insurance. Also, they should read the documents about insurance by the American Institute of Architects; e.g., AIA Document G610—*Owner's Instructions for Bonds and Insurance*, and AIA Document A511—*Guide for Supplementary Conditions* (latest editions). Individuals outside the United States also will find these and other AIA documents helpful. Publications by insurance companies and related organizations are another valuable information source.

Often an owner needs to occupy part of a building under construction before substantial completion; or during construction he needs to have temporary access and partial occupation to install his equipment. Such occupancy could cause property insurance coverage to become void. To ensure that it does not affect insurance coverage, it is imperative to talk with the insurer before allowing occupancy or to plan earlier.

There is much ignorance and carelessness with regard to insurance in construction. Many who prepare construction contracts are not knowledgeable about construction insurance, and many project manuals contain general conditions about insurance from past projects used again and again without much thought as to the specific needs for insurances and the minimum amounts of coverage required. Also, designers and construction managers usually are not qualified as insurance counsellors, but who ignore at their peril the importance of adequate insurance protection for an owner, a contractor, and for themselves.

The best procedure for owners' agents is to ask an owner to complete a form such as AIA Document G610—*Owner's Instructions for Bonds and Insurance*, or something similar, which puts the onus for making insurance decisions on the owner. Insurance coverages and exclusions from coverage vary greatly among insurance companies and different localities; therefore, it is most important that every business, no matter the size, should get the best advice possible on insurance matters. Not to do so is to take unnecessary risks.

Workers' Compensation Insurance

Workers' compensation insurance is similar to no-fault automobile insurance; its purpose is to enable monetary compensation to be made to accident victims and survivors without the need for court action. Coverage varies by location, and different states and provinces have different legislation, but the principle is the same everywhere: the doctrine is one of liability without fault for employers, since they have the greater means of preventing accidents, and since the purpose is to compensate those in need.

Employers (contractors) pay most of the insurance costs because they can pass them on as an overhead cost of construction, and because they can best set up measures to prevent accidents. Some states have their own obligatory and monopolistic insurance schemes, while others allow for coverage by private insurance carriers. Compensation for workers is of three kinds:

1. Cash benefits according to injury or disability
2. Medical benefits
3. Rehabilitation and training.

Before doing construction in a state or province for the first time, a builder might look at the statistics for workers' compensation insurance in a locality and learn something about its insurance costs and apparent working conditions. Statistics for specific trades also are indicative. For example, why are the costs of this insurance so high in the District of Columbia and the state of Hawaii? There they are more than double the national average, according to one source.[15] Demographics, and local customs and practices may be involved. Similarly, the widely different rates among certain trades also raises questions.

Other Types of Insurance

Employers' liability insurance and common-law liability have not been replaced completely by workers' compensation insurance.[16] Employers' liability insurance is an insurance for employers against common-law liabilities. A common-law liability arises from common law, such as the liability of an employer for injuries to an employee incurred at work. Contingent liability insurance, or protective liability insurance, pays on behalf of an insured owner or contractor to a third party for injury, sickness, or death arising from construction work performed for the insured by independent contractors.[17]

In the United States, the Social Security Act requires old age, survivors' disability, and health insurance (OASDHI), and the act gives it its name. In Canada, the equivalent is the Canada Pension Plan, Old Age Security, Old Age Assistance, and the different provincial health plans. Also, in the United States, the federal Unemployment Tax Act calls for unemployment insurance. In Canada, it is the federal Unemployment Assistance Act and provincial programs.

Excess liability insurance extends the normal coverages for liabilities particularly where the usual liability insurance coverages are subject to large proportions of so-called self-insurance,[18] which leaves an insured company exposed to that extent. The purpose of this insurance is to provide even greater coverage against loss, and therefore the policies issued are not standard policies and should be explained and read with care.[19]

Wrap-up Insurance for Construction Projects

Wrap-up insurance using comprehensive master policies arose from the increasing complexity of construction and construction insurance and from the simple fact that an owner always pays, directly or indirectly, all the costs of all insurance required by the performance of construction work. Why then not eliminate much complexity, doubt, and confusion, and the risk of having too little or too much insurance coverage, by having the owner purchase all the necessary insurance in one policy to protect and indemnify all the persons involved in a particular project? In this way, an owner can directly get what he needs and he does not have to worry about whether a contractor has obtained the necessary insurance. Of course, a contractor also needs to know whether the owner has purchased adequate insurance, and this should be accomplished by communication among the owner, the contractor, and the insurance broker.

Wrap-up insurance covers all construction insurance included under the two main headings: (1) liability insurance, and (2) property insurance. As with all construction insurance, wrap-up insurance requires the experience and assistance of an experienced insurance consultant who is knowledgeable about comprehensive insurance especially designed for individual construction projects. For larger projects, wrap-up insurance may be cheaper than traditional insurance if all the alternative premium payments are considered. Some people disagree and point to the standard policies often carried by contracting companies that may overlap with wrap-up insurance. The most important benefit of wrap-up insurance specially designed for a project is that it provides comprehensive coverage without gaps, overlaps, or inadequate coverage for certain kinds of work.

Errors and Omissions Insurance

Professional designers (architects, engineers, and other professional designers) and certain other consultants (cost consultants and construction managers) need this professional liability insurance to give them protection against claims arising from the design and supervision of work and other professional services. For increasingly complex construction and contractual arrangements, there is now a new kind of liability

insurance with policies for individual projects. Perhaps there is a need for a kind of wrap-up liability insurance that will protect everyone against the effects of errors and omissions and avoid the problems of allocating responsibility among those involved.

22.3 BONDS AND INSURANCE IN CM PROJECTS

In Chapter 21, we mentioned a construction manager's responsibilities for protection and indemnification in CM projects. We saw that to the extent that a construction manager fills the position of a contractor in a CM project, to that extent he is liable to third parties and required to indemnify the owner and others against loss from claims for damages. Therefore, to that extent, a construction manager requires liability insurance and may have to provide performance and payment bonds.

Under the *General Services Administration System for Construction Management*, and according to the published form of CM contract between the federal government and a construction manager, a construction manager is liable for damage arising from the work of all general condition items provided by him to the government. He also has to provide a 100 percent performance bond and a 50 percent payment bond in the standard formats to guarantee that work.

As a professional consultant and contract administrator, a construction manager also may need insurance protection against claims arising from his own errors and omissions, particularly if he participates in the design stage of construction work as a consultant–adviser. A construction manager may be, however, a professional consultant and agent of an owner only, in which case his position is comparable with that of an architect or professional engineer.

22.4 COMPUTER APPLICATIONS TO BONDS AND INSURANCES

The end of Chapter 21 referred to computer applications protection and indemnification, particularly in containing the costs of litigation. The same emphasis is relevant regarding bonds and insurance. Checklists are an important tool in construction management, contract administration, and field engineering. Their use in other sectors (e.g., bonds and insurance) is open to further development. For example, a construction company might develop a data base of outlines and checklists for the different kinds of insurances it needs for different types of work in various localities and under different circumstances. Thirty years ago, Aird's study[20] found that efficiency in construction management was lacking because information and informed personnel were lacking. The means now exist to change this situation.

REFERENCES

1. Robert F. Cushman and John P. Bigda, eds. *The McGraw-Hill Construction Business Handbook,* 2d ed. (New York: McGraw-Hill, 1985).

SUMMARY OF MAIN POINTS

- Construction bonds involve: (1) An owner, who requires a guarantee, or bond, that, (2) a contractor, will perform as agreed, from (3) a guarantor, or surety, who will ensure performance or pay damages to the owner if the contractor defaults.

- Three main kinds of construction bonds include: (1) a bid bond, (2) a performance bond, and (3) a payment bond.

- Bid bonds guarantee that a bidder whose bid is accepted by an owner will enter into a contract; failing which, the surety will pay as damages to the owner the difference between the bid first accepted and the next higher bid the owner accepts to make a contract, up to the bond's face amount (usually 5 or 10 percent of the bid).

- Withdrawal of a bid before it is accepted is legal, except in the case of some public works, for which bids can be withdrawn only before bid opening, or otherwise according to certain regulations. Public authorities generally must always accept the lowest proper bid. A private owner, however, can accept any or no bid.

- A bid is seen as an option for the valuable consideration of the privilege of bidding and of the possibility of being awarded a contract, by at least one court.

- A contracting company's bidding capacity is assessed by consideration of its capacity to do work, its cash and other assets, and the character or reputation (i.e., the Three Cs of bonding).

- Bonding companies sell bonds for profit, but sometimes they make mistakes, and sometimes go out of business. Therefore, check the viability of a surety company and the validity of its bonds.

- Performance bonds are most common; their face amount usually is 50 or 100 percent of the contract sum; their costs are rated per thousand according to amount and proportion (50 or 100 percent); their cost is a job overhead cost. If a bonded contractor does not perform a contract, the surety is required to do so to the extent of the bond's face value. Later, the surety will collect from the contracting company and its principals (who usually have a personal liability).

- Payment bonds are common in public works because lien claims cannot be made against government property. If a contractor makes payments as obliged, his payment bond is void. The Miller Act provides for bonding of performance and payment on certain federal projects; similarly, some state public works require bonding.

- The two main kinds of construction insurance are (1) general liability insurance against claims by workers and other third parties, and (2) property insurance against losses due to damage to the construction work.

- General liability insurance is taken out by a contractor to insure against claims by employees and others arising from the work; contractual liability (by indemnifying owner); and other claims arising from other causes and sources (e.g., vehicles, equipment, and operations).

- Comprehensive general liability insurance is not fully comprehensive. Post-contract liability insurance is required by some contracts.

- Property insurance (known as fire, builder's risk, all-risks, etc.) is for protection against loss resulting from damage to the work from several named causes, including vandalism and theft; this coverage is for all who have an insurable interest in the work.

- Different owners, contracts, and contractors have different insurance requirements. Consult an insurance consultant, and buy through a broker.

- Completed operations insurance is required for a stipulated period after final completion of some projects.

- Workers' compensation insurance provides for income and worker rehabilitation for injured workers and also death benefits; it is required from employers according to different state statutes and different rates.

- Wrap-up insurance is devised for comprehensive coverages for all involved in a specific project in one policy.

- Designers (and some others) carry errors and omissions (professional liability) insurance to protect them against claims arising from their services.

- A construction manager needs liability insurance and may be required to provide workers' compensation insurance and bonds to the extent that he acts as a contractor.

- Bonds and insurance, like other construction contractual matters, given the large amount of information and data involved, are subjects for computer data bases.

NOTES

[1]For a detailed and expert source of information, see, Robert F. Cushman, Esq., and Kenneth E. Lewis, Esq., "Surety Bonds," in *The McGraw-Hill Construction Business Handbook*, 2d edition, Robert F. Cushman, Esq. and John P. Bigda, Esq., eds. (New York: McGraw-Hill, 1985), Chapter 42.

[2]Persons are either individuals or corporations. Most persons involved in construction are corporations. However, usually it is more concise and covenient to refer to them as individuals.

[3]In turn, a prime contractor may require a subcontractor to furnish a bond.

[4]One might argue that an owner's loss in having to accept the next highest bid also is an apparent one. In construction there is really no such thing as a fixed price until a contract is made.

[5]See William Jabine, *Case Histories in Construction Law* (Boston, Mass.: Cahner Publishing Company, 1973), Chapter 8, "*Is it Possible to Get Out of a Low Bid?,*" pp. 179–182; also, Collier, *Construction Contracts*, 2d ed. (Prentice-Hall, 1987), 2.2.13 "*Accepting and Rejecting Bids,*" pp. 264–268.

[6]William Jabine, *Ibid.,* p. 179–182 (*Modany* vs. *State Public School Building Authority*, 208 A, 2d 276).

[7]William Jabine, *Ibid.,* p. 187.

[8]The Miller Act, 40 U.S.C.A. & 270a–270f.

[9]For a detailed account see Robert E. Cushman, Esq., and Kenneth E. Lewis, Esq., "Surety Bonds," *The McGraw-Hill Construction Business Handbook*, 2d ed. (New York: McGraw-Hill, 1985), pp. 42-3–42-30.

[10]A third party is one who is neither the first nor the second party. The first and second parties are the parties to a contract; in this case, a construction contract.

[11]Apparently it is not uncommon for a designer's staff without much expert knowledge or understanding of real needs to include incomplete or inappropriate insurance requirements in bidding/contract documents.

[12]An insurance agent represents one or more insurance companies. An insurance broker-consultant supposedly represents a purchaser of insurance and is unbiased.

[13]Reference here is to Robert G. Warren, "Why Contractors Need Special Insurance Programs," Robert F. Cushman and John P. Bigda, eds., *The McGraw-Hill Construction Business Handbook*, 2d ed. (New York: McGraw-Hill, 1985).

[14]CCDC2, the Canadian standard form of stipulated-price contract, requires a contractor to provide this kind of post-contract insurance over a six-year period following the date of total performance of a contract.

[15]Means, *Building Construction Cost Data*, 1989 (Kingston, MA).

[16]Robert G. Warren, "Why Contractors Need Special Insurance Programs," *The McGraw-Hill Construction Business Handbook*, 2d ed., 1985. pp. 9-4, 9-18, 9-19.

[17]Independent contractor is a legal term to identify a person who does work for another, but not as an employee.

[18]Self-insurance is a euphemism for no insurance coverage, except that which a person provides for himself by setting aside a cash reserve.

[19]*Ibid.,* pp. 9-21, 9-23.

[20]See Chapter 5, Section 5.2, *Management by Contractors*.

QUESTIONS AND TOPICS FOR DISCUSSION

1. a. Name and briefly describe the three kinds of bonds most commonly used in construction.

  b. Name and briefly describe two other kinds of surety bonds.

2. Explain in outline the fundamentals of bonding and insurance in construction, and point out the main differences between them.

3. Present a reasoned argument why a surety company should not have to pay an owner damages because the surety company's client has refused to enter into a formal construction contract with an owner.

4. Present a reasoned argument why a surety company should not have to pay on a bid bond an amount equal to the difference between the lowest bid and the next lowest bid (but not more than the face amount of the bond).

5. a. Explain briefly the Three Cs of bonding.

  b. Who ultimately pays any monies paid out to an owner by a surety company under a performance bond? Explain how and why.

6. a. Briefly describe the two main kinds of construction insurance and their purposes.

  b. Explain which contracting party usually carries each of these two main kinds of construction insurance, and why.

c. Briefly explain wrap-up insurance.

7. a. Identify four different kinds of liability insurance, stating who usually carries it, and against which risks.

  b. Identify four different kinds of coverage obtainable with property insurance, stating who usually carries it and against which risks.

8. Describe a situation in which third-party liability insurance coverage might be voided or jeopardized. (This situation is commonly referred to on construction signs.)

9. What are the purposes of wrap-up insurance? Explain in general terms what it usually gives protection against.

10. Make innovative suggestions for other kinds of insurance in construction, bearing in mind the principles of insurance and the high risks inherent in construction work.

11. Describe briefly the significance of exclusions listed in a liability insurance policy.

12. Explain the concept of a bid as an option by describing the consideration involved. What are the implications?

13. What is post-construction insurance and what does it insure against?

14. What are the primary details and purposes of workers' compensation insurance?

23

LAWS AND LIENS IN CONSTRUCTION

Reason is the life of the law;
nay, the common law itself
is nothing else but reason...
Sir Edward Coke (1552–1634)

Two legal realities affect construction. On the one hand, there is the great freedom from constraint in the making of contracts; on the other, the large body of statute law that governs construction work once a contract is made. Each reality is considered in this chapter. First, however, is an examination of a legal anomaly—the right of lien.

23.1 LIENS IN CONSTRUCTION

Liens exist only by right of statute, and lien statutes vary. As applied to construction, liens seem mostly limited to North America. The word lien means a legal charge against the property of another until that person or another satisfies a debt or duty owed to the lienholder. In effect, the property becomes a form of security for the debt or duty owed. In commerce, the lien has broad application, but in construction its use is in claims for payment, the security for which is the real property that is the work site. The anomaly is that the site belongs to an owner who usually is neither the debtor nor the defaulter. Generally, liens cannot be filed against public property, but some states have enacted municipal lien statutes for claims against municipal contract funds.

Some lien statutes still use the term mechanic's lien, but now, others who are not mechanics, or workers, (e.g., contractors, subcontractors, and certain suppliers) also may have a right of lien. Originally, lien acts were to protect the rights of workers to be paid their wages by ensuring that they had some recourse if they were not. Construction always has employed itinerant workers, or journeymen, so often it was easy for an employer or foreman to abscond with the payroll.

Other than a payment bond, the only effective security for wages is the property that is the site; even though the site's owner usually is not at fault if workers are not paid. However, an owner does get the benefit of the work, and once done it becomes part of the land and cannot be removed. Nevertheless, liens appear to contravene the usual fairness that is expected of the law.

A lien is a registerable claim, and when properly filed it creates a legal encumbrance or cloud on the title of the property such that it may hinder its sale or use as security. One effect of filing a lien, therefore, may be to cause a mortgage company (i.e., mortgagee or lender) to stop advancing money to the owner (the mortgagor, or borrower). Therefore, an owner usually cannot afford to have lien claim against a site as it may obstruct the cash flow from a lender, or it may interfere with other plans that include the property in question.

Filing a Lien

When filing a lien, it is important to follow the procedures laid down in the particular lien statute in force at the place of work. The procedures for filing generally make it easy to file without the need for legal counsel. Fewer workers now file liens; suppliers and subcontractors file more. A lien has to be filed within a stipulated period following substantial completion of the contract, or following physical completion of the actual work, or the delivery of materials. Statutes have different filing periods (e.g., 30, 60, or 90 days). Under some statutes, a claimant must give written notice to the owner when filing a lien, but an owner cannot assume he will get a notice. Proof of a valid claim may not be required to file a lien, and the existence of a recorded lien may be enough to encumber a title and block a transaction, and possibly interrupt cash advances to the owner by a mortgage company. Therefore, in some jurisdictions the revision of lien statutes to tighten up filing procedures and to discourage frivolous and malicious claims is considered necessary by some.

In some jurisdictions, filing a lien can preclude a person from subsequently taking action in a small debts court to collect the money owed. Therefore, before filing, anyone seeking to make a claim should find out about liens locally and the alternatives for collecting debts by asking a lawyer.[1]

All engaged in construction should know the local lien act, and those in their districts in which they work or supply materials, and how to file a lien in each jurisdiction.

Foreclosure of a Lien

After the filing of a valid lien, one of three things may occur: (1) The debt is paid, and the reason for the lien no longer exists; in which case the lien is withdrawn, or allowed to lapse, depending on the statute and the length of time involved; (2) the debt is not paid, but no further action is taken by the lienholder, who must proceed with an action within the period stated in the lien statute; so, ultimately, the lien becomes void and no longer exists; (3) the debt is not paid, and the lienholder takes the proper action within the stated time to enforce the lien and to foreclose if necessary.

A foreclosure action by a lienholder does require legal counsel, and a property with a lien registered against it may be sold at auction to raise the money to settle the debt that caused the claim and the lien. More often, the owner of the property settles the claim and avoids sale of the property.

Retention from Payments to Contractors

Under certain lien statutes, an owner must retain a stipulated percentage of all payments made to a contractor and to hold the **retainage** (retention, holdback) for a stated period following substantial completion of the work.[2] This period is longer than the period within which a lien must be filed; if no liens are filed, the retainage may then be released to the contractor. If someone files a lien against the site within the stipulated period, the owner must then follow the specific requirements of the lien statute (usually, to pay the retainage into court). That action usually is all that is required of an owner. If many liens are filed against a property, the retained money may be insufficient to cover all debts, so there is no assurance that all the lienholders' debts will be settled in full. The specific requirements of a lien statute must be fulfilled, and different statutes state different priorities.

Waiver of a Lien

Most construction contracts, including the standard documents, refer to a waiver of lien[3] that may be required by an owner from a contractor before final payment and release of any retained money. An owner may not wish to release money to a contractor without some assurance that there will be no liens filed afterward, leaving the owner to settle with the lienholders to clear the title. If the contract so provides, an owner may require waivers of lien from the contractor and from all suppliers and subcontractors who might have cause to file a lien. Such waivers must be consistent with the appropriate lien statute. Some lien statutes say that a right to file a lien cannot be waived by prior agreement.

Release of Liens

A contractor, his subcontractors, and suppliers may be required by some contracts to submit to the owner an affidavit, or statutory declaration,[4] to the effect that they have met all payment obligations. Again, the purpose of the owner is to ensure that no liens will be filed after the final payment to the contractor. Most people believe affidavits are significant and mean what they say. However, some individuals will sign affidavits and then treat them as Hitler did treaties, as mere scraps of paper. Waivers and releases cannot always be taken at face value, and the experienced take the precaution of a lien search to ensure there are no liens registered against a property. No final payment should be made until

- The owner–designer gets an affidavit of release of liens from the contractor and all the subcontractors and suppliers or, alternatively, waivers of lien are received
- The owner–designer obtains an affidavit from the contractor stating that there is no indebtedness connected with the work. (This affidavit may be combined in one document with an affidavit of release of liens.)[5]
- The statutory period within which liens must be filed has expired
- The owner–designer has an independent lien search made as an assurance that no liens exist on the site's title.

Liens on Public Works and Property

Generally, government property cannot be the subject of a lien claim. The alternative protection for mechanics, contractors, and others doing public works is a payment bond (see Chapter 22). Further, some jurisdictions have statutory provisions for liens against funds still held by a government or other public agency, instead of against the property. Again, statutes vary among jurisdictions and legal advice should be obtained.[6]

Trust Fund Statutory Provisions

The idea of a trust fund is that of money received by one person and held in trust for the benefit of another or others. In some jurisdictions, there are statutes that declare that all funds paid by an owner of a project to the project's contractor are trust funds to be held by the contractor, as a trustee, to the benefit of all the subcontractors and suppliers on that project. In some jurisdictions, the lien act itself contains trust fund provisions in tandem with the provisions for lien claims.[7] In other jurisdictions there are different statutory trust fund provisions for public and private works. The duties of a contractor as a trustee of a trust fund vary with different statutes. Generally, payments to a contractor for work done are recognized by law as a trust fund that the contractor cannot himself use until he makes all the payments due to workers, subcontractors, and suppliers.

Protection for Persons Owed Payment

Construction, generally, affords several kinds of protection to those entitled to payment:

- Liens against real property or funds

- Payment bonds issued by a surety
- Trust fund provisions in a statute
- The general law governing payment of debts

The scope of these protections for a particular class of person (i.e., worker, contractor, subcontractor, supplier, or designer) varies in different jurisdictions. With some statutes, right of lien does not extend to a supplier, and there the distinction between supplier and subcontractor becomes significant.[8] Therefore all engaged in design and construction should know about the pertinent statutes in force in the places where they do business and work. Since statutory provisions and case precedents vary so, legal counsel should be sought.

23.2 A BRIEF REVIEW OF THE LAW AND CONSTRUCTION

As discussed in Chapter 1, the law does little to restrict or hinder the creation of contracts; instead it makes it as simple as possible because contracts are the means to almost everything. Once a contract is made, however, the law expects it to be acted on—unless the parties mutually decide to abandon it. The competent can contract to do anything, providing it is legal. Also, not all contracts must be written, although usually it makes things easier if they are.

Construction Work

The law is concerned with the outcome of construction contracts: with the work on-site as improvements made on the land. There are at least two important reasons for this concern:

1. Construction work in progress is a potential source of harm to workers and to public safety and health
2. Land is uniquely special: the source of all wealth, and the place of abode; it is real property.

Buildings under construction are dangerous places, and even when completed and occupied they have a continuing effect on the health and safety of people. Buildings are more permanent than most things, and they are part of the land upon which they stand. The statutes governing real property development and construction are many and vary from place to place, so only an indication of the headings of relevant subjects is possible. Specific statutes in specific jurisdictions should be obtained and their content understood. Relevant subjects of such laws include

- Real estate sales, licensing powers, trust funds, agreements of sale, validity of contracts, deposits and stakeholders, developers' prospectus requirements
- Condominium developments with strata titles, leasehold strata lots, condominium corporations, and condominium bylaws
- Agricultural land reserves, parks, and preserved areas and reservations
- Municipal statutes governing property assessment and taxation, fire protection and control, community planning, zoning, subdivision of land, and building regulations

The range is large and varied. No one can afford to be in a business related to property and development and not have a broad general knowledge of the relevant laws and regulations.

23.3 HOUSING AND BUILDING LAWS AND STANDARDS

The fundamental purpose of the laws that create building codes and regulations governing construction is the protection of public health and safety. Codes and regulations accomplish this by the establishment of minimum standards for the construction and maintenance of buildings. Notice that standards in building codes are minimum standards. In the minds of many, all too often they soon become no longer the minimum to be surpassed, but standards to be achieved. These minimal standards of building codes do not necessarily satisfy the requirements of owners who contract for building work.

EXAMPLE:

The kitchen floor of a new house supported a large island work-counter located near its center. Subsequently, the floor sagged because the joist size, taken from a building-code table, although correct for the joist type, span, and normal loads, was insufficient for a large load in the middle of the span.

Even without eccentric loads, joists of sizes listed in some building codes may eventually show unacceptable bending. Although the structure is stable and safe no owner would find the result acceptable. Even if they will never collapse, floors should not sag.

Building regulations usually do not deal with the quality of building construction. Instead, regulations deal with whatever is important to health and safety, such as fire protection, structural stability (e.g., safe floors), sanitation, ventilation, and lighting. Codes apply not only to the construction of new buildings, but also to the alteration of existing buildings when the work is beyond a certain extent. New building codes usually are not retroactive; however, if there are extensive alterations to an existing building, it is usual for the law to require that the altered building conform to the current code; particularly if the value of alteration work exceeds a stipulated proportion of the original building's value.

Laws governing building generally are of municipal origin and application, although some state and housing laws (i.e., those of New York and Michigan) and some state- and province-initiated building codes exist for adoption by municipalities. Other municipalities have adopted (often with modifications) other models codes, such as the National Building Code[9] and the Basic Building Code[10] in the United States, and the National Building Code in Canada.[11] Other model codes and standards in the United States include

- The Uniform Building Code (International Conference of Building Officials, Los Angeles, California)
- The Southern Standard Building Code (Southern Building Code Congress, Atlanta, Georgia)
- The Model Minimum Housing Standards Ordinance (National Institute of Municipal Law Officers, Washington, D.C.)

In common talk, building laws and codes are virtually synonymous, but a building code is not necessarily a law, and it usually takes a legislative body to pass a law to adopt a particular code. Generally, building codes (like most specifications) are mostly prescriptive in nature and stipulate the choices and qualities of the materials and the methods of construction to be used in different buildings of various occupations and sizes and in different locations. As with some specifications, more building codes now require specific standards of performance, leaving the choice of materials and methods to those doing the work.

Because of changes and developments in construction materials and methods, some codes and ordinances are not up to date. Yet, in other instances, building codes have given a lead in setting standards by requiring such features as better fire prevention and accessibility for handicapped persons.[12]

Plumbing, heating, ventilation, and electrical work in buildings have their own codes and regulations and inspections by official specialists. As population densities in urban areas increase, and as they build more multi-unit and multistory buildings, and as the demand for this kind of building space increases, so the need for more complex service systems in buildings and more stringent health and safety requirements increases, which increases the need for more technically advanced building codes and regulations.

Management and supervision of construction require a detailed knowledge of local building codes and regulations. The fact that a professional person designs the work, and that a building inspector's staff check the drawings and specifications, will not nullify a builder's responsibility to perform work according to the laws and codes in force.

Computer Applications to Codes

Computers create an opportunity to make it easier and quicker to ensure a design conforms to a building code and to issue building permits by putting a building code and the contract documentation of projects into a computer so that they can be quickly searched and analyzed and compared (as described for legal documents in Chapter 21). Also, when it comes to the necessary calculations from data in building codes to decide such things as minimum setbacks related to building use, total areas of openings allowed in exterior walls, and other such design criteria, a computer system can prove useful. With a CADD component, code requirements can be displayed and solved graphically like other complex equations.

23.4 ZONING LAWS

Zoning makes an impact on development long before the time for construction, and those builders who offer design–build services or speculative construction must get involved with zoning and other regulations affecting property development. Whereas the first concern of housing and building laws is with public health and safety, zoning goes further and controls, among other things, activities that in some places would be a nuisance (e.g., a car-wrecking business in a residential area). Zoning laws also may control

- Land use and social functions
- Site planning and architectural design
- The height and mass of buildings
- The density of buildings and population
- Congestion in communities
- Conservation of property values
- Fire and chemical hazards
- Pollution of air and water
- Public nuisances
- Access to light, air, and views
- Parks and other amenities
- Consolidation and development of land

Zoning laws also create fortunes, bureaucracies, and, according to some, sterile neighborhoods. Sometimes they destroy amenities. It depends a lot on one's point of view—and the zoning authority. Increasingly, the acronym NIMBY is heard across the land (Not In My Back Yard!). Everyone is glad to be rid of nuisances in their own neighborhoods. Although zoning is primarily a means to city planning, it is now extending into rural areas in an attempt to control the conversion of agricultural land to other uses (usually residential estate developments and golf courses).

Planning and zoning are subjects of continuous controversy between city planners and councils, and between those in city hall and the many affected outside. The success of planning and zoning is not easily judged. Its existence does not appear to guarantee a better environment, nor does its absence always appear to ensure a worse one. In one way or another, for good or bad (being the bureaucratic process that it is) zoning does have a great effect on property development, land costs, and construction.

By definition, zoning usually is a municipal function operating through municipal laws, but metropolitan and regional planning have supplemented zoning in many areas. With the effects of increasing environmental concern and increasing population, zoning will increasingly become a hot issue among developers, politicians, and the public at large. This in turn will have its effect on the construction industry.

For certain works on a site, special permits may be needed (e.g., burning rubbish and debris). In some places there may be noise restrictions between certain hours. Work may be banned on certain days. Special parking permits may be necessary, and where work encroaches onto streets (e.g., hoardings, walkways, and other temporary protections) there may be municipal charges for the loss of revenue from obstructed parking meters or facilities.

23.5 TORT (CIVIL OFFENSES)

A tort is a civil offense, and the term covers a wide range of civil offenses (other than breach of contract) for which the law provides relief. The law of tort protects citizens' interests in property, personality, and against threats and harms of many kinds including

- Trespass: entry onto the land of others, or dumping material or rubbish on another's property
- Nuisance: an act or a negligence that endangers or injures life, safety, comfort, and the enjoyment of property
- Negligence: the failure to use reasonable care, as in the use of equipment and in providing a professional service
- Conversion: the appropriation of another's property, including its destruction

These are some examples of classes of tort that might have a direct bearing on construction work. Other torts include offenses against a person's right of privacy or civil rights. The usual remedy at law for tort is money damages, but remedies also include an injunction, forcible ejection, and restitution. One legal writer says: "The modern law of torts must be laid at the door of the industrial revolution, whose machines had a marvellous capacity for smashing the human body."[13]

Trespass

In construction terms, trespass is most likely to be an invasion of real property, but its meaning goes much further and includes personal injury. Actions for trespass, nuisance, and negligence tend to overlap as their common purpose is to protect person, property, trade, and personal relations. Although trespass is the longer established tort, nuisance and negligence especially are now more common.

Nuisance

An action for nuisance is often for the protection of a property owner against certain activities on adjoining property, such as a construction site. Excessive noise, dust, vibration, and seepage of water, all might be a private nuisance against which an action might be brought. Public nuisances are a threat to the public at large, and may also be a crime. Liability in nuisance rests with the person causing the nuisance and with the occupier of the land on which a nuisance exists, although the occupier himself may not be responsible for the cause of the nuisance. As an occupier of a site, therefore, a contractor might be liable for a nuisance such as seepage.

Negligence

A legal historian claims that the great increase in torts, especially negligence, came with the railways in the nineteenth century.[14] Negligence is doing something a reasonable person would not do, or not doing something a reasonable person would. It is a failure to exercise due care and attention, and if it results in damage, it is actionable by the one who suffers that damage. Actions for negligence must show that

- The defendant owed the plaintiff a duty of care
- The defendant did not take care
- That as a result, the plaintiff suffered damage

The necessary degree of care is a matter for legal judgment, but sometimes it is a matter of *res ipsa loquitur* (the facts speak for themselves). If a worker is careless and knocks a tool off a scaffold and it falls and does damage or injury, probably the law will assume that the occupying contractor, or his or her employee is responsible and it will be up to the defendant in an action for negligence to prove that negligence did not occur. (Refer to Chapter 22 for liability insurance against claims by third parties.)

Apart from negligence, the doctrine of strict liability says certain things always are potentially dangerous, and therefore if damage results the defendant, who has a strict liability, does not have to be proven negligent: the fact of its existence speaks for itself. Storing certain things that are potentially dangerous (e.g., explosives, or even a large volume of water) may create a strict liability. Special aspects of negligence may touch on typical construction activities. By their nature, some activities are inherently dangerous (such as using high explosives). Courts have found that these activities require a higher standard of care, and those who undertake them must take special precautions, including carrying third-party liability insurance with high coverages. Another aspect of negligence that may touch on construction is product liability. Apart from negligence, some courts have favored the principle of strict liability for manufacturers: that they guarantee their products are free of defects. Vicarious liability may exist if an employee at work does something to cause another injury and the employer is liable for damages; although the employee as well is liable. The principle is one of fairness; that the one who stands to make the profit (from the employee's work and actions) should bear the greater liability for

loss. Any of these special cases of negligence might occur with construction work.

Conversion

Conversion is the wrongful exercise of control over goods. Examples include a seller who wrongfully disposes of goods and a common carrier who deliberately disobeys instructions and delivers goods to the wrong person. Also, a purchaser of goods who disposes of them before paying for them may be guilty of the tort of conversion.

Inducing Breach of Contract

It is a tort to induce another person to break an existing contractual duty and thereby to breach a contract. This might take the form of awarding a contract to an individual already committed to another to make the performance of the first contract impossible.

23.6 STATUTES AFFECTING CONTRACTING AND CONSTRUCTION

Some more important United States statutes affecting the construction industry include the following:

Buy American Act. Enacted in 1933, this act is applicable to government contracts, and requires government to use materials produced in the United States, with certain exceptions.

Clayton Anti-Trust Act. Enacted in 1924, this act provides for triple damages for offenses that involve "exclusive dealing arrangements" detrimental to competition, and arrangements that force a customer to buy from a supplier other goods as a condition to purchasing the goods the buyer needs. In Canada there is the Combines

Investigation Act against monopolies, unfair trade practices, and conspiracy to fix prices.

Davis-Bacon Act. Enacted in 1931, this act requires that in a contract for construction work for the United States government in the United States, there shall be stated the wage rates and benefits for workers that the contractor and subcontractors undertake to pay, and that they shall not be less than those prevailing in the locality.

Equal Employment Opportunity Act. This act involves levels of employment of minorities and women and has had an impact on construction, especially on union companies. As an authority on the subject says: "Accordingly, contractors bidding on federally involved construction contracts should carefully review the general affirmative action and nondiscrimination requirements stipulated in contract EEO clauses and the federal EEO bid conditions..."[15]

Fair Labor Standards Act. Enacted in 1938, this act specifies minimum pay and maximum hours of work and prohibits wage discrimination because of age or sex.

Federal Trade Commission Act. This act is against unfair methods of competition in interstate commerce.

Miller Act. This act was referred to in Chapter 22, and requires bonding on certain federal projects.

Occupational Safety and Health Act. Enacted in 1970, OSHA requires freedom from safety hazards and health risks in the workplace. Compliance with OSHA Standards is a requirement of virtually every employer, and records must be kept of work-related injuries and sickness. Employers also must display certain OSHA posters and notices. In Canada, working conditions are generally the subject of provincial legislation.

Robinson-Patman Act. Enacted in 1936, this act prohibits certain unfair and discriminatory practices not prohibited by the Clayton Anti-Trust Act and promotes equal opportunity in business by prohibiting certain differences in the prices of goods to different purchasers that detract from competition.

Service Contract Act. This act deals with wages and working conditions on government contracts.

Sherman Anti-Trust Act. Enacted in 1890, this act provides triple damages caused by restraint of trade, monopolization, and combinations and conspiracies to monopolize. Reportedly, the act was only really used effectively against labor unions.[16]

The Uniform Commercial Code comprehensively deals with the sale of goods and related contracts. In Canada, there is the Sale of Goods Act.

Walsh-Healy Public Contracts Act. Enacted in 1936, this act deals with the purchase of materials by government and wages and working conditions of companies who contract to supply materials to government.

Participation of the Public

State law is the law that mostly deals with tort and the laws of property and contract, but increasingly, as the limits of geography disappear, better and more uniform laws and codes are needed. Surely (for good or ill) such laws and codes will come. In Seattle, Washington, and Portland, Oregon, the recent development of departments of neighborhoods shows an increasing public concern with such things as planning and zoning and other things related to development and the environment. Public involvement is the best solution. Meanwhile, the best marketing for developers and builders is to show an awareness and care for the environment, both natural and built.

Contract Law

Given the thrust of this book, there are references to contracts and contract law throughout. The references listed at chapter ends provide some other sources of information about this topic. Above all else, however, is the wording of a valid and enforceable contract, for which the law insists to uphold. Like the sea, the subject is vast and deep and ever-changing, and to cross it one needs a navigator.

REFERENCES

1. Robert F. Cushman, Esq. and John P. Bigda, Esq., *The McGraw-Hill Construction Business Handbook*, 2d ed. (New York: McGraw-Hill, 1985).

2. Lawrence M. Friedman, *A History of American Law* (New York: Simon and Schuster, 1973).

SUMMARY OF MAIN POINTS

- Construction contracts are easily made and the constraints are few. Once a contract is made, there are many laws and regulations that govern construction work, including: lien statutes, building and zoning laws and regulations, and the common law of tort.

- A lien is a registerable legal claim on property; in construction, the property is the site; liens exist through statutes that vary in different states.

- Mechanic's (worker's) lien acts were legislated first to protect wages, but now contractors and subcontractors are more commonly claimants; also, some suppliers, and sometimes designers, depending on the local statute.

- Filing a lien often can be done without a lawyer, but all the requirements must be precisely met. After filing, the debt is paid, and lien is no longer needed; or, the debt remains, and the lien holder fails to take action within the statutory period; or, the debt remains and the proper action is taken to foreclose. Usually, the claim then is settled by payment of the debt, so foreclosures are not common.

- Waiver of lien by a contractor usually is required before final payment in a construction contract, but this is not allowed by some lien statutes; also, affidavits and statutory declarations by those with payment obligations are not always valid; therefore a title search is necessary to ensure no liens are registered.

- Liens on government property usually are not possible, so the alternative protection is a municipal lien on funds or a payment bond (e.g., under the Miller Act on federal projects, and under state statutes for other public projects).

- Trust fund statutory provisions require all money paid to a contractor to be held in trust for the benefit of all who have a legal right to payment.

- In construction, those entitled to payment have three kinds of protection: liens, payment bonds, and trust fund provisions. Not all have lien rights; however, everyone has other legal recourse.

- The law applicable to construction is extensive because it involves land and buildings and the health and safety of the public.

- Housing and building laws establish minimum standards for health and safety that often are inadequate for an owner's specific requirements in a building. Building codes are not law until so made.

- Computer systems can facilitate the procedures involved in checking contract documents and construction projects for compliance with laws; they also can provide graphic solutions to questions of code application.

- Zoning laws are local, they control real property development and conditions in built-up areas, and increasingly in rural areas. Changes in zoning may create wealth or destroy amenities. For certain site works, special permits may be needed.

- Torts are civil offenses and breaches of duty (other than breach of contract); they include a variety of actions and inactions that may cause harm and give rise to civil actions, usually for damages. Injunctions and court orders for specific performance also are remedies for tort. Common torts include trespass, nuisance, and negligence of a duty or obligation.

- Strict liability exists for certain things considered always potentially dangerous (e.g., storing explosives).

- Federal and state (provincial) statutes affecting construction and development are numerous; public concern demands more. Public involvement at the neighborhood level is the best solution.

NOTES

[1]Many law firms offer free a first brief consultation.
[2]Retainage under a lien act is the case in British Columbia and other provinces. Check locally.
[3]See AIA Document A201-1987, Subpara. 4.3.5.
[4]AIA Document A201-1987, Subpara. 9.10.2. CCDC2-1982, GC 14, Para. 14.4, calls for "a sworn statement."
[5]See AIA Documents G706 - *Contractor's Affidavit of Payment of Debts and Claims*, and G705A - *Contractor's Affidavit of Release of Liens* (latest editions).

[6]See, Armen Shahinian, Esq., "Mechanic's Liens of Public Projects," in *The McGraw-Hill Construction Business Handbook*, 2d ed., Chapter 41.
[7]As in British Columbia.
[8]See, Collier, *Construction Contracts*, 2d edition, (Englewood Cliffs, New Jersey: Prentice-Hall, 1987), pp. 29–32, for a discussion on the differences between subcontractor and supplier.
[9]Prepared by the National Board of Fire Underwriters, New York City, Chicago, and San Francisco.

[10]Prepared by the Building Officials' Conference of America, Chicago.

[11]Prepared by the National Research Council, Ottawa, for adoption by provincial and local governments.

[12]As in the case of the Provincial Building Code of British Columbia.

[13]Friedman, *A History of American Law*, (New York: Simon and Schuster, 1973), p. 409.

[14]Friedman, *Ibid.*, p. 262.

[15]Ronald M. Green, Esquire, "The Continuing EEO Challenge," *The McGraw-Hill Construction Business Handbook*, 2d ed., p. 20-4.

[16]"United States (of America)," *Encyclopaedia Britannica* (1972), 22, 656.

QUESTIONS AND TOPICS FOR DISCUSSION

1. Write an essay on the need for building departments in local government, and the possible alternative of putting responsibility for ensuring that buildings are built according to laws and ordinances on the designers and contractors.

2. Make a list of all the laws, ordinances, and regulations that directly affect construction in your district.

3. a. Obtain a copy of the local building code and find in it and report on as many examples as possible of obsolete building practices.

b. Obtain a plumbing or electrical code and do the same as in (a) above.

4. Obtain a copy of the local lien statute in your district, and report on what it says about

a. Who can file a lien

b. The procedure to file a lien

c. Within what period liens must be filed

d. Within what period liens must be acted upon

e. The amount required (if any) by the statute to be held back from payments to contractors as retainage for lien purposes.

5. Research and report on the lien statute in a particular state and discover what it says about those who have lien rights; those who do not; and the essential requirements for registering a lien.

6. Research and report on a lien statute's requirements for foreclosure procedures.

7. Define the following terms, and give examples:

a. Mechanic's lien

b. Affidavit

c. Waiver of lien

d. Miller Act

e. Lien search.

8. Regarding the quality of work, explain why building codes are not an adequate substitute for project specifications.

9. Write a report on your local lien statute concerning the following:

a. Limitations on lien rights

b. Limitations on scope of application

c. Limitations on time to file liens

d. Limitations on time to take action on a lien.

10. Select a construction project, obtain permission, and make a lien search of the property of the project. Write a report of your actions, the procedures followed, and the results.

11. Compare trust funds, liens, and payment bonds, and their pros and cons as protection for persons in construction who are owed money.

12. Define the following terms, with examples:
- a. Zoning regulations
- b. Building code
- c. Building law
- d. The Miller Act.

13. Define the following terms, with examples:

- a. Tort
- b. Breach of contract
- c. Trespass
- d. Nuisance
- e. Breach of duty.

14. In outline, list the main laws that apply to construction projects before and after a construction contract is made.

GLOSSARY OF CONSTRUCTION TERMS

In the text, certain words and phrases are typeset in boldface to indicate that their definition is included in this glossary. Many of the terms have an ordinary nontechnical meaning as well as a special meaning in construction. This glossary originated in an earlier text[*]; it provides a useful means by

which to review and, in conjunction with the *Questions and Topics for Discussion* at the end of each chapter, to make up tests and examinations. The primary purpose is clearer expression and better understanding. For example, the word **work** has an ordinary meaning and also a more specialized contractual meaning in construction. Also, the terms, **plans**, and **general conditions** like many others, are often used inaccurately. Other terms may be new to the reader: terms such as **quantity surveyor** and **bills of quantities**. A few terms, such as **primordial agreement**, were coined by the author.

---

[*] Keith Collier, *Fundamentals of Construction Estimating and Cost Accounting* (Englewood Cliffs, N.J.: Prentice-Hall, 1974). The glossary has been edited for this text, but some terms in the glossary may not be found therein.

Activity: A portion of the total work identified in a **work breakdown structure**, and in a **work plan** and a **work schedule.** (See also **Work activities** for a fuller description.)

Act of God: Operation of uncontrollable natural forces. (See also **Force majeure.**)

Addendum: An addition to **bidding documents** issued to **bidders.**

Advanced purchasing: Purchasing for **construction** by an **owner** prior to awarding contracts for the **construction work** to ensure timely delivery.

A/E: Architect or **engineer** (see also **designer**).

A/E/C: Architect, and **engineer,** and **contractor** (i.e., those primarily involved in construction).

A/E/CM: Architect, and/or **engineer,** and/or **construction manager.**

A/E/QS/CM: Architect, and/or **engineer,** and/or **quantity surveyor,** and/or **construction manager** (i.e., one of the owner's **agent–consultants** indicated).

Agent–consultant: One who acts as both a consultant to and an agent for an **owner** in construction.

Agent (of owner): See **Agent–consultant.**

AIA: The American Institute of Architects; publishers of the **AIA standard contract documents.**

Alteration work: Certain **new work** done to or in conjunction with **existing work,** other than complete demolition.

Applications for payment: These are made periodically by a contractor to a **designer** or **owner,** according to the terms and conditions of a construction contract, prior to and as the basis of (subject to checking and approval) the **certificates of payment** subsequently issued by the **designer** to the **owner;** applications for payment are required to be based on the approved **schedule of values** previously submitted by the contractor.

Architect: a person registered as such; named in some **standard contracts** as the representative and **agent–consultant** of the **owner.**

Authorities with jurisdiction (over the work): Those government authorities with some statutory power over construction design and work.

Back charges: Charges by a **prime contractor** to a **subcontractor** for the use of facilities, services, or equipment; often controversial because of an ill-defined subcontract.

Bar chart: See **Gantt bar chart.**

Basic item (of work): An **item of work** identified in specifications and in cost codes and common to a particular type of construction work, which, therefore, can be part of a basic cost code or a basic specification for that type of construction (as opposed to a **particular item of work**). The criterion is the basic item's practically invariable recurrence in that type of construction (e.g., concrete footings in building construction), even though the dimensions and specific details may vary from job to job. The recurrence of basic items makes basic specifications and cost codes possible and useful.

Basic work item: See **Basic item (of work).**

Bid: An offer to do construction work for payment, the acceptance of which constitutes a contract between the contractor who made the bid (the bidder) and the owner who accepted it. Also known as a proposal or a tender; often called a **prime bid** when made by a construction company that hopes to become the **prime contractor,** or a **sub-bid** when made by a company that hopes to become a **subcontractor;** known as an **offer** in legal terminology. A written bid is not a **contract document** unless the contract says so.

Bid bond: A bond provided by a surety company on behalf of a **bidder** to guarantee to an owner that the bidder will enter into a construction contract with the **owner** in accordance with his **bid** if it is accepted by the owner. If the bidder does not enter into a contract when his bid is accepted or if, alteratively, the bidder does not pay to the owner an amount equal to the difference between the defaulting bidder's bid and a larger bid amount, for which the owner shall contract with another bidder, up to the maximum of the face amount of the bid bond (usually 10 percent of the bid) the bid bond amount is forfeited to the owner.

Bid depository: A system set up by industry and authorized by a **bidding authority** to regulate sub-bidding by receiving and distributing sub-bids as required by the **sub-bidders.**

Bidder: One who makes a **bid**.

Bidding authority: Someone who solicits bids for construction work and provides bidding documents for that purpose; usually an **owner** (private or public), or an **owner's agent**, such as an architect or engineer.

Bidding documents: Those issued by an **owner–designer** to bidders that subsequently become the **contract documents** (assuming that a **bid** is accepted and a contract is made), plus certain other documents required for bidding purposes (e.g., the **bid** and the **instructions to bidders**), but not for a contract.

Bid shopping: The practice of some contracting companies, which having received **sub-bids**, attempt to privately negotiate lower prices with sub-bidders by setting one sub-bidder against another.

Bills of materials: Lists or schedules of materials required for construction work prepared by a contractor and subcontractors after a construction contract is awarded, prior to purchasing. Also, prepared by a **designer** or other **agent–consultant** as part of the bidding documents in some contracts (usually not building construction contracts), or as a means to **advanced purchasing.** (Not the same as **bills of quantities**.)

Bills of quantities (BOQs): Documents used in **contracts with quantities** containing the specifications and accurately measured quantities of the required work, which are priced by **bidders** in the calculation of their bids. Bills of quantities are prepared by an **agent–consultant** of the owner, usually by a **quantity surveyor** (sometimes a **designer**), often in accordance with a published national **standard method of measurement** (outside the United States); they are roughly equivalent to a **project manual**, except for the insertion of quantities and the cash columns for the pricing of the measured quantities of work by the several trades; hence the use of the term "bills." Bills of quantities are not unlike the **schedules of unit prices** used in some engineering contracts made in North America, but are more detailed and specific, particularly when made for building construction work.

Bonus: See **Penalty** and **Liquidated damages**.

Building construction work: (as distinct from **engineering** and **industrial construction work**) Generally work in or on custom-designed, residential, commercial, and industrial buildings that involve the work of a number of trades.

Building elements: See **Elements of construction**.

Building equipment: Machinery and equipment permanently installed in, as part of, a building (as distinct from **construction equipment**).

CAD(D): Computer-aided drafting (and design).

Cash allowance: An amount of money specified by a **designer** to be allowed by all **bidders** in their estimates and bids to cover certain specified parts of the work of a project for which the **owner–designer** is unable or unwilling to provide sufficient design information to enable bidders to estimate the costs prior to bidding; which amount is the owner–designer's best estimate of the probable costs. Subsequently, the **contract sum** is adjusted according to the amount of variation between the amount expended and the specified cash allowance. (See also **Prime cost sum** and **Provisional sum.**)

Cash discount: A discount given to a customer by a supplier for payment (for goods supplied) by a stipulated date. (See also **Trade discount** and **Volume discount.**)

Cash flow: Commonly, an income stream from a specific source, or sources; as an accounting term, net income plus non-cash charges against income (e.g., depreciation); a measure of liquidity.

Cash-flow schedule: A graph with "cash income" and "time" on the axes, showing a project's projected cash flow, typically as a lazy-S curve.

CCDC: The Canadian Construction Document Committee, Ottawa, Canada; publishers of the standard construction documents in Canada.

Certificates for payment: Periodically issued by the **designer** or the **construction manager,** following approval of the **application for payment,** according to the terms and conditions of the contract, to certify to the owner that the certified amount is due for payment to the contractor.

Change (in the) work (of a construction contract): Contractually the subject of a **change order,** or a **minor change in (the) work,** as defined by the contract; as in the AIA Document A201, *General Conditions of the Contract for Construction,* a national **standard construction contract.**

Change order: An order issued in writing by a **designer** or an **owner** to a **contractor** according to the conditions of the contract to make a change in some part of the work, or of the contract that may or may not result in a change in the scope of the **construction work, contract sum,** and **contract time,** depending on the purpose and substance of the change order. Also, a **modification** of the contract (as in the AIA Document A201), and a **variation** (in some countries).

Charge-out rate: That determined by adding **overhead** and **profit** to a **labor rate.**

Chartered quantity surveyor: A member of the Royal Institution of Chartered Surveyors (RICS) qualified in quantity surveying and entitled to use the designation ARICS (Professional Associate), or FRICS (Fellow). (See also **Quantity surveyor.**)

CIQS: The Canadian Institute of Quantity Surveyors.

Clerk of (the) works: An inspector and monitor of construction employed by an **owner,** usually under the direction of the **designer,** according to the conditions of the contract for construction. Generally, a term not now used in North America.

CM: See **Construction management; Construction Manager.**

CM project: One for which the **owner** employs a **construction manager** as an

agent–consultant for **construction management.**

Completion: See **Substantial completion, Total completion.**

Completion documents: Those required in a construction contract by the **owner–designer** from the **contractor** prior to **completion** (as defined in the contract conditions).

Component: A **material** of construction (as distinct from raw and unassembled materials, such as lumber); a portion of **work** usually made off the site (i.e., **prefabricated**), often according to a **special design** for the project. (See also **Products**.)

Conceptual estimate: An estimate of construction costs made from preliminary design sketches and outline specifications; usually by a **quantity surveyor** or other **cost consultant**. While controlling costs during the **design phase** (of construction), usually more detailed cost estimates are made as the design develops.

Conditions: The special, supplementary, or **general conditions** of a contract.

Construction: The **design** and **production** of **construction work**.

Construction change directive: Under AIA Document A201, a **designer** and **owner** can issue such a directive in the absence of total agreement by the **contractor** with a **change order**.

Construction costs: See **Costs of (construction) work**.

Construction equipment: Mobile machinery used in the performance of **construction work**, such as a bulldozer. (See also **Plant, Equipment,** and **Building equipment**.)

Construction management: In the ordinary and traditional sense, management of **construction work** as a normal part of construction in the traditional mode. In a more recent and specialized sense, **Construction Management (CM)** (capitalized, to distinguish it from construction management in the ordinary sense) involves a contractual arrangement in which an **owner** employs an **agent–consultant** called a **construction manager** and has a number of **separate contracts** (instead of one **prime contract**) for the several parts of the construction work of the project coordinated and managed by the construction manager. (See also **Development management** and **Project management**.)

Construction manager: A person (corporate or individual) appointed by an **owner** (or by an owner's **project manager**) as the owner's **agent–consultant** to work with the owner's **designer** in the design of construction work, to prepare the necessary bidding documents and contract documents, to arrange the necessary construction contracts, and to manage the several **separate contractors** to ensure that all the work is completed within the scheduled time and within the financial budget for the **CM project**, according to the terms and conditions of a Construction Management contract between the construction manager and the owner (or his project manager).

Construction materials: See **Materials**.

Construction work: See **Work**.

Consumable items: Material items that are worn out or used up by doing work; especially fuel and parts of tools (saw blades) and equipment (fan belts and plugs).

Contingency allowance/sum: An allowance made in a cost estimate for some or any contingency. (N.B.: **Documents** may require a contingency allowance to be included in a bid and contract sum, or a contractor may make one unilaterally.)

Contract amount: See **Contract sum**.

Contract documents: The drawings, specifications, conditions, agreement, and other documents prepared by the **designer** (in the first instance as **bidding documents**) that illustrate and describe the **work** of the construction contract and the terms and **conditions** under which it shall be done and paid for; and that should contain nothing that is not in the original bidding documents, except by the mutual agreement of the **owner** and the **contractor;** as identified and listed in the contract's agreement, and as modified by any subsequent **modification** (a contract document) made after the execution of the contract.

Contract manager: An individual hired by an **owner** to manage one or more projects and to represent the owner on the construction site(s) as a **project manager;** or one hired by a **contractor** or by a **construction manager** to administer a contract. Generally, not a common term in North America.

Contract quality: That specified for all parts of the **work.**

Contract quantity (of work): That shown or implied by the **contract documents.**

Contract sum: The total sum of money paid by an owner to the contractor, usually in **progress payments**, for the construction **work** done according to the terms and conditions of the construction contract between them. In **stipulated-sum contracts,** the contract sum is explicit in the contract agreement, but subject to **modification.** In some other kinds of contracts, the contract sum is only implicit, and not finally known until the work is completed and the **construction costs** are accounted for according to the contract.

Contract time: The period stipulated in a construction contract for the performance and completion of the **work** of the contract; or, the actual time taken if no contract time is stipulated, as in some **cost-plus-fee contracts**.

Contract with quantities: A construction contract in which the contract documents and the bidding documents include **bills of quantities** prepared by a professional **quantity surveyor** employed by the **owner** as an **agent–consultant**.

Contractor: The party (of the second part) to a construction contract who does the **construction work** (or part of it), who performs the contract, and who usually has one or more **subcontracts** with **subcontractors** to do some of the work that he (the contractor) has undertaken to perform. (See also **General contractor, Prime contractor.**)

Contractor's estimate: (as distinct from a **designer's estimate** or a **conceptual estimate**) An estimate (of construction costs) made on the basis of more or less complete **design information** (depending on the type of construction contract intended), measured quantities of work, and the contractor's own **experiential information**, generally used as the basis of a **bid.**

Cost accounting: That part of **construction management** in which actual **costs of (construction) work** are segregated and attributed to specific **items of work**, or groups of items, and to specific items of **job overhead costs**; after which the cost information is analyzed and combined with other data for use in **planning and scheduling**, in **cost control**, and in estimating the costs of other projects (also, **job costing**).

Cost-benefit analysis: a technique for appraising investments in projects that attempts to evaluate all benefits and costs; not only the monetary but also the social; as distinct from a **feasibility study** that deals only with business aspects.

Cost consultant: A general term for a **quantity surveyor**, a **cost engineer**, and others who provide cost-consulting services and expert advice on construction costs and economics and often on contracts and contracting.

Cost control: The part of **construction management** that seeks to ensure that construction costs incurred do not exceed the estimated costs, or that seeks to do **construction work** for the lowest possible costs, or both.

Cost engineer: A person with an engineering or construction education and background who uses his or her knowledge and skills in the application of scientific principles and techniques to matters involving costs estimates, cost control, and construction management, particularly as it involves the costs and economics of construction.

Cost estimate: See **Estimate (of construction costs)**.

Cost-plus-fee contract: A construction contract in which the **owner** agrees to pay the **contractor** (usually monthly) all the actual, **direct costs (of construction work)**; in other words, the direct, **reimbursable costs**, plus a fee—either a stipulated and fixed fee paid in installments pro rata the actual costs, or a stipulated percentage of the actual costs, to cover the **indirect costs (of construction work)**; i.e., the indirect, **nonreimbursable costs**. Generally, this kind of contract is made because the owner or designer is unable to provide bidders with more de-sign **information** about the work required and because the owner is unable to obtain another kind of construction contract with less risk at an acceptable price (such as a **fixed-price contract**).

Costs of (construction) work: All of the **direct costs** and the **indirect costs**; generally classified as **labor costs, material costs, plant and equipment costs, job overhead costs, operating overhead costs**, and **profit**.

CPM: See **Critical path method**.

Crash(ing): Speeding up a number of activities in a **work schedule** in order to complete in the least possible time. The object is to crash only those activities necessary for the economically optimum solution, since crashing costs more; and usually not all activities need to be crashed.

Critical path: The longest irreducible sequence of **activities** that determines the least possible duration of a project.

Critical path method (CPM): A method of planning and scheduling a project using a list of **activities** (or, a **work breakdown structure**) that are represented graphically in a network diagram in order to discover the critical path.

Critical phases (activities), (tasks), (items of work): Those on the **critical path**.

Custom designed (components, products, items of work): Those made to a **special design** for a project; not standard. (See also **Subcontractor** and **Supplier**; i.e., those who make either custom-designed and standard items respectively.)

Data: (as distinct from **information**) Similar information from several sources analyzed and synthesized to provide reference levels of productivity and costs, as guides in estimating and planning work (i.e., the plural of datum, a reference level).

Defects liability period: That period following **substantial completion of the work** during which the contractor is required by the contract to make good any defects; usually a one-year period.

Depreciation: The loss in value of tangible assets due to any cause, including: aging, wear and tear, and obsolescence.

Design: The conceptual part of **construction** and the process of bringing it to the stage of **production**; including communicating the design and the **design information** to a builder, or to **bidders**, by means of the **bidding documents** so as to effect the design of the work.

Design–build: A term to describe a construction service provided by a company that includes both the **design** and **production** of buildings or other structures.

Design–build drawings: A term that describes a type of **shop drawing** (in that they are submitted by a **prime contractor** for approval of conformance with the general design of the work), but more comprehensive in scope than shop drawings, and possibly extending to complete working drawings; excluding the drawings made by the **designer (A/E)** to show the general design of the work with which the design–build drawings must conform.

Design information: That information about a project provided to a builder or bidders by the **owner** or **designer**, as distinct from the **experiential information** together with which the design information comprises all of the information needed to perform the contract(s) of a project.

Design phase (of construction): The earlier phase, usually followed by the **production phase**. The two phases are sequential in traditional construction, but in CM projects with **fast-track construction** usually the two phases overlap.

Design responses: A term used to embrace all those things submitted by a **contractor** in response to a contract's **general conditions** and specifications that pass to the contractor responsibility for the design of minor parts of the work or for the provision of information about specific **materials**; i.e., **samples, shop drawings**, and **product data**.

Design team: Usually, a **designer** and the **designer's consultants**; possibly including a **construction manager**, or a **quantity surveyor**, or other **agent–consultants**.

Designer: A party to a contract to provide professional design services to an **owner** (the other party to the contract); often an **architect** or a **professional engineer**. Also, one (individual or corporate) who performs the design function in construction, as in a **package deal**, a **turnkey project**, or a **development management project**.

Designer's consultant: A party to a contract to provide professional engineering design services, cost-consultant's services, or other consultant's services to a **designer** who, in turn, has undertaken to provide design services to an owner of which the services provided by the designer's consultant are a part.

Designer's estimate: As distinct from a contractor's estimate as the basis for a bid for a lump-sum contract, an estimate of construction costs made on the basis of incomplete information during the **design phase (of construction)** and prior to obtaining **bids**; generally made by means of costs per unit (per unit of area, unit of volume, or unit of use), or by means of **elements (of construction)**, or approximate quantities of **items of work**, or both, or by combinations of any of these; made by a **designer**, or a **cost consultant**, or a **construction manager**, or by a **precontractor** as a basis for negotiations, or for a bid for a contract (other than a **lump-sum contract** or **unit-price contract**).

Designer's instructions: Those given to a contractor by the designer named in a construction contract.

Developer: A person (corporate or individual) who develops land through construction and who, therefore, becomes an **owner** to this end; one who seeks a profit through development either by turning over the developed property or by obtaining a return on the investment.

Development management: Professional services wider in scope and at a higher level of responsibility than either **construction management** or **project management**, and embracing both of them. The total management of an investment in real property, including land assembly and acquisition (if necessary), **feasibility studies**, advice on taxation, design, **estimates (of construction costs), value engineering**, production of the **construction work**, and possibly subsequent property management.

Development manager: A corporation that provides development management services for a fee.

Direct costs (of construction work): Those costs of (construction) work generally classified as **labor costs, material costs, plant and equipment costs**, and **job overhead costs**, all of which are directly attributable to a specific **construction contract** or **project**. (See also **indirect costs (of construction work**.)

Direct labor costs: Those paid by a contractor directly to a worker. (See also **indirect labor costs**.)

Discounts: See **Cash discount, Trade discount**, and **Volume discount**.

Division (of work in a specification): One of the 16 standard divisions of construction work in the **Masterformat**. Divisions are divided into nonstandard **sections of work** for a **project** by a specification writer, according to the nature and extent of the work specified, to facilitate the writing, production, and use of construction specifications.

Documents: As in **bidding documents,** or **contract documents,** or both. (Most bidding documents become contract documents without a change of content.)

Element (of a contract): A term that embraces, **contract quantity, contract quality, contract time,** and **contract cost**.

Elemental cost analysis: The allocation of all costs of (construction) work to the selected **elements (of construction)**.

Elements (of construction): A part of a structure that always performs the same function. At the macro-level, functional elements are of three groups: (1) those related to building area; (2) those related to building perimeter; (3) those elements unrelated to either. At the micro-level, the subelements are: **labor, materials,** and **tools, plant,** and **equipment. Elemental cost analyses** and cost estimates are made at all levels. Most are made with functional elements (at intermediated levels) consisting of one or more **items of work**.

Employer: In countries outside North America, an owner in a construction contract.

Engineer: A professional engineer registered to work as such in one of several disciplines related to construction, including structural, civil, mechanical, and electrical engineering.

Engineering construction work: (as distinct from **building construction work and industrial construction work**). Generally civil and structural work (other than that done in buildings) and heavy construction (e.g., dams).

Entire contract: One in which the entire work of the contract must be completed before any payment is made.

Equipment: Mobile machinery used in the performance of **construction work,** such as a bulldozer; sometimes referred to as construction equipment, to distinguish it from **machinery and equipment** installed in a building; a construction resource. (See also **Building equipment, Machinery, Plant,** and **Plant and equipment costs.**)

Errors and omissions insurance: A popular term for **professional liability insurance,** which gives protection to a **designer** and **designer's consultants** against claims arising from errors and omissions in the designer's work as an **agent–consultant.**

Estimate (of construction costs): The measurements and **quantities of work** and the estimated **costs of work.** Measurements and quantities are derived from design drawings. Prices and costs are derived from experience, preferably through cost accounting. Some estimates are based on measured **elements (of construction),** and some on measured **items of work.** (See also **Contractor's estimate** and **Designer's estimate**).

Estimating: The process of making an estimate that consist of two parts: (1) measurement, and (2) pricing.

Estimator: One who makes estimates for contracting companies (usually for bidding purposes) as distinct from a **cost consultant.**

Event: In network diagrams for scheduling, the finish and/or start of one or more **activities;** events are represented by nodes when activities are represented by arrows, and vice versa.

Existing work: That which already exists when a construction contract is made and which has some physical relation or connection with the **new work** of a contract; e.g., a new addition to an existing building. (See also **Alteration work** and **New work.**)

Experiential information: That information about a project already known by bidder–contractors from experience; as distinct from the **design information,** together with which the experiential information comprises all of the information needed to perform the contract(s) of a project.

Expressed warranty: One expressed in writing in a construction document. (See **Implied warranty,** and **Warranty.**)

Fast-track construction (project): Construction that is started before the **design** is completed, so that both occur simultaneously until the design is completed. A contracting arrangement to shorten the duration of a project from concept to conclusion; usually under the direction of a **construction manager;** therefore, the usual kind of construction in a **CM project.**

Feasibility study: A study of the economic feasibility of a development project. Usually based on a **conceptual estimate of the construction costs,** the cost of the land, the available resources and finances, the estimated income from the development, the costs in use, the financing costs, and taxes. (See also **Cost-benefit analysis.**)

Final completion of work: Total comple-tion (performance) and fulfillment of a contract. (See also **Substantial comple-tion (performance) of work.**)

Fixed-price contract: A common term for a **stipulated-sum** or **lump-sum contract**.

Fixture: A removable item installed and fixed in place in such a way (more or less permanently) and for such purposes that legally it is considered part of the building or land (e.g., a sink, a cabinet, or a vene-tian blind).

Float: Extra time theoretically or actually available in a project's **work schedule** for a specific **task**; by definition, such a task is therefore not on the critical path.

Flow-down condition: A term for a condi-tion in a **prime contract** that is required by that contract to be part of any related **subcontract** (e.g., a requirement to pro-vide a **performance bond**, if required by the **owner**).

Force majeure: An irresistible and unfore-seeable event, or course of events.

Gantt bar chart: A diagrammatic chart used for scheduling, invented early this century, and attributed to Henry L. Gantt and Frederick W. Taylor. **Activities** are graphically represented by "bars," the length and position of which relate to activities' durations. Usually, the vertical axis of a bar chart shows the activity titles and the horizontal axis shows the days and weeks. Probably the most common type of schedule diagram used in con-struction.

General bid: A **bid** made by one seeking to be a **general contractor;** a **prime bid**; not a **sub-bid.**

General conditions: Those that generally apply in a contract; of which standard editions are published. (See also **Condi-tions Standard form of contract.**)

General condition items: A popular but imprecise term used to describe those items that give rise to **job overhead costs,** some of which are required by the general conditions of a contract (e.g., a performance bond). Many **job overhead** costs, however, are not mentioned in **gen-eral conditions.** (See also **General re-quirements.**)

General contractor: A popular but noncon-tractual term used to describe a **prime contractor** (a party to a construction contract) who has a number of **subcon-tractors** to do some or all of the work that the contractor has undertaken to do for the **owner.** (The term once referred to a contractor who employed workmen of several different trades and who under-took building projects, as distinct from a **specialist contractor,** who normally un-dertakes the work of only one or two trades.)

General requirements: Those temporary facilities, temporary services, and similar prerequisites for work which are provid-ed on site by a **contractor**, which because of their general nature, are related to a project's work as a whole rather than to specific **items of work.** Properly specified and referred to in documents in Division 1, General Requirements, of **Masterfor-mat**. (N.B.: Some general requirement items are referred to in the general condi-tions of contracts, but it is recommended that general conditions be limited to con-tractual-legal items, as distinct from the administrative and technical provisions that should be referred to either in Divi-sion 1, General Requirements, or in sub-sequent divisions.)

GSA/PBS: The initials of the United States federal government's General Services Administration, Public Buildings Service;

the administrators of construction management services purchased by the federal government.

Hard costs of a development: The total costs of construction work, including design fees; as distinct from the **soft costs of a development** that include all the other costs.

Heavy construction: See **Building construction work** and **Engineering construction work.**

Holdback: See **Retainage.**

Implied warranty: One implied by law and the work done or the service provided, i.e., not an **expressed warranty**.

Improvement: A legal term referring to anything erected on and affixed to land (e.g., buildings, roads, fences, and services), which legally becomes part of the land, according to common law and statutory definition.

Indemnification: The act or process of protecting a person against harm, claims, or loss, by agreement and obligation in a contract.

Indirect costs (of construction work): (as distinct from **direct costs** that can be entirely attributed to specific **projects**) Those costs of work generally classified as **operating overhead costs** that cannot be entirely attributed to the work of specific projects, and **profit**. Their magnitude is, in part, determined by the competitive market for work.

Indirect labor costs: Labor costs paid by an employer on an employee's behalf for such things as insurance, Social Security (pensions), and vacations. (See also **Direct labor costs.**)

Industrial construction: (as distinct from **building construction** and **engineering construction**) That concerned with industrial plants.

Information: (as distinct from **data**) Specific information about a project or its work.

Interim payment: See **Progress payment.**

Interpretation (by a designer): The designer's interpretation of a contract; as required in the AIA Document A201-1987 (Subpara. 4.2.11), and by a written request from either the **owner** or the **contractor.**

Item of work: A portion of **work** that can be observed, identified, and separated for purposes of estimating, **cost accounting**, and management. **Direct costs (of construction work)** can be segregated and allocated to specific items (e.g., masonry walling; the masonry units and the mortar joints are not because they are inseparable parts of the wall). Items of work usually involve the work of only one trade. (See also **Basic item (of work)** and **Particular item (of work).**)

Job: A popular term for a project, or for part of the work therein (e.g., as in **Job costing).** (See also **Project.**)

Job costing: in construction, **cost accounting** of projects.

Job overhead costs: Those **direct costs (of construction work)** that, cannot be allocated to specific **items of work,** but which can be properly allocated to a specific **project**; as distinct from **operating overhead costs** (e.g., costs of temporary facilities and services, permits, and a performance bond).

Labor: As distinct from **supervision,** those workers whose work the costs of which can be allocated to specific **items of work** as a **direct cost (of construction work)**; a construction resource.

Labor and materials payment bond: See **Payment bond.**

Labor contract: A contract for labor only, or for workers supplied to a site.

Labor costs: That part of the total **costs (of construction work)** expended on **labor**, dependent on the **labor rates** paid to workers and their productivity; including both **direct** and **indirect labor costs.** The **costs of work** other than the **material costs, plant and equipment costs, overhead costs,** and **profit.**

Labor item (of work): An item the costs of which include no **material costs** (e.g., cutting a chase).

Labor rate: The total costs for labor paid by an employer, including all **direct** and **indirect labor costs** for a specific period (in a specific place) divided by the total number of hours worked during that period. (See also **Charge-out rate.**)

Lag: A deliberate delay between tasks, built into a **work schedule.**

Lien: A legal charge against real property for **work** or services done on or for that property, or for **materials** delivered to the property, until payment is made for the work or services, or for the material's delivered; commonly known in construction as a mechanic's lien. Liens are allowed by and subject to local statutes which vary with locale. Liens were intended to give protection to workers against loss resulting from unpaid wages, but this protection has now been extended and more often protects contractors and subcontractors, and sometimes designers and suppliers.

Liquidated damages: (as distinct from damages that may subsequently be obtained from a **contractor** by a legal action initiated by an **owner,** and as distinct from a **penalty** for late completion bearing no relation to the actual damages incurred) A settled and stipulated sum payable to an owner for damages suffered, usually because of late completion of construction by a **contractor.** The amount of the payment is settled in advance (liquidated), often at so much a day, and included in a construction agreement.

Logic diagram: Made to show the logical sequence and arrangement of **work activities** for scheduling and other management purposes (usually either activity-on-arrow or activity-on-node).

Long-lead item: A **material** that is a subject of long-lead procurement.

Long-lead procurement: The same as **advanced purchasing.**

Low(est) bidder: An imprecise but convenient term for the person who submits the lowest bid.

Lump-sum: A fixed or stipulated sum; as in a **lump-sum contract.**

Lump-sum contract: A popular term for a stipulated-sum or **fixed-price contract.**

Lump-sum item: An item priced by a **lump-sum** (often, an overhead item, such as the cost of a permit; or an item of work, such as a gate or door).

Machinery (and equipment): A class of **material** incorporated into **construction work.** (See also **Equipment.**)

M & E (sub)contractors: Those who do mechanical and electrical work.

Management contractor: One who contracts to manage a project and to bring it to timely completion within the budget, who (unlike a **general contractor**) does none of the **work** with his own forces, but instead has **subcontractors** to do all the work; and who (unlike a **construction manager**) guarantees performance and costs.

Markup: A popular but convenient term for the **indirect costs** (i.e., **operating overhead costs** and **profit**) added to the **direct costs** (often as a percentage) to arrive at the total estimated **costs of construction work** as a basis for a **bid** (or for negotiations). (*verb*) The action of calculating and adding **indirect** to **direct costs** in an estimate.

Material costs: That part of the total **costs (of construction work)** expended on **materials;** including the costs of delivery, handling, storage, sales and other taxes, and the costs resulting from **laps (in construction work)** and **waste.** The costs of work other than the **labor costs, plant and equipment costs, overhead costs,** and **profit.**

Materialman: An old term for a **supplier.**

Materials: Everything required to be installed and permanently incorporated in **construction work** according to the construction contract, including **products, components, building equipment,** and **machinery,** but excluding **equipment** (as in **plant and equipment costs**). A class of construction resources.

Material supplier: See **Supplier.**

Maximum cost-plus-fee contract: One fundamentally the same as a **cost-plus-fee contract,** except that the **contractor** agrees to complete the **work** at a total cost not greater than the maximum cost stipulated in the contract; often containing a sharing clause whereby the contractor shares in any savings made by completing the work at an actual total cost that is less than the stipulated maximum cost.

Methods engineering: A technology primarily concerned with the study of industrial (construction) methods; a part of industrial engineering.

Minor change in (the) work (of a construction contract): Contractually, the subject of an order by a **designer** with authority under the contract to order minor changes in the work that do not involve an adjustment to either **contract sum** or **contract time,** and that are not inconsistent with the intent of the contract. (See also **Change in (the) work (of a construction contract)** and **Change order.**)

Modification: Defined in AIA Document A201-1987 as a written amendment to a construction contract signed by both parties (**owner** and **contractor**); or a **change order;** or a **construction change directive;** or a written order for a **minor change.**

Negative float: An **activity** with negative float has a required start date earlier than the activity's scheduled start date.

Net, in place: A term used to refer to the officially recommended method of measuring construction work as set down in national **standard methods of measurement (for construction work),** published in Canada and England; to measure work according to the dimensions shown on the drawings or, when no dimensions are shown, according to certain minimum dimensional allowances (such as for excavations) as laid down in the published standard method of measurement and, as a result, to make all necessary allowances for **shrinkage and swell,** and **waste,** as required, in an item's **unit price** and not in its measured quantities of work.

New work: Construction work, as defined, as opposed to **existing work.**

Nominated subcontractor, or **nominated supplier:** A subcontractor or a supplier selected and named (nominated) by the **owner** or **designer** in a project's specifications, or subsequently in the **designer's instructions** to the **contractor,** with whom the contractor is required to enter into a subcontract or a supply contract (provided the contractor may make no reasonable objection). A nominated subcontractor or supplier is paid out of **prime cost sums** or **provisional sums (cash allowances)** stipulated by the designer in the specifications. The purpose of nomination is to give an **owner** and a **designer** the opportunity to delay design decisions about work or materials, or both, which are covered by **prime cost sums** and provisional sums and which are to be executed by or supplied by nominated subcontractors or suppliers, respectively; and to give an owner and a designer greater control over the work than they would have under a simple **lump-sum contract**. The term and practice are common in Britain and most other English-speaking countries, but are less so in North America.

Nonreimbursable costs of work: Those construction costs so defined in a **cost-plus-fee contract** and covered by the fee, as stipulated in the contract. Usually the **indirect costs (of construction work)** as defined. (See also **Reimbursable** costs of work.)

Notice of change: A written notice, without contractual significance, issued to a **contractor** by an **owner** through the **designer,** giving notice of an intention to make a **change in (the) work (of a construction contract)** and intended to initiate the necessary negotiations without making a commitment.

Notice to proceed: A written notice by a **designer** to the **contractor** to proceed and start the work on site; important to determining the duration of a project.

Offer: See **Bid.**

Office overhead costs: A popular but imprecise term that is synonymous with **operating overhead costs** (as distinct from **job overhead costs**) and that refers to the costs that are incurred in a contractor's main office (as distinct from those incurred in temporary site offices); sometimes called "office overhead costs."

Operating costs of equipment: See **Owning and operating costs.**

Operating overhead costs: As distinct from **job overhead costs, plant and equipment costs, materials costs,** and **labor costs,** all of which are **direct costs** (of construction work); operating overhead costs, with **profit,** the **indirect costs** (of construction work); those costs of operating a construction contracting business which, because of their general nature, cannot be allocated to specific projects; instead, they are charged to projects as a percentage (usually) of the direct costs as part of the **markup.**

Other contract: (See **Separate contract.**) One performed by an other contractor.

Other contractor: See **Separate contractor.**

Outline chart: A list of **work phases, tasks,** or **work items,** and other work **information** from a project's cost estimate, made prior to making a **work breakdown structure** and a **work schedule.**

Outline specifications: Incomplete project specifications; those that cover only the major items of work, often accompanying preliminary design drawings.

Overhead costs: An imprecise term that includes both **job overhead costs** and **operating overhead costs.** The more specific terms should be used.

Overhead and profit: An imprecise term (see **Overhead costs** and **Markup**).

Owner: The first party to a construction contract, who pays the **contractor** (the second party) for the **construction work;** also, the party who owns the rights to the land upon which the work is done and who, therefore, owns the work; also, the client of a **designer**, a **construction manager**, a **project manager**, or a **development manager.**

Owner–designer: A convenient term where purpose rather than precise responsibility is to be indicated.

Owner's agent: As distinct from an employee of an owner; a general term that includes **a designer, a quantity surveyor, cost engineer** or similar **agent–consultant** (e.g., a **construction manager, a project manager,** or a **development manager.**)

Owning and operating costs: The total of **plant costs** or **equipment costs.** Owning costs are incurred simply by ownership of **plant** or **equipment,** and consist primarily of the costs of depreciation, maintenance, and investing in ownership; operating costs are incurred by actually operating and using plant and equipment—over and above the owning costs; they primarily consist of the costs of repairs, fuel, lubricants, **consumable items,** the operator's labor costs, and the costs of mobilization and demobilization.

Package deal: Also called a design and construct contract. One that includes the necessary design services for the construction work; usually involving a negotiated contract; often a **maximum cost-plus-fee contract;** sometimes includes purchasing the land upon which the work is done. Some make a distinction between a **package deal** and a **turnkey project,** sometimes called a design and manage contract, but general usage is loose and specific differences in terminology are not well-established.

Particular item (of work): Also known as "rogue items" or "maverick items," as distinct from **basic items of work,** or standard items of work. An item that is not a basic item and that therefore requires an original and unique description in specifications and cost codes for the projects in which it occurs. Particular items are much less common than basic items and are specified and described as needed in specifications (i.e., they are not boiler plate). Similarly, in estimates, particular items are identified by special code numbers for cost accounting and other construction management procedures.

Parol-evidence rule: A rule of law that says that a written agreement precludes any previous oral agreement.

Payment bond: A bond in which the surety company guarantees that the **contractor** named in the bond will properly pay all legal and valid debts arising from the **construction work** or the bond will be in default and paid to the **owner.**

P.C. sum: See **Prime cost sum.**

Penalty: A monetary penalty payable by a **contractor** to an **owner** for late completion of **construction work** according to the contract agreement, irrespective of the amount of actual damages suffered by the owner, or whether no damages are suffered by the owner because of late completion. Maybe considered by a court as invalid, especially if not equitably balanced by a bonus for early completion.

Performance bond: A bond issued by a surety company on behalf of a **contractor** to guarantee an **owner** proper performance of the construction contract.

Performance specification: One in which the subsequent performance of the work is specified, rather than the specific materials and methods. Much work is specified by a combination of performance and prescriptive specifications. (See also **Prescriptive specification.**)

PERT: See **Program evaluation and review technique.**

Phased construction: That in which **design** and **production** more or less overlap, thus shortening project time; usually practiced in **CM projects** (see text for other contractual means).

Planning and scheduling: First, planning list all activities in a logical order. Next, scheduling calculates the durations of activities and the duration of the whole project and putting dates on their starting and finishing times. (See also **Work plan, Work schedule.**)

Plant: As distinct from **construction equipment,** which is mobile; machinery and other operated equipment planted in a more or less permanent place, such as a concrete batch plant.

Plant and equipment costs: All owning and operating costs of plant and equipment; **small tools** supplied by a contractor are economically similar to plant and equipment but usually less significant.

Precontractor: As distinct from a bidder and a contractor (who has already entered into a construction contract); similar to a **bidder**, except that a precontractor negotiates with an owner, or his representative, with the intention of arriving at an agreement and a construction contract; or, one who has made a successful bid and is likely to be the contractor.

Prefabricated (component): One made off the site, and subsequently delivered for installation in the work. (See also **Subcontractor** and **Supplier**).

Prescriptive specification: (as distinct from a **performance specification**) A specification in which the materials and methods are prescribed by the **owner–designer.** Many items of work are specified by a combination of prescriptive and performance specifications, but generally the prescriptive form has dominated; al-

though there now is a move toward performance specifications, as materials and methods become varied, innovative, and complex.

Primary contract: See **Prime contract.**

Primary contractor: See **Prime contractor.**

Prime agent: The agent of an owner named in a construction contract; usually an **architect, engineer,** or **construction manager.**

Prime bid: One made by a **bidder** seeking to be a **prime contractor**; not a **sub-bid.**

Prime contract: A construction contract between an **owner** and a **prime contractor.**

Prime contractor: A less common but more precise term for a **general contractor;** one who has a contract with an **owner** and several **subcontractors.**

Prime cost: The **direct costs of work,** or of **materials** supplied, as charged by a (sub)contractor doing the work, or by a supplier supplying the materials; and without a markup added by the prime contractor. The original cost of materials or work.

Prime cost sum: A term used outside North America for a **cash allowance.** (See also **Provisional sum.**)

Primordial agreement: The tacit and partial agreement that exists during the early stages of negotiations for a construction contract.

Procurement: In construction, the procuring or purchasing of **materials.** (See also **Advanced purchasing.**)

Product data: A term used in the AIA Document A201 in referring to information about specific **material** to be provided by the **contractor.**

Production phase (of construction): In traditional construction, the later phase preceded by the **design phase.** In **CM**

projects, the two phases usually more or less overlap, as in **phased construction.**

Production rate: See **Productivity rate.**

Productivity: The amount of **work** done in a given period; usually measured in units of work per man-hour.

Productivity rate: A unit rate of production; the total amount produced in a given period divided by the number of hours (e.g., placing concrete in footings, at a rate of 0.5 man-hour per cubic yard).

Products: As distinct from raw **materials,** such as yard lumber and cement; construction materials produced and finished by a manufacturer away from the site. (See also **Component, Machinery (and equipment),** and **Materials**).

Profit: The excess of income from construction over the total expenditures for **materials, labor, tools, plant and equipment cost,** and **job** and **operating overhead costs.** For an **owner,** the profit is a cost of the work. For a **contractor,** it is a reason for doing the **work** and taking the risks involved.

Profitability: The net return on an investment in business; often represented by a percentage obtained by dividing the profit (times 100) by the tangible net worth of the business.

Program evaluation and review technique (PERT): A method of **planning and scheduling activities** and **work** when little historical information is available on which to base the estimation of activity and project durations; not widely used in ordinary construction; its distinction is in the use of the "three times" estimate formula,

$$\frac{(a + 4m + b)}{b} = \text{task duration;}$$

when a = pessimistic estimate (10 percent probability); m = most likely; and b = optimistic (10 percent probability). (See also **Critical path method.**)

Progress payment: A payment made to a **contractor** by the **owner** during the course of construction according to the terms and conditions of the construction contract (usually every month), on the basis of the value of work completed to date, less any required **retainage,** less the total of all previous payments.

Project: A construction undertaking of which the **work** of a **construction contract** may be the whole or part. In the latter case, the several parts of a project may be performed by **separate contractors** (the traditional model), or by **specialist (trade) contractors** (as in a **CM project**).

Project management: In the ordinary and looser sense, the term is practically synonymous with **Construction Management (CM).** In a more precise sense, it means construction done under a particular contractual arrangement in which an **owner** employs an agent as his representative (sometimes an employee, as in a government department) called a **project manager.** PM involves professional services at a higher level of responsibility than **CM,** and often includes or requires supervision of the latter; but not as comprehensive as **development management.**

Project manager: A person (corporate or individual) employed or appointed by an **owner** as his agent in a construction project and to do more or less all those things the owner would otherwise have to do, including (sometimes) appointing the **designer,** a **construction manager,** and other agents of the owner (such as a **quantity surveyor**), making payments to the contractor(s), and making any changes in the work. Also, one who provides project management services for a fee. Also, one employed by a contractor.

Project manual: The written parts of **bidding documents** and **contract documents,** as distinct from the drawings (although project manuals increasingly contain detail drawings and graphic schedules); sometimes consisting of more than one volume; popularly called the **specifications** (which it contains, along with the contract agreement, general and other conditions, and all other material required for estimating and bidding provided by the **owner** and **designer**).

Proposal: See **Bid.**

Provisional sum: Similar to a **prime cost sum,** or a **cash allowance,** but included in a construction contract for work that may or may not be necessary, such as possible additional work needed in a substructure, or work possibly required by a contingency; hence, also a **contingency sum.**

Punch list: A list of **items of work** or deficiencies to be attended to prior to **completion.**

Quantities of work: Measured quantities of **construction work** (not only construction materials) in **estimates (of construction costs)** and **bills of quantities.**

Quantity surveying: Translating construction drawings into **bills of quantities,** including specifying **items of work** and **job overhead items,** measuring and calculating **quantities of work,** and preparing cost estimates. The professional **quantity surveyor** also provides services other than those described here. (See also **Taking off (quantities).**

Quantity surveyor: One who surveys **quantities of work,** prepares **bills of quantities** and other contract documents, arranges for **bids** and for their review, advises on the selection of contractors, administers the financial aspects of **construction contracts,** negotiates and settles with contractors the value of **changes in (the) work,** checks **applications for payment,** settles construction accounts, and generally acts as an **agent–consultant** (or employee) of an **owner,** or of a **contractor.** In addition, professional quantity surveyors also undertake **feasibility studies, conceptual estimates,** the preparation of studies and reports, and generally perform the functions of **cost engineers** and **construction managers** (and, to some extent, of appraisers) in all fields of construction and development. (See also **Chartered quantity surveyor** and **Cost engineer.**)

Reimbursable costs of work: Those **construction costs** so defined in a **cost-plus-fee contract;** usually the **direct costs (of construction work),** as defined. (See also **Nonreimbursable costs of work.**)

Resource schedule: One that shows when certain quantities of a particular resource (e.g., **labor, material,** or **equipment**) are required.

Retainage: Those portions of cash amounts due to be paid to a **contractor** for **work** completed that are held back (retained) by the **owner** and not paid until some later date; often at **substantial completion** (performance) or at **final completion of the work,** according to the terms and conditions of the contract and any relevant legal statute (such as a mechanic's lien act); as a security for proper performance of work and fulfillment of a contract's requirements.

RICS: The Royal Institution of Chartered Surveyors; a professional body with headquarters in London, England, whose members offer services of all kinds related to real property and its use and development, including: building and quantity surveying, and construction management and administration. (See also **Chartered quantity surveyor.**)

Samples: Representative examples of a specific **material** selected to show the ranges of variation in characteristics, provided by a contractor to the **owner–designer** for selection of the precise material and its characteristics required for the **work.**

Schedule of quantities: Similar to a **bill of quantities,** but whereas a single bill of quantities is usually for the work of only one trade, the **bills of quantities** (for all trades) are part of the contract documents for a **contract with quantities.** A schedule of quantities usually refers to a list of items of work the unit prices of which are submitted with a bid as for a **unit-price contract.** Schedules of quantities are more common in North America than bills of quantities; they also are more common in contracts for **engineering construction work** than in contracts for **building construction work.**

Schedule of unit prices: Similar to a **schedule of quantities,** but often without quantities, as in a **lump-sum contract** in which the **unit prices** are to be used for the valuation of **changes in (the) work (of a construction contract).** When included in a unit-price contract, and when it contains quantities, a schedule of unit prices often is practically the same as a **schedule of quantities.**

Schedule of values: A written breakdown or analysis of a contract sum, usually required of a **contractor** in a **stipulated-sum contract** prior to his first **application for payment** for checking and approval by the **designer** or other **agent–**consultant, after which the approved schedule of values is the basis for all applications for payment. It usually shows the various parts of the work, the names of the contractor (or subcontractor) who will perform each part, the value of all parts of the work, the total of which equals the contract sum, except for **cash allowances,** which usually are shown separately.

Scheduling: See **Planning and scheduling.**

Section (of a specification): A part of a **division** of a specification, with its own title and reference; usually numerical–alphabetical, consisting of a number (1 to 16) from the 16 standard divisions of work followed by an alphabetical letter that varies with the project. The work included in a section depends on a specification writer, but usually the work in any section should be by one **trade contractor** and the subject of not more than one construction trade's **sub-bid;** so that the scope of all sub-bids consists of one or more sections, and so that no sub-bid contains only part of the work specified in a section.

Separate contract: One performed by a separate contractor.

Separate contractor: (not a subcontractor) A term used in construction contracts to describe a person who has another **separate contract** with the same owner to do other construction work at the same site, thereby creating a need for cooperation among the owner's several contractors on that site.

Services: Water, gas, electrical, drainage, sewerage, and other lines carrying supplies to and wastes from buildings and other structures, and also within structures themselves. Usually classified as either private (within the site boundaries) or public services (either on-site or off-site).

Shop drawings: Drawings of specific details of **work** as required for production and installation, submitted by the **prime contractor** for approval by the **designer** for conformity with the **contract** and the **design** of the **work.**

Small tools: Generally, hand tools and other relatively small items of equipment provided by a **contractor** (i.e., other than those provided by tradesmen), as distinct from **plant and construction equipment**; usually allowed for in an estimate as a proportion of the labor costs, as determined by **cost accounting.** (N.B.: In estimating, the distinction between small tools and some items of construction equipment is not hard and fast. It is a matter of expediency in both estimating and cost accounting.)

Soft costs (of a development): All development costs but the **hard costs of development.**

Special design: One made specially for a particular **project**, of a part or the whole; a custom design; not standard. (See also **Subcontractor** and **Supplier.**)

Specialist (trade) contractor: A contracting company with a contract to do **trade work** in a project (and usually the work of not more than one or two trades, hence the use of the words "trade" in the title); not a **general contractor.** Often referred to loosely as a **subcontractor,** whether or not there is a subcontract.

Specialized construction: That distinct from **building,** and **engineering,** and **industrial construction**; e.g., highway and pipeline construction.

Special warranty: One for a certain part of the **work** (e.g., roofing) that usually is for a period greater than that of the **warranty period,** or **the defects liability period.**

Specifications: The major part of a **project manual,** but excluding the **bidding documents, contract agreement,** and the **conditions of the contract**; the written descriptions of **items of work** that complement the construction drawings. (See also **Performance specification** and **Prescriptive specification.**)

Standard (form of) (construction) contract: A contract usually consisting of an agreement and a set of general conditions published by an authoritative body such as an institute of architects (**AIA**) or engineers (NSPE/PEPP/ASCE), or by a board made up of a number of institutes and organizations (**CCDC**); intended for use by **owners** and **designers** in making construction contracts; usually endorsed or authorized by one or more construction organizations (AGCA, CCA), if not actually produced with their direct cooperation.

Standard method of measurement (for construction work): A document prepared and published by an institute of quantity surveyors (e.g., the **CIQS,** and the **RICS,** with or without the cooperation of construction organizations; or published by a committee made up of representatives from such an institute and from construction organizations) that sets down the agreed methods of measurement for **construction work,** trade by trade, for purposes of standardization, and to facilitate and increase the understanding and use of **bills of quantities,** estimates (of construction costs), **schedules of quantities,** and **schedules of unit prices** based upon the specified standard methods of measurement.

Stipulated sum: The sum stipulated in a **bid** for a **stipulated-sum contract** (also called a fixed-price or lump-sum contract), for which the bidder offers to do the **work,** which sum becomes the contract sum if the offer is accepted and a contract is made.

Sub-bid: An offer to a **contractor** (or to a **precontractor**) to do **trade work** for payment; the acceptance of which constitutes a **subcontract** between the **specialist (trade) contractor** who made the sub-bid and the contractor who accepted it; a contract subsidiary to a **prime contract** between an **owner** and a **contractor.** (See also **Bid** and **Subcontractor.**)

Subcontract: See **Subcontractor.**

Subcontractor: A party to a **subcontract** who does **trade work** for a **contractor** (the other party), which work is part of the work of a **prime contract** between the same **contractor** and an **owner;** one who is defined as a subcontractor by a prime contract. (See also **Sub-bid, Specialist (trade) contractor,** and **Supplier.**)

Subproject: Part of a **project;** possibly the work of a **separate contractor,** or of a **subcontractor,** or of a **phase** of a project; often with its own **work plan** and **schedule,** which is a part (**phase, activity**) in a master schedule.

Substantial completion (performance) of work: Completion (performance) such that the work is ready and usable for the purpose for which it was constructed, even though some minor items may remain to be completed that do not significantly detract from its readiness for use; something less than total, absolute completion, or **final completion;** completion so certified by the **designer** or other **agent–consultant** as substantial completion, according to the **general conditions**

of the contract. (Final completion of work follows the completion of those outstanding minor items listed at the time of substantial completion, according to the contract.) Substantial completion generally is most significant because certain other contractual matters turn upon it (e.g., warranty periods), and because it is the first step to final completion.

Substructure (work): That which is mostly below the surface of the site; often designated for contracting purposes as all work below a certain level (e.g., lowest floor level).

Sub-sub-bid: An offer to a **subcontractor** to do **trade work** for payment, the acceptance of which constitutes a **sub-subcontract** between the **specialist (trade) contractor** who made the sub-sub-bid and the subcontractor who accepted it; a contract subsidiary to a subcontract between a subcontractor and a contractor. (See also **Sub-bid.**)

Sub-subcontract: See **Sub-subcontractor.**

Sub-subcontractor: A party to a **sub-subcontract** who does **trade work** for a **subcontractor** (the other party). (See also **Sub-sub-bid.**)

Subtrade: A construction trade the **work** of which usually is performed by a **specialist (trade) contractor** and so called because traditionally the work is done by a **subcontractor.** An abbreviation of "subtrade contractor" often used in reference to a **specialist (trade) contractor.** In **CM projects,** such trade work usually is done by **separate contractors.**

Subtrade contractor: As distinct from a **prime contractor,** a term used loosely usually in reference to a **specialist (trade) contractor,** because often (but not always) such a person is a **subcontractor.**

Subtrade work: That normally performed by a **subcontractor** or a **specialist (trade) contractor.** (See also **Subtrade.**)

Super: Popular abbreviation of superintendent; used in the text as a common designation for a superintendent (employed by a **contractor**) and for a supervisor (employed by a **construction manager**), particularly when the reference is to both.

Superintendent: A person employed to represent a **contractor** on a construction site, as required by the **construction contract,** who is in charge of **labor,** receives instructions, and supervises and manages the **work.** (See also **Supervision.**)

Supervision: (as distinct from labor) Management staff, including **superintendents** and other staff on sites (e.g., assistants, cost accountants); primarily, the distinction is for cost accounting and estimating purposes as supervision costs are a **job overhead cost.**

Supervisor: A person employed to represent a **construction manager** on-site (usually, as required by the Construction Management contract), who receives instructions, and oversees and manages the work of the separate contractors on a **CM project.** (N.B.: Depending on a project's size, this person may be called a **project manager.**)

Supplier: A person who supplies materials for **construction work,** who is not a **subcontractor** as defined in the **prime contract.** (See also **Subcontractor** and **Supply contract.**)

Supply bond: A bond given to guarantee proper and timely delivery of **materials.**

Supply contract: a contract between a **supplier** and an **owner, contractor, subcontractor,** or **sub-subcontractor,** for the supply of **materials.** (N.B.: The nature of the **materials** supplied often is the point upon which the contractual distinction between a supplier and a subcontractor turns.)

Taking off (quantities): Measuring **construction work** from drawings. (See also **Quantity surveying.**)

Target-figure contract: One in which an **owner** receives **construction work** for a sum not greater than a stipulated target-figure; similar to a **maximum cost-plus-fee contract.**

Task: A **work activity** indicated in a **work schedule**; a portion of the total work of a project identified in a **work breakdown structure,** and a component of a **work plan** and a **work schedule.**

Task lag: A waiting period between **tasks** built into a **work schedule.** (Also Assignment lag.)

Tender: See **Bid.**

Third party: A person who is not a party to the contract in question.

Tool, plant, and equipment costs: See **Plant and equipment costs.**

Tort: A civil wrong; a breach of duty (but not a breach of contract); e.g., trespass, nuisance, and negligence.

Total completion: See **Final completion** and **Substantial completion.**

Trade contract: A contract for the work of usually one trade made with a **specialist (trade) contractor.**

Trade contractor: See **Specialist (trade) contractor.**

Trade discount: A discount allowed by a **supplier** to a customer who is a **contractor** or **subcontractor,** the amount of which is discounted (deducted) from a list price or from an already discounted price (e.g., list less 30 percent, less 5 percent). (See also **Cash discount** and **Volume discount.**)

Trade work: See **Subtrade work.**

Turnkey project: Also called a design-and-management project. A project for which the contract between **owner** and **contractor** makes such provisions for land acquisition, design, and production of the **work** that the owner need only pay the contract amount to receive the key and turn it to enter a completed building. In ordinary usage, practically synonymous with a **package deal**.

Unit cost: An average cost per unit calculated by dividing total costs of an **item of work** by the quantity (number of units) of the item. Costs may include: **material costs, labor costs, plant and equipment costs, job overhead costs, operating overhead costs,** and **profit**. As an **item of work** may have separate unit costs for materials and labor, and some or all other costs may or may not be included, the constituents of unit costs must always be defined.

Unit-price contract: A contract in which **unit prices** for the specific **items of work** are stipulated by **bidders,** based on and applied to the quantities of those items given in the document. **Quantities of work** done are later confirmed and priced at the contract's unit prices as the basis for payment. (See also **Unit cost** and **Unit prices**). May or may not be a contract for a fixed price.

Unit prices: Similar to **unit costs,** but based on the costs of work of past projects, unit prices are for pricing work in estimates (of construction costs), in **unit-price contracts, contracts with quantities,** and in **fixed-price contracts** for pricing **changes**. Unit costs are based on actual costs; unit prices on unit cost data.

Value engineering: The economic evaluation and comparison of different construction applications.

Variation: Another term for a **change**.

Volume discount: A discount, or rebate, allowed by a supplier to a regular customer because of a certain minimum volume of business transacted between them over a certain period. (See also **Cash discount** and **Trade discount**.)

Warranty: A written guarantee or promise that things will be as they should be (i.e., according to the contract). (See also, **Expressed, Implied,** and **Special warranty**.)

Warranty period: A specified period (usually one year) immediately following **substantial completion** during which a **contractor** undertakes to correct defective work or work found not to be in accordance with the construction contract. (See also **Defects liability period**.)

Waste: Construction **material** that is additional to the actual quantity of material required in the work, as indicated by the contract, which is, nevertheless, required by or used in performing the work, or is somehow lost as a result of doing the work, and therefore contributes to the **material costs**.

Weasel clause: A pejorative term for those clauses in contracts and specifications which unreasonably pass on the risk inherent in doing indeterminate work to the **contractor** in a **fixed-price contract**.

Work: The subject of a construction contract: **labor, materials,** and the use of **small tools, plant, equipment,** and all other things and services required of the **contractor** in a contract, for which the owner pays. (See also **Alteration work, Costs of (construction) work, Existing work, Item of work,** and **New work**.)

Work activities: A term used in **planning and scheduling** to indicate those parts into which the total work is divided for planning and scheduling purposes. In some projects, work activities may be large and may consist of the entire work of one trade on the job. Commonly, shown in **Gantt bar charts** for smaller projects, and in network diagrams for larger projects. For planning purposes, in engineering projects in which there are large quantities of a relatively small number of items of work, each major **Item of work** may be divided into a number of work activities (e.g., laying a pipeline may be divided into one-mile lengths). For expediency, in other projects such as for buildings, some work activities may constitute an entire item of work, whereas others may be fractions of items, or a combination of several items. (See also **Tasks, Work breakdown (structure),** and **Work phases.**)

Work breakdown (structure): A list or chart of **work items,** or **work phases,** or other appropriate groupings of work items, or **tasks** (taken from a cost estimate, or from a preliminary **work outline**), such as are useful for planning and scheduling work of a contract, **subproject**, or a **project.**

Work items: See **Item of work.**

Work phase: A group of contemporaneous **work items** in a **work breakdown structure** and **work schedule.**

Work outline: An intermediate step from a cost estimate to a **work breakdown structure.**

Work plan: One practical and expedient arrangement of the contents of a **work breakdown structure,** made prior to scheduling. There may be several alternative work plans to consider.

Work schedule: A **work plan** showing **task** or **phase** durations and dates for the start and completion of tasks or phases and of the entire project.

Wrap-up insurance: A method of combining all necessary insurance protection in a project in one policy, usually taken out by the **owner.** The objectives are to ensure that proper and adequate insurance coverage exists for all those involved and to reduced the total costs of insurance for a project. The details often are complex, making necessary the services of an insurance consultant–broker.

INDEX

An index brings together ideas and topics and through cross-referencing provides other views of a complex subject and other ways to examine and study the text.